Cognitive Diagnostic Assessment for Education

With the current push toward educational reform, there is great potential for innovation and change, particularly in large-scale testing. One area where change is possible is in cognitive diagnostic assessment (CDA). Researchers in educational measurement and cognitive psychology are finally in a position to design tests targeted specifically to providing valuable information about students' cognitive strengths and weaknesses. This book organizes into one volume what is known about CDA in education, including its conceptual and philosophical basis, methods, and applications. The complete list of topics includes educational demand, philosophical rationale, construct validity, cognitive methods, test construction, statistical models, and unresolved issues (e.g., how to best translate diagnostic information into teaching practices). The book presents a comprehensive and up-to-date examination of CDA in education.

Dr. Jacqueline P. Leighton is Associate Professor of Educational Psychology at the University of Alberta and a registered psychologist by the College of Alberta Psychologists. Her specialization is cognitive-based assessment, in particular the design of educational and psychological testing instruments to measure higher-level thinking skills. Professor Leighton's current research is focused on examining the usability of cognitive models for informing educational tests. She is a member of the American Educational Research Association, National Council on Measurement in Education, and Canadian Society for the Study of Education. Her research is funded by the Social Sciences and Humanities Research Council of Canada and the Natural Sciences and Engineering Council of Canada.

Dr. Mark J. Gierl is Professor of Educational Psychology and Director of the Centre for Research in Applied Measurement and Evaluation (CRAME) at the University of Alberta. His specialization is educational and psychological testing, with an emphasis on the application of cognitive principles to assessment practices. Professor Gierl's current research is focused on differential item and bundle functioning, cognitive diagnostic assessment, and assessment engineering. His research is funded by both the College Board and the Social Sciences and Humanities Research Council of Canada. Dr. Gierl holds the Canada Research Chair in Educational Measurement.

Cognitive Diagnostic Assessment for Education

Theory and Applications

Edited by

JACQUELINE P. LEIGHTON

Associate Professor,
Educational Psychology,
University of Alberta

MARK J. GIERL

Professor and Canada Research Chair,
Educational Psychology,
University of Alberta

CAMBRIDGE
UNIVERSITY PRESS

CAMBRIDGE UNIVERSITY PRESS
Cambridge, New York, Melbourne, Madrid, Cape Town, Singapore, São Paulo

Cambridge University Press
32 Avenue of the Americas, New York, NY 10013-2473, USA

www.cambridge.org
Information on this title: www.cambridge.org/9780521865494

First published 2007

Printed in the United States of America

A catalog record for this publication is available from the British Library.

Library of Congress Cataloging in Publication data

Cognitive diagnostic assessment for education: theory and applications / edited by
Jacqueline P. Leighton, Mark J. Gierl.
    p. cm.
Includes bibliographical references and index.
ISBN 978-0-521-86549-4 (hardback)
ISBN 978-0-521-68421-7 (paperback)
1. Educational tests and measurements.   2. Cognition – Testing.   I. Leighton,
Jacqueline P.   II. Gierl, Mark J.   III. Title.
LB3051.C622 2007
371.26′2 – dc22   2006035160

ISBN 978-0-521-86549-4 hardback
ISBN 978-0-521-68421-7 paperback

Contents

List of Contributors

Denny Borsboom Assistant Professor of Psychology, University of Amsterdam

Louis V. DiBello Research Professor of Psychology, University of Illinois at Chicago

Susan E. Embretson Professor of Psychology, Georgia Institute of Technology

Mark J. Gierl Professor of Educational Psychology and Director of the Centre for Research in Applied Measurement and Evaluation, University of Alberta

Dean P. Goodman Assessment Consultant

Joanna S. Gorin Assistant Professor of Psychology in Education, Arizona State University

Sarah M. Hartz Resident, Department of Psychiatry, University of Iowa

Robert A. Henson Assistant Professor of Education Research and Methodology, University of North Carolina at Greensboro

Kristen Huff Senior Director, K-12 Research & Psychometrics, The College Board, New York

Stephen M. Hunka University Professor of Educational Psychology, University of Alberta

Jacqueline P. Leighton Associate Professor of Educational Psychology, Centre for Research in Applied Measurement and Evaluation, University of Alberta

Richard M. Luecht Professor of Education Research and Methodology, University of North Carolina at Greensboro

John S. Macnab Teacher, Jasper Place School, Edmonton Public Schools

Gideon J. Mellenbergh Professor of Psychology, University of Amsterdam

Robert J. Mislevy Professor of Measurement, Statistics, and Evaluation, University of Maryland

Stephen P. Norris Professor of Educational Policy Studies and Director of the Centre for Research in Youth, Science Teaching and Learning, University of Alberta

Linda M. Phillips Professor of Elementary Education and Director of the Canadian Centre for Research on Literacy, University of Alberta

Louis A. Roussos Senior Psychometrician, Measured Progress

William Stout Professor of Statistics, University of Illinois at Urbana-Champaign

André A. Rupp Professor, Institute for Educational Progress (IQB), Humboldt-Universität zu Berlin

Jonathan L. Templin Assistant Professor of Psychology, University of Kansas

Xiangdong Yang Research Associate, Center for Educational Testing and Evaluation, University of Kansas

PART I

THE BASIS OF COGNITIVE DIAGNOSTIC ASSESSMENT

1

Why Cognitive Diagnostic Assessment?

Jacqueline P. Leighton and Mark J. Gierl

Cognitive diagnostic assessment (CDA) is designed to measure specific knowledge structures and processing skills in students so as to provide information about their cognitive strengths and weaknesses. CDA is still in its infancy, but its parentage is fairly well established. In 1989, two seminal chapters in Robert Linn's *Educational Measurement* signaled both the escalating interest in and the need for cognitive diagnostic assessment. Samuel Messick's chapter, "Validity", and the late Richard Snow and David Lohman's chapter, "Implications of Cognitive Psychology for Educational Measurement", helped solidify the courtship of cognitive psychology within educational measurement. The ideas expressed in these chapters attracted many young scholars to educational measurement and persuaded other, well-established scholars to consider the potential of a relatively innovative branch of psychology, namely, cognitive psychology, for informing test development.

CDA can be traced to the ideas expressed in the previously mentioned chapters and, of course, to the many other authors whose ideas, in turn, inspired Messick, Snow, and Lohman (e.g., Cronbach, 1957; Cronbach & Meehl, 1955; Embretson, 1983; Loevinger, 1957; Pellegrino & Glaser, 1979). Since 1989, other influential articles, chapters, and books have been written specifically about CDA (see Frederiksen, Glaser, Lesgold, & Shafto, 1990). Most notably, the article by Paul Nichols (1994) titled "A Framework for Developing Cognitively Diagnostic Assessments" and the book coedited by Paul Nichols, Susan Chipman, and Robert Brennan (1995) appropriately titled *Cognitively Diagnostic Assessment*. This book, in particular, brought together a wide-ranging set of perspectives on how cognitive diagnosis might be implemented in educational measurement, including tutoring systems and job knowledge testing.

Since the mid-1980s, the marriage of *cognitive psychology*, which is focused on studying the mind in terms of the mental representations and processes that underlie observable behavior (Sternberg, 1984), and *psychometrics* has appealed to researchers and practitioners because of what it can offer. But what can it offer fundamentally? We argue that the union of cognitive psychology and psychometrics generally, and CDA in particular, offers a convincing avenue to establishing test validity. In the first section, we describe why the goal of CDA, as a way to resolve questions about test validity, is worthy of interest, investigation, and also scrutiny. To this end, we revisit some important concepts outlined by Messick (1989), Snow and Lohman (1989), and Nichols (1994) pertaining to the interest and need for unifying cognitive psychology and educational measurement. We quote, in some cases, from the original sources to illustrate and emphasize the prescience of their ideas in anticipation of CDA. We conclude this section by presenting a case for the interest and perceived need for CDA as an avenue for achieving a strong program of test validity (Cronbach & Meehl, 1955; Kane, 2001, 2006) and the information such a program offers about students' cognitive processes. In the second section, we introduce the chapters in this volume, and describe how they provide a rationale for the development of CDA and how they afford the building blocks for making such an endeavor occur in practice.

INFORMATION, TEST VALIDITY, AND COGNITIVE PSYCHOLOGY

It might be somewhat surprising that some of the most influential psychometricians in the history of testing have also been psychologists and vice versa. Robert Sternberg (1984) recounts that Sir Francis Galton was not only the inventor of the correlational method, but also an enthusiastic experimentalist in psychology, and that Alfred Binet not only created the quintessential intelligence test, but also wrote avidly about mental processes. Even Charles Spearman, who originated factor analysis, theorized intensely about cognitive processes, writing in 1923 about the "principles of cognition." And, of course, Lee Cronbach developed the most widely used measure of test reliability, while also advocating for the match between learning environments and student abilities. That some of the most prominent psychometricians in history have also been psychologists is surprising only because one would think that such complementary disciplines would be the norm today rather than the exception. However, this is not the case. Anastasi (1967) warned that "those psychologists specializing in psychometrics have been devoting more and more of their efforts to refining techniques of test construction, while losing sight of the behavior they set out to measure" (p. 297). And R. J. Mislevy (1993) added 25 years later "it is only a slight exaggeration to describe the test theory that dominates educational measurement today as the application of 20th century statistics to 19th century psychology" (p. 19). Perhaps, as Sternberg (1984) describes, the impediment has been more fundamentally "a sociological one and resides primarily (but not exclusively) in the professional identification of the investigator and of the methods he or she uses" (p. 41). In other words, psychometricians at the end of the day must focus on *metrics* and not on *psychology*.

We are now at a moment in time, however, when even sociological impediments must be overcome. There is increasing pressure to make assessments more informative about the mental processes they measure in students. In particular, there is increasing pressure to adapt costly large-scale assessments (Organisation for Economic Co-operation and Development [OECD], 2004; U.S. Department of Education, 2004) to be informative about students' cognitive strengths and weaknesses. In the United States, for example, the No Child Left Behind Act of 2001 has made completing high-stakes, large-scale state assessments a rite of passage for almost all students and teachers. These tests are intended not only to determine students' learning outcomes and needs, but also to evaluate instructional programs (school effectiveness). In other parts of the world, the zest for educational accountability and standards to ensure that students are prepared and competitive for knowledge-based work environments has also shepherded an appetite for informative large-scale testing (OECD, 2004). What are these large-scale tests supposed to inform stakeholders of? The information being sought from these tests is essentially about students' cognitive strengths and weaknesses in thinking and learning. That is, to what extent do test scores reflect certain forms of thinking and higher-order cognitive processes associated with meaningful learning, as opposed to misconceptions and localized testwise strategies associated with lower-level understanding? Large-scale assessments are increasingly scrutinized about what they can deliver for pinpointing why students perform as they do and how students' opportunities to learn can be maximized.

Wanting to Make Inferences about Psychological Process: A Substantive Approach

In 1989, Messick already anticipated the importance of providing information about students' mental processes (as opposed to simply content-based behaviors) from test scores:

Thus, the heart of the notion of so-called content validity is that the test items are samples of a behavioral domain or item universe about which inferences are to be drawn. But these inferences are likely to invoke, even if only tacitly, psychological processes or behaviors rather than mere surface content. (p. 36)

With these words, Messick openly expressed a reasonable observation – that the real, but unspoken, targets of inference in which many educators are interested are about students' psychological or mental processes. And why should this not be the case? Many problem-solving behaviors are known to be related to, and in some cases a direct consequence of, cognitive antecedents such as insufficient knowledge or unsophisticated strategy selection (Newell & Simon, 1972). It is sensible to want to draw test-based inferences about students' mental processes if only to increase the likelihood of providing the most effective and timely instruction to students in a way that cuts to the origin of behavior. With such information, teachers could alter students' misconceptions and replace faulty strategies. According to Messick (1989), understanding test performances substantively in terms of the mental processes students use to answer and/or solve test items is a core feature of construct validity theory. In particular, he regarded the substantive approach in construct theory as having a definitive role in the domain specification of a test:

In the substantive approach, items are included in the original pool on the basis of judged relevance to a broadly defined domain but are selected for the test on the basis of empirical response consistencies. The substantive component of construct validity is the ability of the construct theory to account for the resultant test content.... the internal structure and substance of the test can be addressed more directly by means of causal modeling of item or task performance. This approach to *construct representation* attempts to identify the theoretical mechanisms that underlie task performance, primarily by decomposing the task into requisite component processes (Embretson, 1983). Being firmly grounded in the cognitive psychology of information processing, construct representation refers to the relative dependence of task responses on the processes, strategies, and knowledge (including self-knowledge) that are implicated in test performance. (pp. 42–45)

However, grounding test-based inferences in the cognitive psychology of information processing is not straightforward. There is a catch, and the catch involves developing and pursuing a fairly rigorous program of construct validation (Cronbach, 1988; Kane, 2001; Messick, 1989). The test developer must begin with a well-grounded construct theory from which items will be generated and selected, and from which predictions about score relationships will be made. In considering data and analyses relevant to such a program of construct validation, Messick suggested including (a) judgmental and logical analyses to discover alternative hypotheses of score interpretation, (b) correlational or covariance analyses to search for convergent and discriminant evidence to the patterns expected from construct theory, (c) analyses of process to probe construct representation, (d) analyses of group differences and changes over time, (e) responsiveness of scores to experimental treatment and manipulation of conditions, (f) generalizability of score interpretation across contexts, and (g) threats to the tenability and generalizability of research conclusions. Notice that not only do these steps pertain to CDA, but they also directly seek to identify how students of different ability or achievement levels mentally represent and manipulate test information over time, in differing contexts, and in response to instructional interventions and test variable manipulations. However, these steps also require a committed effort of time and resources from test developers to understanding the psychology of test taking. This is the catch.

A commitment to these seven steps requires a radical shift in how testing is viewed and developed. It requires that we consider testing as a concrete, scientific endeavor instead of a circumstantial enterprise, where it is largely correlational evidence that is collected in ad hoc fashion (often after the test has been administered) to justify the interpretation of test scores (Borsboom, Mellenbergh, & Van Heerden, 2004). A quote used by Messick, which also bears repeating here, was offered by Peak (1953) more than 50 years ago: "a protest must be entered . . . against the proliferation of blindly empirical validities which are without the disciplined guidance of theory, for the increment of meaning from the accumulation of miscellaneous correlations may ultimately approach zero" (p. 288). In sum, CDA requires us to pursue a rigorous program of validation, one that is focused on measuring students' mental processes as they engage in test-taking behaviors and then using this information for improving students' opportunity to learn.

Exploring the Substantive Approach with Cognitive Psychology

Even more so than Messick, Snow and Lohman (1989) were explicit in their statements of how cognitive psychology could be used to inform educational measurement:

First, the cognitive psychology of problem solving is a central concern for educational measurement because all mental tests are, in some sense, problem-solving tasks. Hence, existing or proposed test designs ought to be evaluated as such. . . . *Second*, the two most general purposes of educational measurement, the assessment of student aptitudes and achievements, would appear to cut across the matrix of cognitive psychology in different ways. . . . Thus, different slices across the field of cognitive psychology might be needed to inform test design and evaluation . . . (p. 265)

Snow and Lohman indicated that the ideas, theories, and methods of cognitive psychology could contribute to the advancement of educational measurement by (a) informing analyses of existing tests to elucidate their underlying constructs; (b) clarifying the goals of testing in terms of the knowledge and skills that are genuine indicators of mastery and understanding; and (c) enhancing theories of aptitude, achievement, and learning across different domains.

In documenting the ways in which cognitive psychology could be useful, Snow and Lohman (1989, p. 267) also recognized the important distinction between an investigator's conceptualization of a person's reasoning and problem solving versus the actual reasoning and problem solving used by the individual when responding to test items. This is a subtle but essential distinction. Such a distinction must be acknowledged in order to fully integrate the psychology of cognition in measurement. Cognitive psychologists, at least in principle, acknowledge that the most sophisticated computer models of what is expected of individual cognitive functioning must be verified with experimental studies on how individuals actually think and reason (e.g., Ericsson & Simon, 1993). Computerized models are, at best, complex hypotheses of how humans are expected to reason in the face of specific constraints. However, for computer models to truthfully inform us of the nature of human reasoning and problem solving, they must approximate real-life human thinking. This is a perspective that is not often taken into account in traditional educational psychometric models such as those embodied in classical test theory and item response theory, although it is directly applicable to developments of CDAs (Snow & Lohman, 1989; see also Embretson & Gorin, 2001; Frederiksen, Glazer, Lesgold, and Shafto,

1990; Irvine & Kyllonen, 2002; Leighton & Gierl, in press; Mislevy, Steinberg, & Almond, 2003; Nichols, 1994).

Adapting Educational Psychometric Measurement Models for Psychological Theory: Structural Fidelity

Although there is some variety in the particular assumptions made across different educational psychometric measurement (EPM) models, as Snow and Lohman refer to them, in general they aim to approximate a person's location on an underlying variable of interest such as science achievement or spatial aptitude. The location at which the person is finally placed is often interpreted as reflecting the sum or amount of the variable that that person has acquired, such as 67% of science achievement or 85% of spatial aptitude. EPM models such as those based on item response theory have contributed greatly to educational and psychological measurement by overcoming important technical obstacles (e.g., an examinee's ability estimate being dependent on the particular sample of test items chosen). However, this groundbreaking measurement has exhibited limitations in the face of changing educational contexts and climates, in which there is ever-increasing demand for information about students' cognitive processing. Serious limitations with EPM models were identified by Snow and Lohman specifically in relation to their failure to incorporate (a) substantive psychological theory to explain item responses; (b) realistic assumptions about the psychological dependencies and variables influencing test item performance (e.g., Lord's [1980] three-parameter logistic model and the assumption that only three parameters influence student item responses); and (c) explicit delineation of the psychological processes that collectively reflect the construct measured by a test. In addition, the implicit cognitive models that inform many educational tests are still reflective of investigators' *expectations* of how students will reason and solve problems in test-taking situations; they are not based on empirical evidence of how students actually think in these circumstances (Leighton & Gierl, in press; Nichols, 1994).

The limitations that EPM models exhibit must be addressed and ultimately overcome for the successful use of CDA. Of course, the most sophisticated of substantive theories would likely be of little use to the development of CDA if such theories could not be incorporated into psychometric models. However, EPM models must now be *adapted* to assimilate and accommodate substantive components of test-taking behavior. Messick (1989) described the value of developing the proper EPM models:

Subsequently, Loevinger (1957) formalized the call for rational scoring models by coining the term *structural fidelity,* which refers to "the extent to which structural relations between test items parallel the structural relations of other manifestations of the trait being measured" (p. 661). The structural component of construct validity includes both this fidelity of the scoring model to the structural characteristics of the construct's nontest manifestations and the degree of interitem structure. (p. 43)

It is tempting to imagine that cognitive psychology can be infused in EPM models directly and, with minor but clever tweaking, transform EPM models completely. Unfortunately, it is not quite that simple. Cognitive theories exist for many phenomena, including perception, memory, attention, reasoning, problem solving, intelligence, and even special abilities (Healy, 2005). However, there are few, if any, cognitive theories about assessment in particular; or about the multifaceted and complex test-taking processes and behaviors that educational tests aim to measure; or about achievement generally as measured by educational assessments. What this means is that the challenge Snow and Lohman (1989) saw for cognitive psychology to "develop improved substantive theories of the aptitudes and achievements that are the goals of education and that educational measurements should be designed to assess and promote" (p. 269) is still true today. That is, substantive theories and empirical studies are still in demand. Borrowing theories from cognitive psychology and importing them into educational measurement initiatives is possible but difficult because these theories are largely developed within narrow learning contexts and in the absence of formal assessment frameworks (e.g., John R. Anderson's ACT programming tutor; see Anderson, Corbett, Koedinger, & Pelletier, 1995, and Anderson & Gluck, 2001). It would be ideal if cognitive psychologists were to develop such theories solely for educational measurement tasks or at least with educational measurement in mind. But we think the reality is largely the same as Sternberg (1984) described it – scholars identify quite narrowly with their own domains of interest and methods. Consequently, the onus is on educational researchers to adapt our methods, techniques, and tools to incorporate cognitive theory and, more important, to actively create, modify, and test theories of cognition for educational measurement purposes. In other words, *we* need to put educational tests under the "cognitive microscope."

A Conceptual Recipe for Developing Cognitive Diagnostic Assessments

The cognitive microscope magnifies the substantive component of educational assessments (Messick, 1989; Snow & Lohman, 1989). This focal point forces us to explicitly consider the construct representation and the structural fidelity of the assessment against the learning process we aim to measure. Putting educational assessments under the cognitive microscope emphasizes the appeal of CDAs as Nichols (1994) articulated so well:

These new assessments [cognitive diagnostic assessments] make explicit the test developer's substantive assumptions regarding the processes and knowledge structures a performer in the test domain would use, how the processes and knowledge structures develop, and how more competent performers differ from less competent performers. (p. 578)

In other words, educational tests designed for cognitive diagnostic purposes are different from traditional approaches in that they do not rely solely on logical taxonomies and content specifications to describe their objectives. This is because "efforts to represent content are only vaguely directed at revealing mechanisms test takers use in responding to items or tasks" (p. 585). Instead, educational tests designed for cognitive diagnosis rely largely on, and are informed by, the psychology of learning, reasoning, and problem solving to describe their purpose. To this end, Nichols outlined five steps for psychology-driven test development:

1. *Substantive theory construction*: This first step requires the development of a model or theory that characterizes the hypothesized knowledge structures and processes required to perform (respond to) the assessment. In addition, the item variables that invoke particular cognitive processes and knowledge structures must be identified.
2. *Design selection*: This second step, guided by the model or theory developed in step 1, requires the test developer to choose the observation and measurement design. The test items chosen will be selected (or created) with the expectation that test takers will respond in predictable ways, with the processes and knowledge structures identified in step 1, to the items.
3. *Test administration*: This third step involves important details of the environment and context in which test takers complete their assessments such as item format, medium of item presentation,

and setting of the test. It is recommended that decisions about the test administration should be informed by research on how different test administration variables influence performance.

4. *Response scoring*: This fourth step involves assigning scores to test takers that are informative of the construct measured by the test. Nichols indicates that response scoring (as design selection) operationalizes the assessment design.

5. *Design revision*: This fifth step involves reexamining the assessment design to see whether it supports the model or theory on which it is based. The results of the assessment are used to revise the substantive base of the assessment. Nichols states, "As with any scientific theory, the theory used in development is never proven; rather, evidence is gradually accumulated that supports or challenges the theory" (p. 587).

These five steps represent a contract for following a substantive approach and ensuring structural fidelity in the development of CDAs. Nichols (1994) emphasizes that the substantive base is developed not only from original research and literature reviews, but also from *"assumptions* about how best [to] represent learning and individual differences" (p. 587, italics added). Care must be taken, however, with what is exactly assumed, how central the assumption is to the substantive component of CDA, and how much confidence it should be assigned. Given the commitment to explicitly identifying the substantive component of CDAs, the use of assumptions, hunches, or best guesses to define the knowledge structures and cognitive processes used by test takers seems overly risky. Central assumptions about the specific knowledge structures and processes to measure might be better put to empirical scrutiny. Otherwise, the very theory guiding CDA may fail to have unequivocal empirical grounding and may, from the outset, become a wavering house of cards. Pilot studies seem especially important in ensuring that the substantive component used to guide the assessment design is as solid as scientifically possible.

Cognitive Diagnostic Assessments: A Strong Program of Validity?

Ensuring that the substantive base in CDA is well researched and articulated (in addition to verifying its structural fidelity) requires a nontrivial commitment to understanding the construct that is being measured. This commitment is by no means small because it involves adhering to

Cronbach and Meehl's (1955; see also Cronbach, 1988) strong program of validity (see also Kane, 2001, 2006; Messick, 1989), as well as developing and testing a *theory of the construct* (Messick, 1989). Cronbach (1988; also reproduced in Kane, 2001, p. 326) distinguishes the strong program against a weak program by indicating that

The weak program is sheer exploratory empiricism; any correlation of the test score with another variable is welcomed.... The strong program, spelled out in 1955 (Cronbach & Meehl) and restated in 1982 by Meehl and Golden, calls for making one's theoretical ideas as explicit as possible, then devising deliberate challenges. (pp. 12–13)

The strong program of validity required by CDA is, in effect, both the allure and the possible downfall of this form of assessment. As a matter of principle, one would expect the pursuit of CDA to be irreconcilable with a weak program of validity because of what cognitive diagnosis necessarily entails. As mentioned previously, cognitive diagnosis entails providing individualized information about students' knowledge structures and cognitive processes to improve instruction. Nichols (1994) underscores this point by stating "CDA provides instructors and policymakers with information on *strategies* students use to attack problems, *relationships* students perceive among concepts, and *principles* students understand in a domain" (p. 579). The specificity of the information Nichols is referring to, namely, *explanatory* information as to why students respond as they do, could only be generated with confidence from a strong program of validity (Cronbach, 1988; Kane, 2001). This information must "have teeth" as Kane (p. 326) asserts; otherwise, who would believe it, and what use would it have?

Explanatory information "with teeth" should be able to explicitly link a student's test performance to inferences made about his or her cognitive strengths and weaknesses. This link is established with investigations into the psychology that underwrites test-based inferences. Such investigations, moreover, are those that reflect studies of group differences, studies of change over time, and, most important, studies of process (Cronbach & Meehl, 1955, pp. 62–64). However, it is the strong program of validity that may also be the downfall of CDA because it places a heavy burden on test developers due to the need for a well-researched and articulated theory of the construct (Cronbach & Meehl, 1955; Kane, 2001). As Snow and Lohman (1989) mentioned, the challenge for cognitive psychologists is to produce such theories, based on sound scientific studies, for use in educational measurement. But this challenge has not been met. Not because cognitive psychologists are uninterested in measurement, because indeed many are (e.g., J. R. Anderson, R. J. Sternberg), but because scholars focus first on investigating the research questions of their own discipline using their own methods and tools (Sternberg, 1984) before embarking on research questions in other disciplines.

Snow and Lohman (1989) wrote optimistically that cognitive psychology had implications for educational measurement. And indeed it does because cognitive psychology is an essential entry point into CDA. However, we cannot wait any longer for this entry point to become available. The challenge is for measurement specialists to make this entry point accessible by extending psychological investigations into the assessment domain. This means that greater differentiation is needed in what psychometricians do. We need psychometricians who not only focus on the technical wizardry of assessments, but who also focus on the development of theories of constructs for CDAs. We can implore cognitive psychologists to help us in this mandate, but, in the end, we must take ownership of the investigations required to make particular forms of assessments available.

OVERVIEW OF BOOK

This volume is an account of where we are in the process of developing CDAs. To this end, the first part of this volume presents some of the foundational issues associated with CDAs, such as the need and philosophical rationale for developing strong substantive accounts for CDAs. The second part of this volume presents some of the principles of test design and analysis for helping ensure the structural fidelity of CDA with substantive components. The third part of this volume presents psychometric procedures and applications for making CDA a reality. Instead of providing an extensive account of each chapter, for the sake of brevity, we highlight only the overall purpose of each chapter and how it serves the objective of this volume.

Part I: The Basis of Cognitive Diagnostic Assessment

The first part of the volume begins with chapter 2, *The Demand for Cognitive Diagnostic Assessment* by Kristen Huff and Dean P. Goodman. This chapter describes the nature and origins of the demand for cognitive diagnostic tests. To provide empirical grounding for their claims, the authors describe the results from a survey developed by the College Board for informing the specific aspects of what stakeholders need from large-scale educational assessments. Chapter 3, *Cognitive Modeling of Performance on Diagnostic Achievement Tests: A Philosophical Analysis and Justification* by Stephen P. Norris, John S. Macnab, and Linda M. Phillips, provides a compelling account for understanding the desire to explain student test performance in terms of causes. This chapter also elucidates how cognitive models of achievement can provide insights into students' understanding of content domains. Chapter 4, *Test Validity in Cognitive Assessment* by Denny Borsboom and Gideon J. Mellenbergh, describes an innovative outlook on test validity. The authors explain the necessity for seeking an explicit understanding of the mechanisms being measured by psychological and educational assessments and the reasons that CDAs are tools for meeting this requirement. All three chapters set the stage for both the practical and the theoretical appeals of CDA.

Part II: Principles of Test Design and Analysis

The next three chapters present avenues for generating explicit accounts of the knowledge structures and cognitive processes measured by educational assessments. In particular, chapter 5, *Construct Validity and Cognitive Diagnostic Assessment* by Xiangdong Yang and Susan E. Embretson, presents a discussion of the cognitive design system approach to item design and how it relates to construct validity issues for CDA. Chapter 6, *Verbal Reports as Data for Cognitive Diagnostic Assessment* by Jacqueline P. Leighton and Mark J. Gierl, presents two methods for generating verbal reports, and indicates how these data inform different kinds of cognitive models for generating and validating educational assessment. Chapter 7, *Test Construction and Diagnostic Testing* by Joanna S. Gorin, explores the item and test construction procedures required to generate assessments measuring specific knowledge structures and cognitive processes.

Part III: Psychometric Procedures and Applications

After chapters 2 through 7 expound on the justification and motivation for investigating, debating, and developing CDAs, the third part of the volume presents some of the exciting new technical advances in psychometrics that hold promise for allowing us to achieve the goal of this new form of assessment. Without these technical advances, the goal of CDA, notwithstanding its strong rationale and desirability, could not become a reality. For example, chapter 8, *Cognitive Foundations of Structured Item Response Models* by André A. Rupp and Robert J. Mislevy, describes the theoretical underpinnings that have informed the development and use of a group of psychometric models, structured item response theory (SIRT) models. The authors describe the complex evidentiary arguments that can be constructed and supported with SIRT models. Chapter 9, *Using the Attribute Hierarchy Method to Make Diagnostic Inferences About Examinees' Cognitive Skills* by Mark J. Gierl, Jacqueline P. Leighton, and Stephen M. Hunka, introduces and illustrates the attribute hierarchy method (AHM) for cognitive assessment, a new psychometric method based on Tatsuoka's rule-space model. The AHM is used to classify examinees' test item responses into a set of structured attribute patterns associated with different levels of mastery specified in a cognitive model of task performance. Chapter 10, *The Fusion Model Skills Diagnosis System* by Louis A. Roussos, Louis V. DiBello, William Stout, Sarah M. Hartz, Robert A. Henson, and Jonathan L. Templin, presents an alternative statistical technique for classifying students into knowledge or skill categories based on their test item responses. The authors also illustrate the sequence of steps for generating the cognitive categories, developing the assessment, and classifying students for diagnostic purposes. Chapter 11, *Using Information from Multiple-Choice Distractors to Enhance Cognitive-Diagnostic Score Reporting* by Richard M. Luecht, illustrates some of the new methods of extracting diagnostic information from multiple-choice distracters to inform the classification of students' strengths and weaknesses. The chapter also discusses how information about students' cognitive misconceptions can inform the generation of test items. Collectively, chapters 8 though 11 illustrate some of the new techniques for incorporating cognitive information about students into psychometric models. Finally, chapter 12, *Directions for Future Research in Cognitive Diagnostic Assessment* by Mark J. Gierl and Jacqueline P. Leighton, presents a summary of the chapters and a look to the future.

Before we conclude, we want to acknowledge the contributors to this volume – Kristen Huff, Dean P. Goodman, Stephen P. Norris, John S. Macnab, Linda M. Phillips, Denny Borsboom, Gideon J. Mellenbergh, Xiangdong Yang, Susan E. Embretson, Joanna S. Gorin, André A. Rupp, Robert J. Mislevy, Stephen M. Hunka, Louis A. Roussos, Louis V. DiBello, William Stout, Sarah M. Hartz, Robert A. Henson, Jonathan L.

Templin, and Richard M. Luecht – for their time, expertise, and vision. Without their collective efforts, this volume would not have been possible. Thank you for being part of this project and helping us communicate new developments in the theory and applications of CDA. We have learned greatly from your work and continue to learn. Also, we want to pay tribute to the many psychometricians and psychologists who have, through their writings, lectures, and deeds, striven to achieve a much closer collaboration between educational measurement and cognitive psychology. We are indebted to your labors and achievements. We also extend a heartfelt thank you to Phillip Laughlin, Eric I. Schwartz, and Armi Macaballug, who supported and guided this project enthusiastically at Cambridge University Press.

References

Anastasi, A. (1967). Psychology, psychologists, and psychological testing. *American Psychologist, 22*, 297–306.

Anderson, J. R., Corbett, A. T., Koedinger, K. R., & Pelletier, R. (1995). Cognitive tutors: Lessons learned. *Journal of the Learning Sciences 4*, 167–207.

Anderson, J. R., & Gluck, K. (2001). What role do cognitive architectures play in intelligent tutoring systems? In S. M. Carver & D. Klahr (Eds.), *Cognition and instruction: Twenty-five years of progress* (pp. 227–261). Mahwah, NJ: Erlbaum.

Borsboom, D., Mellenbergh, G. J., & Van Heerden, J. (2004). The concept of validity. *Psychological Review, 111*, 1061–1071.

Cronbach, L. J. (1957). The two disciplines of scientific psychology. *American Psychologist, 12*, 671–684.

Cronbach, L. J. (1988). Five perspectives on validation argument. In H. Wainer & H. Braun (Eds.), *Test validity* (pp. 3–17). Hillsdale, NJ: Erlbaum.

Cronbach, L. J., & Meehl, P. E. (1955). Construct validity in psychological tests. *Psychological Bulletin, 52*, 281–302.

Embretson (Whitley), S. (1983). Construct validity: Construct representation versus nomothetic span. *Psychological Bulletin, 93*, 179–197.

Embretson, S., & Gorin, J. (2001). Improving construct validity with cognitive psychology principles. *Journal of Educational Measurement, 38*, 343–368.

Ericsson, K. A., & Simon, H. A. (1993). *Protocol analysis.* Cambridge, MA: MIT Press.

Frederiksen, N., Glaser, R., Lesgold, A., & Shafto, M. G. (Eds.). (1990). *Diagnostic monitoring of skill and knowledge acquisition.* New Jersey: Lawrence Erlbaum Associates.

Healy, A. F. (Ed.). (2005). *Experimental cognitive psychology and its applications.* Washington, DC: American Psychological Association.

Irvine, S. H., & Kyllonen, P. C. (2002). *Item generation for test development.* New Jersey: Lawrence Erlbaum.

Kane, M. T. (2001). Current concerns in validity theory. *Journal of Educational Measurement, 38*, 319–342.

Kane, M. T. (2006). Validation. In R. L. Brennan (Ed.), *Educational measurement* (4th ed., pp. 17–64). Westport, CT: National Council on Measurement in Education and American Council on Education.

Leighton, J. P., & Gierl, M. J. (in press). *Defining and evaluating models of cognition used in educational measurement to make inferences about examinees' thinking processes*. Educational Measurement: Issues and Practice.

Loevinger, J. (1957). Objective tests as instruments of psychological theory. *Psychological Reports, 3*, 635–694 (Monograph Suppl. 9).

Lord, F. M. (1980). *Applications of item response theory to practical testing problems.* Hillsdale, NJ: Erlbaum.

Messick, S. (1989). Validity. In R. L. Linn (Ed.), *Educational measurement* (3rd ed., pp. 1–103). New York: American Council on Education/Macmillan.

Mislevy, R. J. (1993). Foundations of a new test theory. In N. Frederiksen, R. J. Mislevy, & I. I. Bejar (Eds.), *Test theory for a new generation of tests* (pp. 19–39). Hillsdale, NJ: Erlbaum.

Mislevy, R. J., Steinberg, L. S., & Almond, R. G. (2003). On the structure of educational assessments. *Measurement: Interdisciplinary Research and Perspectives, 1*, 3–67.

Newell, A., & Simon, H. A. (1972). *Human problem solving.* Upper Saddle River, NJ: Prentice Hall.

Nichols, P. (1994). A framework for developing cognitively diagnostic assessments. *Review of Educational Research, 64*, 575–603.

Nichols, P. D., Chipman, S. F., & Brennan, R. L. (Eds.). (1995). *Cognitively diagnostic assessment.* Hillsdale, NJ: Erlbaum.

No Child Left Behind Act of 2001, Pub.L. No. 107–110, 115 Stat. 1435 (2002).

Organisation for Economic Co-operation and Development (OECD). (2004). *Learning for tomorrow's world: First results from PISA 2003.* Paris: Author.

Peak, H. (1953). Problems of observation. In L. Festinger & D. Katz (Eds.), *Research methods in the behavioral sciences* (pp. 243–299). Hinsdale, IL: Dryden Press.

Pellegrino, J. W., & Glaser, R. (1979). Cognitive correlates and components in the analysis of individual differences. *Intelligence, 3*, 187–214.

Snow, R. E., & Lohman, D. F. (1989). Implications of cognitive psychology for educational measurement. In R. L. Linn (Ed.), *Educational measurement* (3rd ed., pp. 263–331). New York: American Council on Education/Macmillan.

Sternberg, R. J. (1984). What psychology can (and cannot) do for test development. In B. S. Plake (Ed.), *Social and technical issues in testing: Implications for test construction and usage* (pp. 39–60). Hillsdale, NJ: Erlbaum.

U.S. Department of Education. (2004, September 16). *Stronger accountability: Testing for results: Helping families, schools, and communities understand and improve student achievement.* Retrieved February 15, 2006, from http://www.ed.gov/nclb/accountability/ayp/testingforresults.html

2

The Demand for Cognitive Diagnostic Assessment

Kristen Huff and Dean P. Goodman

In this chapter, we explore the nature of the demand for cognitive diagnostic assessment (CDA) in K–12 education and suggest that the demand originates from two sources: assessment developers[1] who are arguing for radical shifts in the way assessments are designed, and the intended users of large-scale assessments who want more instructionally relevant results from these assessments. We first highlight various themes from the literature on CDA that illustrate the demand for CDA among assessment developers. We then outline current demands for diagnostic information from educators in the United States by reviewing results from a recent national survey we conducted on this topic. Finally, we discuss some ways that assessment developers have responded to these demands and outline some issues that, based on the demands discussed here, warrant further attention.

THE DEMAND FOR COGNITIVE DIAGNOSTIC ASSESSMENT FROM ASSESSMENT DEVELOPERS

To provide the context for assessment developers' call for a revision of contemporary assessment practices that, on the whole, do not operate within a cognitive framework, we offer a perspective on existing CDA literature, and we outline the differences between psychometric and cognitive approaches to assessment design. The phrases *working within*

---

[1] The term *assessment developers* is used here to refer to psychometricians, cognitive psychologists, curriculum and instruction specialists, and learning scientists who are practitioners and/or members of the assessment research community.

a cognitive framework, cognitively principled assessment design, and *cognitive diagnostic assessment* are used interchangeably throughout this chapter. They can be generally defined as the joint practice of using cognitive models of learning as the basis for principled assessment design and reporting assessment results with direct regard to informing learning and instruction.

Perspective and Overview of Cognitive Diagnostic Assessment Literature

One way to portray the history of CDA is to start with Embretson's (1983) publication in *Psychological Bulletin*, where she effectively integrated advances in cognitively psychology and contemporary notions of construct validation: "construct representation refers to the relative dependence of task responses on the processes, strategies, and knowledge stores that are involved in performance" (p. 180). Although cognitive psychologists had been working for quite some time modeling the relationship between item difficulty and cognitive processes (Fischer & Formann, 1982), Embretson's publication was significant in its application of developments from cognitive psychology to measurement theory. Messick (1989) notes Embretson's contribution in his hallmark chapter on test validity:

As cognitive psychology in general and information-processing models of cognition in particular have advanced over the years, producing powerful experimental and quantitative techniques of task decomposition, this modeling approach has become much more salient in measurement circles. Although in one form it has only recently been incorporated into the validity literature under the rubric of construct representation (Embretson, 1983), the explicit probing of the processes productive of performance has long been part of the validation repertoire. (Cronbach, 1971; Cronbach & Meehl, 1955, p. 27)

In the same volume of *Educational Measurement*, others challenged the educational measurement community to reconceptualize testing theory and practice to reflect student cognition more broadly than a single latent trait (Snow & Lohman, 1989), and to better integrate testing with instruction and learning (Nitko, 1989). These chapters voiced a clear demand for more discourse among obvious collaborators: educational measurement specialists (psychometricians) and cognitive psychologists. Since the late 1980s, several researchers, theorists, and practitioners echoed the demand for more cognitively informed test design, scoring, and reporting to better inform teaching and learning (e.g., Bennett, 1999;

Chipman, Nichols, & Brennan, 1995; Feltovich, Spiro, & Coulson, 1993; Mislevy, 1996; National Research Council [NRC], 2001; Pellegrino, Baxter, & Glaser, 1999). In response, many promising complex, cognitively based scoring models have been proposed, such as Tatsuoka's (1983, 1995) rule-space method; DiBello, Stout, and Roussos' (1995; see also Roussos et al., this volume) unified model; and Leighton, Gierl, and Hunka's (2004; Gierl, Leighton, & Hunka, this volume) attribute hierarchy method. In addition, much research has been devoted to developing innovative (e.g., performance-based, computer-based) item types that purportedly measure higher-order thinking skills (e.g., Bennett, 1999; Bennett & Bejar, 1998; Bennett, Steffen, Singley, Morley, & Jacquemin, 1997; Sireci & Zenisky, 2006). Item difficulty modeling research has built on Embretson's work in task decomposition and construct representation (Embretson, 1999; Gorin, 2005; Sheehan, 1997; Sheehan, Ginther, & Schedl, 1999). Last, one of the most persistent themes to emerge from this area is how assessments developed from a psychometric perspective differ substantially from assessments designed within a cognitive framework. Much of the *demand* for CDA originates from discussion about the potential to inform teaching and learning by changing the way in which we design assessments.

Psychometric versus Cognitive Assessment Design Frameworks

Nichols (1993, 1994) paints a picture of two starkly different approaches to assessment design and use of assessment results in his discussion of tests developed from psychometric versus cognitive frameworks. Psychometrically developed tests are primarily developed by evaluating the statistical properties of items because the chief purpose of these assessments is to rank-order examinees along a highly reliable scale (which implies the measurement of a largely unidimensional construct) for the purpose(s) of selection, classification, and/or summative evaluation. Such an approach is contrasted with assessments developed from within a cognitive framework, which are primarily used to diagnose the learning state of the examinee and to inform remediation. Nichols (1994) and others (NRC, 2001; Pellegrino et al., 1999; Snow & Lohman, 1989) have compellingly argued that educational assessments designed from psychometric models are not optimal for informing instruction because the assessment tasks were not designed from an explicit model of how students learn, and scoring models that are primarily used to rank-order examinees are severely limited in their ability to reflect the complexity of the learner's cognitive strengths and weaknesses. Consequently, the test results are not necessarily connected to classroom learning and instruction, and accordingly, have limited utility for educators and students.

Researchers have argued that to maximize the educational benefits from assessments, these exams should be situated within an aligned and integrated system of curriculum, instruction, and assessment (Nichols, 1993, 1994; NRC, 2001; Pellegrino et al., 1999). In this system, *curriculum* should sequence learning objectives that reflect our understanding of how students build knowledge structures and expertise in the specified domain, *instruction* should employ strategies that facilitate knowledge building and active learning, and *assessment design* should be informed by the same cognitive framework that shapes the curriculum and should provide feedback to teachers that informs instruction. That is, learning and instruction are optimized when a cognitive model of learning not only provides the framework for assessment design, but also provides the framework for the educational system in which the assessment is used.

Pellegrino (2002) elaborates this integrated system of curriculum, instruction, and assessment by suggesting a cognitive assessment framework that consists of three interrelated elements:

- A model of student learning in the specified academic domain
- A set of beliefs (or hypotheses) about the kinds of observations that will provide evidence of student competencies in the domain, where such competencies are defined by the cognitive model
- A framework for interpreting the results of the assessment

This general cognitive assessment framework is operationalized through evidence-centered design (Steinberg et al., 2003) or, as it has been more recently described, principled assessment design (Mislevy & Riconscente, 2005). Principled assessment design is an approach to designing assessment tasks that are explicitly linked theoretically and empirically to the targets of measurement through the use of detailed design templates (Riconscente, Mislevy, & Hamel, 2005). Design templates require specific attention to what kind of knowledge is being measured, how the target of measurement is related to proficiency in the domain, how the various assessment task features are related to different levels of proficiency, and how the scoring model supports valid interpretations about student proficiency. Such precise articulation and documentation of the assessment argument facilitates a transparency in test design that is too often missing from exams developed from a psychometric perspective.

Some may argue that assessment design practices, whether working from within a cognitive framework or a psychometric framework, are essentially the same because psychometrically developed tests require that items are written to test specifications, and such specifications typically span both content and "cognitive" skills, such as problem solving, reasoning, analysis, and application. However, this position is not necessarily correct. In practice, test specifications for large-scale assessments often only specify content requirements and give little or no explicit consideration to the types of cognitive skills that underlie a curriculum. For example, in our review of test development material from several state departments of education Web sites (Massachusetts Department of Education, 2004; New Jersey Department of Education, 2006; Washington State Office of Superintendent of Public Instruction, 2006), we found general references to the assessment of various cognitive skills, but no explicit application of these skills in each state's test specifications. The lack of any explicit consideration to cognitive skills in the development of items and test forms for a state assessment has also been reported in the work of O'Neil, Sireci, and Huff (2004).

In contrast to psychometrically developed tests that do not explicitly assess cognitive skills, principled assessment design ensures that the cognitive skills of interest are explicitly targeted during item and test form development. This explicit targeting of cognitive skills has three key benefits. First, it helps ensure that all relevant cognitive skills are considered during item and test form development, and that the test forms assess an appropriate balance of cognitive skills (something that cannot be ensured by psychometrically developed tests that only explicitly consider content). Second, it helps ensure that the rationales supporting task designs are clearly documented (something that would facilitate transparency and would give assessment developers some useful evidence to support the validity of their assessments). Third, and perhaps most important, it helps ensure that the resulting scores lead to meaningful and valid interpretations about students' cognitive skills and abilities.

The research supporting the instructional potential of principled assessment design within a cognitive framework is convincing and growing. Since 1999, the NRC has commissioned three compelling volumes that summarize the vanguard in this area. In 1999, *How People Learn: Brain, Mind, Experience, and School* outlined the latest developments in the science of learning and how learning environments can be designed to take advantage of what we know about how students build proficiency. *Knowing What Students Know: The Science and Design of Educational Assessment* (NRC, 2001) followed soon after and addressed how educational assessment can be designed to reflect modern principles of learning by embodying five principles: designing assessments from a model of cognition and learning, making explicit the relationships among task design elements and the cognitive model, collecting evidence for the cognitive processes elicited by the tasks (i.e., construct validation), considering score reporting issues at the beginning of the assessment design phase, and ensuring comparability and fairness across all learner groups (p. 176). Then, in 2002, *Learning and Understanding: Improving Advanced Study of Mathematics and Science in U.S. High Schools* was published. In this volume, the authors argued that the cognitive-based instructional and assessment principles outlined in the two previously mentioned volumes were the most promising guidelines for improving science and mathematical achievements in secondary education.

Although assessment developers' demands for the implementation of CDA principles are compelling, do their demands reflect the needs of the primary users of assessment data – classroom teachers? To what extent are teachers making use of diagnostic information that is currently available from large-scale assessments, and how could this information be improved to better meet teachers' needs? We explore these questions next.

THE DEMAND FOR COGNITIVE DIAGNOSTIC ASSESSMENT FROM EDUCATORS

When assessing the demand for CDA from educators, it is important to recognize that they are *not* actually demanding that assessment developers use cognitive models as the basis for assessment design and reporting. What educators are demanding is that they receive instructionally relevant results from any assessments in which their students are required to participate and that these assessments be sufficiently aligned with classroom practice to be of maximum instructional value. In this section, we explore this demand by highlighting results from a national survey conducted by Goodman and Huff (2006) that examined U.S.

teachers' beliefs about, and practices relating to, the use of diagnostic information from state-mandated and commercial large-scale assessments.

For the purposes of the survey, *state-mandated* assessments were defined as standardized tests that states require schools to administer at specific grade levels (e.g., tests that satisfy the terms of the No Child Left Behind [NCLB] Act of 2001). In most cases, these state-mandated assessments would be developed by or for the state, but they could also include commercial assessments that are administered to satisfy state and federal accountability requirements. Typically, these assessments are designed to assess student proficiency in relation to state curriculum standards, and the resulting scores are reported as proficiency levels (e.g., Basic, Proficient, or Advanced). Proficiency level results are typically defined by general descriptions of the types of knowledge and skills students in each level possess (e.g., students at the Proficient level "demonstrate a solid understanding of challenging subject matter and solve a wide variety of problems" [Massachusetts Department of Education, 2005, p. 9]) or by more detailed, subject-specific descriptions (e.g., eighth-grade mathematics students at the Proficient level are able to "predict from data displays; apply measures of central tendency; describe patterns and relationships using algebraic equations" [Missouri Department of Elementary and Secondary Education, 2005, p. 15]).

Commercial large-scale assessments were defined as standardized tests, such as the Iowa Test of Basic Skills (ITBS), California Achievement Test, and the Stanford Achievement Test, that schools and districts may administer to groups of students for their own *local* use (i.e., assessments not required by the state), or tests such as the Preliminary Scholastic Aptitude Test (PSAT)/National Merit Scholarship Qualifying Test (NMSQT), Scholastic Aptitude Test (SAT), or American College Test (ACT) that students may take in preparation for college admission. Typically, these commercially available tests are norm-referenced, and the feedback consists primarily of various subscores and nationally based percentile ranks.

The survey respondents were a nationally representative random sample of 400 elementary and secondary mathematics and English language arts teachers in U.S. public and nonpublic schools. Results of this survey are estimated to be within 4.90 percentage points of the true population value 95% of the time.

How Many Teachers Receive Large-Scale Assessment Results?

With the implementation of NCLB (2001) and the proliferation of testing and results-based accountability in both public and nonpublic schools, one should expect that the number of teachers in the United States who receive large-scale assessment results is high. The findings of our survey bear this out, showing that the vast majority of elementary and secondary mathematics and English language arts teachers receive results from state-mandated and commercial large-scale assessments. As shown in Figure 2.1, of the 400 teachers who participated in the survey, only 5% reported that they did not receive assessment results from state-mandated assessments, and only 7% reported that they did not receive results from commercial large-scale assessments. Only 3% of teachers reported that they did not receive results from either one of these types of large-scale assessments.

How Often Do Results from Large-Scale Assessments Inform Instruction?

Although it appears that most mathematics and English language arts teachers in the United States have access to large-scale assessment results, to what extent are these results being used? Data we have collected suggest that large-scale assessment results are being used, although not always as regularly as assessment developers and policy makers would like and, perhaps, believe.

In our survey, 45% of teachers who received state-mandated assessment results indicated that these results inform their instruction daily or a few times a week, and 81% stated that these results informed their instruction a few times a year or more (see Figure 2.2 for a more detailed breakdown of these results). A much lower, but still substantial, percentage (27%) of teachers who received commercial large-scale assessment results indicated that these results inform their instruction daily or a few times a week, and 68% of teachers who received these results stated that these results inform their instruction a few times a year or more (see Figure 2.2 for a more detailed breakdown of these results).

Given the stakes that are attached to many large-scale assessment results today, the use of these results by large proportions of teachers is not surprising. What is surprising, however, is that significant proportions of teachers who receive large-scale assessment results appear to *never* use them to inform their instruction or do so only *once* a year. As shown in Figure 2.2, 14% of teachers who received results from

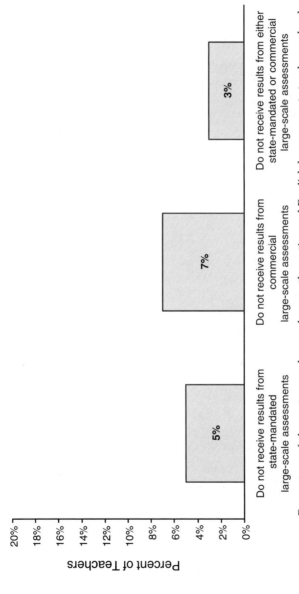

FIGURE 2.1. Percentage of elementary and secondary mathematics and English language arts teachers who do not receive state-mandated and/or commercial large-scale assessment results.

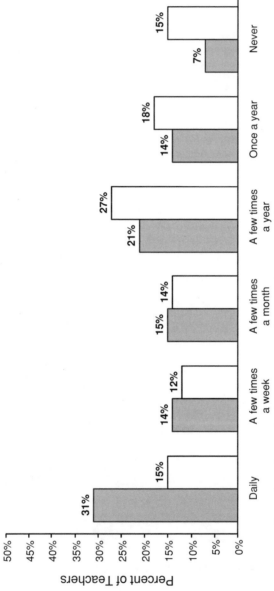

FIGURE 2.2. How often do results from state-mandated and commercial large-scale assessments inform teachers' instruction? White bars represent commercial large-scale assessments. Gray bars represent state-mandated large-scale assessments.

state-mandated assessments reported that they use these results only once a year, and 7% never use these results at all. The findings for commercial assessments should be an even greater cause of concern for assessment developers: 18% of teachers who received results from commercial assessments reported that they use these results to inform their instruction only once a year, and 15% reported that they do not use these results at all (see Figure 2.2).

Although it is encouraging to see that many teachers are using large-scale assessment results to inform their instruction on a regular basis, our findings suggest that far too many teachers who currently receive these results never use them, or use them only once a year for their ultimate purpose – to inform instruction. Clearly, a more concerted effort by assessment developers is needed to make these results more instructionally relevant and useful to all teachers, especially to those teachers who receive the results but rarely or never use them, presumably because they do not find the results to be relevant to their instruction.

To What Extent Do Teachers Believe It Is Appropriate to Collect Diagnostic Information Using a Variety of Assessment Methods?

Teachers have an assortment of assessment options that can inform their instructional practice. As part of our research, we were interested in finding out to what extent teachers believe it is appropriate to collect diagnostic information using a variety of assessment methods.

Based on our experience working with K–12 teachers, we were not surprised to find that the vast majority (93%) of teachers believed that it is moderately appropriate or very important to collect diagnostic information using assessments produced by the classroom teacher (see Figure 2.3F). Clearly, most teachers believe that the assessments they develop are well suited for identifying students' specific strengths and weaknesses. Indeed, the results in Figure 2.3 suggest that teachers believe classroom assessments are the *best* way to collect diagnostic information (with 59% of teachers stating that assessments produced by the classroom teacher are *very* appropriate for collecting diagnostic information).

Given their potential for being ongoing, integrated with instruction, and tailored to the specific needs of individual students, it is hard to deny that well-designed classroom assessment practices (especially those that are designed for formative purposes) can offer valuable diagnostic information. Unfortunately, however, not all assessment practices used by classroom teachers are well designed. Indeed, considerable research

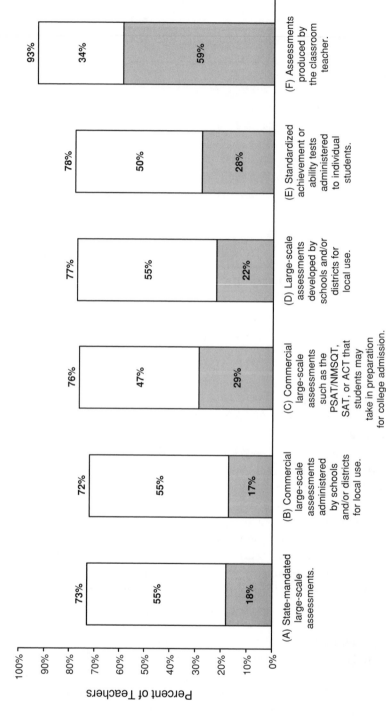

FIGURE 2.3. How appropriate do teachers believe different assessment methods are for collecting diagnostic information? White bars represent the percentage of teachers who think the methods are moderately appropriate for collecting diagnostic information. Gray bars represent the percentage of teachers who think the methods are very appropriate for collecting diagnostic information.

exists on the various ways in which classroom assessment practices can be improved (see Black & Wiliam, 1998a, 1998b; Stiggins, 2001), including better specifications of the types of cognitive skills and abilities that should and will be assessed (Mathematical Sciences Education Board, 1993; Notar, Zuelke, Wilson, & Yunker, 2004). Efforts to help teachers incorporate CDA principles into the design of classroom assessment practices would therefore appear to have some clear benefits.

In addition to classroom assessments, high percentages of teachers believed it is also appropriate to collect diagnostic information using state-mandated and commercial large-scale assessments. Seventy-three percent and 72% of teachers, respectively, believed it is moderately appropriate or very appropriate to collect diagnostic information using state-mandated large-scale assessments or commercial large-scale assessments such as the ITBS or Stanford Achievement Test (see Figures 2.3A and 2.3B). Seventy-seven percent of teachers believed that it is moderately appropriate or very appropriate to collect diagnostic information using large-scale assessments developed by schools and school districts for local use (see Figure 2.3D). Surprisingly, 76% of teachers had a similar view about collecting diagnostic information from college admission assessments such as the SAT or ACT (see Figure 2.3C). These results are especially noteworthy given that only a slightly higher percentage of teachers (78%) shared similar views about the appropriateness of collecting diagnostic information using standardized achievement or ability tests administered to individual students (the latter of which are typically designed and used for the purpose of providing diagnostic information; see Figure 2.3E). Based on these findings, it appears that any efforts to collect diagnostic information using large-scale assessments would be consistent with the general views of most teachers.

What Types of Information Do Teachers Consider Diagnostic?

Under NCLB (2001, Section 111[b][3][c][xiii]), states are required to produce diagnostic score reports that allow parents, teachers, and principals to understand and address the specific needs of students. We believe that this requirement is a step in the right direction because it emphasizes the need to make score reports both meaningful to the intended audience and directly relevant to addressing student needs. Unfortunately, the legislation does not provide any guidance as to what kinds of information are considered diagnostic and how this requirement could be best accomplished.

We found that very high percentages of teachers consider existing types of large-scale assessment results to be diagnostic (see Figure 2.4). Seventy-two percent of teachers surveyed considered even the most basic type of large-scale assessment results, overall subject-level scores, to be diagnostic information. Eighty-seven percent of teachers considered subdomain scores to be diagnostic information. Eighty-five percent and 82% of teachers, respectively, considered descriptions of specific skills or knowledge a student demonstrates on a large-scale assessment and descriptions of specific skills or knowledge that a student should develop to be diagnostic information. Eighty percent of teachers considered item-level results to be diagnostic information. These results indicate that teachers are quite willing to regard large-scale assessment results as being diagnostic; the extent to which they believe that these results actually serve to inform instructional practice is explored next.

Does Diagnostic Information from Large-Scale Assessments Play a Valuable Role in Informing Instruction?

In our survey, we explored the roles that diagnostic information[2] from state-mandated and commercial large-scale assessments play in informing instruction. In almost all cases, a majority of teachers indicated that diagnostic information from state-mandated and commercial large-scale assessments plays a valuable role in informing instructional practices at all levels of the K–12 school system: individual student, classroom, grade, school, and district (see Figures 2.5 and 2.6). The only exception to this pattern was for commercial assessments, where less than half (46%) of the teachers reported that diagnostic information from commercial large-scale assessments plays a valuable role in informing instruction at the individual student level.

The results in Figures 2.5 and 2.6 also show that more teachers believe that diagnostic information from state-mandated assessments plays a valuable role in informing instruction at each level of the K–12 school system than diagnostic information from commercial large-scale assessments. The percentage of teachers who agreed or strongly agreed with statements that diagnostic information from state-mandated assessments plays a valuable role in instruction at different levels of the K–12 school system ranged from 59% at the individual student level to 79% percent at the classroom level (see Figure 2.5). The percentage

---

[2] *Diagnostic information* was operationally defined for these survey items as any information provided by a large-scale assessment that is more detailed than overall subject-level scores.

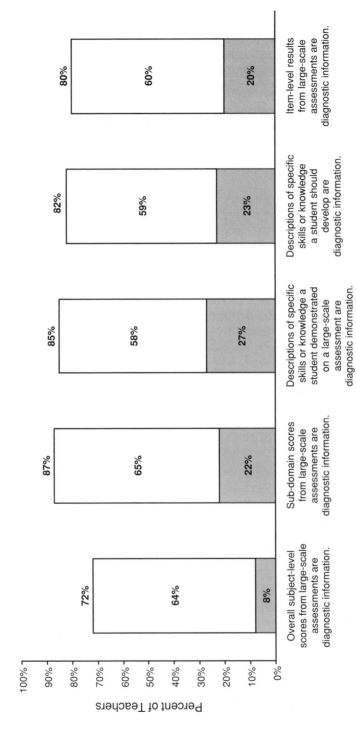

FIGURE 2.4. Extent to which teachers believe that different types of large-scale assessment results are diagnostic information. White bars represent the percentage of teachers who agree. Gray bars represent the percentage of teachers who strongly agree.

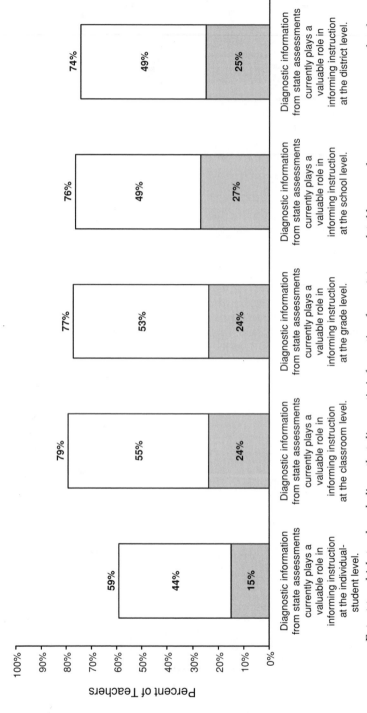

FIGURE 2.5. Extent to which teachers believe that diagnostic information from *state-mandated* large-scale assessments currently plays a valuable role in informing instruction at the individual student, classroom, grade, school, and district levels. White bars represent the percentage of teachers who agree. Gray bars represent the percentage of teachers who strongly agree.

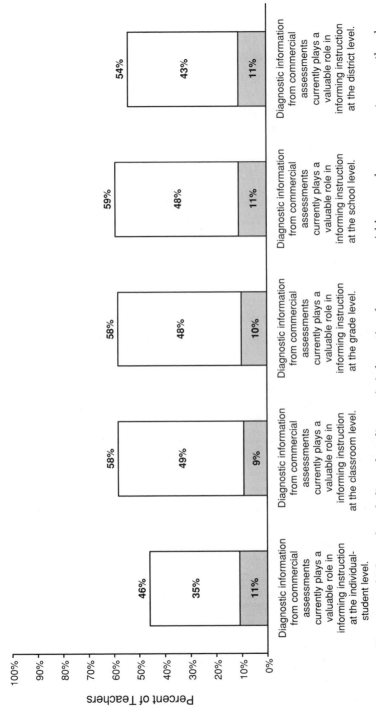

FIGURE 2.6. Extent to which teachers believe that diagnostic information from *commercial* large-scale assessments currently plays a valuable role in informing instruction at the individual student, classroom, grade, school, and district levels. White bars represent the percentage of teachers who agree. Gray bars represent the percentage of teachers who strongly agree.

of teachers who shared a similar view toward diagnostic information from commercial large-scale assessments was 13% to 21% lower across the various levels, ranging from 46% at the individual student level to 59% at the school level (see Figure 2.6). Based on these results, it appears that teachers believe that diagnostic information from state-mandated and commercial large-scale assessments have *less* instructional value at the individual student level than at the classroom, grade, school, and district levels. One can infer from these results that classroom teachers are more likely to use assessment results to inform general instructional practices rather than informing instruction with individual students.

How Is Diagnostic Information from Large-Scale Assessments Being Used by Teachers?

To help improve the utility of diagnostic assessment results, it is important to determine how the results are being used by teachers who receive them. As part of our research, we explored how often teachers use diagnostic information from state-mandated and commercial assessments across a variety of educational activities. Some of our findings are presented in Table 2.1.

Teachers reported similar patterns in their use of diagnostic information from state-mandated assessments and from commercial assessments, although information from commercial assessments is used less frequently overall. Approximately one-third (36%) of teachers who receive results from state-mandated assessments indicated that they use diagnostic information from these assessments regularly (i.e., daily or a few times a week) when planning their instruction and selecting instructional strategies. The percentage of teachers who use diagnostic information from commercial large-scale assessments to plan instruction and to select instructional strategies dropped by half to 18% and 17%, respectively. Although these findings suggest that some teachers make regular use of diagnostic information from large-scale assessments, given the intent of diagnostic feedback and the objectives of NCLB (2001), it is important to note that significant percentages of teachers who receive state-mandated assessment results *never* use them to inform instructional planning (13%), select instructional strategies (18%), assess their teaching effectiveness (20%), give feedback to students (22%), evaluate student progress (17%), or remediate students (29%). The percentages almost double when the same questions are asked about the

TABLE 2.1. *How often teachers use diagnostic information from state-mandated and commercial large-scale assessments across a variety of educational activities*

	% of teachers who use results daily or a few times a week		% of teachers who never use results	
	State-mandated assessments	Commercial assessments	State-mandated assessments	Commercial assessments
Planning my instruction	36	18	13	32
Selecting instructional strategies	36	17	18	33
Assessing my teaching effectiveness	21	10	20	39
Giving feedback to students	18	9	22	38
Remediating students	18	8	29	49
Evaluating student progress	16	7	17	38

use of commercial assessment results, where between 32% and 49% of teachers report that they *never* use diagnostic results to inform these activities. Overall, these results suggest that the teachers' current use of diagnostic information is limited, and that further effort is required to make assessment results from both state-mandated and commercial assessments more suitable for informing these types of important educational activities.

Obstacles That Inhibit the Use of Diagnostic Information from Large-Scale Assessments

Although it is encouraging that a majority of teachers believe that diagnostic information plays a valuable role in informing instructional practices, it is clear that substantial percentages of teachers never use diagnostic information for key educational activities. To help address the issue of nonuse of diagnostic information, it is important to consider what obstacles inhibit teachers' use of this information. Findings relevant to this issue are presented in Figures 2.7 and 2.8 and are discussed in this section.

Teachers reported that the most significant obstacles in using diagnostic assessment information were (a) not receiving the assessment results back in time to use them and (b) a lack of resources to inform the proper use of diagnostic information from large-scale assessments. In our survey, 68% of teachers reported not getting results back in time as an obstacle that inhibits the use of diagnostic information from state assessments, and 57% of teachers reported the same obstacle for using diagnostic results from commercial assessments (see Figures 2.7A and 2.8A). Approximately half (50% and 49%) of the teachers considered a lack of resources to inform the proper use of results as an obstacle that inhibited the use of diagnostic information from state-mandated assessments and commercial assessments, respectively (see Figures 2.7G and 2.8G). Given these high percentages, efforts by assessment developers to reduce the amount of time required to release assessment results and to provide classroom teachers with more resources to inform the proper use of diagnostic information from large-scale assessments are clearly warranted.

Approximately one-fourth of teachers (27% for state-mandated assessments and 24% for commercial assessments) indicated that the diagnostic information that is currently reported for large-scale assessments is not useful (see Figures 2.7D and 2.8D). Approximately one-third

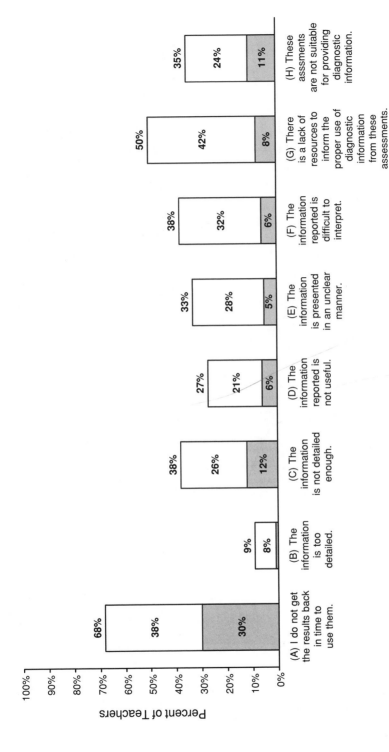

FIGURE 2.7. Obstacles that inhibit the use of diagnostic information from *state-mandated* large-scale assessments. White bars represent the percentage of teachers who agree. Gray bars represent the percentage of teachers who strongly agree.

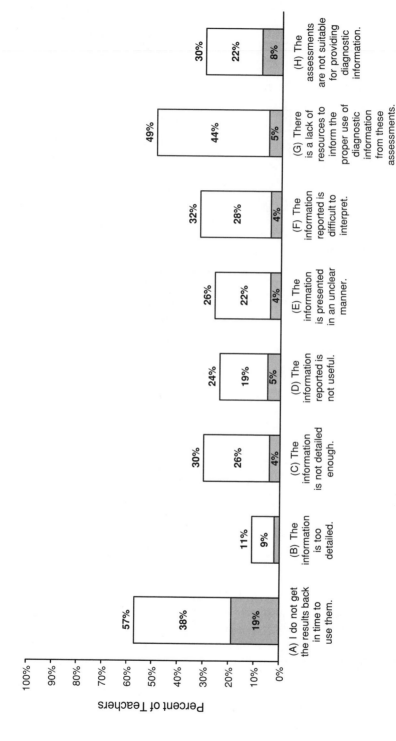

FIGURE 2.8. Obstacles that inhibit the use of diagnostic information from *commercial* large-scale assessments. White bars represent the percentage of teachers who agree. Gray bars represent the percentage of teachers who strongly agree.

of teachers (38% for state-mandated assessments and 32% for commercial assessments) also reported that the information reported on state-mandated and commercial large-scale assessments is difficult to interpret (see Figures 2.7F and 2.8F). Thirty-three percent of teachers believed that diagnostic information from state-mandated assessments is presented in an unclear manner (see Figure 2.7E); 26% of teachers had similar views regarding diagnostic information from commercial large-scale assessments (see Figure 2.8E). Based on these results, further efforts to make diagnostic information from large-scale assessments more useful to teachers and easier for all teachers to understand appear to be necessary.

In a more positive light, assessment developers should be encouraged to see that a majority of teachers do not believe that large-scale assessments are unsuitable instruments for providing diagnostic information. Sixty-five percent of teachers disagreed or strongly disagreed with the statement that "[State-mandated assessments are] not suitable for providing diagnostic information" (results derived from Figure 2.7H). Seventy percent of teachers who receive commercial assessment results disagreed or strongly disagreed with a comparable statement about commercial large-scale assessments (results derived from Figure 2.8H). These results suggest that most teachers regard large-scale assessments as an appropriate vehicle for collecting diagnostic data and are in keeping with results discussed previously. Still, considerable percentages of teachers (35% and 30%) agreed or strongly agreed with this statement for state-mandated and commercial assessments, respectively, so further efforts to better align large-scale assessments with their intended use appear to be warranted.

Do Large-Scale Assessment Results Currently Providing Sufficient Information about Students' Strengths and Weaknesses?

Another important finding of our survey was that a majority of classroom teachers believe that large-scale assessment results do not provide sufficient amounts of information regarding students' strengths and weaknesses. As shown in Figure 2.9, 51% of teachers believed that state-mandated large-scale assessments results *do not* provide sufficient information about students' strengths and weaknesses, and 53% of teachers held similar beliefs about commercial large-scale assessment results. Also, as shown in Figure 2.10, 74% and 71% of teachers believed that it would be valuable to have more diagnostic information than is typically

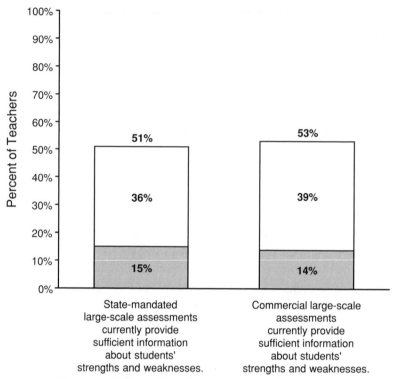

FIGURE 2.9. Extent to which teachers *do not* believe that state-mandated and commercial large-scale assessments currently provide sufficient information about students' strengths and weaknesses. White bars represent the percentage of teachers who disagree. Gray bars represent the percentage of teachers who strongly disagree.

provided by large-scale assessments at the individual student and classroom levels, respectively; 62%, 56%, and 49% of teachers believed it would be valuable to have more diagnostic information available at the grade, school, and district levels, respectively (see Figure 2.10). Based on these results, demand for more diagnostic information from large-scale assessments appears to be strong, particularly at the individual student and classroom levels.

What Kinds of Diagnostic Information Do Teachers Want from Large-Scale Assessments?

In our survey of teachers, it was clear that most teachers wanted not only *more* diagnostic information than is typically provided on large-scale

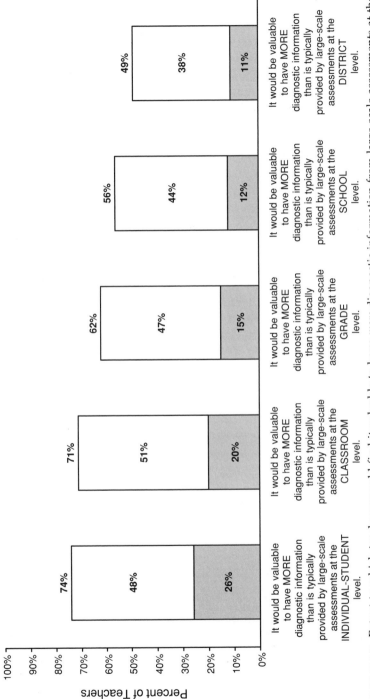

FIGURE 2.10. Extent to which teachers would find it valuable to have *more* diagnostic information from large-scale assessments at the individual student, classroom, grade, school, and district levels. White bars represent the percentage of teachers who agree. Gray bars represent the percentage of teachers who strongly agree.

assessments, but also *different* kinds of diagnostic information. As shown in Figure 2.11, 79% and 73% of teachers believed that it would be valuable to have different diagnostic information than is typically provided by large-scale assessments at the individual student and classroom levels, respectively. A majority of teachers (68%, 61%, and 56%) also believed that it would be valuable to have different diagnostic information at the grade, school, and district levels, respectively (see Figure 2.11).

A number of results from our survey provide insight into the types of diagnostic information that teachers want from large-scale assessments. As indicated in Figures 2.7C and 2.8C, approximately one-third of teachers (38% for state-mandated assessments and 30% for commercial assessments) believed that the diagnostic information currently reported for large-scale assessments is not detailed enough. Much smaller percentages (9% for state-mandated assessments and 11% for commercial assessments) held the contrary view that existing diagnostic information is too detailed (see Figures 2.7B and 2.8B).

We also asked teachers to indicate the importance of reporting assessment results using various points of reference. Although approximately one-half (51%) of teachers indicated that it is important or very important to report norm-referenced diagnostic information (see Figure 2.12I), a larger majority of teachers (between 64% and 89%) believed that it is important or very important to report diagnostic information using a variety of criterion-referenced approaches (see Figures 2.12A to 2.12H). Teachers appear to be especially interested in receiving descriptions of specific skills or knowledge individual students demonstrated on a large-scale assessment, as well as descriptions of specific skills or knowledge individual students should develop (with 89% and 85%, respectively, of teachers stating that it is important or very important to report diagnostic information in these ways) (see Figures 2.12A and 2.12B). Similarly, a majority of teachers indicated that it was important or very important to receive suggested strategies individual students might use to improve their skills or knowledge (81%), as well as to receive suggested strategies a teacher might use to address student needs (83%). Eighty percent of teachers believed that it was important or very important to report results in multiple ways. Seventy-four percent of teachers indicated that it was important or very important to report students' performance on individual items, and 68% and 64%, respectively, had similar beliefs for reporting diagnostic information using number and percentage of items correct (i.e., subscores) and standards-based information (i.e., results in relation to state performance standards).

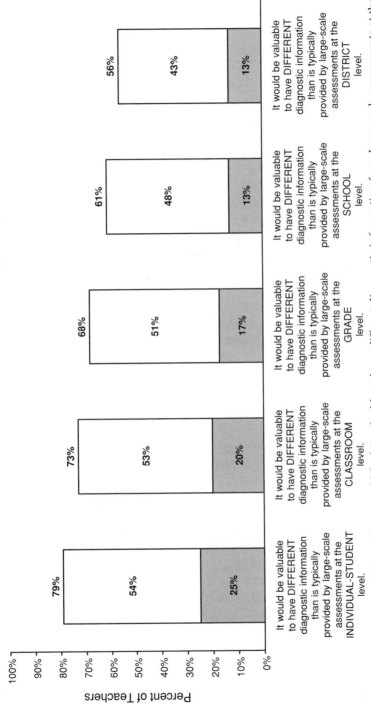

FIGURE 2.11. Extent to which teachers would find it valuable to have *different* diagnostic information from large-scale assessments at the individual student, classroom, grade, school, and district levels. White bars represent the percentage of teachers who agree. Gray bars represent the percentage of teachers who strongly agree.

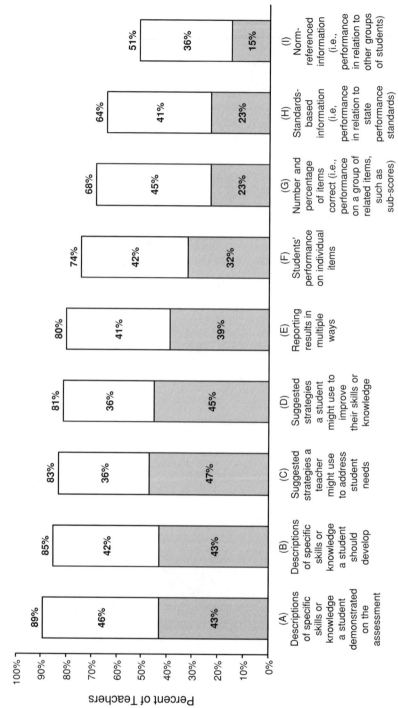

FIGURE 2.12. Extent to which teachers find various points of reference important for reporting diagnostic information. White bars represent the percentage of teachers who find various points of reference important. Gray bars represent the percentage of teachers who find various points of reference very important.

The high levels of importance that teachers give to these various methods of reporting diagnostic information, as well as research that indicates many of these reporting methods are not typically used in existing assessment programs (see Goodman & Hambleton, 2004), offer some important insight into ways that current reporting practices could be improved.

Summary of Educators' Demand for Diagnostic Information

The results of our survey demonstrate that educators are demanding both more and different diagnostic information from large-scale assessments. Although teachers are currently using the results of these assessments, there is a clear need to improve on existing diagnostic assessment reporting practices. In recent years, assessment developers have been modifying their practices to help address these needs. Some of these efforts are explored next.

SOME CURRENT EFFORTS TO ADDRESS EDUCATORS' NEEDS

Although educators appear to have become accustomed to receiving and using large-scale assessments results in their classrooms, the results of our survey suggest further efforts to provide improved and more relevant diagnostic information from these assessments is warranted. Assessment developers are currently responding to these issues in at least two ways: (a) by finding ways to better integrate large-scale assessment results into classroom practice, and (b) by using CDA principles and practices to improve diagnostic reporting procedures for existing assessments. Although neither approach reflects a full consideration of the principles that underlie CDA, we believe that they represent some promising ways to help address educators' needs and, especially if applied jointly, to implement some key CDA principles in practice.

Efforts to Help Integrate Diagnostic Assessment Results into Classroom Practice

In recent years, we have seen some promising efforts to better integrate diagnostic assessment results into classroom practice. These include the development of (a) classroom-based assessments that are directly related to state standards, and (b) guides for classroom and instructional planning that are aligned to information in the score reports of large-scale assessments.

An example of how diagnostic assessment results can be better integrated into classroom practice comes from Ohio. The Ohio Department of Education requires diagnostic testing of all first- and second-
grade students in reading, writing, and mathematics. These assessments
are designed to give teachers information about students' progress
toward the state's standards (Ohio Department of Education, 2005). The
assessments are designed to be flexible and thus vary in how they can be
administered (e.g., assessments can be integrated into regular classroom
activities, administered individually or to a group, and/or administered
orally or written). For each state standard measured, students are classified into one of three categories – clearly on track, further assessment
may be needed, or needs further assessment and/or intervention – based
on the number of items they answered (Ohio Department of Education,
2005). Teachers are provided with recommended activities that are tailored to the needs of students who fall within a given category.

The Stanford 10 Achievement Test (SAT 10) provides another example of how diagnostic assessment results can be better integrated into
classroom practice. The SAT 10 is a commercial large-scale assessment
that reports diagnostic information in the form of general subscores (e.g.,
Word Study Skills, Reading Vocabulary, Reading Comprehension on the
Grade 4 Reading test) and more detailed subcategories of each subscore
(e.g., Literary, Informational, Functional, Initial Understanding, Interpretation, Critical Analysis, Strategies, Thinking Skills; Harcourt Assessment, 2006a). A lot of data (e.g., number correct, scale score, national
percentile rank, national grade percentile, grade equivalent) are provided for each subscore. Further information (number of items, number
answered, and number correct) is provided for the more detailed subcategories of each subscore. Given the large amounts of data that are
provided, there is a clear risk that teachers may find the information
difficult to properly interpret and use (a position that is informed by the
results of our survey, as well as by research of Impara, Divine, Bruce,
Liverman, and Gay, 1991). However, the availability of resources that
go beyond traditional interpretive guides should help in this regard.
Along with the score reports, educators can also receive guides for classroom and instructional planning that are aligned to the information in
the score report (Harcourt Assessment, 2006b). Although our research
did not specifically address the efficacy of these specific supplementary
materials, it is clear from our results that teachers are currently lacking
resources to inform the proper use of diagnostic information from large-
scale assessments. Based on this finding, we believe that any responsible

attempts to develop resources that link classroom practices with diagnostic assessment results is a step in the right direction and should be explored by all assessment developers.

Using Cognitive Diagnostic Assessment Principles and Practices to Improve Diagnostic Reporting Procedures for Existing Large-Scale Assessments

The number of assessment developers who discuss, research, and implement principles and practices that have been informed by the CDA literature is growing. Nichols (1994) and NRC (2001) provide several examples of diagnostic assessment systems designed and built completely within a cognitive framework (e.g., HYDRIVE, GATES, Automated Cognitive Modeler). However, because most large-scale assessments have been developed through a psychometric approach to assessment design and often were not originally designed to provide diagnostic feedback, it is helpful to consider what steps, if any, can be taken to improve the instructional relevance of the results from these assessments when the full implementation of CDA principles is not feasible. We explore this issue by examining some ways in which CDA principles have been applied to improve the scoring and reporting procedures of existing psychometrically designed assessments.

Testing programs of all types are exploring alternative approaches to scoring and reporting that will allow them to report sufficiently reliable information at smaller and smaller grain sizes in the hope that such feedback can inform instruction. Methodologies that are frequently researched include augmenting subscores with Bayesian techniques (Wainer et al., 2001) or multidimensional item response theory (Thissen & Edwards, 2005), as well as comparing individual item response patterns to item-by-skill matrices to classify students as masters or nonmasters of each skill, such as with rule space methodology (Tatsuoka, 1983, 1995). These approaches are a departure from the typical methods of providing diagnostic information using number and percent correct or performance on individual items, and are of interest as assessment developers seek to improve current practice.

CDA principles are also influencing testing programs that were not designed to be diagnostic by enabling them to provide test candidates with more than just a scale score and the associated percentile rank, and to identify different skills for which they can report results. Some recent efforts by the College Board help illustrate this fact.

The PSAT/NMSQT Score Report Plus, which was first provided to students and educators in 2001, employed a cognitive-centered approach in its development. Researchers and test developers identified the multiple skills required to solve each item (Buck et al., 1998), and then used a modified rule-space approach (DiBello, 2002; DiBello & Crone, 2001) to classify students as either masters or nonmasters on each of the skills according to their individual item response patterns. Suggestions for how to improve on weak skills are also provided on the score report. The PSAT/NMSQT was not defined from an explicit cognitive model, but this CDA-influenced approach to providing individualized score reports was seen as a more effective way to provide instructionally useful information than approaches that do not differentiate strengths and weaknesses among students with the same total score, or subscores grouped by content or skill.

A second example of CDA influence on large-scale testing programs is the College Board research initiative to identify cognitive skills for the critical reading and mathematics sections of the SAT in an effort to make SAT results more informative to both students and educators. In 2003, as the development for the revised SAT was underway, research began on how to better describe student performance in ways that could help inform instruction. At the time, the current SAT score report only provided raw number correct and estimated percentile scores for items grouped by item type on the Verbal section (i.e., Critical Reading, Analogies, and Sentence Completion) and items grouped by content category on the Mathematics section (i.e., Arithmetic and Algebraic Reasoning, and Geometric Reasoning). The value of this type of feedback was questionable, especially when one tries to imagine how such feedback could inform instruction. Although the SAT was not designed within an explicit model of cognition in reading or mathematics, in an effort to improve the diagnostic utility of the test results, the College Board initiated research to determine the types of cognitive skills that underlay the test (Huff, 2004; O'Callaghan, Morley, & Schwartz, 2004; VanderVeen, 2004). As a result of this research, the College Board is able to demonstrate that the critical reading section can be theoretically and empirically supported as measuring the following clusters of text comprehension skills: determining the meaning of words; understanding the content, form, and functioning of sentences; understanding the situation implied by a text; understanding the content, form, and function of larger sections of text; and analyzing authors' purpose, goals, and strategies (VanderVeen et al., 2007). As noted by VanderVeen et al., these five clusters generally align with extensively researched cognitive processing models of text comprehension, such as the ones proposed by Kintsch (1998) and Perfetti (1985, 1986), providing evidence to support the validity of these potential new reporting classifications and demonstrating that the test as a whole assesses the types of cognitive processes that underlie text comprehension. Thus, in addition to providing additional skill areas for which results can be reported, this type of post hoc analysis offers useful ways for test developers to show that their assessments align with the cognitive models that underlie the construct of interest (a powerful piece of evidence for establishing test validity).

These examples of improving the instructional relevance of large-scale assessments are encouraging. In the next section, we discuss future directions for those interested in improving the instructional utility of assessment results.

FUTURE DIRECTIONS

In this chapter, we explore the demand that exists for CDA from within the assessment community and educators' demands for diagnostic feedback from the assessments for which their students regularly take part. We have also outlined some promising ways to make diagnostic results more relevant to instructional practice, as well as some efforts to improve the types of diagnostic information that can be derived from existing large-scale assessments. We end this chapter by highlighting some issues that, based on the demands discussed here, warrant further attention. These include efforts to develop more coherent, comprehensive, and continuous assessment systems that are based on the same underlying model of learning, and take advantage of recent technological advancements. Also, to maximize potential, assessment results must be provided to educators in a timelier fashion, and the assessment results must be presented in a more useful and meaningful manner.

Develop Assessment Systems Based on the Same Underlying Model of Learning

The intent of providing detailed diagnostic feedback from large-scale assessments is to facilitate valid interpretations with regard to students' strengths and weaknesses on the material tested, as well as to aid in generalizing from the assessment context to the domain of interest. Presumably, the value of assessment results increase as their interpretability in the context of classroom instruction and learning increases. As mentioned previously in the chapter, when curriculum, instruction, and assessment are part of a coherent system that is based on a common model of learning, then the assessment results, per force, will be instructionally relevant. The application of CDA principles in the design and development of assessments is certain to help in this regard, and should be the ultimate goal of assessment developers. However, in situations where this is not immediately feasible (e.g., in the case of well-established assessment programs), we propose that adapting CDA principles in the analyses and reporting of results (e.g., what has been done for the PSAT/NMSQT and SAT) is a reasonable and practicable response to address some important demands from assessment developers who advocate CDA and from educators who are demanding better diagnostic information from large-scale assessments.

Although the primary focus of this chapter was to explore the demands for CDA from the perspective of large-scale testing, it is clear from the results of our survey that teachers overwhelmingly view classroom-based assessments as being the best way to gauge student strengths and weaknesses. Unfortunately, however, a body of research exists that shows that classroom assessment practices do not always provide accurate and valid information, measure a full complement of cognitive skills (see, e.g., Notar et al., 2004, and Stiggins, 2001), or are as well integrated with instruction as they could be (Black & Wiliam, 1998a, 1998b). Consequently, a more concerted effort by the measurement community and teacher training programs to provide teachers with a full array of assessment tools (particularly those that serve a formative function) appears warranted. Many have discussed the benefits of using a cognitive model of learning as the basis for an integrated system of curriculum, instruction, and assessment in the classroom (e.g., Nichols, 1993, 1994; NRC, 2001; Pellegrino et al., 1999). Consistent with the views of NRC (2001), we argue that extending the application of CDA principles to the development of large-scale assessments would enable the creation of a comprehensive assessment system, where results from all levels would provide complementary pieces of evidence that can be readily linked to and interpreted within a common model of student learning.

Take Advantage of Recent and Upcoming Technological Advancements

As noted by NRC (2001), technological advancements are helping remove some of the constraints that have limited assessment practice in the past. Assessments no longer need to be confined to a paper-and-pencil format. Computer-based platforms will help assessment developers use innovative item types that have the potential to measure the kinds of knowledge and skills that are more reflective of the cognitive models of learning on which assessments should be based (Huff & Sireci, 2001; Sireci & Zenisky, 2006). The implementation of computer-based assessment systems will also enable assessment developers to move away from traditional scoring methods that only consider whether a student provided the correct response to an item by allowing them to collect data on such things as the choices that students make in items that have multiple components, auxiliary information accessed when answering an item, and the length of time students take to complete an item (Luecht, 2002). Of course, these advancements also introduce a number of technical challenges outside the more general challenges (e.g., cost and the current lack of suitable equipment in many K–12 schools) that currently limit the widespread application of computer-based assessments in the K–12 environment. These include developing complex scoring models that can make use of all data that are available from computer-based assessments to make valid inferences about the cognitive strategies employed by the examinee, to diagnose the learning state of the examinee, and to provide instructionally relevant feedback that can be made available to teachers and students in a time frame that will increase the use and value of these results. Furthermore, it is hoped that other creative solutions that exploit technological advances, such as automated scoring that minimizes or removes the need for human scorers, can be refined and used within the operational constraints of K–12 large-scale assessments. Thus, although more general issues such as cost and the limited availability of necessary equipment in the K–12 system are being addressed by policy makers, researchers should ready themselves for the day when computers are accessible to each examinee and should investigate ways to use technology to assess new and important skills of interest, such as the ability to transfer knowledge to new situations.

Improve Operational Procedures to Minimize the Delay in Reporting Results

In our survey, we found that a key factor that inhibits teachers' use of diagnostic information from large-scale assessments is the significant delay between test administration and the availability of results. We see this as major obstacle for effective use of large-scale assessment data, and one that deserves greater attention if these assessments are to provide useful diagnostic information to educators, parents, and students.

The need to minimize lag time between administering the test and reporting results is something of which most assessment developers and policy makers are well aware. Still, it is the unfortunate reality that many large-scale assessment results are released months after the tests are administered, and often are not released until the subsequent school year (after students have moved on to another teacher and possibly to another school). If assessment developers want to provide educators with meaningful and useful diagnostic information, they must find ways to do this in a timelier manner, without sacrificing the quality and integrity of the assessments. It is encouraging to note that some departments of education have made significant progress in this area. For example, the British Columbia (BC) Ministry of Education, which serves approximately 575,000 K–12 public school students (BC Ministry of Education, 2005a, p. 11), has refined its assessment cycle and administration and reporting procedures so they are able to release results only 4 *weeks* after an assessment session (BC Ministry of Education, 2005b, pp. 33–34). In addition to offering multiple testing sessions throughout the year, the BC Ministry of Education (2005b, 2006) delivers student-, school-, and district-level results electronically through secure Internet portals, and now provides schools with the option of administering a number of large-scale assessments on computers. We are encouraged by these developments, and it is hoped that other K–12 assessment programs will effectively improve the speed with which they are able to release assessment results, while maintaining (and even improving on) the quality of their assessments.

Present Assessment Results in a More Useful and Meaningful Manner

Many techniques can be applied to improve the types and clarity of information that are provided on large-scale assessment score reports. In their review of existing student-level score reports from state-mandated and commercial assessments, Goodman and Hambleton (2004) outlined some weaknesses in current reporting practices that should be addressed. These include reporting an excessive amount of information in some reports and not reporting other essential pieces of information (e.g., the purpose of the assessment and how the results will and should be used) in others, not providing information about the precision of the test scores, using statistical jargon that will not be readily understood by users of the reports, and reporting a large amount of information in too small of a space. Further guidance is also available in the work of Hambleton and Slater (1997), Impara et al. (1991), Jaeger (1998), Wainer (1997), and Wainer, Hambleton, and Meara (1999).

The research presented here shows that teachers are eager for both more and different types of diagnostic information. Suggestions have been provided on how this type of information could be made available using CDA principles. Presenting this information in a useful and meaningful manner is another challenge that assessment developers must face and address.

CONCLUSION

Large-scale assessments for summative and high-stakes purposes are an integral part of the K–12 educational system. Although these assessments are typically developed for the purposes of accountability or to rank-order students, redesigning these assessments from a cognitively principled approach could help integrate these assessments with teaching and learning in the classroom without necessarily jeopardizing their primary purposes. Similarly, CDA principles and practices can be used post hoc to identify new types of information that can be reported for assessments developed from within a psychometric framework. Results from our survey show that teachers are searching for as much information as possible about their students from various sources. It is our responsibility as educators to respond creatively to their needs by taking advantage of new knowledge about instruction and learning when designing assessments and when analyzing and reporting assessment results. The application of CDA principles would be an important advancement in this regard.

References

Bennett, R. E. (1999). Using new technology to improve assessment. *Educational Measurement: Issues and Practice, 18*(3), 5–12.

Bennett, R. E., & Bejar, I. I. (1998).Validity and automated scoring: It's not only the scoring. *Educational Measurement, 4*, 9–17.

Bennett, R. E., Steffen, M., Singley, M. K., Morley, M., & Jacquemin, D. (1997). Evaluating an automatically scorable, open-ended response type for measuring mathematical reasoning in computer-adaptive tests. *Journal of Educational Measurement, 34*(2), 62–176.

Black, P., & Wiliam, D. (1998a). Assessment and classroom learning. *Assessment in Education: Principles, Policy and Practice, 5*(1), 7–74.

Black, P., & Wiliam, D. (1998b). Inside the black box: Raising standards through classroom assessment. *Phi Delta Kappan, 80*(2), 139–148.

British Columbia (BC) Ministry of Education. (2005a). *2004/05 Service plan report.* Retrieved June 26, 2006, from http://www.bcbudget.gov.bc.ca/Annual_Reports/2004_2005/educ/educ.pdf.

British Columbia (BC) Ministry of Education. (2005b). *Handbook of procedures for the graduation program.* Retrieved June 26, 2006, from http://www.bced.gov.bc.ca/exams/handbook/handbook_procedures.pdf.

British Columbia (BC) Ministry of Education. (2006). *E-assessment: Grade 10 and 11 – Administration.* Retrieved June 26, 2006, from http://www.bced.gov.bc.ca/eassessment/gradprog.htm.

Buck, G., VanEssen, T., Tatsuoka, K., Kostin, I., Lutz, D., & Phelps, M. (1998). *Development, selection and validation of a set of cognitive and linguistic attributes for the SAT I verbal: Sentence completion section* (ETS Research Report [RR-98–23]). Princeton, NJ: Educational Testing Service.

Chipman, S. F., Nichols, P. D., & Brennan, R. L. (1995). Introduction. In P. D. Nichols, S. F. Chipman, & R. L. Brennan (Eds.), *Cognitively diagnostic assessment* (pp. 1–18). Mahwah, NJ: Erlbaum.

College Board. (2006). *Passage-based reading.* Retrieved January 15, 2006, from http://www.collegeboard.com/student/testing/sat/prep_one/passage_based/pracStart.html.

Cronbach, L. J. (1971). Test validation. In R. L. Thorndike (Ed.), *Educational measurement* (3rd ed., pp. 443–507). Washington, D.C.: American Council on Education.

Cronbach, L. J., & Meehl, P. E. (1955). Construct validity in psychological tests. *Psychological Bulletin, 52,* 281–302.

DiBello, L. V. (2002, April). *Skills-based scoring models for the PSAT/NMSQT^{TM}.* Paper presented at the annual meeting of the National Council on Measurement in Education, New Orleans.

DiBello, L. V., & Crone, C. (2001, April). *Technical methods underlying the PSAT/NMSQT^{TM} enhanced score report.* Paper presented at the annual meeting of the National Council on Measurement in Education, Seattle.

DiBello, L. V., Stout, W. F., & Roussos, L. A. (1995). Unified cognitive/psychometric diagnostic assessment likelihood-based classification techniques. In P. D. Nichols, S. F. Chipman, & R. L. Brennan (Eds.), *Cognitively diagnostic assessment* (pp. 361–390). Hillsdale, NJ: Erlbaum.

Embretson (Whitely), S. (1983). Construct validity: Construct representation versus nomothetic span. *Psychological Bulletin, 93*(1), 179–197.

Embretson, S. E. (1999). Generating items during testing: Psychometric issues and models. *Psychometrika, 64*(4), 407–433.

Feltovich, P. J., Spiro, R. J., & Coulson, R. L. (1993). Learning, teaching, and testing for complex conceptual understanding. In N. Frederiksen, R. J. Mislevy, & I. I. Bejar (Eds.), *Test theory for a new generation of tests* (pp. 181–218). Hillsdale, NJ: Erlbaum.

Fischer, G. H., & Formann, A. K. (1982). Some applications of logistic latent trait models with linear constraints on the parameters. *Applied Psychological Measurement, 6*(4), 397–416.

Goodman, D. P., & Hambleton, R. K. (2004). Student test score reports and interpretive guides: Review of current practices and suggestions for future research. *Applied Measurement in Education, 17*(2), 145–220.

Goodman, D. P., & Huff, K. (2006). *Findings from a national survey of teachers on the demand for and use of diagnostic information from large-scale assessments.* Manuscript in preparation, College Board, New York.

Gorin, J. (2005). Manipulating processing difficulty of reading comprehension questions: The feasibility of verbal item generations. *Journal of Educational Measurement, 42,* 351–373.

Hambleton, R. K., & Slater, S. (1997). *Are NAEP executive summary reports understandable to policy makers and educators?* (CSE Technical Report 430). Los Angeles: National Center for Research on Evaluation, Standards, and Student Teaching.

Harcourt Assessment. (2006a). *Stanford achievement test series, tenth edition: Critical, action-oriented information.* Retrieved January 29, 2006, from http://harcourtassessment.com/haiweb/Cultures/en-US/dotCom/Stanford10.com/Subpages/Stanford+10+-+Sample+Reports.htm.

Harcourt Assessment. (2006b). *Support materials for parents, students, and educators.* Retrieved January 29, 2006, from http://harcourtassessment.com/haiweb/Cultures/en-US/dotCom/Stanford10.com/Subpages/Stanford+10+-+Support+Materials.htm.

Huff, K. (2004, April). A practical application of evidence centered design principles: Coding items for skills. In K. Huff (Organizer), *Connecting curriculum and assessment through meaningful score reports.* Symposium conducted at the meeting of the National Council on Measurement in Education, San Diego.

Huff, K. L., & Sireci, S. G. (2001). Validity issues in computer-based testing. *Educational Measurement: Issues and Practice, 20*(4), 16–25.

Impara, J. C., Divine, K. P., Bruce, F. A., Liverman, M. R., & Gay, A. (1991). Does interpretive test score information help teachers?*Educational Measurement: Issues and Practice, 10*(4), 16–18.

Jaeger, R. (1998). *Reporting the results of the National Assessment of Educational Progress* (NVS NAEP Validity Studies). Washington, DC: American Institutes for Research.

Kintsch, W. (1998). *Comprehension: A paradigm for cognition.*Cambridge, MA: Cambridge University Press.

Leighton, J. P., Gierl, M. J., & Hunka, S. (2004). The attribute hierarchy method for cognitive assessment: A variation on Tatsuoka's rule-space approach. *Journal of Educational Measurement, 41,* 205–237.

Luecht, R. M. (2002, April). *From design to delivery: Engineering the mass production of complex performance assessments.* Paper presented at the annual meeting of the National Council on Measurement in Education, New Orleans.

Massachusetts Department of Education. (2004). *2004 MCAS technical report.* Retrieved January 15, 2006, from http://www.doe.mass.edu/mcas/2005/news/04techrpt.doc#_Toc123531775.

Massachusetts Department of Education. (2005). *The Massachusetts comprehensive assessment system: Guide to the 2005 MCAS for parents/guardians.* Malden: Author.

Mathematical Sciences Education Board. (1993). *Measuring what counts: A conceptual guide for mathematics assessment.*Washington, DC: National Academy Press.

Messick, S. (1989). Validity. In R. L. Linn (Ed.), *Educational measurement* (3rd ed., pp. 13–103). New York: American Council on Education/Macmillan.

Mislevy, R. J. (1996). Test theory reconceived. *Journal of Educational Measurement, 33*(4), 379–416.

Mislevy, R. J., & Riconscente, M. M. (2005). *Evidence-centered assessment design: Layers, structures, and terminology* (PADI Technical Report 9). Menlo Park, CA: SRI International and University of Maryland. Retrieved May 1, 2006, from http://padi.sri.com/downloads/TR9_ECD.pdf.

Missouri Department of Elementary and Secondary Education. (2005). *Missouri assessment program: Guide to interpreting results.* Retrieved June 24, 2006, from http://dese.mo.gov/divimprove/assess/GIR_2005.pdf.

National Research Council (NRC). (1999). *How people learn: Brain, mind, experience, and school.* Washington, DC: National Academy Press.

National Research Council (NRC). (2001). *Knowing what students know: The science and design of educational assessment.* Washington, DC: National Academy Press.

National Research Council (NRC). (2002). *Learning and understanding: Improving advanced study of mathematics and science in U.S. high schools.*Washington, DC: National Academy Press.

New Jersey Department of Education. (2006). *Directory of test specifications and sample items for ESPA, GEPA and HSPA in language arts literacy.* Retrieved June 24, 2006, from http://www.njpep.org/assessment/TestSpecs/LangArts/TOC.html.

Nichols, P. D. (1993). *A framework for developing assessments that aid instructional decisions* (ACT Research Report 93–1). Iowa City, IA: American College Testing.

Nichols, P. D. (1994). A framework for developing cognitively diagnostic assessments. *Review of Educational Research, 64,* 575–603.

Nitko, A. J. (1989). Designing tests that are integrated with instruction. In R. L. Linn (Ed.), *Educational measurement* (3rd ed., pp. 447–474). New York: American Council on Education/Macmillan.

No Child Left Behind (NCLB) Act of 2001, Pub. L. No. 107-110, § 1111, 115 Stat. 1449–1452 (2002).

Notar, C. E., Zuelke, D. C., Wilson, J. D., & Yunker, B. D. (2004). The table of specifications: Insuring accountability in teacher made tests. *Journal of Instructional Psychology, 31*(2), 115–129.

O'Callaghan, R., Morley, M., & Schwartz, A. (2004, April). *Developing skill categories for the SAT® math section.* In K. Huff (Organizer), Connecting curriculum and assessment through meaningful score reports. Symposium conducted at the meeting of the National Council on Measurement in Education, San Diego.

Ohio Department of Education. (2005). *Diagnostic guidelines.* Retrieved February 1, 2006, from http://www.ode.state.oh.us/proficiency/diagnostic_achievement/Diagnostics_PDFs/Diagnostic_Guidelines_9–05.pdf.

O'Neil, T., Sireci, S. G., & Huff, K. L. (2004). Evaluating the content validity of a state-mandated science assessment across two successive administrations of a state-mandated science assessment. *Educational Assessment and Evaluation, 9*(3–4), 129–151.

Pellegrino, J. W. (2002). Understanding how students learn and inferring what they know: Implications for the design of curriculum, instruction, and assessment. In M. J. Smith (Ed.), *NSF K–12 Mathematics and science curriculum and implementation centers conference proceedings* (pp. 76–92). Washington, DC: National Science Foundation and American Geological Institute.

Pellegrino, J. W., Baxter, G. P., & Glaser, R. (1999). Addressing the "two disciplines" problem: Linking theories of cognition and learning with assessment and instructional practice. *Review of Research in Education, 24,* 307–353.

Perfetti, C. A. (1985). Reading ability. In R. J. Sternberg (Ed.), *Human abilities: An information-processing approach* (pp. 31–58). New York: W. H. Freeman.

Perfetti, C. A. (1986). *Reading ability.*New York: Oxford University Press.

Riconscente, M. M., Mislevy, R. J., & Hamel, L. (2005). *An introduction to PADI task templates* (PADI Technical Report 3). Menlo Park, CA: SRI International and University of Maryland. Retrieved May 1, 2006, from http://padi.sri.com/downloads/TR3_Templates.pdf.

Sheehan, K. M. (1997). A tree-based approach to proficiency scaling and diagnostic assessment. *Journal of Educational Measurement, 34*(4), 333–352.

Sheehan, K. M., Ginther, A., & Schedl, M. (1999). *Development of a proficiency scale for the TOEFL reading comprehension section* (Unpublished ETS Research Report). Princeton, NJ: Educational Testing Service.

Sireci, S. G., & Zenisky, A. L. (2006). Innovative item formats in computer-based testing: In pursuit of improved construct representation. In S. M. Downing & T. M. Haladyna (Eds.), *Handbook of test development* (pp. 329–348). Mahwah, NJ: Erlbaum.

Snow, R. E., & Lohman, D. F. (1989). Implications of cognitive psychology for educational measurement. In R. L. Linn (Ed.), *Educational measurement* (3rd ed., pp. 263–331). New York: American Council on Education/Macmillan.

Steinberg, L. S., Mislevy, R. J., Almond, R. G., Baird, A. B., Cahallan, C., DiBello, L. V., Senturk, D., Yan, D., Chernick, H., & Kindfield, A. C. H. (2003). *Introduction to the Biomass project: An illustration of evidence-centered assessment design and delivery capability* (CRESST Technical Report 609). Los Angeles: Center for the Study of Evaluation, CRESST, UCLA.

Stiggins, R. (2001). The unfulfilled promise of classroom assessment. *Educational Measurement: Issues and Practice, 20*(3), 5–15.

Tatsuoka, K. K. (1983). Rule space: An approach for dealing with misconceptions based on item response theory. *Journal of Educational Measurement, 20,* 345–354.

Tatsuoka, K. K. (1995). Architecture of knowledge structures and cognitive diagnosis: A statistical pattern recognition and classification approach. In P. D. Nichols, S. F. Chipman, & R. L. Brennan (Eds.), *Cognitively diagnostic assessment* (pp. 327–359). Hillsdale, NJ: Erlbaum.

Thissen, D., & Edwards, M. C. (2005, April). *Diagnostic scores augmented using multidimensional item response theory: Preliminary investigation of MCMC strategies*. Paper presented at the annual meeting of the National Council on Measurement in Education, Montreal.

VanderVeen, A. (2004, April). *Toward a construct of critical reading for the new SAT*. In K. Huff (Organizer), Connecting curriculum and assessment through meaningful score reports. Symposium conducted at the meeting of the National Council on Measurement in Education, San Diego.

VanderVeen, A., Huff, K., Gierl, M., McNamara, D. S., Louwerse, M., & Graesser, A. (2007). Developing and validating instructionally relevant reading competency profiles measured by the critical reading section of the SAT. In D. S. McNamara (Ed.), *Reading comprehension strategies: Theory, interventions, and technologies*. Mahwah, NJ: Erlbaum.

Wainer, H. (1997). Improving tabular displays: With NAEP tables as examples and inspirations. *Journal of Educational and Behavioral Statistics, 22*(1), 1–30.

Wainer, H., Hambleton, R. K., & Meara, K. (1999). Alternative displays for communicating NAEP results: A redesign and validity study. *Journal of Educational Measurement, 36*(4), 301–335.

Wainer, H., Vevea, J. L., Camacho, F., Reeve, B. B., Rosa, K., Nelson, L., Swygert, K. A., & Thissen, D. (2001). Augmented scores: "Borrowing strength" to compute scores based on small numbers of items. In D. Thissen & H. Wainer (Eds.), *Test scoring* (pp. 343–387). Hillsdale, NJ: Erlbaum.

Washington State Office of Superintendent of Public Instruction. (2006). *Test and item specifications for grades 3–high school reading WASL*. Retrieved June 24, 2006, from http://www.k12.wa.us/Assessment/WASL/Readingtestspecs/TestandItemSpecsv2006.pdf.

3

Cognitive Modeling of Performance on Diagnostic Achievement Tests

A Philosophical Analysis and Justification

Stephen P. Norris, John S. Macnab,
and Linda M. Phillips

To interpret and use achievement test scores for cognitive diagnostic assessment, an explanation of student performance is required. If performance is to be explained, then reference must be made to its causes in terms of students' understanding. Cognitive models are suited, at least in part, to providing such explanations. In the broadest sense, cognitive models should explain achievement test performance by providing insight into whether it is students' understanding (or lack of it) or something else that is the primary cause of their performance. Nevertheless, cognitive models are, in principle, incomplete explanations of achievement test performance. In addition to cognitive models, normative models are required to distinguish achievement from lack of it.

The foregoing paragraph sets the stage for this chapter by making a series of claims for which we provide philosophical analysis and justification. First, we describe the philosophical standpoint from which the desire arises for explanations of student test performance in terms of causes. In doing this, we trace the long-held stance within the testing movement that is contrary to this desire and argue that it has serious weaknesses. Second, we address the difficult connection between understanding and causation. Understanding as a causal factor in human behavior presents a metaphysical puzzle: How is it possible for understanding to cause something else to occur? It is also a puzzle how understanding can be caused. We argue that understanding, indeed, can cause and be caused, although our analysis and argument are seriously compressed for this chapter. Also, in the second section, we show why understanding must be taken as the causal underpinning of achievement tests. Third, we examine how cognitive models of achievement might provide insight into students' understanding. This section focuses on what cognitive models can model. Fourth, we discuss what cognitive models cannot model, namely, the normative foundations of achievement, and refer to the sort of normative models that are needed in addition. Finally, we provide an overall assessment of the role and importance of cognitive models in explaining achievement test performance and supporting diagnostic interpretations.

CAUSATION AND EXPLANATION

A justification is required for turning to cognitive models in the development and use of diagnostic achievement tests because there has been a long-standing view in the testing field with a contrary leaning. That view is *nominalism*. Nominalism in various guises has had a great deal of influence on educational testing. It is the view that ability and achievement concepts, and the theoretical terms and constructs used in educational and psychological testing and in science more generally, are labels for sets of direct observables, such as classes of behaviors exhibited under certain conditions. Nominalism contrasts to a view of theoretical terms as referring to unobservable entities, structures, and processes for which direct observables are but manifest signs. According to the strongest versions of nominalism, the *entire* meaning of constructs such as "intelligence" or "critical thinking" can be given by reference to observable behaviors, such as performances on tests. The view leads to the use of a statistical generalization model for making inferences from scores. Roughly put, test items are selected randomly from a domain, and the proportion of items an examinee answers correctly is used to infer the proportion of the domain of items that the examinee would answer correctly if given the opportunity. This proportion of the domain of items is then equated to a level of achievement.

This inference model faces insurmountable theoretical difficulties. The classes of items needed to define achievement are unbounded, and it is impossible to select randomly from unbounded sets. One nominalist response to this problem is to shift the target of the examination. Although the set of possible addition problems is unbounded, the set of possible pairs of three-digit numbers is finite. So, instead of testing for understanding or ability in addition, the nominalist might test for the ability to add three-digit numbers. Regardless of whether this response is adequate (and we believe it is not), the properties of those items about which we want to make inferences are conditional properties that the items have in some possible future (e.g., whether a student would answer them correctly). Statistical generalization cannot handle properties of sets in possible futures but deals with the properties of sets at the time they are sampled. Ultimately, it is about properties of students that we want to infer, for instance, about their levels of achievement, but statistical generalizations can sanction inferences only about the properties of the objects selected, which are test items and not students. These and other problems are described at length by Norris, Leighton, and Phillips (2004) and Tomko (1981).

Tomko (1981) also pointed to some peculiarities of this view when set against established testing practices. One such practice is the treatment of guessing. The nominalist view does not provide a means for making a distinction between an examinee who guesses the test answers and gets 25% of them correct by chance and an examinee who knows the answers to the same 25% but not the remaining 75%. Both exhibit the same behavior and would be said to have the same level of achievement, according to the nominalist view. Yet, as revealed in the use of corrections for guessing and in instructions not to guess, there is a frequent desire among test developers and users to make a distinction between these two examinees, presumably because the manner in which examinees arrive at their answers makes a difference to judgments of their achievement.

Another peculiarity of nominalism when set against testing practice arises from the fact that educators often use examinees' performance on tests to motivate and guide attempts to improve examinees' achievement. The assumption underlying such uses of scores is that examinees' performance indicates both possible sources of their behavior and possible points of intervention. However, because on the nominalist view the source or genesis of behaviors is not of interest and does not figure in nominalist theorizing, there is a glaring disjunction between the nominalist theory of testing and the diagnostic and remedial uses to which achievement test results actually are put.

It is also difficult for nominalism to account for the scientific practice of psychologists and other social scientists. MacCorquodale and Meehl (1948) illustrated the problem well when they distinguished between intervening variables and hypothetical constructs. The former involve no assumptions about the existence of an underlying reality but are "simply [quantities] obtained by a specified manipulation of the values of empirical variables" (p. 103). The latter, in contrast, are intended to impute underlying processes, structures, or events. Hypothetical constructs "are not reducible to sentences about impressions" (p. 96); that is, they cannot be defined in terms of observable behaviors. The connection is that nominalists understand psychological constructs as intervening variables that do not impute any reality underlying overt behavior. A key question raised by MacCorquodale and Meehl is whether science can get by using only intervening variables. They argued that scientific practice defies this conclusion:

> We would find it rather difficult to defend the ingenious conditioning hypotheses developed in Hull's series of brilliant papers (1929–) in the *Psychological Review* on the ground that they merely provide a 'convenient shorthand summarization of the facts'.... We suspect that Professor Hull himself was motivated to write these articles because he considered that the hypothetical events represented in his diagrams may have actually *occurred*. (pp. 104–105)

Similarly, we find it rather difficult to understand performance on a test without appealing to underlying mental processes, structures, or events that may actually have occurred or may actually exist.

It is even doubtful that the narrowest conception of criterion-referenced testing, a field of testing that relies on statistical generalization to justify inferences from test performances, can find a sufficiently strong theoretical footing within the nominalist position that undergirds it. We have argued already that the statistical generalization model cannot support the inferences about future performance desired by test users. Nevertheless, users *intend* to use the tests for prognostication. However, such inferences about the future need to depend on some assumption of stability or lawfulness in the phenomenon under study. Would it, then, be legitimate to infer an examinee's future performance from a present performance on the basis of stability in the test? Clearly, stability in the test is not enough because there must also be some form of stability in the examinee and in the interactions between the examinee and the context, including the test. This conclusion points to one of the greatest peculiarities between nominalist-based theories and testing practice because, according to criterion-referenced testing, performances are properties of the items. However, for the generalization to hold across those performances, stability in some underlying properties of the examinees and in their interaction with items must be invoked, but such a conception of underlying properties cannot be contemplated within a nominalist theory.

In addition to the problems mentioned previously, we want to highlight in some detail another problem with nominalism that is more crucial to educational testing. That problem is the stance on causation and explanation that goes along with nominalism. According to the nominalist conception, ability and achievement terms "label" or "summarize" categories of observed behavior (Mischel, 1973, p. 262). What happens when these descriptive labels are put into an explanatory context and used to state causes or explanations of behaviors? An example might be as follows: "Critical thinking causes or explains performance on the *Cornell Critical Thinking Test, Level X*". This statement would be no more than a description of a coincidence between the presentation of a stimulus (the Cornell test) and the exhibition of a class of behaviors. If constructs are conceived nominalistically, then there is a necessity to view causation and explanation as regularity relationships, famously articulated by Hume (1748/1955) more than 250 years ago.

More recently, the regularity view of causation has been elaborated into the deductive-nomological (D-N) model or the covering law model, and adopted by prominent early theorists of construct validation (e.g., Cronbach, 1971). Contemporary deliberations on this type of scientific explanation widely reference a 1948 seminal article by Hempel and Oppenheim. According to them, "The question '*Why* does the phenomenon happen?' is construed as meaning 'according to what general laws, and by virtue of what antecedent conditions does the phenomenon occur?'" (p. 136). Hempel and Oppenheim posited that what is being explained must be logically deducible from the antecedent conditions and the general laws. This type of explanation they labeled "causal", and the explanations themselves were deductive arguments. That is, for Hempel and Oppenheim, just as for Hume, causal explanations for particular events are provided when empirical regularities (general laws) connect a particular set of antecedent conditions with the occurrence of the particular event.

Rescher (1962) argued that if scientific explanations, as Hempel and Oppenheim would have them, were confined to deductive arguments from general laws, many modern scientific discussions would be defined as "outside the pale of *explanations proper*" (Rescher, 1962, p. 50). In a move away from a regularity view of explanation, Rescher and others (e.g., Reichenbach, 1971; Salmon, 1971), and after 1948, even Hempel (1966), stressed that the concept of scientific explanation needed to be extended to include explanations based on statistical probability. As McErlean (2000) states, "while deductive arguments have universal laws which necessitate their conclusions, the conclusion of an inductive argument is not guaranteed, it is at best rendered highly probable" (p. 20). According to Salmon (1989), the most important development in the second of his *Four Decades of Scientific Explanation* was the explicit study and advancement of models of statistical explanation. In statistical explanation, an event is explained by showing that its occurrence is highly probable on the basis of given facts and known statistically general laws.

In addition to the critique of deductivism, there have been other, more significant critiques of the D-N view. One critique, and this was known to Hempel, is that functional explanations do not fit the D-N pattern or the probabilistic refinements to it. Functional explanations are closely associated with questions in biology and studies of human affairs (Nagel, 1961). Here the question concerns the purpose or function of something: Why do Os have P? (Kitcher, 1989, p. 417). Examples of questions requiring a functional explanation include the following: Why do test developers use four-alternative, multiple-choice items? Why do people guess when they do not know the right answers? In answering these questions, attention must be paid to consequences, ends, functions, and purposes. A possible explanation for the test developers' practice is that four alternatives reduce the chances of guessing to an acceptable level. The problem for the D-N model in accounting for this explanation is that there is little chance of finding a general law as required by that model that can be used in a derivation of the fact that developers use four-alternative items. The possible candidates, such as that 25% is an acceptable level of chance among test developers, simply are not true generally. Different test developers have different reasons for their practice: some might judge 25% to be an acceptable risk of guessing; some might simply choose four alternatives because it is common to do so, or because it is too difficult to think of more.

An additional critique of deductivism comes from historians who insist there is a narrative or genetic explanation that relates the story leading up to the event to be explained. Scriven (1959, 1962, 1963) championed this critique and others of the D-N model in a series of papers. The classic example that Scriven used concerns the mayor who contracted paresis. In the example Scriven constructs, he believes we can explain the mayor's contracting paresis by pointing out that he previously had syphilis that was left untreated. The problem for the D-N model in accounting for this explanation is that there is only a low probability of contracting paresis from untreated syphilis. Therefore, there is no possibility of constructing the general law required of the model, and the low probability of the connection between syphilis and paresis challenges even the probabilistic refinements to the model, which depend on the existence of high probabilities.

Nagel (1961) considered the distinctiveness of genetic explanations debatable, because he believed it likely that they were "by and large probabilistic" (p. 26). As he explained,

the task of genetic explanations is to set out the sequence of major events through which some earlier system has been transformed into a later one. The explanatory premises of such explanations will therefore necessarily contain a large number of singular statements about past events in the system under inquiry. (p. 25)

He noted that because not every past event is mentioned, those events that are included must be selected "on the basis of assumptions (frequently tacit ones) as to what sorts of events are causally relevant to the development of the system" (p. 25).

A final problem with the D-N model that we mention is that it does not respect the asymmetry of the explanatory relation. If A explains B, then, unless we are dealing with the special case of a feedback loop, B does not explain A. We can explain examinees' performance on an item by the difficulty of the item. However, we cannot explain the difficulty of the item by examinees' performance on it (although we could estimate the level of difficulty from their performance). The D-N model cannot block this type of unwanted explanation, primarily because it is based on a constant conjunction view of causation that is bidirectional.

Contemporary alternatives to the D-N view designed to avoid such critiques have been offered by Kitcher (1989), an explanatory unification view, and van Fraassen (1980), a pragmatics of explanation view. According to Kitcher's view, the value of explanations resides in their enabling us to unify and organize knowledge. Scientific knowledge is unified to the extent that our explanations fit the phenomena into a general world view with few independent assumptions. According to van Fraassen's view, an explanation is an answer to a question, specifically to a why question. In addition to the pragmatic element introduced by viewing explanations as speech acts in this manner, van Fraassen developed pragmatic theories of questions and of answers. His theory of questions shows that they must be interpreted in context, making their meanings pragmatic. These views are too elaborate to specify in detail in this chapter. Suffice it to say that they were both developed as responses to the overwhelming critiques of the D-N view and that neither fully addresses all concerns about the meaning of explanation.

A fundamental problem with the D-N view and its nominalist relative is that they provide no means of having confidence in the regularities that occur in nature and society, including educational testing contexts. If we rely on Hume, we are left with mere sequences of events, one type following another, which, as far as we have reason to believe, could alter their pattern at any time or cease to occur altogether. Set against this unsettling view is a practical confidence in the continuance of patterns of events when science is settled on why they occur. As an alternative to the D-N view, we adopt in this chapter a model of causation and explanation inspired by Harré (1970, 1993). Harré (1993) provides a convincing argument about the source of such confidence:

> It turns out that when people argue about the force of some correlation, say that between smoking and the twenty-odd diseases which have been found to be connected with it statistically, the issue turns almost always on the mechanism by which the inhaling of tobacco smoke induces the cancerous proliferation of cells, the furring of the arteries, the wrinkling of the skin, the development of cataract and so on. In the absence of an understanding of the mechanism or mechanisms involved, it is always open to the critic of the force of the correlation to suggest that the statistics are mere coincidence, or that they reflect the joint effects of a common cause. (p. 89)

Harré's (1970, 1993) view of causation and explanation stands in stark contrast to the nominalist view. On the nominalist account, scientific investigation does not theorize more deeply than direct observable behaviors, except to classify and name them and compile how such classes might coincide. Such coincidences then serve as the basis of prediction but without the confident knowledge of why we should expect past coincidences to occur in the future. Harré sees the establishment of regularities among observed phenomena as only the first phase of scientific investigation. The second phase consists of postulating and testing mechanisms by which the classes of events are connected. "These mechanisms usually consist of hypothetical entities which are referred to in the theory that is constructed to account for the experimental results. At the heart of a theory is a model or representation of the relevant mechanism" (p. 91). Scientific investigation proceeds by trying to establish (or not) the existence of the modeled entities and their functioning in bringing about the observed regularities. According to Harré's view, we can explain an event when we can point to the causal mechanism that led to its occurrence.

Harré's (1970, 1993) theory of causation and explanation shows how to remove the peculiarities that arise when testing is studied through the lens of nominalism. Guessing, according to Harré's account, would be construed as a strategy that examinees employ and that, at least in theory, could be identified by the lines of thinking they follow when answering items. An examinee asked to choose the largest proper factor of 24, guesses when he chooses 12 just because it is the largest option provided. An examinee who systematically identifies the factors of 24 starting at the smallest by testing them through division, and who continues testing beyond what seems to be the largest factor, exhibits a mechanism that shows understanding. A teacher who examines not only students' answers to the question, but who also looks to the reasons they provide, is able to decide whether a review of the basic concepts of factoring is needed based on whether students' reasons point to guessing or understanding. Explanations in accord with Harré's conception are also able to support (or not) assumptions of stability within examinees that are needed for prediction of future performance. The causal mechanisms to which Harré refers are stable properties. Although they do admit to change over time, the types of thinking that examinees exhibit in dealing with mathematical factoring are unlikely to change without either some instructional intervention or time sufficient for forgetting. Therefore, there is a period of time over which predictions can be expected to hold based on stability of understanding.

For the purpose of summation and context setting, it is helpful to note that the history of educational testing theories has paralleled the history of epistemology. During the early and mid-20th century, construct validation was framed in terms of the most widely accepted epistemology of the time, which was logical positivism mingled with some post-positivistic thought. Central to positivism was the doctrine that theoretical constructs were useful fictions. Constructs had a functional role in making predictions, and because prediction and explanation were seen as the same processes except in time-reversed order, constructs were tied in the same functional manner to explanations. Explanations thus conceived were deductive arguments. That is, explanation was achieved through derivation of observations from general laws, with no ontological commitments beyond the observable level. This epistemology foundered when theorists searched within such explanations for causative agents – that which makes things happen. Scientists find underlying mechanisms for why things occur as they do, an accomplishment quite at odds with a theory that looks no deeper than surface behavior. Similarly, testing theorists find it useful, as well as an aid to understanding, to think of guessing as an underlying cognitive strategy and to imagine interventions to improve students' test performance by targeting what underlies their overt behavior. We turn next to the attempt to characterize the causal underpinnings of students' performance in terms of their understanding.

UNDERSTANDING AND CAUSATION

We began this chapter with the claim that cognitive models can provide causal explanations of performance on diagnostic achievement tests in terms of examinees' understanding. Now that we have introduced Harré's (1970, 1993) theory of causation and explanation, we need to show how understanding can be conceptualized as a causal mechanism.

It is instructive to begin with a physical phenomenon where the relationship of cause to effect is reasonably well known. We might explain a forest fire by saying that it was caused by an unattended campfire. If pressed, we can expand the explanation to include the proximity of combustible materials to the campfire as being part of the cause. At another level, we might appeal to the chemical properties of the combustible materials to explain why they burned with a certain heat and rapidity. Note that each causal account of the forest fire has been given in naturalistic terms. All causes invoked are natural entities and processes that are themselves causally determined. A complete causal explanation of the forest fire in naturalistic terms is possible, at least in principle, even if it is impossible to provide in practice.

If we ask why the campers abandoned their fire, however, a new problem arises. An appeal to the chemical properties of wood points to an explanatory mechanism that accounts for why wood burns. However, an appeal to the chemical properties of the campers would never be sufficient to explain their actions. An appeal to their belief properties could explain why the campers did what they did, but beliefs are very different from chemical properties. Significantly, beliefs make reference and have semantic properties, which lie outside the realm of the physical. A belief bears an informational relationship between its holder and something in the world. One does not simply have a belief; one has a belief *about* something.

The fact that beliefs bear an informational relationship to the world is not sufficient to explain their causal properties. Unlike the combustibility of wood, beliefs can be mistaken or unjustified. The campers might have believed that the campfire was put out when in fact it was not. They might have believed they had no responsibility to be sure the campfire was extinguished, when that responsibility was theirs alone. Even if beliefs are false or unjustified, they can still have causal influences on behaviors. The causal efficacy of beliefs is unlike what is required for naturalistic explanation. In the naturalistic case, it is only the true chemical and physical properties of wood, regardless of our beliefs, that have any causal influence on its burning. We can assume that the campers acted based on their appraisal of the situation, regardless of whether that appraisal was accurate. The campers would have related their beliefs about the campfire to a much larger network of other beliefs, including facts about the world and norms governing what constitutes the right thing to do. It is such networks of beliefs, norms, and actions that constitute understanding.

To explain why the campers were careless, we interpret their actions in a way that we did not have to interpret the physical components of the fire. People choose to do things, and there is always the possibility that they could have chosen to do otherwise. Wood does not choose to burn, but simply burns when conditions are right. To make sense of what caused the campers to do what they did, we have to grasp what would count as motivation for another person. We imaginatively place ourselves in what we believe to be a position relevantly similar to the campers'. This position is immersed in the world, physically and socially. An explanation from understanding is an explanation *from within a life*.

The same issues arise in testing contexts. Consider the situation of a multiple-choice test of critical thinking. The standards and criteria of critical thinking are rarely sufficient to define correct solutions on such a test because different background beliefs can lead to different correct answers (e.g., Norris, 1988). That is, more than one answer for a given task might reflect critical thinking, which can lead to difficulties. If the background beliefs of some examinees are different from those of the test developer, then examinees would be penalized for choosing answers different from those judged as good by the test developer, even when the examinees follow the standards and criteria of critical thinking. Alternatively, examinees thinking uncritically might be rewarded for choosing the same solutions the test developer reached solely on the grounds of a common set of background beliefs. Again, an explanation based on understanding, or lack of it, must be made from within a life, particular view of the world, set of background beliefs, or however you wish to frame it.

Jürgen Habermas's (1984, 1998, 2003) theory of communicative action provides a model of understanding that can bring us to explanation from within a life and thence back to cognitive models. Habermas grounds understanding in the fundamental competencies that make communication possible. The causal power of understanding is at once at the forefront. Briefly, the central idea is that human understanding and rationality are consequences of the human capacity for communicative action. Communicative action is any action in which two persons attempt to come to a position of mutual understanding about some matter. For mutual understanding to occur, cooperation is necessary. The reliance on cooperation in communicative action requires that two people can take the same stance regarding a state of affairs.

Communicative action can be intelligibly reconstructed in terms of three validity claims that are necessarily raised by interlocutors. When person A uses language to come to a mutual understanding of some matter with B, A simultaneously and implicitly raises three claims to which B must assent for the communicative action to be successful: (a) A claims that A's words truthfully depict some matter in the world (this claim can allow for indirect use, such as irony), (b) A claims to be in a position to make such a claim, and (c) A claims to be sincere. B must accept these three claims, even provisionally, for mutual understanding to occur. These claims—to truth, normative rightness, and sincerity—are universal claims, transcending all local standards of evaluation. That is, when I claim to be telling the truth, I expect that other people are, in principle, able to see my claim as true. Even if I modestly claim that I am reporting things as they seem to me, it is a universal claim to truth in that I expect that anyone who understood my position would see that I am truly reporting things as they seem to me. When I claim to be normatively authorized to make a claim, I expect that anyone who examined my position would agree. Again, I can make a weak claim to authorization and still expect that my reasons are binding on other rational agents. Even if I believe that my authority is debatable, *that* position is intended to be acceptable to anyone relevantly placed to look at the situation. Finally, the sincerity condition is such that I am claiming not to be deliberately deceiving my interlocutor. The interlocutor who doubts my sincerity can come to some understanding of the matter about which I speak, but cannot come to a mutual understanding with me, as we ultimately believe different things about our collective situation.

To understand a concept, proposition, or justification, one must adopt a stance that recognizes the claims to universal validity on which the concept, proposition, or justification is contingent. That is, one must see the concept, proposition, or justification as understandable by other rational agents. I understand a concept, proposition, or justification when I know the conditions under which another person can accept it as true. Suppose that a student were faced with a mathematical problem that can be solved in a number of distinct ways. Whichever method of solution the student chooses, the choosing itself indicates a publicly assessable rationality. Suppose further that the student wonders why this particular method is good for this particular problem. The very asking of that question implies its universality. The question makes no sense unless the student holds out the possibility that there are ego-transcendent reasons for using one method rather than another. Without holding out that possibility, the student could not even formulate the question, "Why ought I do it this way?" The word "ought" in this context points to the fundamental normativity of understanding. There are right ways and wrong ways to proceed, and as soon as one enters into consideration of right and wrong, one has gone beyond the first person, into a second-person stance. "Right" in such contexts is not just right for me, or for us, but right for anyone who enters into a relevantly similar position.

For two people to come to a position of mutual understanding, they must take the stance with one another that the rational agent takes with him- or herself. For a student to understand a concept, he or she must be able to bring forth reasons about the concept's propositional content to which someone else could give assent. To reach mutual understanding with another person about the concept in question, he or she must either convince the other person that his or her reasons are good ones, or at least that he or she could relate such reasons if required to do so. Some reasons are known in advance to the person who understands, but many are not. If pressed, we often can formulate novel justifications for our beliefs or actions with which we can even surprise ourselves. The reason that we can do this is that much of what we believe and do is unarticulated; we believe and do many things without giving them our full attention. Part of our understanding is encoded in our daily lives, in the ways that we engage with the physical world in action (Taylor, 1995), and in the ways that we engage the symbolically structured lifeworld that we socially share with others (Habermas, 1998). If this were not so, intellectual creation would not be possible. Students can answer questions that they have never seen before because they can relate them to other thoughts and experiences. If this relating is acceptable to an interlocutor, then the interlocutor is justified in making the judgment that the student understands. Alternatively, the interlocutor may be satisfied that the student could provide such justifications if pressed on the matter.

To make the judgment of acceptability, the interlocutor must make inferences about the interlocutor's and student's overlapping life-worlds. Some of this is nonproblematic. There are ways of living in the world that are taken for granted, including language and certain types of physical and educational experience. In the case of classroom assessment, this background is likely to be well understood on the basis of shared experiences, as well as on the basis of periodic communicative action that brings the student and teacher into shared understanding on relevantly similar matters. Standardized achievement tests pose a much more difficult theoretical and practical challenge. The assessor must make inferences about a student whom he or she has never met, and of whose educational and other life experiences the assessor has only a vague notion. One way out of this situation is to enter into discourse with the student. Why did you do this? Explain what you are attempting here? Through the giving of reasons, the student is able to demonstrate the relevant understanding required on the test and how that understanding affected his or her performance. Of course, there are institutional barriers to this approach, often making communication between the student and the assessor impossible. Examiners typically do not have sufficient resources to engage in comprehensive questioning with each student in regard to each desired educational outcome.

Testing theorists are aware of this difficulty, but they must take all practical steps that are possible within the constraints imposed by testing contexts to ground their interpretations of test scores in terms of examinees' understanding. Given the institutional barriers to genuine discourse, it is desirable that a proxy for discourse be developed in which understanding is idealized as the communicative processes that underwrite a discourse between two people directed toward mutual understanding. We are proposing a model of understanding that is a simulation of communicative action. To model a person's understanding, one can model an idealized internal dialog in which a person self-reflexively poses questions from the second-person perspective. Thus, for example, if a student is responsible for constructing meaning in a reading comprehension achievement test, then the relevance of the student's background beliefs to interpreting a text cannot be specified in advance from an outside perspective. Relevance must be judged by the soundness of the specific interpretive inferences that the student makes (Norris & Phillips, 1994), and those inferences cannot be pre-judged or known without asking the student to reveal them. What the examiner should want to know is not simply the student's interpretation of the text, but how that interpretation was derived—what judgments the student made, and what connections the student forged between his or her background beliefs and the text information.

These models of students' understanding, however they are structured, may be validated through detailed discursive practices between assessors and students relevantly similar to those who will be tested. We recognize that relevant similarity likely will prove to be a difficult criterion to develop. The validation group that will serve as proxies for the tested group will need to be chosen such that their lifeworlds match the test group's lifeworlds in ways that provide overlap between relevant educational experiences. The nature and extent of this overlap is as much an empirical question as it is a philosophical one, and the latter is the focus of this chapter.

COGNITIVE MODELS AND UNDERSTANDING

In the preceding section, we argued that a person's understanding of some matter can be the causal basis of their actions. In the model of understanding we proposed for adoption, the researcher attempts to appreciate the meaning of an action from within the form of life in which it is experienced by construing understanding in terms of an idealized internal dialog. We now apply this conception to the game of chess to illustrate the connection between understanding and possible objects of cognitive models.

Consider the claim, "Garry understands how to play chess." If the claim is justified, it indicates that Garry has propositional knowledge of the rules of the game, that he is able to play with some proficiency, and that he is able to give some accounting of these matters. That is, Garry is able self-reflexively to give an accounting of chess from the point of view of a person engaged in chess; he is able to provide reasons for his beliefs that would satisfy an appropriately placed interlocutor. While playing the game, he is his own interlocutor; when presenting analysis, his interlocutors are his listeners or his readers. His interlocutors make judgments of Garry's understanding, based on their ability imaginatively to place themselves in relevantly similar situations. Such judgments of understanding typically are not precise. People can disagree about what understanding entails and how much understanding someone shows because judgmental norms can be very flexible.

The judgment that Garry understands chess implies more than that he can move the pieces such that his games are intelligible. The judgment also implies that when he plays, he is meaningfully engaged in a form of life. One could, for example, teach two actors to move the pieces in accord with a chess game. They do not need to know the rules that govern how the pieces move, nor do they need to have any intentions or planning beyond the script. To make the judgment that these actors do not understand chess, one must have access to more than their chess performance. There must be evidence that they are unable to provide a rational accounting for making some moves and not others. In this case, the cause of the actors' moves has nothing to do with understanding how to play chess. Rather, their actions are causally related to their participation in the form of life that we call "acting." Similarly, a computer program does not understand chess and does not even play chess in the normal sense of the word. The computer program's workings can be completely explained in naturalistic terms because the program does not intend or choose anything.

Faced with a chessboard configuration and being asked to make the next move, different players might suggest different moves. Some players might agree on what constitutes the best move but might provide different reasons for making that move. If the different reasons are defensible, then the same rationally motivated move can have different causes arising from different players' understandings. Thus, cognitive models must allow for the same phenomenon to emerge from a number of different causal networks. This is not an unusual requirement. Forest fires, for example, can be caused by a number of different circumstances, although the chemical and physical properties of combustion are invariant. Yet, if understanding provides a causal explanation of chess moves, and even if it is clear that one person's understanding can be strongly divergent from another person's, it is nonetheless possible that some portions of the causal explanation of move choice are consistent across different persons. If certain cognitive processes can apply generically to different networks of understanding and causation, then a role for cognitive models in assessment emerges.

A cognitive model of the chess player or test taker needs to be concerned with only a subset of the range of issues that underwrite understanding. Once an activity such as chess or the writing of an achievement test is understood within the context of a form of life, the details of the intellectual components of the activity are plausibly interpreted and modeled. If we want to know why Garry moved the knight to a particular square, we need to know in what activity he is engaged. If we know that he is playing a competitive game of chess against a peer, then we can substantially narrow the explanatory possibilities we consider. Still, we are not yet fully prepared to model his cognitive processes. As we argued in the preceding section, models of Garry's cognitive process must be sensitive to his overall understanding, which in turn can be understood only in terms of the background against which he is thinking, including his physical and social engagement in the world and his previously held beliefs and concepts. To see that this is so, compare the identical knight move in identical positions in two different games. In the first game, Garry Jones is a relative beginner to chess and is playing against a player equally matched to him. In the second game, Garry Kasparov is playing against Anatoly Karpov for the world championship. It is highly unlikely that Garry Jones and Garry Kasparov have strongly similar understandings of the position as they make what appear to be identical choices. From the participant perspective, the situations are very different. In a sense, the two Garrys are engaged in different activities. The same physical move bears a different informational relationship to two different networks of understanding. Cognitive processes are part of the causal network that leads from understanding to the move, and it is desirable to use the move to assist us in inferring some significant features of understanding. To trace this relationship backward from the move to the understanding, however, more information than just the particular knight move is required.

The chess example is intended to highlight the complicated relationship between understanding and action, as well as to acknowledge that cognitive processes of some sort are involved in the causal link between the two. To build a cognitive model, one constructs a causal mechanism that links understanding to action by showing how this causal mechanism performs the desired tasks. Although understanding itself cannot be naturalized, there are no similar barriers to naturalizing cognitive processes. Thus, it could be that a chess computer offers a good cognitive model of the causal link between understanding and action. Just as the computer does not play chess, but merely performs a series of syntactic manipulations, it is conceivable that the cognitive process portion of the movement from understanding to action is also a matter of syntactic manipulations. Naturalizing cognitive processes is not inconsistent with our arguments, but as we argue in the following section understanding cannot be modeled in this way.

It might be believed that cognitive processes cannot be modeled without taking into account the entirety of a person's understanding. However, models need not be so comprehensive. It is possible that, despite the contextuality of individual networks of understanding, many cognitive processes that allow action to arise from those networks may be generically described. The two chess-playing Garrys likely have differing amounts of chess information on which to base their judgments. They likely visualize and calculate to differing depths. They likely evaluate the quality of their opponents' moves differently. None of these differences entail that the processes by which they relate their current beliefs and norms to their actions cannot be meaningfully compared. Such comparisons could be a primary function of cognitive models.

As it is for chess, a test for student understanding ought to include provisions for making inferences against the backgrounds that students bring to their thinking about the content of the test questions. Suppose a diagnostic test item asked students to calculate the length of the hypotenuse of a plane right-angled triangle with legs of length 5 cm and 12 cm. The question permits only one correct answer, namely, 13 cm. Yet, the correct answer in isolation provides little evidence of the examinee's mathematical understanding. Compare the examinee who recalls the fact that (5,12,13) is a Pythagorean triple to one who finds the squares of 5 and 12 and extracts the square root of their sum, to one who enters the vector [5,12] into a calculator and presses the button for the modulus function. It is clear that all three examinees understand something mathematical about the content of the question, but it is not clear that they understand the same thing. As we argued in the previous section, a communicative situation in which an interlocutor's questions can be suitably addressed is required to make sense of the examinees' understanding. Within that situation, questions of cognitive process can arise. By what means does the first examinee apply previously acquired knowledge of Pythagorean triples to the problem at hand? How does the second examinee judge that the memorized formula is the right one for this problem? What connection does the third examinee see between a vector and right triangles? If diagnostic achievement testing is to provide a means of inferring understanding, then the challenge is to acquire information that relates examinee understanding to examinee performance. The solution to the triangle problem is not sufficient to underwrite an inference to understanding. What is required is a rich set of information in which examinees reveal details of the context to which cognitive processes are applied in linking understanding to performance.

The invocation of cognitive processes and building them into cognitive models of performance enriches the interpretive framework within which understanding can be inferred. If cognitive models can provide plausible links between features of performance and features of understanding, then it becomes possible to think well beyond what is possible with sampling models. Rather than go from "x got $n\%$ of the questions correct" to "x will get $(n \pm \varepsilon)\%$ correct in other trials", as sampling models purport to allow, cognitive models provide the possibility of moving from "x made performance p" to "x understands salient features f_1, $f_2, \ldots f_k$ of concept c, which provides a partial causal explanation of performance p". The cognitive model potentially has explanatory powers that a sampling model cannot have.

COGNITIVE MODELS ARE INCOMPLETE MODELS OF UNDERSTANDING

It is our contention that cognitive models can provide just the sort of causal mechanisms that Harré believes are required for explanation. Cognitive models of performance tend to cover features of thought such as patterns of attention; patterns of dependence, overdependence, and underdependence on various sources of information; completeness and incompleteness of thinking; reference to and reliance on norms and principles of thinking; strategy use and metacognition; the generality of thinking; and knowledge structures (Norris et al., 2004). Yet, insofar as cognitive models are empirical theories, they can give only partial accounts of understanding. Cognitive models can link understanding to performance in causal terms, but they cannot account for the phenomenon of understanding itself; that is, they cannot be used to determine whether understanding has been demonstrated. Understanding not only has elements that can be empirically modeled, as we have shown, but it also has normative features that fall outside the empirical. Furthermore, the objects of cognition cannot be captured fully by cognitive models. Reasoning with basic principles such as *modus tollens*, for example, can be described by such models, but no cognitive model can say what *modus tollens* is, when it has or has not been followed, or why it is a valid mode of reasoning.

Let us consider the following three simple addition problems:

2 +3 ?	2 + 3 = ?	If John has 2¢ and Linda has 3¢, how many cents do they have altogether?

Somewhat different cognitive models might be needed to explain performance on each task because the proportion of students getting such items correct tends to vary from task to task. Nevertheless, the tasks have exactly the same normative underpinning found within mathematics. The cognitive models might tell us how children reason when they face each task, and how that reasoning leads to or detracts from their understanding. However, what counts as understanding on these tasks must come from outside the cognitive models and from within the field of mathematics. This latter claim applies not only to determining the right answer, but also to determining which routes to that answer are legitimate and illegitimate. The cognitive models must work together with normative models to fully account for understanding.

Imagine a logic test with the following task:

Does the conclusion in the argument follow necessarily? Yes or No.
If bats are mammals, then bats have lungs.
Bats are mammals.
Therefore, bats have lungs.

Similarly to the mathematics example, a cognitive model can account for the reasoning steps and strategies that examinees follow in determining their answers. Yet, the right answer itself is not something that the cognitive model can tell us, say by telling us the answer that most examinees choose, the answer that most expert logicians choose, or the routes that any of these people take to find a solution. The right answer is something that falls outside the scope of any empirical theory. In both the case of the mathematical operation of addition and the case of *modus ponens*, understanding cannot be accounted for by what people do when they work on the tasks. Understanding resides in seeing the infinite normative implications present in each case. As a consequence, a cognitive model cannot tell us what a test is testing because the model cannot be used to determine which implications are normatively acceptable.

Even considering the general features of thought mentioned in the first paragraph of this section, cognitive models cannot provide a complete explanation of performance displaying these features. Cognitive models can capture the features themselves and tell us that they occur. However, it is not enough to know that examinees followed certain principles and strategies when arriving at their answers. An account is needed of the appropriateness of those strategies and principles in context, and cognitive models cannot provide such an account. Cognitive models can represent the use of information and what examinees' thinking covers, but they cannot tell whether appropriate use was made of the information or whether examinees' thinking was complete. Such normative judgments fall outside the model.

As a final note, we acknowledge that both cognitive models and normative theory must allow for degrees of understanding. One rarely wants to claim that understanding is an all-or-nothing affair. One can understand many things about addition of integers and be able to add pairs of integers in a variety of situations but be unable to add complex numbers, or to say anything about them at all. In such a case, it would be absurd to say that the person understands nothing about addition. Details about the depth of the person's understanding, including contextual detail, are required to make sense of what is going on. As with our previous point, cognitive models alone cannot be used to specify degrees of understanding.

OVERALL ASSESSMENT

In this chapter, we argue that the use of cognitive models of performance on diagnostic achievement tests is justified if the models can help provide explanations in terms of examinees' understanding. Cognitive models, built on data from examinees' reported internal dialogs while they engage in achievement test items, can help describe their level of understanding. However, we argue that cognitive models cannot provide complete explanations of understanding because understanding involves a normative element that empirical theories cannot capture.

We have not yet said why we want to gain insight into examinees' understanding on achievement tests. There are at least five reasons. The first is that understanding is an educational ideal. When we teach students mathematics, science, or logic, we aim not only to get them to solve problems and get the right answers, but also to grasp the reasons why certain answers are right and why certain procedures are legitimate for arriving at them. Setting our sights any lower than this is to show disrespect for students as persons and as potentially autonomous beings. Reliance on a statistical generalization model of inference from performance ignores examinees' understanding and, for that reason, is a practice that does not square with our educational ideals. This ethical consideration alone is grounds for seeking an alternative testing model. The use of cognitive models for explaining performance on achievement tests and making inferences from scores is on an ethically stronger footing, if not also a scientifically stronger one.

Second, appealing to examinees' understanding, or lack thereof, is the most plausible way to explain what they do on tests. If we cannot appeal to their understanding as revealed by the reasoning that they employ, then their performance on tests remains a mystery. Presumably, we do not as educators want to be in a situation in which we have no good idea of why students are responding in the ways that they do to the tests that we give them.

Third, knowledge of what students understand when they take diagnostic achievement tests allows us to more firmly ground predictions of their future performance on tasks requiring the same understanding. Knowledge of what students understand gives us insight into those aspects of their performance that are principled, and hence likely to be repeated in similar future contexts, and those that are arbitrary, and thus less likely of repetition.

Fourth, and following from the third, knowledge of what students understand and do not understand provides a rationale for which instructional interventions might be needed to improve their understanding by capitalizing on what they already do understand.

Fifth, and finally, we know that correct performance can arise from poor understanding. However, even if bundles of items can provide more secure inferences about examinees' understanding and help avoid examiners' being misled by correct answers examinees have stumbled on by poor reasoning, we still need an answer to the question of what precisely it is that examinees are understanding. The answer to such a question can come only from a perspective provided by cognitive models buttressed with normative models. The reason takes us back to our examples: we cannot know why the campers abandoned their fire or what it meant to make a particular move on a chessboard without some view from the inside concerning the campers' and chess players' motives, intentions, and reasons. Similarly, we cannot know from our stance as outsiders why a student chooses a particular answer on a critical thinking test or interprets a passage in a particular way on a reading comprehension test. Cognitive models attempt to provide a view, however partial and fallible, from the inside, and it is this view that makes cognitive models so important in interpreting diagnostic achievement test scores.

References

Cronbach, L. J. (1971). Test validation. In R. L. Thorndike (Ed.), *Educational measurement* (2nd ed., pp. 443–507). Washington, DC: American Council on Education.

Habermas, J. (1984). *The theory of communicative action*. Boston: Beacon Press.

Habermas, J. (1998). *On the pragmatics of communication*. Cambridge, MA: MIT Press.

Habermas, J. (2003). *Truth and justification*. Cambridge, MA: MIT Press.

Harré, R. (1970). *The principles of scientific thinking*. Chicago: The University of Chicago Press.

Harré, R. (1993). *Laws of nature*. London: Duckworth.

Hempel, C. G. (1966). *Philosophy of natural science*. Englewood Cliffs, NJ: Prentice Hall.

Hempel, C. G., & Oppenheim, P. (1948). Studies in the logic of explanation. *Philosophy of Science, 15*(2), 135–175.

Hume, D. (1955). *An inquiry concerning human understanding* (C. W. Hendel, Ed. & Intro.). Indianapolis: Bobbs-Merrill. (Original work published 1748).

Kitcher, P. (1989). Explanatory unification and the causal structure of the world. In P. Kitcher & W. C. Salmon (Eds.), *Minnesota studies in the philosophy of science: Vol. XIII. Scientific explanation* (pp. 410–499). Minneapolis: University of Minnesota Press.

MacCorquodale, K., & Meehl, P. E. (1948). On a distinction between hypothetical constructs and intervening variables. *Psychological Review, 55*, 95–107.

McErlean, J. (2000). *Philosophies of science: From foundations to contemporary issues*. Belmont, CA: Wadsworth.

Mischel, W. (1973). Toward a cognitive social learning reconceptualization of personality. *Psychological Review, 80*, 252–283.

Nagel, E. (1961). *The structure of science: Problems in the logic of scientific explanation*. New York: Harcourt, Brace & World.

Norris, S. P. (1988). Controlling for background beliefs when developing multiple-choice critical thinking tests. *Educational Measurement, 7*(3), 5–11.

Norris, S. P., Leighton, J. P., & Phillips, L. M. (2004). What is at stake in knowing the content and capabilities of children's minds? A case for basing high stakes tests on cognitive models. *Theory and Research in Education, 2*(3), 283–308.

Norris, S. P., & Phillips, L. M. (1994). The relevance of a reader's knowledge within a perspectival view of reading. *Journal of Reading Behavior, 26*, 391–412.

Reichenbach, H. (1971). *The theory of probability, an inquiry into the logical and mathematical foundations of the calculus of probability*. Berkeley: University of California Press.

Rescher, N. (1962). The stochastic revolution and the nature of scientific explanation. *Synthese, 14*, 200–215.

Salmon, W. C. (1971). *Statistical explanation and statistical relevance*. Pittsburgh: University of Pittsburgh Press.

Salmon, W. C. (1989). Four decades of scientific explanation. In P. Kitcher & W. C. Salmon (Eds.), *Minnesota studies in the philosophy of science: Vol. XIII. Scientific explanation* (pp. 3–219). Minneapolis: University of Minnesota Press.

Scriven, M. (1959). Definitions, explanations, and theories. In H. Feigl, M. Scriven, & G. Maxwell (Eds.), *Minnesota studies in the philosophy of science* (Vol. II, pp. 99–195). Minneapolis: University of Minnesota Press.

Scriven, M. (1962). Explanations, predictions, and laws. In H. Feigl & G. Maxwell (Eds.), *Minnesota studies in the philosophy of science* (Vol. III, pp. 170–230). Minneapolis: University of Minnesota Press.

Scriven, M. (1963). The temporal asymmetry between explanations and predictions. In B. Baumrin (Ed.), *Philosophy of science: The Delaware Seminar* (Vol. I, pp. 97–105). New York: Wiley.

Taylor, C. (1995). *Philosophical arguments*. Cambridge, MA: Harvard University Press.

Tomko, T. N. (1981). *The logic of criterion-referenced testing*. Unpublished doctoral dissertation, University of Illinois at Urbana−Champaign.

van Fraassen, B. C. (1980). *The scientific image*. Oxford, UK: Clarendon.

4

Test Validity in Cognitive Assessment

Denny Borsboom and Gideon J. Mellenbergh

INTRODUCTION

Scientific theories can be viewed as attempts to explain phenomena by showing how they would arise, if certain assumptions concerning the structure of the world were true. Such theories invariably involve a reference to theoretical entities and attributes. Theoretical attributes include such things as electrical charge and distance in physics, inclusive fitness and selective pressure in biology, brain activity and anatomic structure in neuroscience, and intelligence and developmental stages in psychology. These attributes are not subject to direct observation but require an inferential process by which the researcher infers positions of objects on the attribute on the basis of a set of observations.

To make such inferences, one needs to have an idea of how different observations map on to different positions on the attribute (which, after all, is not itself observable). This requires a measurement model. A measurement model explicates how the structure of theoretical attributes relates to the structure of observations. For instance, a measurement model for temperature may stipulate how the level of mercury in a thermometer is systematically related to temperature, or a measurement model for intelligence may specify how IQ scores are related to general intelligence.

The reliance on a process of measurement and the associated measurement model usually involves a degree of uncertainty; the researcher assumes, but cannot know for sure, that a measurement procedure is appropriate in a given situation. For instance, personality researchers may use summed item scores (computed from responses to questionnaire items such as "I like to go to parties") as indicators of personality traits such as extraversion, but one should realize that this common practice is based on hypotheses that may be false. For instance, extraversion may not exist, or the items may measure something else altogether. However, this uncertainty is by no means confined to psychological research; it is present, to varying degrees, in all areas of science. For instance, in astronomy, the movement of solar systems is inferred on the basis of spectral analyses of light emitted by such systems; the idea is that the amount of displacement of the wave frequency spectrum indicates the speed with which the system moves away or toward us. Similarly, in neuroscience it is assumed that differences in activity across the brain are systematically related to differences in the amount of blood flow across brain regions (this forms the basis of functional magnetic resonance imaging [fMRI]). In both cases, researchers rely on a system of hypotheses that explicates how theoretical structures (speed and brain activity) are connected to observations (frequency spectra and graphical representations of blood flow); therefore, they make assumptions on the structure of a measurement model. Like all assumptions, these can be questioned.

In questioning the assumption, that a given measurement procedure is doing the job that it is supposed to do, one is confronting the researcher with a special kind of problem. Specifically, one is questioning the most fundamental aspect of the research: the point where theory meets observation. In psychometrics, this problem is called the *problem of test validity*. Here, the term *test* is to be interpreted broadly; that is, a test involves any procedure for gathering observations to determine the position of people or objects on a theoretical attribute. Given this conceptualization, the problem of test validity is not confined to psychology, cognitive assessment, or psychometrics. It rather concerns any situation in which a researcher uses a measurement procedure to connect observations to theoretical attributes. So construed, the problem of validity is a general methodological problem that occurs throughout science.

This chapter clarifies what validity is about, how it can be studied, and what sort of evidence may be brought to bear on it. First, we make a sharp distinction between validity, as a property, and validation, as an activity. The moral of this story is that, although validation practices involve many distinct research procedures, and in this sense are complicated and multifaceted, validity, as a property, is a relatively simple concept that need not cause us headaches. Second, we discuss the most important strategies for test validation. Third, we propose a distinction between measurement concepts (e.g., validity, measurement precision, unidimensionality), decision concepts (e.g., predictive accuracy, optimality), and impact concepts (e.g., the acceptability of a testing procedure in the light of broad societal concerns). We argue that these concepts cover distinct problems in the application of cognitive assessment and should not be conflated. We end the chapter by relating the proposed theoretical system to other conceptualizations of validity that have been proposed in the past century.

THE CONCEPT OF VALIDITY

The aim of psychological measurement is to obtain information about the positions of people on a theoretical attribute by means of a set of observed scores that are gathered through a testing procedure. This simple idea is graphically represented in Figure 4.1. As illustrated in Figure 4.1, in doing measurement one assumes the existence of an attribute that possesses a certain structure. Such a hypothesis on attribute structure can be simple, as it is for instance in standard unidimensional item response theory (IRT) models, which assume that the attribute structure

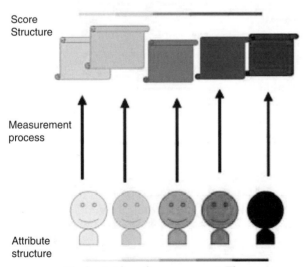

Score Structure

Measurement process

Attribute structure

FIGURE 4.1. The basic idea of measurement. The response processes that a testing procedure elicits transmit the attribute structure into an observational structure. A measurement model formalizes the relation between attribute and observations, and, if correctly specified, can be used to estimate people's positions on the attribute.

is that of a line (dimension) on which people can be positioned, or it can be more complicated, as it is, for instance, in the hierarchical models of Gierl, Leighton, and Hunka (this volume), who propose that a set of attributes combine systematically to account for item responses. The structure can be categorical (as in latent class models) or continuous (as in IRT and factor models), or involve both categorical and continuous parts (as in factor mixture models); it can further be unidimensional or multidimensional. It is important to note that the structure of attributes is not somehow "given" by the data; hence, assumptions on that structure require theoretical and empirical justification.

The testing procedure then elicits a process that gives rise to test scores. The test scores (or possible functions thereof) also possess a certain structure. If the measurement procedure works as it should, then the processes that it elicits are such that different positions in the theoretical structure lead to different positions in the observed structure, and do so in a predictable, systematic manner. A good example of how this may occur is given in Table 9.1 of Gierl et al.'s chapter in this volume (Chapter 9), which formulates a link between attribute structure and item response patterns. Through the response processes evoked by the test, variation in the position on the theoretical attribute causes systematic variation in the test scores. If the theory on the relation between attribute and response patterns is accurate, the observations can then be used to infer the positions of different people on the theoretical attribute.

Let us consider some progressively more difficult examples to identify the problems we may encounter in this process. First, one may set oneself to the task of obtaining information on, say, the attribute of biological sex. There are good grounds for assuming that, in the human population, this attribute has two levels, namely, "male" and "female". There is no further ordering in the structure, so this is a qualitative rather than a quantitative attribute. To find out whether people are male or female, one could for instance ask them which is considered to be a testing procedure in the present context. People's responses to the question "Are you male or female?" are, if all goes well, of two kinds; either a person says that he is male or female. Hence, the structure of the test scores (response: female or response: male) matches the structure of the attribute sex (level: male or level: female). The psychological processes that lie in between sex and test scores are relatively simple and uncontroversial. A person really is male or female, the person knows this, the person understands the question asked by the researcher, and the person answers truthfully. Provided we have no reason to question these assumptions, we accept this testing procedure as valid. And the reason for this is that the response processes can be trusted to transmit variation in the attribute to variation in the responses; that is, variation in the attribute causes variation in the test scores.

It is important to note that, although researchers usually conceptualize sex as an "observed" variable, this way of talking should not be interpreted literally. Sex, as an attribute, is not subject to direct observation in the same sense as concrete objects, such as rocks or trees. When researchers say that sex is observed, they mean that the measurement process that connects the structure of the attribute to answers to the question "What is your sex?" is conceptualized as deterministic; that is, it is assumed that the process is error free. Thus, the practice of equating people's responses to this question about their sex is underpinned by a measurement model; this may be a simple, deterministic, and usually implicit measurement model, but it is a measurement model nonetheless.

Such a deterministic relation between the attribute and the item responses cannot usually be assumed in psychology, where response processes often are subject to error, in the sense that they are influenced by situational and person-specific factors that are not of interest to the researcher. In that case, attributes must be conceptualized as bearing a stochastic rather than deterministic relation to item responses. These attributes are then conceptualized as latent variables. In such cases, the measurement process is rather more complicated than the simple example discussed previously.

As an example of a measurement structure that involves latent variables, consider cognitive assessment as it is used to measure developmental stages. Piaget proposed the theory that children go through several such stages in cognitive development. These stages are considered to be discrete, in the sense that development is considered to be a process of stagewise transitions; a person "jumps" from one stage to another when he or she acquires a new cognitive rule. The transitions in question are thus theorized to involve qualitative changes in the use of cognitive rules. The stages themselves are ordered in the sense that children go through them in a progressive fashion (they may show relapses or skip stages, but the general direction of development is that one goes from stage one, to stage two, to stage three, etc.). A cognitive assessment procedure that is often used to measure these stages is the balance scale task (Inhelder & Piaget, 1958; Jansen & Van der Maas, 1997, 2002). In this task, children have to indicate, for a number of situations, to which

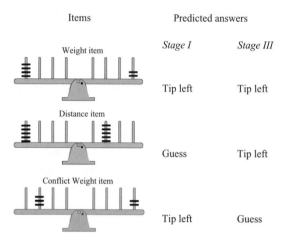

Items	Predicted answers	
	Stage I	*Stage III*
Weight item		
	Tip left	Tip left
Distance item		
	Guess	Tip left
Conflict Weight item		
	Tip left	Guess

FIGURE 4.2. The balance scale test. Children are asked to indicate to which side the balance scale will tip. Predicted item responses for two stages are shown. In stage I, children choose the side that has most weights. In stage III, children take distance into account, but only if the weights are equal; when the weight and distance cues conflict, they start guessing.

side a balance scale will tip, for which they are expected to use cognitive rules. The different situations make up items that are expected to invoke different answers, depending on the stage that a given child occupies because in different stages children use different cognitive rules, which result in different response patterns over the items. Some examples of items are given in Figure 4.2.

This case is, of course, more complicated than the previous example; we are not as confident that we have the structure of the theoretical attribute right, and we may also express doubts on the assumed response processes; hence, there is greater reason to doubt the validity of the testing procedure. However, it is important to realize that although it may be more difficult to refute such criticisms, it remains clear what *should* be the case for the measurement procedure to be valid. Namely, (a) the theoretical attribute should consist of discrete developmental stages and (b) the response process should invoke the associated cognitive rules so that (c) the item response patterns causally depend on the developmental stages measured. Thus, although there is more room for *criticism* of the validity of the testing procedure, the *property being criticized* is exactly the same as in the previous example; namely, the response processes transmit variation in the theoretical attribute so that differences in test scores causally depend on differences in the position of the theoretical attribute.

Let us consider one more example before we draw general conclusions about the property of validity. Consider one of the most important cases of cognitive assessment in our present society, which is the measurement of general intelligence, or *g*. General intelligence is a hypothesized attribute that is invoked to explain the empirical observation that scores on different tests for intelligence tend to be positively correlated; for instance, people, who perform well on a test that requires them to remember strings of numbers (digit span) will on average also perform well on a test that requires them to answer general knowledge questions such as "What is the capital of Italy?" (information); such items make up subtests of well-known IQ testing batteries such as the Wechsler Adult Intelligence Scale (WAIS; Wechsler, 1997) and the Stanford-Binet (Roid, 2003). The idea of general intelligence is that the positive manifold exists because all such tests ultimately depend on general intelligence; hence, individual differences in general intelligence are hypothesized to be the *common cause* of individual differences in subtest scores.

If one thinks about how this measurement procedure is supposed to work, then one encounters two problems. First, it is not entirely clear how the theoretical attribute is structured. In research applications, general intelligence is commonly conceptualized as a dimension (i.e., as a factor in a factor analysis model). This means that it is thought of as a line on which each tested person occupies a definite position. Distances on this line are often considered to be meaningful, in the sense that the difference in general intelligence between Einstein and Bohr may be twice as large as the difference in intelligence between Pascal and Laplace; in such an interpretation, the attribute is considered to possess quantitative structure (Michell, 1997, 1999). However, an alternative conceptualization is that the attribute is ordered but not quantitative; in such a view, we may say that Einstein was more intelligent than Bohr and that Pascal was more intelligent than Laplace, but we cannot say that the first difference is *x* times as large than the second (where *x* is a positive real number). The difference between these two interpretations is not trivial. For instance, if the first is true, then general intelligence may figure in quantitative laws, just like mass, velocity, and time do, and a factor model may be considered to be possibly correct. If the second is true, then quantitative laws cannot pertain to general intelligence; a factor model is then necessarily no more than an approximation of the real measurement structure, which is in fact ordinal. Thus, in a nontrivial sense, the *structure* of the theoretical attribute of general intelligence, and hence the measurement model that relates it to a set of observations, are unclear.

A second problem in this situation is that it is not obvious why the invoked response processes (e.g., remembering the string "3647253947" and answering the question, "What is the capital of Italy?") should transmit variation in the *same* attribute; at least on the face of it, these questions address *different* attributes; the first draws on working memory and the second on general knowledge. So where and how could general intelligence play a role in the response process invoked by *both* of these items? It seems that, if general intelligence exists and affects these response processes, the effect of general intelligence must be *indirect*; for instance, differences in general intelligence may affect both the development of working memory and the acquisition of knowledge, and the individual differences in working memory capacity and general knowledge that originate in this fashion are measured with the subtests in question. Even if this were true, however, it is still unclear how these developmental pathways run and in what way general intelligence affects them.

So to imagine what it would take for IQ scores to measure general intelligence requires at least a serious stretch of one's imagination. Not only are there reasons for doubting the validity of the IQ test for measuring general intelligence; it is not clear what, exactly, should be the case for the test to be valid. The reason for this is that the causal link between the structure of general intelligence and the structure of test scores is not merely speculative, but in fact less than speculative, because we do not even know *what* we are speculating to be the case. Note, however, that this does not imply that general intelligence does not exist or cannot be measured through IQ tests because it may be the case that the causal link that connects IQ scores to general intelligence does exist, even though we are not currently able to specify it. Also note that the property of the measurement procedure that we are questioning here is the same one that we questioned in the example of developmental stages: namely, the existence of a causal link between the structure of the attribute and the structure of the test scores.

The problem that researchers are unable to specify the processes that connect theoretical attributes to test scores is quite widespread throughout the social sciences (for some reason, it seems to be rare in the physical sciences). It also occurs in the specification of measurement models for educational tests. When a set of items involving, say, numerical problems turns out to fit a unidimensional measurement model, it is seductive to suppose that the latent variable in the model must correspond to something real (an ability of some sort). However, unless substantive theory is available to specify the causal link between attributes and test scores, the measurement model remains something of a black box. The ability may then really be nothing more than a reformulation of people's observed performance on a theoretically arbitrary set of items. In such a case, one may fit IRT models and talk about trait estimates, but such parlance may be misleading because there may not be a trait to estimate; if so, the trait estimates, however impressive the statistical machinery that generates them, carry no more theoretical weight than that of a useful summary. Therefore, if one is not in possession of a substantive theory that links attributes to test scores, one must be careful in adopting the rhetoric of measurement and validity.

It is clear that, even though we have been considering very different cases of measurement to which very different criticisms apply, the property of validity comes down to exactly the same thing in each case. So this suggests that this property can be defined in a simple and unambiguous fashion. We indeed think that this is the case. For those who have not guessed already, here it is: *A test is valid for measuring a theoretical attribute if and only if variation in the attribute causes variation in the measurement outcomes through the response processes that the test elicits.* Test validity thus means nothing less and nothing more than that a test can be used to measure a theoretical attribute because the processes that the test elicits transmit variation on the attribute to variation in test scores. It is important to see that, despite the intricate theoretical treatises that have been written on this topic (e.g., Messick, 1989), the property of validity itself is not difficult or complicated; a bright 8-year-old could grasp the general idea.

RESPONSE PROCESSES AND VALIDITY

For a measurement procedure to be valid, the attribute measured must play a role in determining what value the measurement outcomes will take. There are at least three ways in which this may occur. First, the attribute may play the role of a *parameter* in a *homogeneous* response process. Second, the attribute may act as a *moderator* that homogenizes a set of response processes. Third, the attribute may exist as a *composite* of distinct attributes, which causes differences in test scores because these sample from the universe of the distinct attributes that comprise the composite. We discuss the associated mechanisms in turn.

Attributes as Parameters

In many research settings in psychology, measurement processes are assumed to be homogeneous; that is, each person to whom the item is administered follows the same process in responding to it. One can think of a response process as the trajectory, through a continuous or categorical state space, that the tested person follows between item administration and item response. If each tested person follows the same process then the model that describes the trajectory is homogenous, in the sense that it governs every response process elicited in every subject for every item. Systematic variance in the item responses must then reflect differences in one or more parameters of the response model. Theoretical attributes that are assessed in this manner can be conceptualized as (sets of) parameters in a response model.

Response processes for which such a conceptualization is plausible are mainly situated in psychonomic research on basic mechanisms in information processing. An example is a two-choice response task in which a subject has to choose which of two alternatives is correct (i.e., has a certain property such as "being a number" or "being a word"). Such a process can be modeled as a diffusion process, in which the subject accumulates evidence for the alternatives, and chooses one if the accumulated evidence hits a certain boundary (Ratcliff, 1978; Tuerlinckx & De Boeck, 2005). In this research, it is typically assumed that the model is structurally invariant across subjects; hence, intra- or interindividual differences in response patterns must originate from differences in the parameters of the models that govern the response process (e.g., the location of the boundaries; Tuerlinckx & De Boeck, 2005). Note that these differences may either be stable interindividual differences or (possibly experimentally induced) intraindividual differences. If response processes are homogeneous, the role of the theoretical attribute can therefore be conceptualized in terms of parametric differences in these processes. It must be noted that this situation will probably not be encountered often when higher cognitive processes are involved because people are then likely to follow different strategies and hence cannot be described by the same response model. Attributes that can be viewed as response model parameters are not likely to be encountered in educational settings, except perhaps where these concern very basic learning processes (e.g., conditioning).

Attributes as Moderators

In many cases, the differences that we observe in item responses are not likely to result from parametric differences but rather from qualitative differences in response processes themselves. This is the case, for instance, for the balance scale task discussed in the previous section

(Inhelder & Piaget, 1958; Jansen & Van der Maas, 1997, 2002). Children in different developmental stages follow different cognitive rules in responding to the items. Hence, the pool of response processes is heterogeneous, but this is because the population studied includes children in different developmental stages; and *within* each developmental stage the process may be considered to be homogeneous. Thus, the theoretical attribute (developmental stages) *homogenizes* the response processes. If there are no further structural differences among children in any developmental stage, then a standard latent class model is appropriate for the data (Jansen & Van der Maas, 1997, 2002). The theoretical attribute then acts as a *moderator* with respect to the response processes elicited.

Mixed Response Processes – Nested

Parametric differences may be nested under a moderator attribute. In this example, this would be the case if, within the developmental stages, there existed additional parametric differences between children that affect item response patterns. For instance, two children who follow the cognitive rule "the balance scale will tip to the side that contains most weights" may nevertheless differ in performance because one of them is better in counting the weights. In this case, the latent class model will not capture all systematic variation in item responses; an additional individual differences variable may then be postulated within the classes to reflect these parametric differences. This may, for instance, lead to a mixed Rasch model (Rost, 1990) or to a finite mixture model (Dolan, Jansen, & Van der Maas, 2004; Schmittmann, Dolan, Van der Maas, & Neale, 2005; Uebersax, 1999), depending on the relevant theory. In such a conceptualization, the response processes would be qualitatively homogeneous within the classes but quantitatively different.

Mixed Response Processes – Not Nested

The situations considered so far are relatively straightforward. Theoretical attributes either function as a parameter in the response process or they moderate response processes (with possible additional parametric differences obtained within the levels of the moderator). The theoretical structure of such situations is tractable, and psychometric models can be used to formalize the hypotheses that follow from the theory; hence, hypotheses on the way the measurement instrument works are at least indirectly testable. Unfortunately, this situation does not apply to some of the most important psychological tests in use, such as intelligence and personality tests. Such tests contain diverse items that elicit response processes that cannot plausibly be decomposed in terms of parametric and moderator attributes.

Suppose, for instance, that Jane and Dave occupy exactly the same position on the trait extraversion. They now encounter an item in a personality test that purports to measure extraversion; let us assume that it is the item "I like to go to parties". Jane may now consider the few last parties she has attended and assess how much she liked them. Dave may consider the opinion that a friend has just given on his personality; say his friend called him a party animal. They may both circle "5" on the response scale, which is what one should hope for because they are, in fact, equally extraverted; yet they have followed different response processes. Now suppose that John also answers the item in question, and he in fact is somewhat less extraverted than Jane and Dave. He follows the same response process as Jane did; that is, he considered the last few parties to which he has been. It so happens that John's parties were more fun than Jane's. This makes up for the difference in extraversion so John also marks "5" on the response scale. John and Jane have followed the same response process, have a different position on the attribute, and yet they now have the same item response. To make matters worse, consider Mary, who is exactly as extraverted as John and has also been administered the item. She goes through the same response process as Dave; however, in her case a friend has just described her as shy. This causes her to mark "2" on the response scale. Although she has the same position on the attribute as John, she thus gets a different item response, because she has followed a different response process.

The situation is graphically depicted in Figure 4.3. If such a situation obtains, and in the case of personality testing it is very plausible that it does, then we have a situation where, in terms of the connection between response processes and the attributes that are the object of measurement, anything goes. There is no clear relation between response processes and differences on the attribute: the attribute functions neither as a parameter in the response model nor as a moderator of response processes. This is a rather messy situation. It lacks the structure necessary for a firm theoretical treatment of the measurement process, and therefore it cannot form the basis for the explication of a measurement model. The burden of proof for establishing the validity of such testing procedures would exist in spelling out the way that elicited response processes connect variation in the theoretical attribute to variation in the test scores. However, because the elicited processes are not structurally connected to the theoretical attribute, spelling out these relations appears to be

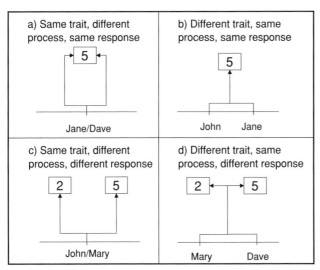

FIGURE 4.3. A measurement procedure without structure? The figure illustrates a case for which the relation between observational structure, response process, and attribute structure is ambiguous. The attribute functions neither as a parameter in a homogeneous response process nor as a moderator of response processes.

difficult at best and impossible at worst. Hence, in such cases, the validity of the testing procedure is bound to remain, to some extent, an article of faith.

Attributes as Composites

Because validity is about the way a test works, and because in psychological tests this usually involves psychological processes, in most cases the evidence for validity must come from the relations between these processes, as they are evoked by the test, and the attribute measured. However, this is not always the case. Consider, for instance, the assessment of people's knowledge of history. Such a knowledge domain can be conceptualized in terms of a large number of facts. A test of a person's knowledge of the domain could then be a sample of these facts (e.g., the person has to indicate whether the statement "Cleopatra and Julius Caesar were lovers" is true). This item, of course, does not directly assess knowledge of Egyptian history; it assesses whether people know that Cleopatra had a romantic relationship with Julius Caesar, which is one of the many facts that define the knowledge domain in question. At this level, the link between the structure of the attribute (knowing versus not knowing the fact in question) and the item response (correctly or incorrectly answering the question) is relatively unproblematic and analyzable in much the same way as the question "What is your sex?". Thus, the attribute plays the role it has to play for validity to hold.

However, now consider composite attributes; that is, attributes that are themselves comprised of other attributes, as "knowledge of Egyptian history" is made up of knowledge of the romantic relationship between Caesar and Cleopatra and many other facts. We may attempt to estimate the proportion of facts that any given person knows by administering a sample of questions taken from the knowledge domain, as is common in educational assessment. Then it is clear that the composite attribute ("knowledge of Egyptian history") does not play a causal role with respect to the item responses to any individual item. That is, a person correctly answers the item in question because he or she knows that Caesar and Cleopatra had a romantic relationship (or is lucky guessing, a possibility that may be readily accommodated in the measurement model; Hambleton & Swaminathan, 1985), but *not* because of his or her standing on the abstract composite "knowledge of Egyptian history". Nevertheless, it is equally clear that one's knowledge of Egyptian history *may* be validly assessed through a set of items such as the above. But if such an assessment measures a composite attribute and the composite attribute does not play a causal role in producing differences in individual item responses, then the assessment appears *not* to be a candidate for validity. So what is going on here?

What occurs in this testing procedure is that differences in the composite attribute do not play a role in producing differences in individual item responses, but do play a role in producing differences in another composite, namely, people's total scores. This is to say that the proportion of facts you know does not make a difference for whether you can answer a particular question (you either can or cannot, which depends on whether you know the answer), but this proportion does make a difference to the *number* of questions you can answer (assuming that they are a representative sample from the domain). Hence, the relation between the attribute and the summed item scores is a universe sampling relation; and the test scores transmit variation in the attribute through their sampling properties, just like differences in sample averages from a set of populations convey differences in the locations of the population distributions. In this conceptualization, the measurement of composite attributes poses no problems to the present approach to validity. However, it must be noted that composite attributes may often be composed of items that require heterogeneous response processes; in such cases, they cannot typically be used to draw inferences about psychological processes and strategies, or about impairments therein, as one often desires in cognitive diagnostic assessment.

TEST VALIDATION

In the previous sections, we attempt to elucidate the meaning of the validity concept. In doing so, we specify the ontological conditions for validity; that is, we say what the world should be like for validity to hold. A second question, which is distinct from the ontological one, concerns the epistemology of validity: how can we investigate whether a test has the property of validity? Obviously, this requires testing the hypothesis that there is a causal effect of a theoretical attribute on test scores; the hypothesis of test validity cannot be taken for granted but must be tested in empirical research. *Validation* is therefore defined as *testing the hypothesis that the theoretical attribute has a causal effect on the test scores.* Here, we briefly discuss several methods that are relevant to establishing the validity of psychological tests.

Test Construction

All cognitive assessment begins with the construction of the measurement instrument. It is, in general, advisable to construct a test in such a way that validity is best built into the test as much as possible. Different methods are used for constructing tests; within the present framework, two methods of test construction are especially relevant. These are deductive and facet design methods (Oosterveld, 1996, chapter 2). The deductive method (Jackson, 1971) starts from the definition of a theoretical attribute, and the test constructor writes items that fit this definition. The facet design method (Guttman, 1965) starts with the decomposition of the theoretical attribute in facets, where each facet has a number of elements. The factorial combination of the facets yields a design for item writing. These two construction methods use the hypothesized structure of the theoretical attribute in item design, but this, in itself, does not guarantee that the test is valid. The validity of a test is a hypothesis that needs to be tested separately. As an example, consider the Dental Anxiety Inventory (DAI; Stouthard, Mellenbergh, & Hoogstraten, 1993). This test was explicitly designed on the basis of considerations on a theory of dental anxiety, as reflected in a facet design. However, such a test construction procedure does not guarantee that variation in dental anxiety causes variation in the DAI scores; this hypothesis must be tested in validation studies.

Content Analysis

The content of the items must fit the theoretical attribute. This type of test validation is typically done by judges who evaluate the appropriateness of the items for measuring the theoretical attribute. Of course, for content analysis to be appropriate, there has to be some level of theory that relates the attribute to the content of items. The theoretical structure of composite attributes, as discussed in the previous paragraph, lends itself most naturally to predictions on the content of test items. An important question is whether the content domain has been sampled adequately; relevant considerations in investigating whether this is the case are discussed by Messick (1989) under the headers of content relevance (the question whether items are elements of the specified universe of behaviors) and representation (the question whether the items have been sampled from the universe in a representative fashion).

Response Process Analysis

The analysis of item response processes may be carried out in two different ways. First, qualitative information is obtained from examinees' introspections or retrospections (see Leighton & Gierl, this volume). The introspection (retrospection) protocols are analyzed, and processes are identified that explain examinees' item response behavior. Second, psychometric models are constructed for the cognitive processes that are involved in item responding, and these cognitive process psychometric models are tested on empirical test data. Discussions of such models are given by, among others, Embretson and Reise (2000, chapter 11), Maris (1995), Snow and Lohman (1989), De Boeck and Wilson (2004), and in the chapters by Rupp and Mislevy (this volume), Roussos et al. (this volume), and Gierl et al. (this volume). It is obvious that these two strategies can be combined in test validation: cognitive processes are derived from protocol analysis and are used to build cognitive psychometric models that are subsequently fitted to empirical test data. Gierl et al. (this volume) present a good example of such a strategy in their treatment of SAT items.

Experimental Manipulation

Experimental validation studies manipulate the theoretical attribute and study the differences in test scores between different experimental conditions. For example, the validation of an anxiety test may be carried out through an experiment, where one group of persons is randomly assigned to an anxiety-provoking condition and the other group to a neutral condition. The validity of the anxiety test is supported if the test scores are higher under the anxiety-provoking condition than under the neutral condition. Normally, experimental research designs analyze data through observed score techniques (e.g., analysis of variance). However, it is advisable to consider incorporating a measurement model into the analysis of experimental designs. This was, for instance, done by Wicherts, Dolan, and Hessen (2005), who analyzed experimental data through a measurement invariance model with latent variables. Such analyses directly subject the measurement structure to experimental tests, and hence provide stronger evidence for validity than observed score techniques can, by themselves, offer.

Group Comparisons

Many attributes (e.g., intelligence) cannot be manipulated, and many attributes that can be manipulated (e.g., phobic anxiety) do not qualify for manipulation because of ethical reasons. Validation of tests for these types of attributes is therefore restricted to quasiexperimental and correlational studies. A quasiexperimental design for test validation may, for instance, compare the test scores of groups of persons that are assumed to differ in the attribute. The validity of the test is supported if the test scores substantially differ between these groups. For example, Stouthard et al. (1993) studied the validity of the DAI in this way. The DAI was administered to two groups of patients: one group was accepted for treatment in a special dental health clinic, and the other group was treated in a regular dental school clinic. The validity of the DAI was supported because the mean DAI score of the special treatment group was substantially higher than the mean score of the regular treatment group. It is generally important to assess whether the mean differences in observed scores can indeed be interpreted as the result of mean differences in the attribute; this can be investigated by using techniques for assessing measurement invariance (Mellenbergh, 1989; Meredith, 1993).

Correlational Analysis

In general, the randomized experiment is the best method for testing causal relations, and, therefore, it is the preferred design for test validation. A randomized experiment manipulates the attribute and randomly assigns participants to conditions (Shadish, Cook, & Campbell, 2002, p. 13). Frequently, attribute manipulation and random assignment of participants are impossible or out of the question because of ethical or practical constraints. In that case, test validation must revert to a correlational design. Test validation in correlational studies follows the guidelines of Campbell and Fiske (1959). A test of an attribute must covary (converge) with test attributes that are theoretically related to the attribute, and the test must not covary with (discriminate from) tests of attributes that are not theoretically related to the attribute. For example, Stouthard, Hoogstraten, and Mellenbergh (1995) assumed that the dental anxiety attribute was related to some personality traits (e.g., neuroticism, inadequacy) and unrelated to some other traits (e.g., conscientiousness, dominance). They correlated the DAI with a set of personality tests and found support for the validity of the DAI. A more advanced method of test validation is the specification of a structural equation model. The model specifies the presence and absence of causal relations between the attribute and other attributes, as well as, possibly, models for the measurement of the attributes (Bollen, 1989; Kaplan, 2000). A good fit of the structural equation model to empirical data increases the plausibility that the test is valid for the measurement of the attribute.

Validity and Validation
In many applications of psychological measurement, the evidence for the validity of tests is either lacking or highly indirect. Hence, the validity of tests that measure psychological constructs is often seriously doubted in scientific and public debates. For example, multiple-choice tests, such as mathematical achievement tests, require recognition of given responses, but they do not ask for the production of new responses. For this reason, critics of such tests sometimes maintain that multiple-choice tests are invalid for the measurement of complex cognitive skills, such as insight in mathematics. This opinion is not widely published in the scientific literature, but in our experience is regularly encountered in informal discussions on educational assessment. In terms of our validity definition, such critics claim that individual differences in insight in mathematics do not causally affect individual differences in multiple-choice mathematics test scores; proponents of multiple-choice tests claim the opposite. Such issues can be settled by deriving diverging empirical predictions based on these respective positions and evaluating these in empirical research. Thus, although debates on test validity are heated and recurrent, they may in many cases be settled by test validation research.

MEASUREMENT, DECISIONS, AND THE IMPACT OF TESTING

An important question that arises related to the present conceptualization of validity is how the validity concept relates to other concepts that figure in the theoretical framework of psychometrics, such as reliability, predictive accuracy, and measurement invariance. At present, the dominant view, as expressed by, among others, Messick (1989), is that most of the psychometric concepts can be subsumed under the umbrella of test validity. In the proposed view, however, validity does not play the role of providing an overarching evaluation of test score interpretations. Instead, we propose to juxtapose psychometric concepts instead of subordinating them to validity. Three types of concepts are distinguished: measurement, decision, and impact concepts.

Measurement Concepts

Measurement concepts are concepts that specifically address features of tests or test scores that are relevant to the inference of people's positions on a theoretical attribute on the basis of observed test scores, that is, the measurement problem. In psychometrics, the most important measurement concepts are unidimensionality, measurement invariance, measurement precision, and test validity.

Unidimensionality
Most tests consist of more than one item, and the responses to n different items are used for scoring the test. In classical psychometrics, the item responses are scored by fiat (e.g., 1 for a correct answer and 0 for an incorrect answer; 1–5 for the five categories of a Likert item). In modern psychometrics, the item responses are used to estimate examinees' latent variable values. Whatever approach is used, a question is whether it is justified to combine the responses to the n items in one test score. Good test construction practice tells that the n items should predominantly measure one and the same latent variable. This unidimensionality requirement of a test can be studied by applying IRT models to the data of the n test items (Hambleton & Swaminathan, 1985; Lord, 1980; Sijtsma & Molenaar, 2002; Van der Linden & Hambleton, 1997).

Measurement Invariance
Another question is whether the test scores of different members of a population can be compared to each other. A test for measuring a latent variable is said to be measurement invariant with respect to a variable

V if the test scores are only caused by the latent variable and are not also affected by V (Millsap & Meredith, 1992). If the variable V also affects the test scores, V is called a violator of the measurement of the latent variable (Oort, 1993). For example, it is plausible that individual differences in Dutch students' responses to the item "$7 \times 13 = \ldots$" are caused by differences in their latent arithmetic skills, but that individual differences in responses to the item "Seven times thirteen is..." will also be affected by differences in their English comprehension skills. Therefore, the numerical item is likely to be measurement invariant with respect to English comprehension, whereas the verbal arithmetic item will be biased with respect to English comprehension. Continuing this line of thought, the ideal measurement situation is that the measurement of the latent variable is invariant with respect to any possible variable V. In practice, this strong requirement is hard to meet, and test constructors are satisfied if the test is measurement invariant between relevant subpopulations of the total population (e.g., males and females, majority and minority groups, age groups, native and nonnative speakers). The validity of a test that is not measurement invariant with respect to the variable V may be restricted to a subpopulation, which is determined by V. For example, the English arithmetic test could be valid for the measurement of the arithmetic skill of Dutch students who sufficiently master English numerals but invalid for Dutch students who do not master these numerals.

Measurement Precision
Two aspects of measurement precision are distinguished: reliability and information (Mellenbergh, 1996). *Reliability* is the precision with which we can discriminate between different latent variable values of different members of a population. In contrast, *information* is the precision of estimating a given person's latent variable value. Reliability is a population-dependent concept, which is clear from the classical definition of reliability as the squared correlation between observed and true scores in a population of persons (Lord & Novick, 1968, section 3.4). In contrast, information is a population-independent concept of measurement precision, which is under the assumption of classical test theory equal to the inverse of the standard error of measurement of a given person (Mellenbergh, 1996).

Test Validity
Unidimensionality, measurement invariance, and precision are important test theoretic concepts. Unidimensionality guarantees that the test

items measure one and the same latent variable, measurement invariance guarantees that the measurement model is invariant across relevant subpopulations (or levels of the variable V), and high precision guarantees accurate discrimination between the latent variable values of different persons of a population and accurate estimation of a given person's latent variable value. However, these three concepts do not guarantee that the test is valid because the latent variable, which the test measures, does not need to coincide with the theoretical attribute that the test is intended to measure. For instance, it is conceivable that one could misinterpret sets of measurements of objects' weights, through a series of balance scales, as measurements of their heights; in such a case, the test scores may be unidimensional, measurement invariant, and precise, but the measurement instrument is not valid for the theoretical attribute of height (even though the scores may be highly correlated with height). The reason for this is that differences in height do not causally affect differences in the test scores. Hence, test validity is not implied by other psychometric properties.

Decision Concepts

In practice, tests are used not only for the purpose of measurement, but also for making decisions; examples are personnel selection, college admission, and medical diagnosis. In such applications, test scores provide a basis for choosing a course of action (e.g., whether to hire a job applicant, which treatment to administer to a patient). Decision concepts are used to describe the quality of test-based decision-making procedures. De Vries (2006) distinguished four types of test score comparisons, and each type yields different psychometric decision situations.

1. *Comparison of the scores of different persons on the same test.* The test scores of the persons are ordered, and decisions are based on this order. An example is the *selection* of applicants for a job, college, or psychotherapy. At the basis of selection is the test-based prediction of persons' criterion performance, such as their future success on the job, in college, or in psychotherapy. A key concept of selection is *predictive accuracy*, that is, the accuracy of the test-based predictions of the criterion performance. In this context, mostly the concept of criterion-oriented validity is used (see, e.g., Cronbach, 1990, chapter 5). However, the accuracy of predictions says little about the relation between the theoretical attribute and test scores, which is suggested by the term criterion-oriented validity. For adequate selection of students, it does not matter whether the WAIS measures *g* or anything else as long as it

accurately predicts college performance. Therefore, the concept of predictive accuracy is preferred over criterion-oriented validity.

Usually, a number of subpopulations of a total population of applicants can be distinguished, such as males and females, and majority and minority group members. Frequently, political and ethical opinions and laws require that selection is *culture fair*, that is, fair with respect to relevant subpopulations of applicants. A relevant concept for culture-fair selection is *prediction invariance*, which means that the prediction model is the same across relevant subpopulations. For example, the linear prediction of criterion performance from test scores is prediction invariant with respect to applicant's sex if the regression lines of males and females have the same intercept, slope, and residual variance. It must be noted that prediction invariance is often inconsistent with measurement invariance, a concept that is also relevant to culture-fair selection. In particular, situations where the latent distributions of subgroups differ in many cases preclude simultaneous satisfaction of measurement and prediction invariance (Millsap, 1997). Hence, predictive invariance does not imply that test scores are unbiased in a measurement sense. In fact, Millsap's work suggests that it commonly implies measurement bias. Whether one should generally favor measurement invariance or prediction invariance in selection settings is open and in need of theoretical investigation.

2. *Comparison of a given person's test score to a standard.* An example is *criterion-referenced testing in education.* A student's test score is compared to a domain of behaviors, for example, different aspects of the arithmetic skill, and the teacher decides whether the student sufficiently or insufficiently masters these aspects.

3. *Comparison of a given person's scores on the same test at different occasions.* This type of comparison is made in the *measurement of change.* An example is the comparison of a patient's pre- and posttreatment depression scores, where the clinician decides whether the patient's gain is of clinical significance.

4. *Comparison of a given person's scores on different tests.* A number of tests or subtests is administered to a person, which results in a *profile* of standardized (sub)test scores, and these scores are compared to each other. An example is a counselor's interpretation of a client's profile of WAIS (verbal and performance) subtest scores, and his or her vocational advice to the client.

Psychometric decisions may also concern other types of units than persons, and the same types of comparison can be distinguished as for persons. Examples are the comparison of mean achievement test scores among countries for policy making, and the comparison of a school's mean achievement test scores at the beginning and the end of the school year for educational policy making.

Psychometric decision theory consists of mathematical models for optimal test-based decision making. Examples are the models for criterion-referenced testing (Van der Linden, 1980), selection (Cronbach & Gleser, 1957), and culture-fair selection (Gross & Su, 1975; Mellenbergh & Van der Linden, 1981). The key concept of psychometric decision making is *optimality* (Mellenbergh & Van der Linden, 1979), which means that decisions are optimal in some sense. For example: How many applicants must be selected to yield maximal profit for the company, and which pass/fail cutting score on an educational test minimizes the proportions of misclassification (false masters and false nonmasters)?

Psychometric decision theory is hardly applied in practice. The models are mathematically formulated and they are hard to explain to practical decision makers. More important, the models require that decision makers express their preferences in terms that are novel to them, for example, in terms of utility functions for different subpopulations in culture-fair selection. However, psychometric decision theory has made some conceptual contributions. Although it is often impossible to strictly implement hard-boiled psychometric decision procedures, psychometrics can help improve the quality of test-based decision making, even though the decisions remain suboptimal.

Psychometric decision theory states that decisions must be optimal in some sense, but it does not say *what* should be optimized. The specification of optimization criteria lies outside the reach of psychometrics (or any other branch of science); rather, it draws on the competence of decision makers. That does not mean that psychometric decision making is ultimately irrational; the choices and specifications that are required to apply psychometric decision-making procedures need to be based on sound and rational (legal, ethical, political, etc.) arguments. The point is rather that these arguments themselves lie beyond the realm of psychometrics.

Impact Concepts

Test-based decision making is well established, especially in Western countries. It has a large impact on, for example, job applicants, students, and schools, and it is the subject of many debates. These debates may concern questions of validity but often also involve broader questions on the appropriateness of testing procedures. Examples are questions such as "Is it ethically defensible to assign children to different educational programs based on their test scores?", "Does the benefit of using the label 'schizophrenic' in diagnosis outweigh its stigmatizing effects?", or "Does the implementation of IQ-based selection and placement have adverse consequences for society at large?". Concepts that refer to the appropriateness of testing procedures in this broader sense are *impact concepts*.

Many of the issues that Messick (1989) discussed under the label of the *consequential basis of validity* fall under this header. In Messick's words, such considerations involve "the appraisal of the value implications of the construct label, of the theory underlying test interpretation, and of the ideologies in which the theory is embedded" (p. 20; see also Messick, 1998). Impact concepts that are often used in the appraisal Messick refers to are, for instance, the *fairness* of testing procedures to test takers, the *beneficial* or *adverse* social consequences of implementing a testing procedure, and the evaluation of an *ideological system* in which the test procedure may be embedded. A detailed framework of impact concepts is currently lacking. However, De Groot's (1970) acceptability concept, which states that a test must be acceptable for examinees, might be a good starting point for further conceptualization.

Impact concepts are, in De Groot's words, "badly needed", and the questions that they address are central to any implementation of assessment methods in the real world. Whatever the importance of such questions, we think that it is a mistake to subsume such concerns under the header of *validity*, as Messick (1989) attempted to do. The problems to which impact concepts refer typically involve evaluative considerations that partly depend on one's ethical and political convictions. In our view, this means that they cannot be resolved by psychometrics, or by scientific research in general. For instance, the question of whether the implementation of a testing procedure will have a given social consequence may be an empirical one that is open to scientific research. However, the question of whether that consequence is "adverse" or "beneficial" is not.

As Popham (1997) noted, the consequences of testing are important issues to consider but have little to do with validity. The reason for this is simply that these issues, although important, are not psychometric. Therefore, presenting them under the psychometric rubric of test validity is, in our view, obscuring rather than clarifying, and we propose to divorce these issues from the concept of test validity.

Validity Again

It is evident that, within the proposed framework, validity addresses an important but restricted issue in assessment. When test scores are used for selection and placement, or when they are used with the goal of bringing about certain politically motivated changes in society at large, validity may play an important role in these processes, but it cannot, by itself, justify them.

For instance, tape measures are presumably valid for measuring length, but that cannot possibly justify the utilization of tape measures for deciding, say, who goes to which university. The reason for this is that we consider using them for college admissions to be *nonsensical* (given that we see no theoretical connection between length and suitability for college) and *unfair* (given our ideological commitment to equal opportunities). However, this does not mean that tape measures, or interpretations thereof, are invalid. It does not even mean that their use in this context is invalid; only that it conflicts with our ideological commitments. We may find the use of test scores to be nonsensical, unfair, irresponsible, or discriminatory, and may decide against it for these reasons. But to discuss such reasons under the header of validity overstretches the coverage of this term, and is moreover unproductive in confounding scientific issues with ideological ones.

Whether a test measures a given theoretical attribute (validity) is a matter distinct from questions such as whether the test scores are precise and measurement invariant (other measurement concepts), whether selection based on the test scores is accurate and prediction invariant (decision concepts), or whether using the test scores in decision making has desirable societal consequences (impact concepts). These matters may be important, but that does not mean that they are all matters of validity.

DISCUSSION

In this chapter, we define test validity in terms of a causal relation between the theoretical attribute and the test scores: a valid test transmits variation in the attribute into variation in test scores. We define test validation as the scientific process of researching whether the test has the property of validity. Finally, we distinguish between measurement concepts (e.g., validity, measurement invariance, precision, unidimensionality), decision concepts (e.g., predictive accuracy, optimality), and impact concepts (e.g., the acceptability of the test procedure to the institutions that use tests, to tested persons, and to society at large).

It is useful to consider the relation of the present stance with previous conceptualizations of validity. With respect to the classic trinity of construct, content, and criterion validity, these relations are straightforward. Our conceptualization is largely in line with a realist interpretation of Cronbach and Meehl's (1955) article on construct validity. This realist interpretation is not explicated in their seminal paper (one can also read it in a positivist interpretation; see, for such a reading, Bechtold, 1959) but was forcefully articulated by Loevinger (1957). The addition to Cronbach and Meehl's (1955) and Loevinger's (1957) ideas is that we propose to conceptualize validity with an explicit appeal to causal relation that has to obtain between the attribute and the test scores.

The case with content validity is different. Content validity does not, in our view, constitute a distinct kind of validity, but rather is a conceptualization of validity for a particular kind of theoretical attribute; namely, a composite attribute, such as a person's universe score for a given knowledge domain. The causal mechanism involved in transmitting the differences in this theoretical attribute into differences in test scores is the (random) sampling of items that assess the constituent knowledge states, which together comprise the knowledge domain. The question of validity then boils down to whether the sampling process has resulted in a set of items that are relevant and representative for the domain in question (Messick, 1989). Thus, content validity is not a different kind of validity but a particular instantiation of validity as it applies to composite attributes.

A still different role is reserved for what is traditionally known as criterion validity. Criterion validity, as conceptualized here, is a decision concept rather than a measurement concept. It concerns the predictive accuracy of test scores with respect to some criterion, and hence can be the basis for decision processes such as personnel selection or college admission. Predictive accuracy of test scores does *not* presuppose or require that the test scores are valid for a particular theoretical attribute in a measurement sense. To see this, one may consider the well-known statistical fact that multicollinearity of predictors (i.e., high correlations between them) is problematic for their predictive adequacy with respect to a criterion variable. Hence, for prediction purposes, it is generally better to have tests or items that are mutually uncorrelated but highly correlated with the criterion, which is exactly the opposite of what one would expect from a set of tests or items that are unidimensional. This presents a good example of how measurement and decision properties need not coincide and may actually be antagonistic. It also shows clearly that criterion validity is distinct from test validity in a measurement sense.

Thus, with respect to the classical trinity, we draw the following conclusions. *Construct validity* coincides with our conceptualization of validity on a realist view of theoretical attributes and a causal interpretation of the measurement process. *Content validity* is validity applied to a particular type of attributes (namely, composite ones) and a particular type of measurement process (namely, a universe sampling process). *Criterion validity* has nothing to do with measurement per se and should not be considered as a measurement concept, let alone a kind of validity. We suggest that the relevant concerns be rephrased in terms of decision concepts, such as predictive accuracy, and that the use of the term *validity* be avoided in this context.

The relation that our proposal bears to more recent conceptualizations of construct validity, such as Messick's (1989), is more difficult. Messick defines validity as "an integrated evaluative judgment of the degree to which empirical evidence and theoretical rationales support the *adequacy* and *appropriateness* of *inferences* and *actions* based on test scores or other modes of assessment" (p. 13, italics in original). It is evident that our definition of validity does not remotely resemble this much broader definition. In our view, test validity may at best be considered an ingredient of, or basis for, the evaluative judgment that Messick mentions. Presumably, this judgment involves not only measurement concepts, but also decision and impact concepts as they relate to test use. However, it is not clear how one should weigh the relative importance of such concepts to arrive at Messick's desired evaluative judgment or how one should assess the "degree" to which it is supported.

The question of how to weigh different psychometric properties to arrive at a judgment of validity is especially difficult when the relevant properties are involved in a trade-off. This can ordinarily be expected for predictive accuracy and undimensionality (Borsboom, Mellenbergh, & Van Heerden, 2004), as well as for measurement invariance and prediction invariance (Millsap, 1997). Moreover, it is easy to imagine situations where the implementation of a testing procedure that has excellent measurement and decision properties leads to a humanitarian disaster (witness some of the eugenics programs of the previous century), or where the implementation of a bad testing procedure has desirable consequences (e.g., a bad selection procedure for college admissions may nevertheless lead students to work harder, and learn more, than they otherwise would). It is all very well to say that everything is important and should be incorporated into a validity judgment, but if no specifics are given on how to do that, the advice is empty. Apart from the fact that nobody knows how measurement, decision, and impact concepts should be "added" to combine into an evaluative judgment, or how to assess the "degree" to which that judgment is supported, we have a more fundamental objection to Messick's conceptualization of validity. By broadening validity to include not only measurement concerns, but also decision concepts and even the consequences of test use, Messick draws considerations into psychometric theory that simply do not belong there. For instance, psychometric theory may give one the technical apparatus to assess the optimality of a decision procedure, but it cannot indicate with which properties the procedure should be optimal. As an example, psychometrics may show how to optimize test use for a given selection ratio in college admission (the proportion of examinees that are to be admitted), but it cannot say which selection ratio should be chosen. It may give one the tools to test the hypothesis that a test measures, say, general intelligence, but it cannot answer the question of whether the use of intelligence tests for personnel selection has adverse consequences for society for the simple reason that psychometric theory cannot determine which consequences should be considered "adverse".

In conclusion, we propose that test validity should be confined to the question of whether a test measures what it should measure. The consequences of test use, such as the impact of implementing tests on society at large, are extremely important issues to consider, but they are beyond the proper realm of psychometric theory or, for that matter, of science itself.

AUTHOR NOTE

The authors thank Conor V. Dolan and Keith A. Markus for their comments on an earlier version of this chapter. The research of Denny Borsboom is supported by a Veni-grant from the Netherlands Organization for Scientific Research. Send correspondence to Denny Borsboom,

Department of Psychology, Faculty of Social and Behavioral Sciences, University of Amsterdam, Roeterstraat 15, 1018 WB Amsterdam, The Netherlands; e-mail: d.borsboom@uva.nl.

References

Bechtold, H. P. (1959). Construct validity: A critique. *American Psychologist, 14*, 619–629.

Bollen, K. A. (1989). *Structural equations with latent variables.* New York: Wiley.

Borsboom, D., Mellenbergh, G. J., & Van Heerden, J. (2004). The concept of validity. *Psychological Review, 111*, 1061–1071.

Campbell, D. T., & Fiske, D. W. (1959). Convergent and discriminant validation by the multitrait-multimethod matrix. *Psychological Bulletin, 56*, 81–105.

Cronbach, L. J. (1990). *Essentials of psychological testing* (5th ed.). New York: Harper & Row.

Cronbach, L. J., & Gleser, G. C. (1957). *Psychological tests and personnel decisions.* Urbana: University of Illinois Press.

Cronbach, L. J., & Meehl, P. E. (1955). Construct validity in psychological tests. *Psychological Bulletin, 52*, 281–302.

De Boeck, P., & Wilson, M. (2004). *Explanatory item response models: A generalized linear and nonlinear approach.* New York: Springer.

De Groot, A. D. (1970). Some badly needed non-statistical concepts in applied psychometrics. *Nederlands Tijdschrift voor de Psychologie, 25*, 360–376.

De Vries, A. L. M. (2006). *The merit of ipsative measurement: Second thoughts and minute doubts.* Unpublished doctoral dissertation, University of Maastricht, The Netherlands.

Dolan, C. V., Jansen, B. R. J., & Van Der Maas, H. L. J. (2004). Constrained and unconstrained normal finite mixture modeling of multivariate conservation data. *Multivariate Behavioral Research, 39*, 69–98.

Embretson, S. E., & Reise, S. P. (2000). *Item response theory for psychologists.* Mahwah, NJ: Erlbaum.

Gross, A. L., & Su, W. H. (1975). Defining a "fair" or "unbiased" selection model: A question of utilities. *Journal of Applied Psychology, 60*, 345–351.

Guttman, L. (1965). Introduction to facet design and analysis. In *Proceedings of the 15th international congress of psychology.* Amsterdam: North Holland.

Hambleton, R. K., & Swaminathan, H. (1985). *Item response theory: Principles and applications.* Boston: Kluwer-Nijhoff.

Inhelder, B., & Piaget, J. (1958). *The growth of logical thinking from childhood to adolescence.* New York: Basic Books.

Jackson, D. N. (1971). The dynamics of structured personality tests. *Psychological Review, 78*, 229–248.

Jansen, B. R. J., & Van Der Maas, H. L. J. (1997). Statistical tests of the rule assessment methodology by latent class analysis. *Developmental Review, 17*, 321–357.

Jansen, B. R. J., & Van Der Maas, H. L. J. (2002). The development of children's rule use on the balance scale task. *Journal of Experimental Child Psychology, 81*, 383–416.

Kaplan, D. (2000). *Structural equation modeling: Foundations and extensions.* Newbury Park, CA: Sage.

Loevinger, J. (1957). Objective tests as instruments of psychological theory. *Psychological Reports, 3,* 635–694.

Lord, F. M. (1980). *Applications of item response theory to practical testing problems.* Hillsdale, NJ: Erlbaum.

Lord, F. M., & Novick, M. R. (1968). *Statistical theories of mental test scores.* Reading, MA: Addison-Wesley.

Maris, E. (1995). Psychometric latent response models. *Psychometrika, 60,* 523–547.

Mellenbergh, G. J. (1989). Item bias and item response theory. *International Journal of Educational Research, 13,* 127–143.

Mellenbergh, G. J. (1996). Measurement precision in test score and item response models. *Psychological Methods, 1,* 293–299.

Mellenbergh, G. J., & Van der Linden, W.J. (1979). The internal and external optimality of decisions based on tests. *Applied Psychological Measurement, 3,* 257–273.

Mellenbergh, G. J., & Van Der Linden, W. J. (1981). The linear utility model for optimal selection. *Psychometrika, 46,* 283–305.

Meredith, W. (1993). Measurement invariance, factor analysis, and factorial invariance. *Psychometrika, 58,* 525–543.

Messick, S. (1998). Test validity: A matter of consequence. *Social Indicators Research, 45,* 35–44.

Messick, S. C. (1989). Validity. In R. L. Linn (Ed.), *Educational measurement* (pp. 13–103). Washington, DC: American Council on Education and National Council on Measurement in Education.

Michell, J. (1997). Quantitative science and the definition of measurement in psychology. *British Journal of Psychology, 88,* 355–383

Michell, J. (1999). *Measurement in psychology: A critical history of a methodological concept.*Cambridge, UK: Cambridge University Press.

Millsap, R. E. (1997). Invariance in measurement and prediction: Their relationship in the single-factor case. *Psychological Methods, 2,* 248–260.

Millsap, R. E., & Meredith, W. (1992). Inferential conditions in the statistical detection of measurement bias. *Applied Psychological Measurement, 16,* 389–402.

Oort, F. J. (1993). Theory of violators: Assessing unidimensionality of psychological measures. In R. Steyer, K. F. Wender, & K. F. Widaman (Eds.), *Proceeding of the 7th European meeting of the Psychometric Society in Trier* (pp. 377–381). Stuttgart: Gustav Fischer.

Oosterveld, P. (1996). *Questionnaire design methods.* Unpublished doctoral dissertation, University of Amsterdam, Amsterdam, The Netherlands.

Popham, W. J. (1997). Consequential validity: Right concern-wrong concept. *Educational Measurement: Issues and Practice, 16,* 9–13.

Ratcliff, R. (1978). A theory of memory retrieval. *Psychological Review, 85,* 59–104.

Roid, G. H. (2003). *Stanford-Binet Intelligence Scales, Fifth Edition.* Itasca, IL: Riverside Publishing.

Rost, J. (1990). Rasch models in latent classes: An integration of two approaches to item analysis. *Applied Psychological Measurement, 14,* 271–282.

Schmittmann, V. D., Dolan, C. V., Van Der Maas, H. L. J., & Neale, M. C. (2005). Discrete latent Markov models for normally distributed response data. *Multivariate Behavioral Research, 40,* 461–484.

Shadish, W. R., Cook, T. D., & Campbell, D. T. (2002). *Experimental and quasi-experimental designs for generalized causal inference.* Boston: Houghton Mifflin.

Sijtsma, K., & Molenaar, I. W. (2002). *Introduction to nonparametric item response theory.* Thousand Oaks, CA: Sage.

Snow, R. E., & Lohman, D. F. (1989). Implications of cognitive psychology for educational measurement. In R. L. Linn (Ed.), *Educational measurement* (pp. 263–311). Washington, DC: American Council on Education and National Council on Measurement in Education.

Stouthard, M. E. A., Hoogstraten, J., & Mellenbergh, G. J. (1995). A study of the convergent and discriminant validity of the dental anxiety inventory. *Behaviour Research and Therapy, 33,* 589–595.

Stouthard, M. E. A., Mellenbergh, G. J., & Hoogstraten, J. (1993). Assessment of dental anxiety: A facet approach. *Anxiety, Stress, and Coping, 6,* 89–105.

Tuerlinckx, F., & De Boeck, P. (2005). Two interpretations of the discrimination parameter. *Psychometrika, 70,* 629–650.

Uebersax, J. S. (1999). Probit latent class analysis with dichotomous or ordered category measures: Conditional independence/dependence models. *Applied Psychological Measurement, 23,* 283–297.

Van der Linden, W. J. (1980). Decision models for use with criterion-referenced tests. *Applied Psychological Measurement, 4,* 469–492.

Van der Linden, W. J., & Hambleton, R.K. (Eds.). (1997). *Handbook of modern item response theory.* New York: Springer.

Wechsler, D. (1997). *Wechsler Adult Intelligence Scale, Third Edition.* San Antonio,TX: The Psychological Corporation.

Wicherts, J. M., Dolan, C. V., & Hessen, D. J. (2005). Stereotype threat and group differences in test performance: A question of measurement invariance. *Journal of Personality and Social Psychology, 89,* 696–716.

PART II

PRINCIPLES OF TEST DESIGN AND ANALYSIS

5

Construct Validity and Cognitive Diagnostic Assessment

Xiangdong Yang and Susan E. Embretson

INTRODUCTION

Cognitive diagnostic assessment (CDA) is increasingly a major focus in psychological and educational measurement. Instead of inferring a general response tendency or behavior consistency of an examinee over a target domain of measurement, diagnostic assessment results provide a detailed account of the underlying cognitive basis of the examinee's performance by mining the richer information that is afforded by specific response patterns. Sophisticated measurement procedures, such as the rule-space methodology (Tatsuoka, 1995), the attribute hierarchy method (Leighton, Gierl, & Hunka, 2004), the tree-based regression approach (Sheehan, 1997a, 1997b), and the knowledge space theory (Doignon & Falmagne, 1999), as well as specially parameterized psychometric models (De La Torre & Douglas, 2004; DiBello, Stout, & Roussos, 1995; Draney, Pirolli, & Wilson, 1995; Hartz, 2002; Junker & Sijtsma, 2001; Maris, 1999), have been developed for inferring diagnostic information.

Although measurement models for diagnostic testing have become increasingly available, cognitive diagnosis must be evaluated by the same measurement criteria (e.g., construct validity) as traditional trait measures. With the goal of inferring more detailed information about an individual's skill profile, we are not just concerned about how many items have been correctly solved by an examinee. We are also concerned about the pattern of responses to items that differ in the knowledge, skills, or cognitive processes required for solution. Similar to traditional tests, empirical evidence and theoretical rationales that elaborate the underlying basis of item responses are required to support the inferences and interpretations made from diagnostic assessments.

Construct validation, as elaborated by Messick (1989), is the continuing scientific process of collecting various kinds of evidence to justify the inferences that are drawn from observed performances of examinees. The covert nature of psychological constructs, however, makes construct validation an inherently difficult process. To make inferences about the unobservable traits or qualities, observable indicators must be either identified or designed to elicit the examinee behaviors. The process of item design and test assembly results in establishing such behavioral indicators for the unobservable latent traits or qualities.

A systematic and defensible approach to item design is especially significant for the construct validity of diagnostic assessment (see Gorin, this volume). However, the traditional item design approach does not achieve such requirements for several reasons. First, traditional item design has been primarily concerned with developing items for stable, self-contained latent traits (Messick, 1989; Mislevy, 1996). Empirical relationships of test items with each other or with other external traits are often deemed to establish item quality in this case. Cognitive diagnosis, in contrast, requires a more direct understanding of the mental processes involved in test items. Second, traditional item design has long been viewed as an artistic endeavor, which mainly depends on the item writer's expertise, language skills, and creativity in the subject domains. The traditional item design approach normally lacks either theories to understand how specific features of items impact the cognitive basis of performance or relevant research methods to test such constructs (Embretson, 1983). As a result, other than some general guidelines or principles about item format, content, and mode, no detailed description or empirical evidence is available to support the relationship between content features of the items and the constructs under investigation.

As noted by Leighton et al. (2004), cognitive item design can provide a basis for diagnostic assessment. In cognitive item design, cognitive theory is incorporated into test design (Embretson, 1994, 1998). If the theory is sufficiently well developed, it elaborates how item stimuli influence the cognitive requirements of solving the item. Therefore, item performance is explicitly linked to its underlying cognitive variables, and the cognitive theory explicates the underlying measurement construct of the test.

This chapter concerns the implications of construct validity for CDA. The material in this chapter is organized as follows. First, current views on construct validity are discussed and summarized. Second, the unique issues of construct validity within the framework of CDA are discussed. The discussion includes a description of the cognitive design system approach to item design and how it relates to construct validity issues of CDA. Third, an example is presented to illustrate and contrast the implications of cognitively designed items for the construct validity of both traditional trait measures and CDA. Fourth, a summary of the approach that is taken in this chapter and discussions of the relevant issues are provided.

CONSTRUCT VALIDITY: GENERAL FRAMEWORK

Construct validity is a multifaceted yet unified concept. *Construct validity* concerns the degree to which empirical evidence and theoretical rationales support the inferences made from test scores. Numerous articles on validity have been published since Cronbach and Meehl's (1955) elaboration of the concept. The most important results from these developments are (a) the presentation in the current *Standards for Educational and Psychological Testing* (American Education Research Association/ American Psychological Association/National Council on Measurement in Education, 1999), in which validity is conceptualized differently than in the previous versions, and (b) an extensive integration of several aspects of validity into a comprehensive framework (Messick, 1989, 1995). According to both developments, no longer may validity be considered to consist of separate types, as emphasized in the prior version of the *Standards for Educational and Psychological Tests*. The separate types of validity were construct validity, criterion-related validity, and content validity, which were differentially appropriate, depending on test use. Instead, the concept of construct validity is now articulated within a unifying framework of construct validity.

Messick differentiated six aspects of construct validity to apply to all tests. Two traditional types of validity – content validity and criterion-related validity – are conceptualized as different sources of evidence for construct validity by Messick (1989). First, the *content* aspect concerns the relevancy and representativeness of test content to the construct. For any test, including ability tests, test content is important to evaluate for appropriateness to the inferences made from the test. Test content may concern either surface or deep structural features of content. Second, the *substantive* aspect concerns the theoretical rationale and evidence about the processes behind test responses. On an ability test, the relevancy of the processes employed by examinees to solve items to the intended construct should be assessed. For example, if solving quantitative reasoning items depends primarily on using information from the distracters, the measurement of reasoning as a general top-down approach to problem solving would not be supported. Third, the *structural* aspect concerns the relationship of the scoring system to the structure of the construct domain. Factor analytic studies are relevant to this aspect of validity. If scores are combined across items and factors, empirical evidence should support this combination. Fourth, the *generalizability* aspect concerns the extent to which score interpretations may be generalized to varying populations, conditions, and settings. Research on adverse impact, use of paper-and-pencil versus computerized testing, are relevant to this aspect of validity. Fifth, the *external* aspect concerns the correlations of test scores with criteria and other tests. Studies of predictability of criteria, as well as multitrait-multimethod studies, are relevant to this aspect of validity. Sixth, the *consequential* aspect concerns the social consequences of test use, such as bias, fairness, and distributive justice.

The *substantive* aspect of construct validity is especially related to item design and interpreting the basis of an examinee's performance. As with other aspects of construct validity, it requires empirical evidence. The type of evidence required for substantive validity goes beyond the individual differences studies that were envisioned as supporting construct validity (Cronbach & Meehl, 1955). Embretson (1983) distinguished an interpretation of construct validity, *construct representation*, that requires evidence previously more typical of experimental psychology studies. That is, *construct representation* refers to the cognitive processing components, strategies, and knowledge stores that persons apply directly in solving items. The evidence that is required to support *construct representation* includes studies on how performance is affected by aspects of the item stimuli that influence various underlying processes. Thus, evidence such as experimental studies to manipulate item stimuli, mathematical modeling of performance, and eye tracker studies are needed to support this aspect of validity. Such studies are also relevant to item design because their results indicate how the cognitive complexity of items can be specified by variations in an item's stimulus features.

For all aspects of construct validity, Messick (1989, 1995) notes two major threats: (a) construct *underrepresentation* and (b) *construct irrelevant variance*. *Construct underrepresentation* occurs when important aspects or facets of what is being measured are omitted. A test of quantitative reasoning, for example, that included only algebra problems would be too narrow and consequently would underrepresent the reasoning construct. *Construct irrelevant variance*, in contrast, occurs when performance depends on qualities that are not considered part of the construct. For example, if a test for quantitative reasoning involves an undue dependence on language, then construct irrelevant variance is introduced. For individuals with less competence in a language, such quantitative reasoning tests become more a measure of language proficiency than of quantitative reasoning.

CONSTRUCT VALIDITY: UNIQUE ISSUES OF COGNITIVE DIAGNOSTIC ASSESSMENT

In addition to the aspects of construct validity for general testing practice, CDA bears its own distinctive issues in terms of construct validity. This section focuses on some aspects of construct validity for CDA. However, it doesn't mean that the aspects of validity that are not given special discussion here are not important. On the contrary, diagnostic assessments that fail to satisfy the fundamental validity requirement of sound measurement instruments most certainly fail to be defensible diagnostic instruments.

The Meaning of Diagnosis

Probably the best place to start the discussion is to ask the following question: "What makes CDA distinctive relative to other type of assessment?" To begin with, we examine the meaning of the word "diagnosis". For example, in the *American Heritage Dictionary of the English Language* (2000), diagnosis is defined as the following:

1. *Medicine.*
   a. The act or process of identifying or determining the nature and cause of a disease or injury through evaluation of patient history, examination, and review of laboratory data.
   b. The opinion derived from such an evaluation.
2. a. A critical analysis of the nature of something.
   b. The conclusion reached by such analysis.
3. *Biology.* A brief description of the distinguishing characteristics of an organism, as for taxonomic classification. (p. 500)

From such a definition, it may be safely inferred that diagnosis has been primarily applied in the field of medicine and biology, while different meanings are attached to the same word in different fields. Ignoring the differences across fields, it seems that at least three aspects of diagnosis can be extracted: (a) a description of the distinguishing characteristics of a thing or phenomenon, (b) identifying or determining the nature of a thing or causes of a phenomenon, and (c) the decision or conclusion that is made or reached by such description or analysis. Such a decision or conclusion could be a decisive classification of the thing into some prespecified categories such as diagnosing a patient as having pneumonia, or it could be an assertive statement of the mechanism that leads to the observed phenomenon, such as failure of the cooling system that leads to the overheating of the car engine.

Goals of Cognitive Diagnostic Assessment

Both the descriptive and causal-seeking approaches of cognitive diagnostic testing have been studied. For example, in his LISP tutor (Anderson, 1990), which is an intelligent tutoring system for teaching programming in LISP, learner's cognitive characteristics are represented by a detailed production system of cognition. Both how students actually execute the production rules and how these rules are acquired are specified in the LISP tutor. Diagnostic evaluation in the system is to assess the set of production rules that have been mastered at a particular stage by a student. Similarly, White and Frederiksen (1987) developed a tutoring system called QUEST that teaches problem solving and troubleshooting of electricity circuit problems. Students' mental characteristics are represented by various qualitatively different mental models, which are mental representations of the students' declarative and procedural knowledge, as well as strategic behaviors afforded by such representations. Other representations that are employed in diagnostic assessments include the conceptual or semantic network of declarative knowledge (Britton & Tidwell, 1995; Johnson, Goldsmith, & Teague, 1995; Naveh-Benjamin, Lin, & McKeachie, 1995). Diagnostic evaluations are conducted by comparing such presentations of domain experts with those of novices to detect possible misconceptions of the latter.

Alternatively, Brown and Burton (1978) represented students' problem-solving processes in basic mathematical skills through a directed procedural network, in which the set of declarative and procedural knowledge is connected with each other in a goal-structured fashion. The various misconceptions student hold in the domain are also represented in the network as incorrect alternatives of the correct procedure. The resulting diagnostic modeling system, the DEBUGGY system, provides a mechanism for explaining why a student is making a mistake in basic algebraic problems, not just identifying the mistake itself. In contrast, Embretson and Waxman (1989) developed several cognitive processing models for spatial folding tasks in which four cognitive components were identified as (a) encoding, (b) attaching, (c) folding, and (d) confirming. By empirically establishing the relationships between task features and the underlying components, specific patterns of examinees' responses to spatial tasks can be explained by identifying the specific sources of cognitive complexity involved in item solution. A similar approach can also be found in the work of Das, Naglieri, and Kirby (1994).

In short, cognitive diagnostic testing in a psychological or educational setting mainly focuses on at least three aspects of cognitive characteristics:

1. Skill profiles or knowledge lists that are essential in a given cognitive domain. Those skill and knowledge sets represent the most important skills and concepts of the domain, and serve as the basic building blocks for developing any other higher-order competency.

2. Structured procedural and/or knowledge network. Knowledge and skills are represented in our minds in a highly structured fashion (Collins & Loftus, 1975; Rumelhart, 1980). Expertise in a domain is represented not only by the number of basic skills or pieces of knowledge possessed in the domain, but also by the structure or organization of such skills and knowledge (Chi, Glaser, & Farr, 1988; Ericsson & Charness, 1994).

3. Cognitive processes, components, or capacities. The information processing paradigm of cognitive research provides methods to tap into the internal processes of cognition so specific cognitive models can be developed for a particular type of cognitive task. Observed performances therefore can be explained by looking into examinees' underlying cognitive processes when they perform such tasks.

These three aspects of cognitive characteristics are not exhaustive. Higher-order thinking skills such as cognitive strategy, strategy shifting, and metacognitive skills, should also be included in diagnostic assessment but may be limited by the development of testing techniques at present (Samejima, 1995; Snow & Lohman, 1993).

Issues of Construct Validity for Cognitive Diagnostic Assessment

The special goals of CDA inevitably bring forth particular issues of construct validity. The following discussion of construct validity focuses on both the representation of measured construct and the design of CDAs.

Construct Representation

As mentioned in the previous section, construct representation refers to the theory or rationale of the specification of the construct itself. For diagnostic purposes, the construct is usually represented in fine-grained forms, such as the procedural networks and processing models, to adequately capture the complexity of examinees' cognitive characteristics.

One important aspect of construct validity is the appropriateness and completeness of construct representation. Appropriateness of construct representation addresses whether the form or the symbol system we adopted to describe the cognitive characteristics is suitable. For example, the traditional latent trait perspective of intelligence, mainly through the dimensional theory of factor analysis, leads to enormous knowledge about the interrelationships among such latent traits, but little knowledge about the representation of the latent traits themselves. Similarly, cognitive psychologists have recognized the necessity of distinguishing between declarative and procedural knowledge because of their distinctive characteristics, which requires different approaches to represent such knowledge appropriately. Therefore, for a specific diagnostic testing purpose, adopting an appropriate representation of the construct is essential.

The completeness of construct representation addresses whether the construct has been identified adequately. As mentioned previously, two threats to construct validity are construct underrepresentation and construct irrelevant variance. For diagnostic assessment, however, complete representation of the construct may not be a practical option given the complexity of the examinee's cognitive characteristics in a given domain. This is exemplified in most of the intelligent tutoring systems that aim to capture the detailed processes of cognitive performance and learning mechanisms. It is a daunting task even for a highly structured cognitive domain. For example, to accurately diagnose students' misconceptions in solving algebraic problems, the diagnostic system has to encode all misconceptions that might appear in students' performances (Brown & Burton, 1978). Alternatively, restrictions on the breath of the construct might have to be imposed to achieve the depth of such representation.

Another important aspect of construct representation for cognitive diagnostic testing is the issue of granularity. Granularity is closely related to the issue of completeness but has its own implications. From a psychometric modeling perspective, granularity might be related to the capacity of measurement models, the affordance of the data, and the availability of computational power that are in contrast with the specificity of the cognitive representation (DiBello et al., 1995). Relative to the detailed representation of examinees' cognitive performance, current development in psychometrics might not provide a practical modeling approach. Thus, some degree of simplification of the cognitive representation might be needed. Besides the technical limitations, granularity has substantial implications that are related to the validity of diagnostic inferences as well. That is, at what level should the construct be represented so that both adequacy of representation and generalizability of the diagnostic inferences are maintained? For example, the production rule system representation of the LISP encodes examinee's problem-solving process in such a detail that 80% of the errors in student performance can be captured (Anderson, 1990). So it is adequate in terms of the construct representation. In contrast, however, the fine-grained diagnoses that are afforded by the representation makes such inferences confined to the highly limited situation, which results in very limited generalizability (Shute & Psotka, 1996). Thus, depending on the purpose of the diagnostic assessment, setting the appropriate level of granularity in terms of the representation is crucial for the validity of the inferences that are made from testing results.

Test Design and Administration for Diagnosis

Once the appropriate representation of the construct for diagnosis has been determined, one step for diagnostic testing is to design the items and to assemble the test to elicit examinees' observable behaviors so desirable diagnostic inferences can be made. This is a central step for defensible CDA, for which several issues will become relevant in terms of construct validity.

As mentioned previously, the covert nature of psychological constructs make the task of measuring such constructs inherently difficult. Two questions are essential to the mapping between observable indicators and the unobservable constructs. The first question is how can we be confident of the fact that the items we designed are actually measuring the construct that we are intending to measure? This indeed is a central question for validity, which has been bothering researchers and test specialists in the field of measurement from the beginning. Traditionally, as mentioned in the previous sections, such confidences come primarily from our faith in the opinions of the subject-matter experts. After the creation of test items, techniques such as factor analysis serve as post-hoc verification of such knowledge with regard to these items. Recent development of item design, however, brings both methodology and findings from cognitive research into the design process (Irvine & Kyllonen, 2002). By modeling the cognitive processes involved in item solution and identifying various sources of item difficulty that are caused by different cognitive components, confidence in the new approach of item design comes from how sound the cognitive theory behind the proposed models is, how well the proposed cognitive models fit the observed data that are collected over the designed items, or both. Such an item design approach has many implications for CDA. More discussion of this point is presented in the next section.

Aside from the effort to design and select items to be valid indicators of the construct, it is also a general concern whether certain aspects of cognitive characteristics are indeed measurable, at least with some item formats or approaches of item administrations. For example, Snow and Lohman (1993) discussed how the conventional approach of item design and administration might not be sufficient to measure cognitive characteristics such as qualitatively distinct strategies, strategy shifting, and the adaptiveness and flexibility that individuals exhibit in their problem-solving processes during testing. However, those aspects are undoubtedly facets of cognitive characteristics that are essential to diagnostic assessment. When an individual faces a cognitively complex task, not only the possession of the basic component skills, but also the ability of dynamically restructuring and innovatively using such component skills are essential to successfully solving the task. Recognizing the importance of incorporating such higher-order thinking skills into diagnostic assessment and the feasibility of assessing such characteristics, Samejima (1995) categorized cognitive processes into three categories: (a) processes that are assessable by conventional paper-and-pencil tests, (b) processes that are assessable by computerized tests with the possibility of using innovative test designs or administration, and (c) processes that are not assessable by either of the two testing methods, which require extensive experimental observations. Clearly, for diagnostic assessment to be valid, the approaches to designing the item, as well as the methods to administering the test, have to be considered.

Another important aspect of the test design and administration for diagnosis is sampling, which is relevant to both construct representation and the content aspect of validity. With the fine-grained representation of cognition, item sampling for diagnostic assessment becomes more complicated than for conventional assessment. In conventional assessment, the goal is to infer the general tendency to solve items in a given domain, where the general tendency is usually defined as a single or a few latent theoretical constructs. A sampling theory to measurement applies in this case, in which item sampling is done through defining a universe of items that are indicators of the latent constructs, and then selecting a random (representative) sample of items from the universe (Kane, 1982). When the goal of assessment is to infer the knowledge structure or procedural network of an examinee in a given domain, as diagnostic assessment does, definition of an item universe is much more sophisticated, if not impossible. For example, to measure knowledge networks or schemas (Marshall, 1990), items have to be sampled to measure both the nodes (i.e., the declarative facts or procedural knowledge) and the lines (that connects the nodes or the set of knowledge points) in the network. There are many unsolved issues in sampling items for this type of construct, such as number of items required for each node or line, how to estimate the prevalence of different nodes (statistical distributions across nodes), and so forth.

If the goal of diagnosis is to identify the mental processes of problem solving like those taken by the cognitive approach to measurement (Embretson, 1994), sampling schema must change accordingly. In such cases, a structural theory of measurement could apply (Guttman, 1971; Lohman & Ippel, 1993). In the cognitive process modeling approach to measurement, systematically varying different features of the tasks and the testing conditions could differentially exert influence on different cognitive processes of solving the task. A structural theory of measurement, therefore, states that measurement should focus on the pattern (structure) of observations under various situations, and not the random sample of observations from a defined universe. For example, in the cognitive processing model developed by Embretson and Waxman (1989) for the spatial folding tasks, two important task features are the number of pieces to be folded and the orientation of the markings on the pieces. These task features will systematically but differentially affect the complexity of different cognitive operations in solving the items.

Therefore, examinee's cognitive processing under various conditions can be elicited through a systematic arrangement of these task features. In this case, variations of responses to different tasks or under different testing situations are not random fluctuations, but rather authentic reflections of the differential requirement of cognitive loadings. Item sampling under this perspective of measurement, therefore, should take into account the structural relations among tasks.

EXAMPLE OF CONSTRUCT REPRESENTATION STUDIES FOR TRAIT MEASUREMENT VERSUS COGNITIVE DIAGNOSIS

In trait measurement, which includes ability testing, the goal is to estimate examinees' standings on one or more latent traits that are postulated to underlie test performance. For example, scores from a particular cognitive test may indicate the examinee's standing on one or more abilities that underlie performance. The link between test performance and the latent trait is established through construct validity studies. Traditionally, trait measurement has been the most popular goal of psychological testing.

Some tests may be appropriate for both trait measurement and cognitive diagnosis. In the following example, items for an intelligence test were designed from a theory about the underlying cognitive sources of complexity. For trait measurement, a construct representation study for construct validity would involve relating the design features of items to item difficulty. For cognitive diagnosis, the same design features can form the basis of classifying examinees in terms of their competences.

In this section, the cognitive design principles behind an intelligence test, the Abstract Reasoning Test (ART; Embretson, 1995) are described. Then, two empirical studies are presented to elaborate the construct representation aspect of construct validity. The first study examines the construct representation of ART for trait measurement, whereas the second study examines the structure of ART for cognitive diagnosis.

Abstract Reasoning Test

The ART was developed by Embretson (1995) using the cognitive design system approach. ART items are matrix completion problems. Matrix completion problems appear on a variety of intelligence and ability tests. They are considered a stable measure of fluid intelligence (Raven, 1965).

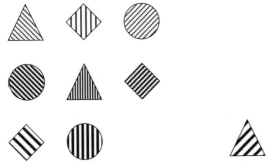

FIGURE 5.1. Example of matrix completion item and the missing entry.

Figure 5.1 gives an example of a matrix completion item. To solve the item, examinees must identify the relationships among the set of entries so the missing entry can be constructed.

Carpenter, Just, and Shell (1990) proposed a theory of processing progressive matrix problems based on results from a variety of experiments. According to their studies, matrix completion problems can be decomposed into different rules or relationships across the rows and columns. Finding and evaluating these relationships are the major processes involved in solving the matrix completion items. Carpenter et al. postulated that five relations are involved in solving matrix completion problems, such as those that appear on the Advanced Progressive Matrix Test (Raven, 1965). These relationships, in order of complexity, are identity, pairwise progression, figure addition or subtraction, distribution of three, and distribution of two. Carpenter et al. (1990) suggested that examinees applied one rule at a time following the hierarchy of these rules. That is, the objects are examined first for identity relationships before considering pairwise progression relationships.

Based on Carpenter et al.'s (1990) processing models for matrix completion problems, Embretson (1995, 1998) developed the ART using the cognitive design system approach. Item structures of ART were specified through the formal notational system (Embretson, 1998), which determines the type and number of relationships in an item. An example of the formal notional system for the item shown in Figure 5.1 is given in Figure 5.2. Two pairwise progressions and one distribution of three are involved in the item. The formal notation system specifies the relations in letters and numbers in which A stands for the triangle, C for diamond, and D for circle. B stands for the grids within the

AB$_{41}$	CB$_{21}$	DB$_{11}$
DB$_{42}$	AB$_{22}$	CB$_{12}$
CB$_{43}$	DB$_{23}$	AB$_{13}$

FIGURE 5.2. Formal notation system for item in Figure 5.1.

objects that show different patterns. The subscripts denote the systematic changes of the grids across rows and columns. Although changes of the first subscript denote the changes of the orientations of the grids, changes of the second subscript denote the changes of their intensities (or weights). Items with the same structure can then be generated by varying different objects or attributes. A set of different item structures can be generated by specifying different combinations of relations and/or abstraction components. The current ART has 30 item structures, each of which has five structurally equivalent items.

Cognitive Psychometric Modeling of Abstract Reasoning Test Item Properties

In this approach, the construct representation aspect is explicated by mathematically modeling ART item properties from the difficulty of the processes involved in item solution. The approach involves postulating a processing model and then specifying the stimulus features in items that determine process difficulty, such as the number of relationships, number of separate objects, and so forth.

The processing theory underlying the cognitive psychometric modeling of ART items was based on Carpenter et al.'s (1990) theory plus an encoding process. In the Carpenter et al. theory, two major processes for matrix completion items such as ART include correspondence finding and goal management. Correspondence finding is primarily influenced by the level of the relationship, as described previously. The highest-level relationship, distribution of two, involves the most abstraction. Goal management, however, depends on the number of relationships in the problem. Carpenter et al. did not include encoding in their theory, primarily because their automatic item solver program required verbal descriptions of the item stimuli.

Embretson (1995, 1998) further developed the processing theory in two ways, that is, combining the relational processing variables into a single variable, namely, memory load, and including an encoding stage that is influenced by several perceptual features of items. The memory load variable includes both the number and the level of relationships. Carpenter et al. (1990) hypothesized that individuals attempted to solve the item with the lowest-order relationships before attempting higher-order relationships. Accordingly, for the highest-level relationship (i.e., distribution of two), all lower-order relationships are assumed to be attempted. The memory load variable is a count of the total number of relationships attempted before reaching the required relationships in the problem. Encoding is influenced by the number of unique attributes, degree of stimulus integration, object distortion, and object fusion. In matrix completion problems, more than one object may appear in a single cell of the design. *Number of unique attributes* refers to the number of separately manipulated objects in the problem stem. *Stimulus integration* refers to the arrangement of the objects. The most integrated display occurs when objects are overlaid, while the least integrated display occurs when two or more objects are displayed around a platform, such as a "+". *Object distortion* refers to corresponding objects for which the shape of one or more is distorted. Finally, *object fusion* occurs when overlaid objects no longer have separate borders.

Estimates of item difficulty from the one-parameter logistic item response theory (IRT) model for 150 ART items were available. The estimates were based on a large sample of young adults. For this set of items, five different items had been generated from each of 30 different item structures. The five variant items differed in the objects or display features. Scores for the items on all cognitive variables were available.

Estimates of item difficulty were regressed on the cognitive variables scored for each item. Table 5.1 presents the overall model summary. Two

TABLE 5.1. *Regression of item difficulty on cognitive model variables*

					Change statistics			
Model	R	R square	Adjusted R square	Std. error estimate	R square change	F change	df1	df2	Sig. F change
1 – Structural only	.758	.575	.569	.92893	.575	99.475	2	147	.000
2 – Structural perceptual	.782	.612	.598	.89737	.036	4.508	3	144	.005

TABLE 5.2. *Coefficients for final cognitive model*

| | Unstandardized coefficients | | Standardized coefficients | | |
	B	Std. Error	Beta	t	Sig.
(Constant)	2.822	.302		−9.332	000
Memory Load	.199	.019	.601	10.664	.000
Number of unique elements	.172	.044	.225	3.923	.000
Object Integration	.387	.168	.129	2.301	.023
Distortion	.507	.260	.105	1.953	.053
Fusions	−.279	.185	−.084	−1.508	.134

variables, memory load and number of unique elements, are specified by the item's abstract structure. These structural variables had a strong and highly significant impact on item difficulty ($R^2 = .575$). The perceptual variables are variations in the display of the objects within a structure. Adding the perceptual variables to the model significantly increased prediction, but the impact was relatively small ($R^2 = .036$).

Table 5.2 presents the standardized and unstandardized regression weights for the final model, which included both structural and perceptual variables. All variables except object fusion had significant weights in prediction. Memory load had the largest beta weight, followed by number of unique elements, again indicating the dominance of the structural variables in predicting item difficulty. Distortion and object integration had smaller and similar beta weights.

In general, the results support the construct representation aspect of construct validity, as specified in the design of the items. The cognitive model variables yielded strong prediction of item difficulty. Of the five variables in the model, ART item difficulty was most strongly affected by the working memory load of the items. These results imply that individual differences in working memory capacity have a strong impact on performance. The pattern of the prediction also supported the feasibility of generating items with predictable properties. That is, the two variables that are specified in the generating structure for ART items, memory load and number of unique elements, had the strongest impact in predicting item difficulty. The perceptual features, which can vary in the same structure, had relatively small impact on item difficulty. Thus, the results support the equivalence of items generated from the same structure, even though specific stimulus features and perceptual displays differ.

Construct Representation Study for Cognitive Diagnosis

Alternatively, the construct of ART may also be represented by the skills of correctly identifying each of the five relationships (rules) involved in solving an ART item. Using a discrete representation of each of the five skills, the ability of a particular examinee to solve an ART item can be regarded as a direct result of whether he or she possesses the required skills to solve the item. For example, the item in Figure 5.1 contains two pairwise progressions and one distribution of three. An examinee is expected to be able to solve the item if he or she possesses the skills of correctly identifying the two relations. To represent the construct measured by ART in this way, however, both the set of skills involved in ART items and the interrelationships among the skills have to be specified. For ART items, the set of skills are the skills associated with identifying the five relations, which constitute the primary source of item difficulty. As for the structural relations among the five skills, Carpenter et al. (1990) speculated that the five relations followed the order: identity (ID) $\rightarrow$ pairwise progression (PP) $\rightarrow$ figure addition and substraction (FA) $\rightarrow$ distribution of three (D3) $\rightarrow$ distribution of two (D2) (letter in parenthesis stands for an abbreviation of the relation and are used hereafter). The arrow $\rightarrow$ stands for the surmise relation between the relation to the left and right of the arrow. For example, ID $\rightarrow$ PP stands for the relation that identification of relation ID is surmised from relation PP. Embretson (1998) found that figure addition/subtraction did not conform to the order given above. Identification of this relation can either be very difficult or very easy. Accordingly, one structural representation among the five relations may be given as follows:

Given the structural relations among the five relations, the following family of admissible subsets of the five skills can be constructed: {Ø}, {ID}, {ID, PP}, {ID, FA}, {ID, FA, PP}, {ID, PP, D3}, {ID, PP, D3, FA}, {ID, PP, D3, D2}, {ID, PP, D3, D2, FA}, where {Ø} refers to the null set

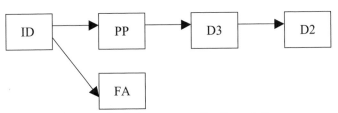

FIGURE 5.3. Structural relations among the five relations.

TABLE 5.3. *Mapping between ability states and ART item structures*

Ability state	Item structure	Ability state	Item structure
{ID}	None	{ID, FA}	10, 12, 19, 21, 23, 24, 27, 28, 32, 34, 35}
{ID, PP}	6, 7, 16, 17, 18, 26, 33	{ID, PP, FA}	{ID, PP} + {FA}
{ID, PP, D3}	8, 9, 13, 20, 25, 29, 39, 40, 41, 46	{ID, PP, D3, FA}	{ID, PP, D3} +{FA}
{ID, PP, D3, D2}	42, 43	{ID, PP, D3, D2, FA}	{ID, PP, D3, D2} + {FA}

that none of the five skills is possessed. We prefer to label each skill set as a latent ability state. In doing so, we imply that a particular latent ability state represents not only a simple list of skills being possessed, but also the higher-order thinking skills that are afforded by the subset of basic skills.

To analyze the ART data under this alternative representation, mapping between different latent ability states and ART item structures needs to be established. Table 5.3 presents the mapping relations for the 30 item structures (see Yang, 2003, for a detailed description of the mapping rules). For illustration, four item structures (7, 21, 29, 42) are selected to measure each of the four skills (PP, FA, D3, D2) (the skill {ID} is excluded because there is no item alone to measure it). For a more detailed analysis of the ART items with regard to inferring diagnostic information from the latent ability-state lattice representation of ART construct, see Yang (2003). From these four item structures, the corresponding ideal response patterns, denoted as the items that can be correctly answered given a particular ability state, are then given as {Ø}, {7}, {21}, {7, 21}, {7, 29}, {7, 29, 21}, {7, 29, 42}, {7, 29, 42, 21}. An intuitive examination of the effectiveness of the hypothesized latent ability structure can be done by simply looking at the proportion of observed response patterns that belong to the ideal response patterns. Table 5.4 gives such an examination based on the data collected from 818 young adults (Embretson, 1998). It can be seen that 88.6% of the examinees fall into one of the eight ideal response patterns, which suggests that the derived ability space fits the data fairly well.

A formal examination of the adequacy of the derived latent ability space to the ART items can be conducted through statistical modeling. Recent developments in both statistical modeling and psychometrics provide the possibility of modeling sets of discrete latent abilities under the framework of latent class/discrete psychometric models (Junker &

TABLE 5.4. *Proportion of examinees falling in ideal response patterns*

Pattern	Item {7, 21, 29, 42}	Observed frequency	Ideal response pattern
1	0000	32	0000
2	1000	63	1000
3	0100	16	0100
4	0010	21	–
5	0001	3	–
6	1100	67	1100
7	1010	115	1010
8	1001	6	–
9	0110	29	–
10	0101	4	–
11	0011	6	–
12	1110	248	1110
13	1101	17	–
14	1011	41	1011
15	0111	7	–
16	1111	143	1111
Total		818	725
Percentage			88.6

Sijtsma, 2001; Templin, 2004). For example, a latent class model for the particular example given Table 5.4 can be given as follows:

$$P(\mathbf{x}) = \sum_{c=1}^{c} \pi(\alpha_c) \prod_{j=1}^{j} \left[(1 - s_j)^{\alpha_j q_j} g_j^{(1-\alpha_j)q_j} \right]^{x_j} \left[1 - (1 - s_j)^{\alpha_j q_j} g_j^{(1-\alpha_j)q_j} \right]^{1-x_j},$$

where $\mathbf{x}, \mathbf{x} = (x_1, x_2, \ldots, x_J)$ is the observed item response pattern; C is the number of permissible latent ability states; $\alpha_c, \alpha_c = (\alpha_{c1}, \alpha_{c2}, \ldots, \alpha_{cK})$, is the vector that represents the latent ability state c; and α_{ck} (1 or 0) indicates whether ability k, $k = 1, 2, \ldots, K$, is included in the latent state c. The probability of being in the latent ability state c is denoted as $\pi(\alpha_c)$. q_{jk} (= 1 or 0) indicates whether item j, $j = 1, 2, \ldots, J$, requires ability k and is collected in the matrix $\mathbf{Q}_{J \times K}$, and s_j and g_j are the slip and guessing parameters, respectively (Embretson, 1985; Junker & Sijtsma, 2001). Alternative models can be derived by imposing constraints on s_j and g_j. Table 5.5 presents the results from three alternative models by imposing that (a) $s_j = s$ and $g_j = g$ (constant error rate across items; Dayton & MaCready, 1976), (b) $s_j = g_j$ (item-specific error rate model), and (c) $s_j = g_j = e$ (Proctor, 1970).

TABLE 5.5. *Latent class models fitted to ART data*

Item[2] {7,29,21,42}	Frequency	Model I[1] Predicted frequency	Model I[1] Pearson residual	Model II Predicted frequency	Model II Pearson residual	Model III Predicted frequency	Model III Pearson residual
0000*	32	32.86	−0.150	33.03	−0.179	33.76	−0.30
1000*	63	60.62	0.306	61.20	0.230	61.82	0.15
0100	21	15.00	1.549	15.06	1.531	15.90	1.28
1100*	115	120.36	−0.489	120.37	−0.490	119.25	−0.39
0010*	16	16.75	−0.184	16.70	−0.171	16.62	−0.15
1010*	67	66.58	0.052	66.71	0.035	66.67	0.04
0110	29	26.56	0.473	27.31	0.322	27.61	0.26
1110*	248	250.39	−0.151	249.63	−0.103	249.36	−0.09
0001	3	3.65	−0.341	3.19	−0.108	2.53	0.30
1001	6	9.11	−1.030	8.53	−0.867	7.88	−0.67
0101	6	4.46	0.732	4.55	0.678	4.58	0.66
1101*	41	40.95	0.008	41.06	−0.010	41.28	−0.04
0011	4	2.86	0.676	2.72	0.773	2.55	0.91
1011	17	18.05	−0.246	17.86	−0.203	18.42	−0.33
0111	7	13.96	−1.864	14.46	−1.962	14.44	−1.96
1111*	143	135.85	0.614	135.60	0.635	135.33	0.66
Total	818	818		818		818	
G^2		9.68		9.55		8.81	
df		7		6		4	
P value		0.208		0.145		0.066	

Note: [1] Model I, Proctor model; Model II, constant error rate across items; Model III, item-specific error rate model.
[2] Response patterns with asterisk (*) are ideal response pattern.

Table 5.5 can be partitioned into two portions. In the top portion, all observable response patterns from the four items, as well as the associated numbers of examinees in each of the 16 response patterns, were given in the first two columns. Then, the predicted numbers of examinees and the associated Pearson residuals for each of the three fitted models were presented. These results provide detailed information about how adequate a particular model fits the data. Specifically, these results inform us which portion of the data is fitted adequately and which is not. Because Pearson residual approximates to a standard normal distribution for large samples, any number in these columns that is greater than 2 in absolute value indicates a statistically significant deviation (at .05 level) of model-predicted frequency from the observed frequency. It can be seen from Table 5.5 that, for all response patterns,

TABLE 5.6. *Parameter estimates from model 1*

Ability state	Ideal response pattern	Probability	Error
{Φ}	{0000}	0.047	0.093
{PP}	{1000}	0.076	
{FA}	{0010}	0.013	
{PP, D3}	{1100}	0.161	
{PP, FA}	{1010}	0.065	
{PP, D3, FA}	{1110}	0.407	
{PP, D3, D2}	{1101}	0.032	
{PP, D3, FA, D2}	{1111}	0.198	

Model I, the Proctor model, fits the data adequately, based on the results of Pearson residual alone.

The bottom portion of Table 5.5 presents values of G^2, degree of freedom (df), and the corresponding P-value for each model. For large samples, G^2 approximates to a chi-square distribution with df $= N - 1 - m$, where N is the number of all possible response patterns in the data (in this case, $N = 2^4 = 16$) and m is the number of parameters in the model. For example, there are eight parameters in the Proctor model (seven class parameters $\pi(\alpha_c)$ and one slip or guessing parameter e). Therefore, the associate df $= 16 - 1 - 8 = 7$. The G^2 represents an overall goodness-of-fit index for a model. Based on the P-value, it can be seen that all three models in Table 5.5 fit the data well. However, combined with results of the Pearson residual, it seems that Model I, the Proctor model, is the model of choice for this data set.

Table 5.6 presents the estimated probability that a randomly sampled examinee belongs to each ideal response pattern under Model I. It can be seen that examinees are more likely to be in the ability state {PP, D3, FA}. The probability of being in {PP, D3, FA} is .407. They also have substantial probability to be in ability states {PP, D3, FA, D2} and {PP, D3}. The corresponding probabilities are .198 and .161, respectively. This is consistent with a previous study, which showed that ART items are relatively easier for the sample (Embretson, 1998). Table 5.6 also shows that the error probability is small (.093), which can be interpreted either as the probability of getting an item correct without possessing the required skills or as the probability of missing the item with the required skills. This is consistent with the ART item format, which has eight options to choose from and primarily relies on rule identification.

TABLE 5.7. *Inference of latent ability state given response pattern* {1011}

Ability state	$\pi(\alpha_c)$	$P(X \mid \alpha_c)$	$\pi(\alpha_c)*P(X \mid \alpha_c)$	$P(\alpha_c \mid X)$
{Φ}	0.047	0.0007	0.0000	0.0015
{PP}	0.076	0.0071	0.0005	0.0244
{FA}	0.013	0.0071	0.0001	0.0042
{PP, D3}	0.161	0.0007	0.0001	0.0053
{PP, FA}	0.065	0.0694	0.0045	0.2036
{PP, D3, FA}	0.407	0.0071	0.0029	0.1307
{PP, D3, D2}	0.032	0.0071	0.0002	0.0103
{PP, D3, FA, D2}	0.198	0.0694	0.0137	0.6201
$\Sigma\pi(\alpha_c)*P(X \mid \alpha_c)$			0.02216	

Given that latent classes in such models are defined theoretically from each latent ability state, a particular examinee's latent ability state can be inferred. In the current example, given the observed response pattern x from a particular examinee i, the likelihood that such an examinee is in a latent class c is given as

$$P\left(\alpha_c \mid \mathbf{x}, \mathbf{s}, \mathbf{g}, \mathbf{Q}\right) = \frac{\pi\left(\alpha_c\right) P\left(\mathbf{x} \mid \alpha_c, \mathbf{s}, \mathbf{g}, \mathbf{Q}\right)}{\sum_{c=1}^{C} \pi\left(\alpha_c\right) P\left(\mathbf{x} \mid \alpha_c, \mathbf{s}, \mathbf{g}, \mathbf{Q}\right)},$$

where $P\left(\mathbf{x} \mid \alpha_c, \mathbf{s}, \mathbf{g}, \mathbf{Q}\right)$ is the probability of observing response pattern x conditional on α_c, $\mathbf{s}$, $\mathbf{g}$, and $\mathbf{Q}$. Table 5.7 illustrates the inference for a particular examinee whose observed response pattern is {1011} under Model I. Given an examinee's observed response pattern {1011}, he or she has the highest posterior probability (.6201) of being in the ability state {PP, D3, FA, D2}.

In general, the latent ability state representation of the ART construct provides an alternative approach to cognitive psychometric modeling. This approach to construct representation decomposes the continuous latent construct of ART, such as the memory load, onto a discrete latent ability space. Results from analysis of ART data using latent class/ discrete psychometric models show that the hypothetical structure of latent skills involved in solving ART items fits the data quite well. Most of the examinees are likely to possess the majority of the four skills in ART. This result is consistent with previous results from cognitive psy- chometric modeling, showing that the ART items are relatively easy for this examinee sample. An individual examinee's likelihood of being in a given latent ability state, conditional on his or her observed response pattern, can be inferred from this approach.

SUMMARY AND CONCLUSIONS

CDA has become increasingly important because of its potential to provide a detailed account of the underlying cognitive basis of an examinee's performance. From a broader perspective, the shift from standardized testing to diagnostic testing reflects the response from the measurement field to the challenges from developments in cognitive and educational psychology in recent decades (Mislevy, 1993). With an adequate representation of the measurement constructs, cognitive diagnostic testing could hopefully capture the complexity of examinees' cognitive characteristics, which are reflected in the types of observations and patterns in the data.

For CDA to be valid and effective, its construct validity must be evaluated thoroughly and systematically. In this chapter, contemporary views of construct validity were presented and elaborated. The substantive aspect of construct validity, and particularly construct representation studies, are especially important for cognitive diagnosis. In construct representation studies (see Embretson, 1998), the processes, strategies, and knowledge behind item responses are elaborated. Although construct representation studies are important for elaborating trait measurement constructs, they are even more important for cognitive diagnostic testing. Because cognitive diagnostic testing requires a more fine-gained representation of the measurement construct, several specific issues for construct validity must be addressed: (a) the appropriateness, completeness, and granularity of the construct representation; (b) the design and selection of observable indicators for a fine-grained measurement construct; (c) the measurability of the construct with regard to item formats or test administration procedures; and (d) the appropriateness of the theoretical measurement foundation that is relevant to the specific purpose of diagnostic assessment. This list is far from complete. Because relatively few studies have been done with regard to cognitive diagnostic testing, especially from the perspective of construct validation, many issues of construct validity for diagnostic assessment are left unexplored. Future research in this aspect is essential for gaining a more comprehensive understanding of the complex landscape for cognitive diagnosis.

A systematic and defensible approach to item design is especially significant for the construct validity of diagnostic testing. For instance, in the cognitive design system approach to item design (Embretson, 1998), the relationship of item stimuli to the cognitive requirements of solving the item is elaborated. Item performance is explicitly linked to its underlying cognitive variables, and the cognitive theory explicates the underlying measurement construct of the test. This approach to item design provides an operational mechanism for bridging measurement constructs with item design, which in turn can provide a foundation for the validity of the resultant diagnostic testing.

In this chapter, the cognitive design principles for a reasoning test were examined empirically to illustrate how construct validity can be supported for trait measurement and cognitive diagnosis. For trait measurement, construct representation related the design features of items to item psychometric properties (e.g., item difficulty or discrimination). For cognitive diagnosis, the same design features form the basis for classifying examinees in terms of their competences. Construct validity was supported empirically in the analyses presented for both measurement goals. For cognitive diagnostic testing, which is the main concern in this chapter, the results have several implications. First, the explicit linkage between item stimuli and the underlying cognitive requirements allows items to be generated with targeted cognitive and psychometric properties, which is a feature that is essential to diagnostic testing. Second, the cognitive theory not only identifies cognitive variables that are sources of item difficulties, but also provides a basis for understanding the structural relationship among them. This is important for interpreting test results and sequencing item administration. Third, combined with modern technology, such as an item generation approach, a validated cognitive theory for items has potential for automating individualized diagnostic testing. That is, adaptive testing for individuals can be based not only on the statistical/psychometric properties of items (e.g, IRT-based difficulty estimates), but also on the substantive properties of the items (e.g., knowledge, skills, or cognitive processes that are required for item solution).

Individualized CDA holds many exciting possibilities. Several models and methods have already been developed for diagnostic testing (e.g., Leighton et al., 2004). What clearly remains to be accomplished are construct representation studies on educationally important domains, such as mathematical competency and verbal comprehension, to support the fine-grained aspects of construct validity required for diagnostic testing.

References

American Education Research Association (AERA), American Psychological Association, National Council on Measurement in Education. (1999). *Standards for educational and psychological testing*. Washington, DC: AERA.

The American Heritage Dictionary of the English Language (4th ed.). (2000). Boston: Houghton Mifflin.

Anderson, J. R. (1990). Analysis of student performance with the LISP tutor. In N. Frederiksen, R. Glaser, A. Lesgold, & M. G. Shafto (Eds.), *Diagnostic monitoring of skills and knowledge acquisition* (pp. 27–50). Hillsdale, NJ: Erlbaum.

Britton, B. K., & Tidwell, P. (1995). Cognitive structure testing: A computer system for diagnosis of expert-novice differences. In P. Nichols., S. F. Chipman., & R. L. Brennan (Eds.), *Cognitively diagnostic assessment* (pp. 251–278). Hillsdale, NJ: Erlbaum.

Brown, J. S., & Burton, R. R. (1978). Diagnostic models for procedural bugs in basic mathematical skills. *Cognitive Science, 2,* 155–192.

Carpenter, P. A., Just, M. A., & Shell, P. (1990). What one intelligence test measures: A theoretical account of the processing in the Raven Progressive Matrices Test. *Psychological Review, 97,* 404–431.

Chi, M. T. H., Glaser, R., & Farr, M. (1988). *The nature of expertise.* Hillsdale, NJ: Erlbaum.

Collins, A. M., & Loftus, E. F. (1975). A spreading-activation theory of semantic processing. *Psychological Review, 82,* 407–428.

Cronbach, L. J., & Meehl, P. E. (1955). Construct validity in psychological tests. *Psychological Bulletin, 52,* 281–302.

Das, J. P., Naglieri, J. A., & Kirby, J. R. (1994). *Assessment of cognitive processes: The PASS theory of intelligence.* Needham Heights, MA: Allyn & Bacon.

Dayton, C. M., & MaCready, G. B. (1976). A probabilistic model for a validation of behavioral hierarchies. *Psychometrika, 41,* 189–204.

De La Torre, J., & Douglas, J.A. (2004). Higher-order latent trait models for cognitive diagnosis. *Psychometrika, 69,* 333–353.

DiBello, L., Stout, W., & Roussos, L. (1995). Unified cognitive/psychometric diagnostic assessment likelihood-based classification techniques. In P. Nichols, S. F. Chipman, & R. L. Brennan (Eds.), *Cognitively diagnostic assessment* (pp. 361–389). Hillsdale, NJ: Erlbaum.

Doignon, J. P., & Falmagne, J. C. (1999). *Knowledge spaces.* Berlin: Springer-Verlag.

Draney, K. L., Pirolli, P., & Wilson, M. (1995). A measurement model for complex cognitive skill. In P. Nichols, S. F. Chipman, & R. L. Brennan (Eds.), *Cognitively diagnostic assessment* (pp. 103–126). Hillsdale, NJ: Erlbaum.

Embretson, S. E. (1983). Construct validity: Construct representation versus nomothetic span. *Psychological Bulletin, 93,* 179–197.

Embretson, S. E. (1985). *Test design: developments in psychology and psychometrics.* Academic Press.

Embretson, S. E. (1994). Application of cognitive design systems to test development. In C. R. Reynolds (Eds.), *Cognitive assessment: A multidisciplinary perspective* (pp. 107–135). New York: Plenum Press.

Embretson, S. E. (1995). The role of working memory capacity and general control processes in intelligence. *Intelligence, 20,* 169–190.

Embretson, S. E. (1998). A cognitive design system approach to generating valid tests: Application to abstract reasoning. *Psychological Methods, 3,* 300–326.

Embretson, S. E., & Waxman, M. (1989). *Models for processing and individual differences in spatial folding.* Unpublished manuscript.

Ericsson, K. A., & Charness, N. (1994). Expert performance, its structure and acquisition. *American Psychologist, 49*, 725–747.

Guttman, L. (1971). Measurement as structural theory. *Psychometrika, 36*, 329–347.

Hartz, S. (2002). *A Bayesian framework for the unified model for assessing cognitive abilities: blending theory with practicality.* Unpublished doctoral thesis, University of Illinois at Urbana-Champaign.

Irvine, S. H., & Kyllonen, P. C. (2002). *Item generation for test development.* Mahwah, NJ: Erlbaum.

Johnson, P. J., Goldsmith, T. E., & Teague, K. W. (1995). Similarity, structure, and knowledge: A representational approach to assessment. In P. Nichols, S. F. Chipman, & R. L. Brennan (Eds.), *Cognitively diagnostic assessment* (pp. 221–250). Hillsdale, NJ: Erlbaum.

Junker, B., & Sijtsma, K. (2001). Cognitive assessment models with few assumptions, and connections with nonparametric item response theory. *Applied Psychological Measurement, 25*, 258–272.

Kane, M. T. (1982). A sampling model for validity. *Applied Psychological Measurement, 6*, 125–160.

Leighton, J. P., Gierl, M. J., & Hunka, S. (2004). The attribute hierarchy method for cognitive assessment: A variation on Tatsuoka's rule-space approach. *Journal of Educational Measurement, 41*, 205–236.

Lohman, D. F., & Ippel, M. J. (1993). Cognitive diagnosis from statistically based assessment toward theory based assessment. In N. Frederiksen, R. J. Mislevy, & I. Bejar (Eds.), *Test theory for a new generation of tests* (pp. 41–71). Hillsdale, NJ: Erlbaum.

Maris, E. (1999). Estimating multiple classification latent class model. *Psychometrika, 64*, 187–212.

Marshall, S. P. (1990). Generating good items for diagnostic tests. In N. Frederiksen, R. Glaser, A. Lesgold, & M. G. Shafto (Eds.), *Diagnostic monitoring of skill and knowledge acquisition* (pp. 433–452). Hillsdale, NJ: Erlbaum.

Messick, S. (1989). Validity. In R. L. Linn (Eds.), *Educational measurement* (pp. 13–103). New York: Macmillan.

Messick, S. (1995). Validity of psychological assessment: Validation of inferences from persons' responses and performances as scientific inquiry into score meaning. *The American Psychologist, 50*, 741–749.

Mislevy, R. J. (1993). Foundations of a new test theory. In N. Frederiksen, R. J. Mislevy, & I. I. Bejar (Eds.), *Test theory for a new generation of tests* (pp. 19–39). Hillsdale, NJ: Erlbaum.

Mislevy, R. J. (1996). Test theory reconceived. *Journal of Educational Measurement, 33*, 379–416.

Naveh-Benjamin, M., Lin, Y., & McKeachie, W. J. (1995). Inferring student's cognitive structures and their development using the "fill-in-the-structure" (FITS) technique. In P. Nichols, S. F. Chipman, & R. L. Brennan (Eds.), *Cognitively diagnostic assessment* (pp. 279–304). Hillsdale, NJ: Erlbaum.

Proctor, C. H. (1970). A probabilistic formulation and statistical analysis for Guttman scaling. *Psychometrika, 35*, 73–78.

Raven, J. C. (1965). *Advanced progressive matrices, set I and II*. London: H. K. Lewis. (Distributed in the United States by The Psychological Corporation, San Antonio, TX).

Rumelhart, D. E. (1980). Schemata: The building blocks of cognition. In R. J. Spiro, B. C. Bruce, & W. F. Brewer (Eds.), *Theoretical issues in reading comprehension* (pp. 33–57). Hillsdale NJ: Erlbaum.

Samejima, F. (1995). A cognitive diagnosis method using latent trait models: Competency space approach and its relationship with DiBello and Stout's unified cognitive-psychometric diagnosis model. In P. Nichols, S. F. Chipman, & R. L. Brennan (Eds.), *Cognitively diagnostic assessment* (pp. 391–410). Hillsdale, NJ: Erlbaum.

Sheehan, K. M. (1997a). *A tree-based approach to proficiency scaling* (ETS Research Report No. RR-97–2). Princeton, NJ: Educational Testing Service.

Sheehan, K. M. (1997b). *A tree-based approach to proficiency scaling and diagnostic assessment* (ETS Research Report No. RR-97–9). Princeton, NJ: Educational Testing Service.

Shute, V. J., & Psotka, J. (1996). Intelligent tutoring systems: Past, present, and future. In D. H. Jonassen (Ed.), *Handbook of educational communications and technology* (pp. 570-600). New York: Macmillan.

Snow, R. E., & Lohman, D. F. (1993). Cognitive psychology, new test design, and new test theory: An introduction. In N. Frederiksen, R. J. Mislevy, & I. I. Bejar (Eds.), *Test theory for a new generation of tests* (pp. 1–17). Hillsdale, NJ: Erlbaum.

Tatsuoka, K. K. (1995). Architecture of knowledge structures and cognitive diagnosis: A statistical pattern recognition and classification approach. In P. Nichols, S. F. Chipman, & R. L. Brennan (Eds.), *Cognitively diagnostic assessment* (pp. 327–359). Hillsdale, NJ: Erlbaum.

Templin, J. (2004). *Generalized linear mixed proficiency models for cognitive diagnosis*. Unpublished doctoral dissertation, University of Illinois at Urbana–Champaign.

White, B., & Frederikson, J. (1987). Qualitative models and intelligent learning environment. In R. Lawler & M. Yazdani (Eds.), *AI and education* (pp. 281–305). Norwood, NJ: Ablex.

Yang, X. (2003). *Inferring diagnostic information from abstract reasoning test items*. Unpublished doctoral thesis, University of Kansas, Lawrence.

6

Verbal Reports as Data for Cognitive Diagnostic Assessment

Jacqueline P. Leighton and Mark J. Gierl

The term *cognitive diagnostic assessment* (CDA) is used in this chapter to refer to a specific type of student evaluation. Unlike classroom-based tests designed by teachers or large-scale assessments designed by test developers to measure how much an examinee knows about a subject domain, CDAs are designed to measure the specific knowledge structures (e.g., distributive rule in mathematics) and processing skills (e.g., applying the distributive rule in appropriate mathematical contexts) an examinee has acquired. The type of information provided by results from a CDA should answer questions such as the following: Does the examinee know the content material well? Does the examinee have any misconceptions? Does the examinee show strengths for some knowledge and skills but not others? The objective of CDAs, then, is to inform stakeholders of examinees' learning by pinpointing the location where the examinee might have specific problem-solving weaknesses that could lead to difficulties in learning. To serve this objective, CDAs are normally informed by empirical investigations of how examinees understand, conceptualize, reason, and solve problems in content domains (Frederiksen, Glaser, Lesgold, & Shafto, 1990; Nichols, 1994; Nichols, Chipman, & Brennan, 1995).

In this chapter, we focus on two methods for making sense of empirical investigations of how examinees understand, conceptualize, reason, and solve problems in content domains. As a way of introduction, we first briefly discuss the importance of CDAs for providing information about examinees' strengths and weaknesses, including the ways in which CDAs differ from traditional classroom-based tests and large-scale tests. Although the preceding chapters have already described the value of CDAs, we reiterate some of these ideas to establish a rationale for collecting verbal reports in the service of developing CDAs. Second, we elaborate on two methods, *protocol analysis* (Ericsson & Simon, 1980, 1993) and *verbal analysis* (Chi, 1997; see Willis, 2005), for guiding the collection and summary of verbal report data for use in the development of CDAs. Although both methods can be used to inform CDAs, we propose that (a) protocol analysis is best used in rule-based, problem-solving contexts (e.g., math, science) for *validating* expectations (hypotheses) of how examinees solve problems, whereas (b) verbal analysis is best used in knowledge-based, problem-solving contexts (e.g., social studies, language arts) for *generating* hypotheses of how examinees think about problems. Third, we provide guidelines for using each method. Fourth, we summarize the limitations of these methods and suggest broader issues that should be explored when designing CDAs.

VALUE OF COGNITIVE DIAGNOSTIC ASSESSMENTS

CDAs cannot be developed from traditional testing practices alone (see also, Gorin, this volume). For example, the quality of an item to be included in a CDA cannot be judged only by considering commonly used psychometric standards (e.g., difficulty, discrimination) or content standards (i.e., whether an item fits one of the cells found in the matrix of test specifications). Item quality in CDAs must also be judged by whether it adequately measures a particular knowledge structure or processing skill. A *knowledge structure* is defined herein as factual information about the meaning or perceptual characteristics of objects. Knowledge structures also include procedural information about how to, for example, pronounce a word or operate a type of machinery (Lohman, 2000). A *cognitive process* is defined herein as a transformation that is performed on a particular mental representation (Lohman, 2000), and it often includes a skill or strategy for manipulating one knowledge state into another. Items in CDAs measure the knowledge structures and processing skills that have been identified, both empirically and theoretically, as important to the acquisition of the construct being measured by the test. One of the goals, then, in administering CDAs is to provide specific and valid information to stakeholders about examinees' depth of understanding within a content domain.

It is easy to say more about what CDA is not than about what it is. This anomaly occurs because CDAs are relatively new (Nichols et al., 1995) and must be carefully distinguished from traditional classroom-based assessments and large-scale tests. First, CDA differs from classroom-based tests in the extent to which empirical and theoretical sources of evidence are used in test development. For example, a CDA developed within mathematics would be expected to contain questions informed by psychological studies of mathematical reasoning, including a careful analysis of the knowledge structures and processes associated with mastery and successful learning outcomes within the domain. In other words, a CDA would be expected to measure knowledge and processing skills with sufficient precision to make an examinee's incorrect response informative about what exactly the student does and does not know. Although classroom-based assessments may be designed in the hope of yielding information about an examinee's level of knowledge or processing skill, these assessments are often developed in the absence of what has been called "assessment literacy," including empirically based rationales for their design and underlying construct (see Lukin, Bandalos, Eckhout, & Mickelson, 2004).

CDAs also differ from large-scale tests such as the Programme for International Student Assessment, Scholastic Assessment Test, School Achievement Indicators Program, and National Assessment of Educational Progress. These large-scale tests, irrespective of their status as high-stakes or low-stakes tests, are developed by test specialists who apply well-established assessment and psychometric practices. However, these large-scale tests are not developed from cognitive models that are backed by studies of human information processing (Leighton, 2004). For example, one simple but well-known practice is for test developers to generate a table of specifications to aid in the design of items that will measure knowledge and skill requirements (Millman & Greene, 1989). Another practice is for test developers to select those items from the pool of test items developed that meet content standards and psychometric standards of difficulty, discrimination, and dimensionality.

To illustrate the difference between CDAs and traditional large-scale tests, consider the table of specifications. In usual test development, the table of specifications illustrates the content and skills that test specialists believe – from their experience with national, state, or provincial curriculum handbooks, and educational standards – are important indicators of expertise within a content domain. Although the table of specifications might include the content and skills to be measured, this does not mean that these are the *actual* content and skills being used by examinees as they respond to items at the time of the test. There is often little, if any, evidence offered to assure stakeholders that examinees are using the content and skills denoted in the table of test specifications or, for that matter, that these content and skills represent psychological processes indicative of mastery within the domain of interest (e.g., Nichols, 1994). Unlike test items for traditional large-scale tests, items designed for CDAs are developed from *cognitive models of task performance* (Leighton, 2004; Nichols, 1994). Such a model represents an empirically verified model of the knowledge structures and cognitive processes examinees use as they respond to classes of test items with specific characteristics. The cognitive model of task performance is usually developed from a review of the theoretical literature and should be followed by empirical studies of human information processing (see Rupp & Mislevy, this volume, and Yang & Embretson, this volume).

Because CDAs are developed from a cognitive model of task performance, they differ from traditional large-scale tests in the information they provide. Large-scale tests are commonly used for summative purposes, providing information about the breadth of examinees' knowledge and skills in the form of a total score. Although this summative approach is seductively succinct, it does not provide unequivocal information about the multifaceted nature of student achievement or the trajectory of their performance (Hamilton, Nussbaum, & Snow, 1997; Snow & Lohman, 1989). If an examinee answers a test question incorrectly, it is virtually impossible to say anything other than "the student didn't know the answer" as an account for the error. Little else can be said because test items are not designed to pinpoint the knowledge and processing skills the examinee may be lacking or where, in their thinking, students lost their way.

Given the wide range of content and skills measured by traditional large-scale tests, it would be very time consuming to measure cognitive components in depth during a single test administration. Notwithstanding the issue of time, developing a greater number of items to create a longer test might permit one to make a comparative argument that an examinee's error was due to a careless mistake (if the error was not made on a remaining set of similar items), a misunderstanding of instructions (if the error was made on items with similar instructions), a misconception about a particular topic or skill, or a lack of knowledge about the topic or skill (if all other items about the same topic were answered incorrectly). However, even with a greater number of items fulfilling the mandate of a longer test, inferences about the nature of examinees' errors would be limited as long as individual items had not been designed explicitly to measure particular knowledge structures and processing skills. As long as individual test items represent a coupling of knowledge structures and processing skills, it is virtually impossible to identify the origins of an examinee's mistake (on an item) as reflecting the absence of a specific cognitive component (see Gorin, this volume). Because CDAs are developed from a psychological framework, CDAs represent a promising alternative for providing information about students' misconceptions and learning in general (Nichols, 1994).

Cognitive models for test development represent new "test theories suited to diagnosing cognitive mechanisms" (Nichols, 1994, p. 579; see also Mislevy, 1996). These new test theories are designed to generate assessments that will improve learning and instruction (Pellegrino, Baxter, & Glaser, 1999). CDAs can also have a summative and formative purpose. These assessments are summative because they could be administered at the end of a school term. But they are also formative because their development takes into account how to generate meaningful information for teachers and parents about students' cognitive strengths and weaknesses within a content domain. The term *cognitive* in CDA then functions as a reminder that (a) the test is designed from a cognitive model of task performance that specifies the knowledge structures and processing skills that are important to perform well in the domain of the test, and (b) these knowledge structures and processing skills can be improved in students by paying attention to the results of the assessment. In the next section, we introduce two methods to validate, and even develop, cognitive models of task performance for CDAs.

VERBAL REPORTS

Investigations of human information processing abound with distinct methods that are associated with a continuum of dependent measures. At the most basic end of the spectrum, students' *response latencies* and *eye fixations* are recorded to measure the length of different cognitive processes and the duration and location of students' attentive gaze, respectively (Lohman, 2000). At the other end of the spectrum, students' *verbal reports* are elicited to identify the knowledge structures and processing skills students are immediately aware of using as they respond to problem-solving tasks, and *extended essay* responses are collected to identify the thinking structures involved in tasks demanding complex organization and planning (Lohman, 2000).

Although response latencies, eye fixations, verbal reports, and extended essays can all be used to investigate human information processing, researchers of educational measurement have gravitated toward the collection of verbal reports to inform construct validation (e.g., Hamilton et al., 1997; Katz, Bennett, & Berger, 2000) and test construction (e.g., Embretson & Gorin, 2001; Tatsuoka, 1990). In this section, we describe two methods associated with the collection of verbal reports: protocol analysis (Ericsson & Simon, 1993) and verbal analysis (Chi, 1997). Although these methods share many surface similarities, there are important points of distinction between them, especially as they pertain to the content domain in which the verbal reports are collected and their epistemic nature.

Protocol Analysis

Protocol analysis involves interviewing students individually as they attempt to solve a task or answer a test item (Ericsson & Simon, 1993). During the interview, a student is asked to *think aloud* while solving a task, and standard probes such as "please, keep talking" are used to maintain the student thinking aloud. If the student remains quiet for 15 seconds or more, the interviewer usually reminds the student to continue thinking aloud. This portion of the interview is normally labeled the *concurrent* interview because the investigator asks the student to verbalize his or her thoughts at the same time the task is being solved. After the student has solved the task and produced his or her final answer, the interviewer may ask the student to recall how he or she remembers solving the task. This latter portion of the interview is normally labeled the *retrospective* interview because the investigator asks the students to think back and recollect the problem-solving processes used. Once the verbal reports are collected, the reports undergo *protocol analysis*. This is where the reports are segmented and coded according to a computational model of information processing (Ericsson & Simon, 1993; see also a cognitive model of task performance in Leighton, 2004). Protocol analysis provides a rich source of data about the nature of student problem solving and, therefore, is well suited to inform the validation of cognitive models of task performance underlying CDAs. In the next two sections, we describe the concurrent and retrospective interviews in greater detail.

Concurrent Interviews

The concurrent interview has a specific objective. It is meant to unveil the processing steps students use to solve a task. These steps include, but are not limited to, encoding and attending to information, selecting, manipulating, and applying background knowledge and strategies, translating information, and generating a response. These processing steps are believed to be available for students to report because (a) the steps are present in students' working memory as they solve the task, (b) working memory is the location where conscious problem solving occurs (see Ericsson & Simon, 1980, 1993; also Baddeley, 1986), and (c) studies have confirmed that asking students to report their problem-solving processes does not significantly alter the nature of their problem solving (known as *nonreactivity*) and does indeed reflect the cognitive processes used (known as *veridicality*; see Ericsson & Simon, 1993; Payne, Braunstein, & Carroll, 1978).

Although collecting concurrent verbal reports seems straightforward, some investigators (e.g., Russo, Johnson, & Stephens, 1989) have challenged the idea that asking students what they are thinking as they solve a task does not alter or change problem solving. For example, investigators such as Russo et al. found that asking students what they were thinking about as they solved a gambling task led these students to exhibit greater accuracy and longer reaction times on the task than students in a control condition. The importance of the Russo et al. study and other similar studies (e.g., Nisbett & Wilson, 1977; Wilson, 1994) is that they remind us of the continuing need to elucidate Ericsson and Simon's (1980, 1993) guidelines for using protocol analysis correctly, especially as the method becomes adopted for use in potentially high-stakes situations, such as in the development and validation of CDAs.

To this end, one of the most basic requirements for the use of protocol analysis is that the tasks used to elicit the verbal reports be amenable to concurrent verbalization. What this means is that the task or problem must be of such a nature, namely, propositional or verbal, that the student can solve the problem *while* describing his or her thoughts aloud. Ericsson and Simon (1980) explain that verbalizations should involve "direct articulation of information stored in a language (verbal) code" (p. 227) or "articulation or verbal recoding of nonpropositional information without additional processing" (p. 227) in order to produce accurate concurrent reports. Again, in Ericsson and Simon's words,

When the subjects articulate information directly that is already available to them, the model predicts that thinking aloud will not change the course and structure of the cognitive processes. When the *information being processed in order to perform the main task is not verbal or propositional,* the model predicts that the performance may be slowed down, and the verbalization may be incomplete ... (p. 227, italics added)

Indeed, there are tasks that fail to meet this basic requirement and that should therefore not be used. These include tasks that are overly easy for students to solve and thus fail to require controlled problem solving; tasks with a large motor-perceptual component; and tasks that require students to attend to complex, visually encoded stimuli that are not easily translated into a verbal code (Ericsson & Simon, 1980, 1993). These tasks fail to elicit verbal or propositional information for students to report. Students participating in think aloud studies should also be familiar with the act of thinking aloud and should be made to feel at ease articulating their thoughts. Students who have difficulty expressing their thoughts may not be the best candidates for producing verbal reports (Chi, 1997; Lohman, 2000).

Retrospective Interviews

The retrospective portion of the interview also has a specific objective. It is designed to confirm that the contents of the concurrent interview are accurate. Standard probes for the retrospective portion of the interview include "Can you tell me all that you can remember thinking as you solved the task." If the student answers this question with a series of steps or processes that fail to match what was said during the concurrent interview, the interviewer has evidence that the concurrent report may be invalid. During the retrospective interview, the student should be able to recall similar processes to those mentioned during the concurrent interview. Retrospective reports collected immediately after engaging students in a concurrent interview have been shown to be accurate indicators of how students solved a task (Ericsson & Simon, 1993; Norris, 1990; Pressley & Afflerbach, 1995). The caution to this, of course, is that the greater the length of time allowed to lapse between the concurrent and retrospective interviews, the greater the likelihood that the retrospective report provided by the student will not be veridical to the processes used to solve the task.

In addition to using retrospective probes to verify the contents of the concurrent interview, the retrospective portion also provides an opportunity for students to mention higher-level or *metacognitive* problem-solving processes that might have been omitted during concurrent verbalization but were genuinely used to guide problem solving (Taylor & Dionne, 2000). Metacognitive processes coordinate problem solving because they involve planning, organizing, and executing localized, lower-level, or basic strategies that are central to regulating and achieving goals, and thus successful performance (Sternberg, 1990). We have already recognized that if a student's concurrent and retrospective reports match in terms of the knowledge and strategies being claimed for solving a problem, the investigator has converging evidence that the reports are veridical descriptions of the student's problem-solving processes. However, it is possible to have some mismatch between concurrent and retrospective reports without necessarily rendering the reports invalid. In particular, consider the possibility of a student mentioning metacognitive processes during the retrospective interview that elucidate the coordination of the basic strategies reported during the concurrent interview. Although these metacognitive processes may not have been verbalized, they do not contradict the contents of the concurrent report and may provide a bird's eye view of the student's overall analysis of the problem.

To understand the role of metacognitive processes, it may be useful to think of these processes as akin to game coaches. Without them, it might be possible to get the job done, but it will probably have more to do with dumb luck than to an organized effort to complete the feat. Much like a winning play, then, the focus for the team is on the brilliance of the players who instantiated the play and not on the strategic pregame analysis conducted by the coach. During a postgame interview, the team may credit the coach with the organization of the brilliant play, but this is not usually the main focus for them as the play is occurring. Likewise, students may know the steps to solving a system of equations but may not articulate how they know or how they planned to use these steps to solve the problem. Instead, they dive directly into setting up and solving the equations. During the retrospective portion of the interview, when the interviewer asks students what they can remember about solving the task, it is only at this time that students may have the perspective to comment on how they organized their problem solving, including how they remembered being taught to set up the equations or how they decided to extract the equations from a word problem. In other words, students are more likely to describe metacognitive processes (i.e., give credit to the coach) during the retrospective portion of the interview because these executive processes are now free to be considered and are not busy directing more localized problem-solving strategies (Taylor

& Dionne, 2000). Investigators recommend using both concurrent and retrospective interview techniques to gather data on students' problem solving (Ericsson & Simon, 1993; Taylor & Dionne, 2000).

Verbal Analysis

Protocol analysis can be distinguished from other methods that share surface similarities, such as verbal analysis (Chi, 1997; Willis, 2005).[1] Verbal analysis is used when the objective is to identify how individuals understand or interpret task information to reach an answer, including the knowledge representations they generate about task objectives and task information. Unlike protocol analysis, verbal analysis is not designed to identify the processing skills individuals use to solve a problem. Instead, verbal analysis is designed to identify the knowledge structures that individuals conjure up in their minds in response to tasks. These knowledge structures are found in explanations of what has been understood or interpreted about a task. As such, verbal analysis is commonly used to identify the kinds of *semantic* or *propositional* networks that individuals generate as they make sense, interpret, and answer tasks that have no immediate or obvious path to a correct solution (Chi, 1997; Desimone & LeFloch, 2004; Willis, 2005). Propositions are the smallest units of knowledge that can be identified as distinct assertions and judged to be either true or false (Anderson, 1990). As shown in Figure 6.1, these propositional networks aim to show the relations among knowledge structures, including concepts and beliefs.

According to Michelene Chi (1997), who has championed this method in establishing differences between novices and experts across a variety of domains, verbal analysis differs from Ericsson and Simon's (1993) protocol analysis in three substantial ways. First, the instructions Ericsson and Simon suggest using for concurrent and retrospective interviews actively *discourage* participants from explaining what they are doing; instead, they encourage participants to report only what is going through their minds as they solve the task:

I would like you to talk aloud CONSTANTLY from the time I present each problem until you have given your final answer to the question. I don't want you to try to plan out what you say or try to explain to me what you are saying.

---

[1] Cognitive interviewing techniques (Willis, 2005) used in the development of surveys and questionnaires share more similarities with verbal analysis than protocol analysis because the goal is to identify how people make sense of a question and whether their interpretations are in line with a specific target meaning.

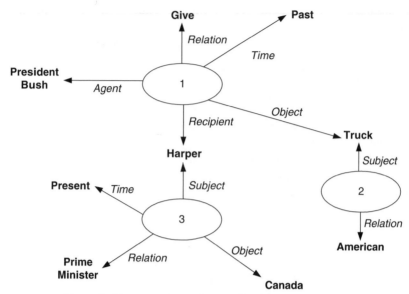

FIGURE 6.1. Example of a propositional network adapted from Anderson (1990). Network corresponds to the sentence *President Bush gave an American truck to Harper, who is the Prime Minister of Canada*. The sentence can be broken down into three propositional units: 1 – President Bush gave a truck to Harper. 2 – The truck was American made. 3 – Harper is the prime minister of Canada.

Just act as if you are alone in the room speaking to yourself. It is most important that you keep talking. If you are silent for any long period of time I will remind you to talk. Do you understand what I want you to do? (p. 378)

This instruction is designed to deter students from explaining the reasons for their thoughts and actions, with the hope of minimizing the possibility that students will learn as they are performing the task and alter the processing skills associated with their task performance (Chi, de Leeuw, Chiu, & LaVancher, 1994).

Second, the problem-solving tasks Ericsson and Simon (1993) suggest using for concurrent and retrospective interviews have a clear solution path from start to finish. With a clear solution path, the processing skills of interest are the strategies used by students to solve the task, along with the sequencing of these strategies from initial state to goal state (Newell & Simon, 1972). Potential tasks undergo a *task analysis* or are scrutinized for the expected sequence of strategies that will distinguish an early stage of problem solving from a middle and final stage of problem solving. The task analysis is then used to define a computational model of information processing, which represents the students' problem-solving path, and also functions to guide the coding and summarizing of the verbal reports once they are collected. In contrast, verbal analysis is used to collect data about the propositional networks students create as they respond to tasks that may not have clear solution paths. Tasks used in verbal analysis are not scrutinized for an expected sequence of stages, and a computational model is not identified a priori. In other words, verbal analysis is more of an exploratory technique used with knowledge-based, problem-solving tasks than is protocol analysis, which is more of a confirmatory technique used with rule-based, problem-solving tasks.

Third, when employing protocol analysis, the bulk of the work is done prior to collecting the verbal reports. The task analysis and the generation of the computational model constitute a significant part of the work that will be used in a top-down fashion to segment and code the verbal reports in order to summarize the processing skills associated with problem solving:

> Even though most cognitive tasks elicit relatively simple behavior and occur in rather static perceptual environments, not all of the relevant information can be retained if the transcription task is to be manageable. Through an analysis of the task itself, the information about behavior and environment that is relevant to task performance can usually be defined fairly well. (Ericsson & Simon, 1993, p. 278)

In contrast, the bulk of the work in verbal analysis is accomplished *after* the verbal reports have been collected. The relevant knowledge structures are identified after the reports are collected; it is at this time that investigators must decide how best to structure and segment the reports and which knowledge structures to code. Structuring, segmenting, and coding the reports is done in an exploratory, bottom-up fashion without a model to guide the process. As a consequence of the three differences between protocol analysis and verbal analysis, conclusions arising from protocol analysis tend to focus on the *sequence* of knowledge and processing skills used to solve problems, whereas conclusions arising from verbal analysis tend to focus on the *structure* of knowledge used to comprehend problems (Chi, 1997).

Both protocol analysis and verbal analysis can be used to collect information about how examinees think about and respond to test items. However, protocol analysis is more appropriately used with tasks that lend themselves to a sequence of strategies or rules for solution, such as in mathematical and scientific domains. Alternatively, verbal analysis is more appropriately used with tasks that require open-ended responses associated with rich knowledge structures and ideas, such as in the humanities, social sciences, and life sciences. In these latter content domains, a standardized sequence of strategies may not be common or even useful to understanding mastery. Rather, the knowledge representations created to understand a task may be the most important element of generating a proper answer (see Chi, 1997; Girotto, 2004; Leighton & Gokiert, 2005a).

PROTOCOL ANALYSIS, VERBAL ANALYSIS, AND COGNITIVE DIAGNOSTIC ASSESSMENT

Both protocol analysis and verbal analysis can guide the development of CDAs. Protocol analysis is better used to validate a computational model of information processing for tasks or test items that have fairly direct paths to a solution, whereas verbal analysis is better used to map the knowledge structures that examinees possess about test items that are largely ill defined and may not be associated with an expected sequence of rules. In the next section, we provide a brief illustration of how a computational model can be validated with evidence obtained from protocol analysis.

Protocol Analysis and Johnson's Laird's Theory of Mental Models

As mentioned previously, protocol analysis is undertaken to validate a computational model of information processing (Ericsson & Simon, 1980, 1993). The computational model represents a hypothetical model comprising an integrated series of cognitive processing steps of how students of a particular ability level solve a class of tasks. In educational measurement, we have called this computational model a *cognitive model of task performance* (Leighton, 2004; Leighton & Gierl, in press). A cognitive model of task performance must illustrate how examinees understand and represent problem-solving tasks, and how they reason about and solve these tasks within a content domain. The cognitive model of task performance is originally created from theoretical reviews and empirical findings of the cognitive processing associated with reasoning and solving a task of interest (Nichols, 1994). In its initial phase, the model might represent a hypothesis of the knowledge structures and processing skills examinees are expected to engage as they perform the task.

Before a cognitive model of task performance is used to design diagnostic test items, however, it must become more than just a hypothesis about how examinees solve test items. The cognitive model of task performance should be validated with empirical evidence of examinees' cognitive processing on the task of interest (Frederiksen et al., 1990; Leighton, 2004; Leighton & Gierl, in press; Nichols, 1994). This means that the model must be sufficiently detailed in its description to make falsification of the model possible with empirical studies. The model should describe the (successful) problem-solving route from initial state to goal state and identify the location of impasses that may afflict some students in their thinking. In some cases, special cognitive models of task performance could be generated to describe common misconceptions and errors in processing that less capable students in a domain possess in their thinking. These special models of task performance could reflect "buggy" models that describe types of faulty processing that may or may not lead to correct responses. These special models could be used to develop multiple-choice distracters (see Luecht, this volume).

One way to illustrate a cognitive model of task performance is with an *attribute hierarchy*. In an attribute hierarchy, the processing skills required to perform well on a set of tasks are labeled attributes and ordered hierarchically[2] in their sequence of operation (Tatsuoka, 1983; see also Gierl, Leighton, & Hunka, 2000). For example, consider the attribute hierarchy shown in Figure 6.2. This attribute hierarchy was created by Leighton, Gierl, and Hunka (2004) to illustrate the sequence of operations required to solve multiple model determinate syllogisms as described by Philip Johnson-Laird (1983) in his theory of mental models. Once specified, this attribute hierarchy is used as a blueprint to develop test items expected to measure increasingly complex aspects of syllogistic reasoning (see Leighton et al., 2004; see also Gierl, Leighton, & Hunka, this volume).

Johnson-Laird's theory of mental models was originally formulated from task analyses of logical reasoning tasks that have clear solution paths (see Johnson-Laird, 1983). The theory has received considerable empirical support as measured by response latencies and accuracy data

---

[2] The hierarchy described here more specifically denotes a *cognitive* attribute hierarchy because it illustrates cognitive structures and functions. A cognitive attribute hierarchy can be distinguished from a *procedural* hierarchy, which illustrates only the behavioral procedures of performance and not its cognitive components. The reader is referred to Leighton et al. (2004) for elaboration of these hierarchies.

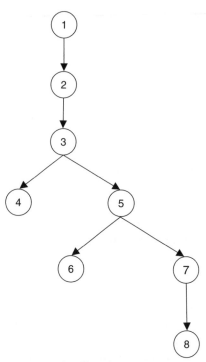

FIGURE 6.2. Attribute hierarchy of Johnson-Laird's (1983) theory of mental models. 1 = understanding all and none, 2 = understanding some and some not, 3 = creation of first mental model, 4 = conclusion for one-model syllogism, 5 = creation of second mental model, 6 = conclusion to two-model syllogism, 7 = creation of third mental model, and 8 = conclusion to three-model syllogism.

(e.g., Byrne, 1989; Evans, Handley, Harper, & Johnson-Laird, 1999; Johnson-Laird & Bara, 1984) but has received equivocal preliminary support from students' self-reports (see Galotti, Baron, & Sabini, 1986; Roberts, 2004). Johnson-Laird's (1983, 2004) theory of mental models suggests that individuals generate inferences (or conclusions) about syllogisms by creating *mental models*. Mental models are representations of the informational content of whatever is being attended to and reasoned about. More specifically, a mental model is "finite, computable, and contains tokens in relations that represent entities in a specific state of affairs" (Johnson-Laird & Bara, 1984, p. 4). A basic idea underlying the theory is that semantic principles oversee the creation of these models such that an inference or conclusion derived from a set of premises is considered valid only if it is true in every possible interpretation of the premises. Although Johnson-Laird did not cast his theory explicitly into the hierarchy of cognitive attributes as illustrated in Figure 6.2, it is clear from his descriptions of the theory (e.g., Johnson-Laird, 2004; Johnson-Laird & Bara, 1984) that there is an ordering of processing skills.

According to Johnson-Laird and Bara (1984), syllogistic reasoning begins with the creation of an initial mental model of the premises. To illustrate this process, consider the following set of premises:

Some accountants are beekeepers.

All beekeepers are chemists.

What can you conclude about accountants and chemists?

Given these premises, Johnson-Laird and Bara propose that a person might construct the following initial mental model:

$A = B = C$

$A \quad B = C$

$\qquad C$

The letters or tokens in the mental model represent the categories of the premises (A = accountants, B = beekeepers, and C = chemists), while the equal signs reflect the relations between tokens. In this example, *some* accountants have been interpreted as equivalent to beekeepers, but not *all* accountants have been interpreted as such (only some As are shown as equivalent [=] to the Bs). Moreover, notice that in this mental model *all* beekeepers are chemists (all Bs are shown as equivalent to Cs). An initial conclusion that could be drawn from the model is that *some accountants are chemists*. This initial conclusion is possible but needs to be checked against all alternate mental models of the premises (i.e., all other interpretations of the relations implied by the premises). Because the goal is to generate a conclusion that can be validly drawn in all potential interpretations of the premises, a successful problem solver is someone who will generate additional models and try to falsify the initial conclusion drawn. For the categorical premises associated with this example, all models of the premises support the conclusion that *some accountants are chemists*. In fact, this is the only conclusion that can be validly drawn from all interpretations of the premises.

Returning to the attribute hierarchy shown in Figure 6.2, this hierarchy portrays Johnson-Laird's theory of mental models for syllogistic reasoning as follows. The first two attributes (1 and 2) correspond to knowledge structures for understanding the quantifiers *All* and *None* (attribute 1) and *Some* and *Some Not* (attribute 2). The knowledge structure for understanding *All* and *None* is considered to be more basic than the structure for understanding the quantifiers *Some* and *Some Not* because students have less difficulty with the former than with the latter (Begg & Harris, 1982). The next two attributes (3 and 4) correspond to the processing skills associated with creating an initial mental model of the categorical premises (attribute 3) and inferring a conclusion to a simple, one-model syllogism (attribute 4). One-model syllogisms are those in which all possible interpretations of the premises support a single conclusion. The next two attributes (5 and 6) correspond to creating at least two distinct mental models of the premises (attribute 5) and inferring a conclusion to a more difficult, two-model syllogism (attribute 6). Two-model syllogisms are those in which an initial model might support one conclusion, but, on creation of a second model, the initial conclusion is falsified and a different conclusion must be drawn. These syllogisms have been found to be more difficult to solve than one-model syllogisms because students have to create multiple models to represent all possible relations implied by the premises (Johnson-Laird & Bara, 1984; Leighton, 2005). The next two attributes (7 and 8) correspond to creating at least three distinct models of the premises (attribute 7) and inferring a conclusion to the most difficult, three-model syllogisms. Three-model syllogisms require the creation of three models to represent all possible relations implied by the premises.

In a study conducted to document the knowledge structures and processing skills used to solve syllogisms, Leighton and Gokiert (2005b) interviewed 16 university students registered in a symbolic logic course. The students were randomly assigned to solve categorical syllogisms of increasing difficulty in both constructed-response and selected-response formats. Examples of the one-, two-, and three-model syllogisms used in the study are listed:

One-model syllogism:	Some librarians are travelers.
	All travelers are counselors.
	What can you conclude about librarians and counselors?
Two-model syllogism:	Some doctors are NOT dancers.
	All chefs are dancers.
	What can you conclude about doctors and chefs?
Three-model syllogism:	Some athletes are nurses.
	No athletes are secretaries.
	What can you conclude about nurses and secretaries?

Adopting the attribute hierarchy shown in Figure 6.2 as their cognitive model of task performance, Leighton and Gokiert (2005b) collected both concurrent and retrospective interviews, and used protocol analysis to summarize the verbal reports. Protocol analysis was used because (a) categorical syllogisms have clear, rule-based solution paths; and (b) the researchers were trying to obtain evidence for the processing skills described in Johnson-Laird's theory of mental models. Two themes were found to characterize students' knowledge structures and processing skills that provide evidence in support of the attribute hierarchy shown in Figure 6.2. First, concurrent and retrospective verbal reports revealed that students solved one-model syllogisms more easily than two-model or three-model syllogisms. More than 75% of students answered the one-model syllogisms correctly, whereas less than 20% of students answered the two- and three-model syllogisms correctly. Moreover, when students were asked to identify the easiest and most difficult syllogisms, 81% of students identified one-model syllogism as the easiest syllogisms to solve, and more than 85% of students identified two- and three-model syllogisms as the most difficult syllogism to solve. Students found one-model syllogisms easier to solve compared to multiple-model syllogisms because the premises associated with one-model syllogisms were found to be easily represented in a single model. The student, N.T., describes why the process is easier for one-model syllogisms:

N.T.: I found the second one [one-model syllogism] the easiest because it was just . . . like once you have *all*, first of all, that makes it somewhat easier because then it's just a direct translation. I don't know . . . it just . . . you can connect the sentences together right away because the first one ends in travelers and the first one starts with travelers, so its basically . . . you can just make them into one and a lot simpler.[3]

Likewise, students found two- and three-model syllogisms difficult to solve because they could not easily represent the relations in the premises:

A.K.: . . . because it's not really apparent because the . . . because you're trying to relate chefs and doctors by an attribute, not necessarily a group. Does that make sense? But you want to relate them as a group of dancers, but because it excludes some doctors . . . that's just confusing. So it takes a while to think of a relationship there. (p. 20)

---

[3] This quote was not illustrated in Leighton and Gokiert (2005b) so a page number is unavailable. Complete interviews can be obtained by contacting the first author.

Students' facility to respond correctly to one-model syllogisms and to identify these syllogisms as the easiest to solve provides evidence in support of the *sequencing* of the attribute hierarchy shown in Figure 6.2.

The second theme found in the concurrent and retrospective verbal reports provided some evidence for the processing demands of single- and multiple-model syllogisms as outlined by Johnson-Laird's theory. Fourteen of 16 (90%) students attempted to solve the syllogisms by generating equivalencies or *relations between tokens or sets of tokens* as described in the premises. After students generated this relation within a model, they attempted to draw a conclusion. The success of generat- ing these equivalencies is essential because it is precisely this processing skill that facilitates the creation of additional and permissible mental models when they are required. In doing so, students must compre- hend the meaning of quantifiers (i.e., some, all, some...not, and no), which delimit the types of equivalencies that can be generated in the models. Consider the verbal report A.L. provides as he reasons through the categorical syllogisms:

A.L.: "Some veterinarians are not runners, some housekeepers are runners". Veterinarians and housekeepers and the reference to runners have nothing in common here if veterinarians are not runners and housekeepers are runners, it does not say anything between them, so nothing. "Some librarians are travelers, all travelers are counselors". Since some librarians are travelers, then all travelers are counselors, that means that some librarians are counselors. *Yes. Yes, because there's a small amount of people of librarians that are travelers and if they're travelers, they're counselors. So some...so some librarians are travelers...or counselors rather.* "Some doctors are not dancers, all chefs are dancers". *This doesn't say there is a relation between doctors* and chefs. Well you could have a doctor that's not a dancer but you can have a doctor that is a dancer, so you can't really conclude between chefs and doctors I don't think. Nothing. "Some athletes are nurses, no athletes are secretaries". *So there's a small amount of athletes that are nurses, so we can split them up between nurses and non-nurses, but no athletes are secretaries. So...but that does not...that doesn't say that nurses can't be secretaries unless they absolutely have no time to do both.* So some athletes are nurses...no athletes are secretaries....I don't think you can conclude anything from this. Some athletes are nurses, no athletes are secretaries. Yeah, I think that's nothing. (Leighton & Gokiert, 2005b, p. 8)

Students attempted to solve the categorical syllogisms by generating relations among the tokens mentioned in the premises (attributes 5, 7, and 9), and then by drawing a conclusion (attributes 6, 8, and 10) from these relations. Students' tendency to generate these relations provides evidence in support of the *processing* demands outlined in

Johnson-Laird's theory and, by extension, the attribute hierarchy shown in Figure 6.2.

Verbal Analysis and Diagnostic Assessment

In the previous section, we described how protocol analysis was used to validate a cognitive model of task performance. Protocol analysis was used because categorical syllogisms are associated with objectively correct solutions and already have an associated cognitive model of task performance (i.e., Johnson-Laird's (1983) theory exemplified by the attribute hierarchy shown in Figure 6.2). If we had not met either of these two conditions, we would not have used protocol analysis to organize our verbal reports and, instead, would have used verbal analysis.

According to Chi (1997), verbal analysis is normally conducted with tasks that are largely knowledge based and ill defined in terms of an objectively correct answer. Verbal analysis is used to *explore* the knowledge structures individuals have and create in response to interpreting and understanding tasks. As such, verbal analysis is a method often used to *generate* a computational model of information processing. The seven steps normally undertaken in verbal analysis consist of the following:

1. Reducing or sampling the protocols
2. Segmenting the reduced or sampled protocols (sometimes optional)
3. Developing or choosing a coding scheme or formalism
4. Operationalizing evidence in the coded protocols that constitutes a mapping to some chosen formalism
5. Depicting the mapped formalism
6. Interpreting the patterns
7. Repeating the whole process, perhaps at a different grain size (optional)

In explaining the rationale for these seven steps, the reader is reminded that an important objective of verbal analysis is to formulate an understanding of the knowledge structures associated with understanding and responding to a task. Without a cognitive model of task performance to guide the coding of verbal reports, investigators are encouraged to follow these steps to impose structure for analyzing a voluminous quantity of data. For example, steps 1 and 2 are designed to make steps 3 and 4 feasible. By temporarily reducing the amount of data considered (step 1), decisions about the unit of analysis and the nature of codes to assign to the verbal reports can be made efficiently without the distraction of too much information (step 2). Reducing the quantity of verbal reports through random sampling is often the most simple and obvious procedure (Chi, 1997). Once the sample is selected (step 1), the investigator segments the reports by the unit of analysis (step 2) desired, such as by a particular level of knowledge structure (e.g., a sentence, an idea, or a reasoning chain) that matches the grain size of the research question being explored.

After the verbal reports are segmented in step 2, each segment must now be assigned a meaningful code in step 3. Although there is no clear algorithm for selecting the appropriate formalism or frame for the codes,

the general rules of thumb are that procedural tasks tend to be more adaptable to production systems, problem spaces (Newell & Simon, 1972), or flow-chart type of formalisms (Siegler, 1976), whereas tasks that tap declarative and conceptual knowledge would more appropriately be represented by semantic and conceptual networks (Johnson-Laird, 1983). (Chi, 1997, p. 290)

The codes in verbal analysis, then, are often shorthand expressions to label and define the propositional networks found in the reports.

Chi (1997) indicates that step 3 is the most difficult step to prescribe to researchers because the nature of codes chosen by investigators will depend on their theoretical point of reference, the hypotheses or research questions being asked, the task, and the content domain. For example, Chi and VanLehn (1991) summarized verbal reports using a taxonomic categorical scheme that included a series of categories for assigning a code to students' explanations as they studied "worked out" examples in physics. Chi and VanLehn coded the segments in the reports as (a) explanations for concepts (e.g., basic physics knowledge – mass, weight, and acceleration); (b) principles (e.g., rules that related mass to acceleration); (c) systems (e.g., the interaction of two or more objects – a block on an inclined plane); and (d) technical knowledge (e.g., algebraic manipulations). They developed this specific coding scheme because they were testing the hypothesis that students can learn to solve problems correctly without a significant understanding of the principles or concepts underlying the problems.

Once the codes are formalized, step 4 involves judging the utterances and statements captured in the verbal reports and deciding which codes should be assigned to represent these student remarks. This step can be straightforward except for two problematic issues. The first difficulty arises from the ambiguity that is sometimes inherent to students' reports and the need to infer what a student "really means" with a particular statement. For example, in a study by Chi et al. (1994), ambiguity arose in deciding the level of complexity that the students were exhibiting in their reported inferences. Because students often reported their thoughts sketchily and without too many elaborations, investigators had to be cautious in how they interpreted ambiguous statements and how they used these statements as evidence to infer sophisticated knowledge structures that may not have been present in students' thinking. The second difficulty arises from the length of students' utterances and the need to decide how much of a verbal report's context to consider when coding the data. When the broader context of a report (many lines before and after a particular segment in a report) is used to code students' statements, the justification for any one of the codes assigned to a segment will likely be convincing. Alternatively, when minimal context is used to code students' statements, the interpretation of reports is kept localized and may expedite coding, but this is achieved at the expense of misrepresenting students' intended meanings. Another option is to code the data twice, once where context is maximized and once where context is minimized, and compare the results. The safest approach is to include as much context as needed to ensure that a student's intended meaning is retained.

Following step 4, steps 5 and 6 require mapping or depicting the results in either tabular form or, more commonly, graphical form with propositional networks. This is done primarily to permit the detection of patterns in the results so general conclusions can be formulated about the ways in which students represent knowledge for responding to a task. During these steps, one does not have to limit conclusions to knowledge structures alone if there are processing skills that emerge from the data. One way to ensure objectivity in the patterns detected in the data is to use multiple sources of evidence, such as coding the data twice with independent raters and calculating an interrater reliability coefficient (see Chi, 1997, for a discussion of the details of this approach).

DISCUSSION AND CONCLUSIONS

The value of CDA rests with the integrity and specificity of information provided about examinees' thinking patterns in relation to classes of problems. For a cognitive diagnostic test to provide accurate information about examinees' strengths and weakness, the test must include items that measure specific knowledge structures and processing skills that reflect genuine competence within a domain, and not simply test wiseness. Moreover, for a cognitive diagnostic test to provide specific information about examinees' strengths and weaknesses, the test must be designed with an empirically substantiated cognitive model of task performance. In this way, examinee performance on test items can be truly informative about the presence or absence of particular cognitive components. If a test is designed without a model of task performance, there is no assurance that the test items are measuring specific knowledge structures and processing skills, and the integrity of inferences is compromised, if not jeopardized completely.

Protocol analysis and verbal analysis are two techniques for securing data on how examinees think about and solve test items. Although these two methods share surface similarities and can be used in the development of diagnostic tests, there are important differences in their instructions, analyses, and conclusions. First, the use of protocol analysis, especially concurrent interviews, discourages the very types of reports that verbal analysis promotes: explanations, descriptions, justifications, and rationalizations. These utterances are discouraged in protocol analysis because they are not expected to reveal the immediate contents of working memory associated with solving the task. Second, protocol analysis is used primarily to identify the sequential processing skills involved in applying permissible rules, whereas verbal analysis is used primarily to capture knowledge structures involved in understanding and generating meaning. In protocol analysis, a task undergoes a thorough review to specify a computational model of information processing that is validated against the verbal reports. In contrast, verbal analysis does not require a thorough review of the task because the precise objective is to explore the ways in which the task is understood by students and the kinds of computational models that are possible. Third, the majority of the work in protocol analysis occurs in generating the computational model *before* verbal reports are collected. After the computational model is generated, the reports are coded directly from the sequence of steps illustrated in the model. Again, in contrast, the majority of the work in verbal analysis occurs at the coding stage *after* the verbal reports are collected. During the coding stage, codes must be generated from a sample of the reports, and then evaluated for whether they are useful in summarizing the reports and answering the question guiding the research. Related to these three points, the primary purpose in protocol analysis is to validate the computational model of information processing (although the criteria for deciding whether the validation has been successful are ambiguous). In verbal analysis, the primary purpose is to generate a cognitive model by identifying patterns among the codes. Consequently, the conclusions drawn from the two methods will be different – protocol analysis is used to validate conclusions primarily about processing skills, and verbal analysis is used to generate conclusions primarily about knowledge structures.

Because problem-solving tasks require students to use knowledge structures and processing skills simultaneously, protocol analysis and verbal analysis are both useful methods in the development and validation of CDAs. Even the categorical syllogism illustration presented previously required students to understand the meaning of quantifiers, along with applying processing skills to generate mental models. However, protocol analysis and verbal analysis are each designed to generate distinct types of conclusions from verbal report data, which address distinct research objectives. Protocol analysis is best used when seeking confirmatory evidence for a model of task performance and/or when working with rule-based, problem-solving tasks that lend themselves to a task analysis. In contrast, verbal analysis is best used when seeking exploratory evidence for a model of task performance and/or with tasks that are ill defined and knowledge based.

There are, of course, limitations with both methods, namely, that one must rely on students' facility to report the thoughts underlying their cognitive performances. Although Ericsson and Simon (1993, pp. 83–107) review a substantial body of evidence to indicate that verbal reports are accurate measures of students' cognitive processing when collected under specific conditions, it is also the case that the onus is squarely on researchers to ensure that the conditions are favorable for collecting accurate data. However, as with any method, it can be misused if not understood (Leighton, 2004). Another limitation rests with a critical assumption in the use of verbal report methods – that students will have conscious access to the most important knowledge structures and processing skills for their responses and solutions. As is well known to anyone who has taken an introductory cognitive psychology course, the processes one is aware of using during problem solving reflect an algorithmic level and may not reflect the most important components of problem solving residing just below awareness at the architectural level of mind (Dawson, 1998). The more we learn about the mind from cognitive psychology, neuroscience, and connectionist simulations, the more we need to scrutinize the methods we use to assess students and the more we need to validate the instruments we use to evaluate them.

Having said this, verbal reports represent a promising method of getting closer to measuring what we want to measure in examinees by facilitating the development of cognitive models that can inform CDAs.

References

Anderson, J. R. (1990). *Cognitive psychology and its implications*. New York: W. H. Freeman.

Baddeley, A. D. (1986). *Working memory*. Oxford, UK: Oxford University Press.

Begg, I., & Harris, G. (1982). On the interpretation of syllogisms. *Journal of Verbal Learning and Verbal Behavior, 21*, 595–620.

Byrne, R. M. (1989). Suppressing valid inferences with conditionals. *Cognition, 31*, 61–83.

Chi, M. T. H. (1997). Quantifying qualitative analyses of verbal data: A practical guide. *Journal of the Learning Sciences, 6*, 271–315.

Chi, M. T. H., de Leeuw, N., Chiu, M. H., & LaVancher, C. (1994). Eliciting self-explanations improves understanding. *Cognitive Science, 18*, 439–477.

Chi, M. T. H., & VanLehn, K. A. (1991). The content of physics self-explanations. *Journal of the Learning Sciences, 1*, 69–105.

Dawson, M. R. W. (1998). *Understanding cognitive science*. Malden, MA: Blackwell.

Desimone, L. M., & LeFloch, K. C. (2004). Are we asking the right questions? Using cognitive interviews to improve surveys in education research. *Educational Evaluation and Policy Analysis, 26*, 1–22.

Embretson, S., & Gorin, J. (2001). Improving construct validity with cognitive psychology principles. *Journal of Educational Measurement, 38*, 343–368.

Ericsson, K. A., & Simon, H. A. (1980). Verbal reports as data. *Psychological Review, 87*, 215–251.

Ericsson, K. A., & Simon, H. A. (1993). *Protocol analysis*. Cambridge, MA: MIT Press.

Evans, J. St. B. T., Handley, S. J., Harper, C. N. J., & Johnson-Laird, P. N. (1999). Reasoning about necessity and possibility: A test of the mental model theory of deduction. *Journal of Experimental Psychology: Learning, Memory, and Cognition, 25*, 1495–1513.

Frederiksen, N., Glaser, R., Lesgold, A., & Shafto, M. G. (Eds.). (1990). *Diagnostic monitoring of skill and knowledge acquisition*. New Jersey: Lawrence Erlbaum Associates.

Galotti, K. M., Baron, J., & Sabini, J. P. (1986). Individual differences in syllogistic reasoning: Deduction rules or mental models? *Journal of Experimental Psychology: General, 115*, 16–25.

Gierl, M. J., Leighton, J. P., & Hunka, S. (2000). Exploring the logic of Tatsuoka's rule-space model for test development and analysis. *Educational Measurement: Issues and Practice, 19*, 34–44.

Girotto, V. (2004). Task understanding. In J. P. Leighton & R. J. Sternberg (Eds.), *Nature of reasoning* (pp. 103–128). New York: Cambridge University Press.

Hamilton, L. S., Nussbaum, E. M., & Snow, R. E. (1997). Interview procedures for validating science assessments. *Applied Measurement in Education, 10*, 181–200.

Johnson-Laird, P. N. (1983). *Mental models. Towards a cognitive science of language, inference, and consciousness.* Cambridge, MA: Harvard University Press.

Johnson-Laird, P. N. (2004). Mental models and reasoning. In J. P. Leighton & R. J. Sternberg (Eds.), *Nature of reasoning* (pp. 169–204). Cambridge, UK: Cambridge University Press.

Johnson-Laird, P. N., & Bara, B. G. (1984). Syllogistic inference. *Cognition, 16,* 1–61.

Katz, I. R., Bennett, E., & Berger, A. E. (2000). Effects of response format on difficulty of SAT-Mathematics items: It's not the strategy. *Journal of Educational Measurement, 37,* 39–57.

Leighton, J. P. (2004). Avoiding misconceptions, misuse, and missed opportunities: The collection of verbal reports in educational achievement testing. *Educational Measurement: Issues and Practice, Winter,* 1–10.

Leighton, J. P. (2005). Teaching and assessing deductive reasoning skills. *Journal of Experimental Education, 74,* 109–136.

Leighton, J. P., & Gierl, M. J. (in press). *Defining and evaluating models of cognition used in educational measurement to make inferences about examinees' thinking processes.* Educational Measurement: Issues and Practice.

Leighton, J. P., Gierl, M. J., & Hunka, S. (2004). The attribute hierarchy model: An approach for integrating cognitive theory with assessment practice. *Journal of Educational Measurement, 41,* 205–236.

Leighton, J. P., & Gokiert, R. (2005a, April). *The cognitive effects of test item features: Identifying construct irrelevant variance and informing item generation.* Paper presented at the annual meeting of the National Council on Measurement in Education, Montreal.

Leighton, J. P., & Gokiert, R. (2005b, April). *Investigating test items designed to measure higher-order reasoning using think-aloud methods.* Paper presented at the annual meeting of the American Educational Research Association (AERA), Montreal.

Lohman, D. F. (2000). Complex information processing and intelligence. In R. J. Sternberg (Ed.), *Handbook of intelligence* (pp. 285–340). New York: Cambridge University Press.

Lukin, L. E., Bandalos, D. L., Eckhout, T. J., & Mickelson, K. (2004). Facilitating the development of assessment literacy. *Educational Measurement: Issues and Practice, 23,* 26–32.

Millman, J., & Greene, J. (1989). The specification and development of tests of achievement and ability. In R. L. Linn (Ed.), *Educational measurement* (3rd ed., pp. 335–366). New York: American Council of Education/Macmillan.

Mislevy, R. J. (1996). Test theory reconceived. *Journal of Educational Measurement, 33,* 379–416.

Newell, A., & Simon, H. A. (1972). *Human problem solving.* Englewood Cliffs, New Jersey: Prentice Hall.

Nichols, P. (1994). A framework of developing cognitively diagnostic assessments. *Review of Educational Research, 64,* 575–603.

Nichols, P. D., Chipman, S. F., & Brennan, R. L. (Eds.). (1995). *Cognitively diagnostic assessment.* Hillsdale, NJ: Erlbaum.

Nisbett, R., & Wilson, T. D. (1977). Telling more than we can know: Verbal reports on mental processes. *Psychological Review, 84*, 231–259.

Norris, S. P. (1990). Effect of eliciting verbal reports of thinking on critical thinking test performance. *Journal of Educational Measurement, 27*, 41–58.

Payne, J. W., Braunstein, M. L., & Carroll, J. S. (1978). Exploring predecisional behavior: An alternative approach to decision research. *Organizational Behavior and Human Performance, 22*, 17–44.

Pellegrino, J. W., Baxter, G. P., & Glaser, R. (1999). Addressing the "Two Disciplines" problem: Linking theories of cognition and learning with assessment and instructional practice. *Review of Research in Education, 24*, 307–353.

Pressley, M., & Afflerbach, P. (1995). *Verbal protocols of reading: The nature of constructively responsive reading*. Hillsdale, NJ: Erlbaum.

Roberts, M. J. (2004). Heuristics and reasoning I: Making deduction simple. In J. P. Leighton & R. J. Sternberg (Eds.), *Nature of reasoning* (pp. 234–272). New York: Cambridge University Press.

Russo, J. E., Johnson, E. J., & Stephens, D. L. (1989). The validity of verbal protocols. *Memory & Cognition, 17*, 759–769.

Snow, R. E., & Lohman, D. F. (1989). Implications of cognitive psychology for educational measurement. In R. L. Linn (Ed.), *Educational measurement* (3rd ed., pp. 263–331). New York: American Council on Education/Macmillan.

Sternberg, R. J. (1990). *Metaphors of mind: Conceptions of the nature of intelligence*. Cambridge, UK: Cambridge University Press.

Tatsuoka, K. K. (1983). Rule space: An approach for dealing with misconceptions based on item response theory. *Journal of Educational Measurement, 20*, 345–354.

Tatsuoka, K.K. (1990). Toward an integration of item-response theory and cognitive error diagnosis. In N. Frederiksen, R. Glaser, A. Lesgold, & M. Shafto (Eds.), *Diagnostic monitoring of skill and knowledge acquisition* (pp. 453–488). Hillsdale, NJ: Erlbaum.

Taylor, K. L., & Dionne, J-P. (2000). Accessing problem-solving strategy knowledge: The complementary use of concurrent verbal protocols and retrospective debriefing. *Journal of Educational Psychology, 92*, 413–425.

Willis, G. B. (2005). *Cognitive interviewing: A tool for improving questionnaire design*. Thousand Oaks, CA: Sage.

Wilson, T. D. (1994). The proper protocol: Validity and completeness of verbal reports. *Psychological Science, 5*, 249–252.

7

Test Construction and Diagnostic Testing

Joanna S. Gorin

Among the many test uses listed in the *Standards for Educational and Psychological Testing* (American Educational Research Association, American Psychological Association, & National Council on Measurement in Education, 1999) diagnosis is perhaps the most complex. Assessment for diagnosis transforms quantitative data into rich qualitative descriptions of individuals' cognitive abilities, psychological pathologies, and personalities. The use of diagnostic tests has historically been applied to psychological assessment for psychiatric and neuropsychiatry diagnosis, with fewer examples of educational tests designed for this purpose. More commonly, educational testing has focused on purposes such as rating, selection, placement, competency, and outcome evaluation. Consequently, the test development procedures included in the majority of the educational assessment literature pertain to test construction for these purposes. Recently, however, educators have recognized educational assessments as missed opportunities to inform educational decisions. Nowhere is this realization more evident than in the No Child Left Behind (NCLB) Act of 2001 in the United States, specifically as it pertains to the development and use of yearly standardized achievement tests.

Such assessments shall produce individual student interpretive, descriptive, and diagnostic reports ... that allow parents, teachers, and principals to understand and address the specific academic needs of students, and include information regarding achievement on academic assessments aligned with State academic achievement standards, and that are provided to parents, teachers, and principals as soon as is practicably possible after the assessment is given, in an understandable and uniform format, and to the extent practicable, in a language that parents can understand. (NCLB, Part A, Subpart 1, Sec. 2221[b]3[C][xii], 2001)

Although the goal of diagnostic testing is promising for educational reform, the necessary assessment tools are lacking. Existing educational tests were, for the most part, developed for traditional uses, such as simple scaling of individuals or rank ordering for selection. The assessments were not designed to provide diagnostic information. To satisfy these new test uses, practical methods for diagnostic test development are essential. This chapter discusses item and test construction procedures specifically tailored for diagnostic tests. In many ways, we rely on traditional test construction procedures. However, given the fundamental difference in testing purpose, some modifications to the test development process are proposed.

WHAT MAKES A GOOD DIAGNOSTIC ITEM?

Having argued that diagnostic score interpretation is a unique challenge and that current tests are not sufficient for this purpose, a description of what *is* a good diagnostic test seems necessary. A good diagnostic test is one that goes beyond estimations of individuals' overall ability levels. Specific information must be available from student responses that isolates weaknesses or inconsistencies in knowledge and provides a fuller picture of student abilities. In other words, information should be available from student responses indicating *why* students responded as they did. Items developed by traditional means provide insufficient information at an appropriate level of description for diagnosis. Good diagnostic tests can be distinguished in terms of *penetration* (Cross & Paris, 1987). Penetration is defined as the resulting psychological information obtained from the test's scores, including information about concepts, knowledge representations, and cognitive processing. Penetrating tests provide information at the level of individual knowledge and processing, including information about the relative abilities of an individual across several different skills. A good diagnostic test is one that helps distinguish between the skills that an individual has mastered, and the ones that have yet to be learned. To do so, an item must produce observable student behaviors at the same level of detail as the target inferences (i.e., observable subskills support subskill inferences). Most current test items provide only one piece of observable student information – the final answer – which is often little more than a blackened circle indicating one of several possible answer choices. Many different processes and skills could have gone into selecting that item. With only the selected answer to score, inferences about the contributing skills cannot be made.

Good diagnostic items provide opportunities to observe the process of student responses and increase the amount of information available from student answers. Two examples of current diagnostic items that adhere to these principles are described as follows.

Computer Networking

Finding examples of operational diagnostic tests in education can be challenging. This is likely a consequence of the relative infancy of diagnosis in educational assessment. One recent example comes from Cisco System's Networking Performance Skill System (NetPASS) project (Behrens, Mislevy, Bauer, Williamson, & Levy, 2004). The goal of Net-PASS was not simply to develop an online performance assessment of networking proficiency. Test creators wanted an assessment tool that could provide useful feedback to stakeholders (e.g., students, instructors). Diagnostic reports of student behavior could ideally fit this need. The task used on the test was based on actual Cisco networking equipment with specific design constraints mimicking real world "scenarios" of network troubleshooting, design, and implementation (Williamson, Bauer, Steinberg, Mislevy, Behrens, & DeMark, 2004). Each scenario was designed in predetermined ways based on typical network failures, configuration requirements, and design constraints. Students were presented with a scenario and then diagramed the structure of a network for a particular problem. Diagrams included elements of a network, as well as the relations and connections between elements. Logs of all computer workstation commands were automatically collected and evaluated based on several characteristics. Each log was examined for completeness and the correctness of procedures while solving the problem, as well as the final outcome. Diagnoses of specific problems were then made by comparing process and outcome of student logs to previously identified processing patterns associated with known weaknesses or misconceptions.

Let us look specifically at one NetPASS task – troubleshooting. In this task, students are introduced to an existing network for which certain failures exist and corresponding "fixes" are needed. Based on user reports, students are required to identify faults and fix them. Once completed, students' commands and sequences of commands are placed into categories that describe the actions – *information gathering about router, changes to router, testing network after fixes*, and *gathering information about commands*. Each category can be further dissected into components of the task (e.g., sequence of actions, help usage, volume of actions). These components are used as a basis of comparison to the "prototypical" performance associated with various diagnostic states. Unlike many traditional test items, for which the outcome is the sole piece of observable information, this process provides supplemental information that may help explain *why* an error may have occurred. For example, if a student fails to fix a particular problem, that outcome alone does not indicate the reason for the missed problem. However, if the additional information regarding procedure suggests that an inefficient search strategy (e.g., serial elimination) was used, it could be useful for instructional design that includes modules on efficient search strategies. In sum, data collected from students' processing increases tests' capabilities to diagnose the source of errors and accompanying misunderstandings, and to provide suggestions for corrections. Good diagnostic test items, such as the NetPASS tasks, are designed to elicit behaviors that provide the necessary data.

Science Assessment

An alternative example of diagnostic test items is provided by Wilson and his colleagues in their work on science assessment with the BEAR Assessment System (Briggs, Alonzo, Schwab, & Wilson, 2006; Wilson & Sloane, 2000). Unlike the technologically sophisticated simulations of NetPASS, the BEAR science items are written as multiple-choice questions – with a twist. By incorporating information regarding common student misconceptions into item distractors, multiple-choice questions were written to obtain diagnostic information. These items, called *ordered multiple-choice questions* (OMCs; Briggs et al., 2006), link response options to a developmental model describing qualitatively distinct understandings of content. Each response option of an OMC item is written to be cognitively consistent with different developmental levels of reasoning about the construct. Figure 7.1 shows an example of an OMC item from Briggs et al.'s (2006) study measuring fifth graders' understanding of the Earth in the solar system. The format of the item is identical to a traditional multiple-choice question. What differs is the information indicated just adjacent to each response option. The various levels (1–4) identify the reasoning level associated with each option. The highest level is the correct answer that characterizes a fully developed concept of the Earth and the solar system, including an ability to coordinate apparent and actual motion of objects in the sky. The other options are written to include specific misconceptions associated with the various developmental levels meant to be captured by the responses. By

	Developmental Level
It is most likely colder at night because	
A. the earth is at its furthest point in its orbit around the Sun.	Level 3
B. the Sun has traveled to the other side of the Earth.	Level 2
C. the Sun is below the Earth and the Moon does not emit as much heat as the Sun.	Level 1
D. the place where it is night on Earth is rotated away from the Sun.	Level 4

FIGURE 7.1. Example OMC item measuring the Earth in the solar system concept as presented in Briggs et al. (2006).

examining individual item responses and patterns of responses across multiple similarly structured items, diagnostic information about where student errors in understanding are occurring can be gained. As in the example from NetPASS, the OMC items are designed such that student behavior provides evidence of why a student responds in a particular way. This information, or penetration as described by Marshall (1990), is exactly what makes a diagnostic item useful. The NetPASS and science OMC examples are used throughout this chapter to provide a context for discussion of diagnostic item writing frameworks and procedures.

FRAMEWORKS FOR DIAGNOSTIC TEST DEVELOPMENT

Many principles of traditional item writing apply equally well to diagnostic tests. For example, unnecessary use of socially or politically charged content in items should be avoided where possible, and item writers should avoid the use of ambiguous wording, unless the handling of such wording is associated with the assessment purpose. At a broader level, desirable items on any test for any purpose should engage individuals in processes relevant to and representative of the construct of interest, an issue central to construct validity. However, several new issues arise for item development that provides more informative and diagnostic information than traditional items. A variety of methods for diagnostic test development have recently been proposed. These methods can generally be divided into two categories: (a) statistical models incorporating parameters for cognitive processing components, and (b) assessment design frameworks that weave cognitive theory into the entire test development procedure.

The statistical models, sometimes called cognitive-diagnostic models (CDMs), are essentially data analysis techniques designed to link cognitive theory with items' psychometric properties. The skills needed to correctly solve problems are specified, and their impact on responses is estimated. Information about skill mastery can be estimated and reported by examining the skills required for each item and the student's response. Incorrect responses suggest that an individual has not mastered the skills required by an item; correct answers suggest that the skills have been acquired. Three CDMs that have received significant attention are the rule space methodology (RSM; Tatsuoka, 1985, 1995), the fusion model (Hartz, 2002), and the attribute hierarchy method (AHM; Leighton, Gierl, & Hunka, 2004). Although the models are relatively new, they have been applied to existing tests with varying levels of success. For example, the RSM was applied to mathematics items from the Trends in International Mathematics and Science Study (TIMSS), an achievement test used to compare students' knowledge of math and science worldwide (Tatsuoka, Corter, & Tatsuoka, 2004). Tatsuoka et al. (2004) examined the skill structure of the items on the TIMMS, and estimated the relationship between requisite skills and item responses. Based on the results of these analyses, student strengths and weaknesses were compared across countries. Several conclusions were then drawn regarding the effects of countries' curriculum design on students' subskill acquisition.

Although these statistical models represent significant psychometric advances, their focus is primarily on post-hoc test and item analysis; that is, these procedures are useful once items have been developed and data have been collected. To date, their applications have primarily been limited to analysis of existing tests and not the development of new assessments. The other category of diagnostic test development methods includes general frameworks that describe entire test development procedures, incorporating cognitive information into test design from the outset. Given that this chapter's focus is on test development, discussion of these models is particularly relevant here. Further discussion of the statistical models and how they assist diagnostic testing can be found in several other chapters of this book.

The two approaches that have been most widely applied are Embretson's cognitive design system (CDS; Embretson, 1994, 1999) and Mislevy's evidence-centered design (ECD; Mislevy, 1994; Mislevy, Steinberg, & Almond, 2002). These approaches, unlike the CDM statistical models, address the use of cognition in the complete process of item and test development, beginning with issues related to construct definition, through item writing, and concluding with validation procedures. Given their extensive use, and their applicability to the complete test development process, CDS and ECD may currently show the most promise for diagnostic test design. Although each procedure is reviewed separately, the reader can find many similarities between them. Most significant is the central role of cognitive theory and evidence gathering through empirical model testing as a basis for item development.

Mislevy's Evidence-Centered Design

The goal in ECD-based test construction is the accumulation of evidence to support inferences about an individual. Unlike traditional assessments limited to inferences about a single competency score, complex assessments based on ECD are amenable to diagnostic inferences regarding student strengths and weaknesses. ECD breaks test development into three components: (a) the claims one wants to make about an individual, (b) the pieces of evidence that can support these claims, and (c) the tasks that produce observations of the evidence (Behrens et al., 2004; Mislevy, 1994; Mislevy et al., 2002). Mislevy (1994) formulates the components as three models: (a) the *student model*, or the type of inferences one wants to make about an individual; (b) the *evidence model*, or the type of evidence that support the target inferences; and (c) the *task model*, the type of task that can elicit the usable pieces of evidence.

The student model specifies the skills, knowledge, or strategies as the focus of inferences. The formulation of this model is tied innately to the purpose of the test. In the case of diagnosis, a student model characterizes knowledge of an individual's strength or weakness (i.e., mastery) on multiple skills or subskills. The evidence model describes the observable behaviors or performances that provide evidence of the student model components. As items on a test are administered and evidence is gathered from student responses, the estimate of an individual's status on the student model variables is updated according to rules in the evidence model. Finally, the task model defines the specific nature of an item, including the conditions under which the task is to be performed, the materials presented, and the nature of the work product generated by the examinee. When selecting a particular task model, the goal is to create an environment in which an examinee generates observable behaviors that correspond most strongly to the evidence model. Once the task model has been generated and linked to the evidence

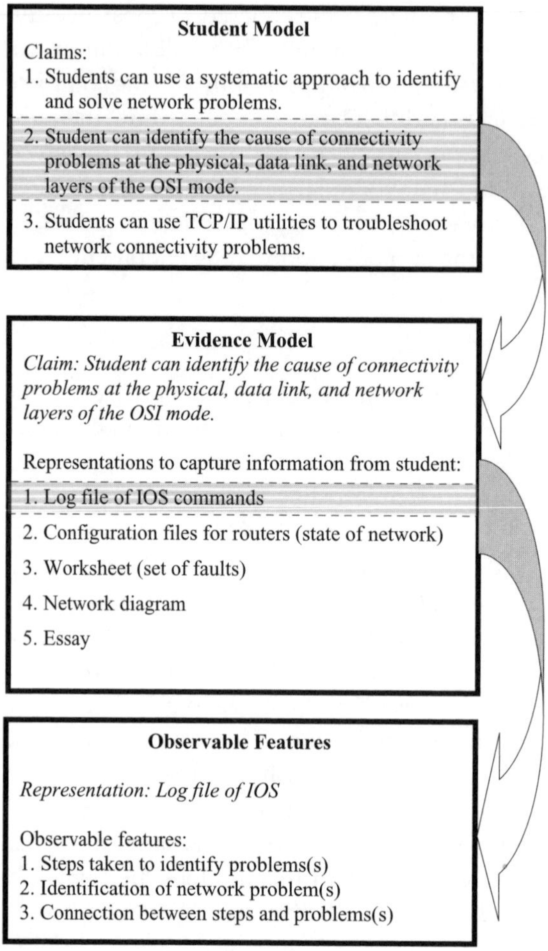

Student Model

Claims:
1. Students can use a systematic approach to identify and solve network problems.

2. Student can identify the cause of connectivity problems at the physical, data link, and network layers of the OSI mode.

3. Students can use TCP/IP utilities to troubleshoot network connectivity problems.

Evidence Model

Claim: Student can identify the cause of connectivity problems at the physical, data link, and network layers of the OSI mode.

Representations to capture information from student:
1. Log file of IOS commands

2. Configuration files for routers (state of network)

3. Worksheet (set of faults)

4. Network diagram

5. Essay

Observable Features

Representation: Log file of IOS

Observable features:
1. Steps taken to identify problems(s)
2. Identification of network problem(s)
3. Connection between steps and problems(s)

FIGURE 7.2. Example claim and evidence chain from NetPASS assessment (Williamson et al., 2004).

and student models, it becomes the basis for generation of an infinite number of items for test assembly.

To make this approach more concrete, let us consider the NetPASS computer networking assessment introduced previously, which was designed using the ECD framework. Figure 7.2 shows an example of the claim evidence chain for network troubleshooting, one of the tasks included on the test. The NetPASS developers reviewed current research, curricular materials, educational texts and networking documentation, interviewed subject matter experts, and examined existing assessments to generate their claims (Williamson et al., 2004). Following the chain of evidence for one of these claims – identifying the cause of connectivity problems – five different student representations are proposed, each of which provides evidence related to the claim. These representations are listed in the evidence model at the center of the diagram. Finally, observable features are identified that provide evidence of each representation. For example, the three features associated with the log file representation include (a) the steps taken to identify the problem, (b) the correct identification of the problem, and (c) the connection between the two. Tasks can then be designed to generate these observable features that can be interpreted as student-level claims by following an evidentiary chain. These inferences are strengthened when the connections between the student model, task model, and evidence models are well defined and supported by empirical psychological research.

Embretson's Cognitive Design System Approach

The CDS was proposed by Embretson (1994) in response to criticism that the typical atheoretical approaches to item design weakened construct validity of score interpretation. The CDS was designed to centralize the role of cognitive theory in test development in order to improve the meaning and use of ability and achievement test scores. The procedural framework of CDS is a series of stages that make explicit the skills targeted in diagnosis in item development, writing, and analysis. Seven test development steps are outlined: (a) specify the goals of measurement, (b) identify the features in the task domain, (c) develop a cognitive model, (d) generate the items, (e) evaluate the model of generated tests, (f) bank the items by cognitive complexity, and (g) validation (Embretson, 1994, 1998). The most unique stages in comparison to traditional test development are the early stages (i.e., stages a–c) and model evaluation (i.e., stage e). Stages a to c are similar to the development of student and task models in the ECD framework. Researchers must dissect a model of the construct or content domain into its most basic units (e.g., subskills, processes, abilities). Items are then written with features that can be empirically tied to components of the model. In model evaluation, psychometric models (e.g., CDMs) are applied to evaluate the fit of item responses to the cognitive model. In other words, researchers can mathematically validate the interpretation of the test scores through a formal test of the item features. Items that fit the cognitive model can be interpreted

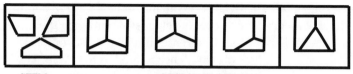

STEM   RESPONSE OPTIONS

FIGURE 7.3. Example assembling objects item.

as providing strong evidence of the construct. When items do not fit the model, test developers should either reexamine the structure of the item or reconsider their proposed definition of the construct they are measuring.

Embretson and Gorin (2001) explain several advantages of the CDS approach similar to those of the ECD approach. First, item parameters may be predicted for newly developed items if the psychometric and mathematical models developed provide adequate fit to the data. Second, construct validity is better understood because processing, strategy, and knowledge information is explicit in the development of the items. Furthermore, construct validity may be understood at the item level and at the test level by specifying the cognitive complexity of each item. Finally, the advantage most related to diagnostic testing purposes, the cognitive information gained at the item and test level from a CDS approach, can be useful for enhanced score interpretations.

Let us consider an example of diagnostic test design for spatial reasoning skills. Embretson and Gorin (2001) applied the CDS approach to generate an item bank that measured specified subskills of spatial reasoning with a specific item type – assembling objects (Figure 7.3). The task here is to identify which of the response options on the right could be correctly assembled by manipulating the individual shapes presented in the stem. In the CDS approach, like the ECD approach, detailed specifications of testing purpose and a model of student cognition are critical at early stages of the CDS process. CDS, however, does not frame the cognitive model necessarily in terms of claims about student behaviors. Applications of CDS to test development have typically been found in cognitive ability domains, such as abstract and spatial reasoning tasks. Student models akin to traditional cognitive information processing models are therefore more often used with CDS than the list of claims used in ECD. Figure 7.4 shows the associated cognitive model describing item processing and a list of item features that drive the cognitive complexity. The

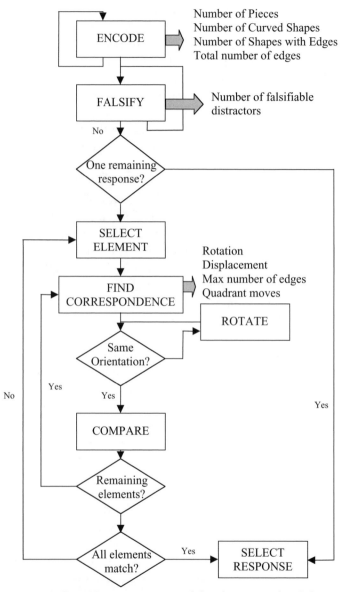

FIGURE 7.4. Cognitive processing model and associated task features for assembling objects item (Embretson & Gorin, 2001).

processing model specifies sources of cognitive complexity that can be explicitly "designed" into an item by manipulating various features of the task. If all features of an item can be ascribed to model processes, such as encoding, then a specific cause for a student's incorrect answer can be identified. Test developers interested in diagnosing skill weaknesses can use this assumption to develop items whose processing is more or less dependent on certain targeted skills. For example, the spatial reasoning model of the assembling objects task specifies that the number of pieces in a question affects the encoding difficulty of an item. Likewise, it indicates that the rotation of the pieces affects confirmation. To diagnose weaknesses in confirmation processes of a spatial task, items could be written with few pieces (i.e., low levels of encoding complexity), all or most of which are rotated 90 degrees or more (i.e., high levels of confirmation complexity). By designing items with an intentional structure (i.e., features associated with cognitive models), student responses can be interpreted in terms of predetermined processes. As with the ECD approach, the CDS approach systematically prescribes intentional item design based on a cognitive model of processing. The result is a set of items that allows for strong diagnostic conclusions to be reached based on student responses.

One final note is in order regarding both the ECD and the CDS approaches to test design. Although steps within both approaches are presented in a suggested order, the entire process is iterative, and the continued improvement of items may require returning to earlier stages of the framework. For example, if at the point of evaluating the cognitive model it is determined that the list of task features does not sufficiently account for processing of the item, several potential problems in the design process are indicated. It is possible that the initial cognitive model is not sufficiently complete or comprehensive to describe the item processing. In this case, it may be necessary to return to model generation, even after having generated items. Alternatively, the test developer may determine that the cognitive model of processing is specified appropriately for the measurement goals and that the problem lies in the design of the item. A reconceptualization of item format may be needed to control for extraneous influences on processing and to strengthen the correspondence between the item and the cognitive model. Overall, the sequence of the ECD and CDS frameworks is meant to emphasize the importance of the earlier stages of assessment development, which should be addressed with the same consideration as the later statistical analysis.

WRITING A DIAGNOSTIC TEST

Construct Definition for Test Design

In most guides to test development, the first step in the process is to generate a clear definition of the construct to be measured (DeVellis, 1991; Netemeyer, Bearden, & Sharma, 2003; Wilson, 2005). The use of cognitive psychology in assessment and psychometrics has added a new dimension to construct definitions. Comprehensive construct definitions help maintain the focus of item and test development on the trait of interest. The linking of items to traits is critical for construct representation, a major component of construct validity.

A construct definition can be reported in several forms. Figure 7.5 provides examples of three different construct definitions of the same construct, ranging in level of detail. The form of the construct definition should in many ways be determined by the ultimate inferences to be made from the scores. For example, to interpret scores purely for selection (e.g., college admissions decision), a general statement describing the construct measured by the test may suffice. However, for complex score interpretations (e.g., identification of subskill weaknesses), a more detailed description is warranted. One way in which test developers provide greater detail in their construct definition is through the use of test specifications (Leighton, 2004). Tables of specifications help define a construct in terms of dimensions (e.g., content areas or abilities) and ensure that a sufficient number of items are developed to measure each. However, item descriptors in test specifications can lack substantive cognitive information needed for diagnosis. In lieu of the traditional specifications, detailed construct definitions, including descriptions of individual cognitive processing and theoretical relationships among trait dimensions, have been advocated (Embretson & Gorin, 2001; Messick, 1989, 1995).

Wilson (2005) describes a tool for organizing cognitive information developmentally called a *construct map*. A construct map details the development levels of a skill and associated knowledge within a particular domain; it is a cognitive model. Its construction is a complex process integrating theory with expert pedagogical knowledge and observational data. Although a construct map can be developed for any skill domain, it is particularly well suited for modeling the cognitive development of mastery in a domain that is structured in a stage-like manner, with typical misconceptions and skill weaknesses at various ordered

(a) Construct definition as a verbal statement.

Reading comprehension questions measure the ability to read with understanding, insight, and discrimination. This type of question explores the ability to analyze a written passage from several perspectives. These include the ability to recognize both explicitly stated elements in the passage and assumptions underlying statements or arguments in the passage as well as the implications of those statements or arguments.

(b) Construct definition as a cognitive processing model.

(c) Construct definition as a list of skills and attributes.

Attribute/Skill List
Encoding Process Skills:
EP1: Encoding propositionally dense text.
EP2: Encoding propositionally sparse text.
EP3: Encoding high level vocabulary.
EP4: Encoding low level vocabulary.
Decision Process Skills:
DP1: Synthesizing large sections of text into a single answer.
DP2: Confirming correct answer from direct information in the text.
DP3: Falsifying incorrect answers from direct information in the text.
DP4: Confirming correct answer by inference from the text.
DP5: Falsifying incorrect answers by inference from the text.
DP6: Encoding correct answers with high vocabulary.
DP7: Encoding incorrect answers with high vocabulary.
DP8: Mapping correct answers to verbatim text.
DP9: Mapping correct answers to paraphrased text.
DP10: Mapping correct answers to reordered verbatim text.
DP11: Mapping correct answers to reordered paraphrased text.
DP12: Mapping incorrect answers to verbatim text.
DP13: Mapping incorrect answers to paraphrased text.
DP14: Mapping incorrect answers to reordered verbatim text.
DP15: Mapping incorrect answers to reordered paraphrased text.
DP16: Locating relevant information early in text.
DP17: Locating relevant information in the middle of the text.
DP18: Locating information at the end of the text.
DP19: Using additional falsification skills for specially formatted items.

FIGURE 7.5. Forms of construct definitions of multiple-choice reading comprehension test questions.

levels of reasoning. Construct maps have been used to develop diagnostic test items such as the science OMC items described previously (Briggs et al., 2006). Recall that in the OMC items, each response option is associated with a different cognitive-developmental level within the domain. Figure 7.6 provides the construct map developed for student

Level	Description
4	Student is able to coordinate apparent and actual motion of objects in the sky. Student knows that • the Earth is both orbiting the Sun and rotating on its axis • the Earth orbits the Sun once per year • the Earth rotates on its axis once per day, causing the day/night cycle and the appearance that the Sun moves across the sky • the Moon orbits the Earth once every 28 days, producing the phases of the Moon COMMON ERROR: Seasons are caused by the changing distance between the Earth and the Sun COMMON ERROR: The phases of the Moon are caused by the shadow of the planets, the Sun, or the Earth falling on the Moon
3	Student is able to coordinate apparent and actual motion of objects in the sky. Student knows that • the Earth orbits the Sun • the Moon orbits the Earth • the Earth rotates on its axis However, student has not put this knowledge together with an understanding of apparent motion to form explanations and may not recognized that the Earth is both rotating and orbiting simultaneously COMMON ERROR: It gets dark at night because the Earth goes around the Sun once a day.
2	Student recognizes that • the Sun appears to move across the sky every day • the observable shape of the Moon changes every 28 days Student may believe that the Sun moves around the Earth. COMMON ERROR: All motion in the sky is due to the Earth spinning on its axis. COMMON ERROR: The Sun travels around the Earth. COMMON ERROR: It gets dark at night because the Sun goes around the earth once a day. COMMON ERROR: The Earth is the center of the universe.
1	Student does not recognize the systematic nature of the appearance of objects in the sky. Students may not recognize that the Earth is spherical. COMMON ERROR: It gets dark at night because something (e.g., clouds, the atmosphere, "darkness") covers the Sun. COMMON ERROR: The phases of the Moon are caused by clouds covering the Moon. COMMON ERROR: The Sun goes below the Earth at night.
0	No evidence or off-track

FIGURE 7.6. Construct map for student understanding of Earth in the solar system as presented in Briggs et al. (2006).

understanding of the *Earth in the solar system* construct, the construct measured by the sample OMC item given in Figure 7.1. At each level of the construct map, information is given regarding the mastered skills, unmastered skills, and typical errors associated with students' cognition. Each level of the map serves as a diagnosis of student understanding that can be associated with individuals selecting a particular response. For example, if a student responds that it is colder at night because the sun has moved to the other side of the Earth (response option B), then one might conclude that he or she is aware that the sun appears to move across the sky every day and thus may believe that the sun moves around the Earth (level 2). The connection between the student response and a given conclusion regarding level of knowledge can be further strengthened by repeated observations of an individual across items based on the same construct map. Notice that the descriptions of knowledge and skills are not tied to any particular task or item. This allows for multiple tasks of similar or different structure to be developed, all of which connect student behaviors to the same set of student-level inferences. In traditional assessment theory, multiple items to measure the same construct are desirable to increase the reliability of measurement. This logic applies similarly to diagnostic measurement, only rather than generating multiple items with a single underlying construct, a common set of items should now share a common construct map.

Selecting Item Types

Successful diagnostic items require two key components: (a) a format that elicits student behaviors at an appropriate level of specificity, and (b) sufficient knowledge of a domain to relate student behaviors to target inferences. The critique thus far of traditional items is that they are based on an insufficient knowledge of the content domain and the items are formatted such that they do not provide information at the appropriate level. Methods of student observation popular in cognitive science and psychology may offer an alternative. Researchers in these fields often apply data-intensive assessment tools that provide direct observations of student cognition such as verbal protocols and visual eye tracking (Cross & Paris, 1987). Admittedly, however, these methods of assessment are time consuming, expensive, and logistically infeasible for large-scale assessment. An ideal diagnostic test should not sacrifice practicability to gain utility. The challenge therefore becomes to develop items that can be administered and scored as efficiently as traditional test items, while still providing information at the same level of description as more cognitively probative methods.

Simulation-Based Assessment
Simulation-based assessments are commonly regarded as one of the most "valid" methods of assessment available. These items, such as

those described on the NetPASS computer networking assessment, engage students in "real world" contexts that require complex solutions, much of which can be observed, recorded, and scored automatically for later analysis. These complex item responses, as compared to typical "single-response" items, are powerful assessment tools for gathering detailed information about task processing and student cognition (Bennett, Jenkins, Persky, & Weiss, 2003; Mislevy et al., 2002). Even large-scale assessment projects such as the *National Assessment of Educational Progress* (NAEP) are exploring the use of simulation-based assessments to augment achievement information available from other traditional item formats (Bennett et al., 2003). The 2009 NAEP Science Assessment Framework includes specific modifications to the test to include simulation-based items that can measure students' declarative, procedural, schematic, and strategic knowledge of science (Champagne, Bergin, Bybee, Duschl, & Ghallager, 2004). For example, the use of student-constructed graphs and figures has been considered to identify student problem representation skills and analysis of student response patterns, while solving problems can provide useful insight into student problem-solving strategies (U.S. Department of Education, 2003). Furthermore, via computer delivery of these items, student responses can be augmented by measures of reaction time to provide richer information regarding student cognitive skills and motivation. Unlike traditional multiple-choice or short-answer questions that provide limited student work product from which to extract information, the realistic context of simulations and the complex behaviors they produce make them ideal candidates for diagnostic assessment.

Multiple-Choice Questions for Diagnosis

Traditional multiple-choice items have two major limitations as diagnostic assessment tools. First, they are generally written at only the knowledge or comprehension level of cognition (e.g., recall of verbatim facts or paraphrasing of information), with few measuring complex skills such as synthesis, analysis, or evaluation (Frederiksen, 1990). Second, they are in almost all cases scored as correct or incorrect, with no use of information from the distractors selected by the students. Multiple-choice items can, in fact, be used for diagnostic purposes if these two features are altered. With respect to processing, although it is difficult, multiple-choice questions can be constructed to measure higher cognitive levels. More important, to gain diagnostic information, the multiple-choice distractors (incorrect responses) can be designed to correspond to specific skill weaknesses or student misconceptions. Student selection of these distractors can thus reveal the cause of the incorrect response. The OMC items are such an example. Other researchers have designed multiple-choice items in similar ways. Pek and Poh (2004) used multiple-choice questions as the assessment component of an intelligent tutoring system in physics. Feedback and subsequent instruction was provided by the "tutor" to the student based on incorrect responses. Consistent with an error analysis approach to diagnosis, examining students' incorrect answers provided insight into specific areas to inform remediation and further instruction. A thorough discussion of multiple-choice items for diagnosis is provided in the chapter by Richard M. Luecht (this volume).

Other Formats

In generating potential item formats for diagnosis, the critical issue is observing behaviors that provide evidence regarding student processing and cognition. Martin and VanLehn (1995) identified five student assessment activities ideal for gathering detailed information about student problem representation and solution planning: (a) problem solving, (b) example studying, (c) problem classification, (d) solution planning, and (e) conceptual problem solving. VanLehn (2001) developed a task design tool that combines these activities to assess student knowledge of physics. The system, called OLAE (online assessment of expertise), has been used in conjunction with intelligent tutoring systems, such as the Andes intelligent physics tutor (Gertner & VanLehn, 2000), to assess student knowledge and deliver tailored instruction that maximizes learning efficiency. Figure 7.7 shows a sample OLAE item. Students are presented with a problem, which in many ways looks similar to those found on traditional physics tests. However, with the OLAE system, students interact with the task in observable ways – asking for help, creating equations, and drawing diagrams. OLAE then compares students' problem-solving behaviors to the behavior of an ideal model, or expert, solving the same problem. At each correct step in the solution process, claims can be made regarding student strengths or mastery of knowledge; at each incorrect step, claims can be made regarding student weakness or nonmastery. Like simulation-based assessments, complex items such as OLAE tasks record behaviors during processing that can provide an evidentiary basis for diagnosis. The need for research on these and other formats for diagnosis is imminent. With progress in available technology and the growing demand for diagnostic tests, it is likely that advances in this area will be rapidly forthcoming.

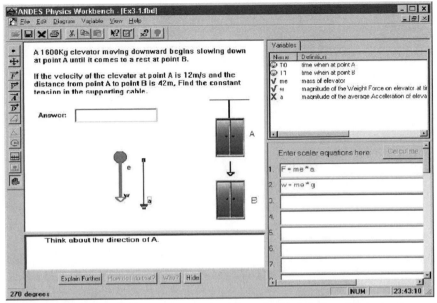

FIGURE 7.7. Sample OLAE assessment item from Andes Intelligent Tutoring System (VanLehn, 2001).

Test Assembly

Up to this point, our discussion of test construction has centered primarily on issues of individual item design. However, in many cases, diagnostic information exists at the level of the test, rather than the single item. For example, many items are constructed such that they only capture information about one or two larger sets of skills targeted for diagnosis. To obtain diagnostic information about all skills of interest, items for a test must be assembled such that all skills are represented. Furthermore, items should be used that represent different combinations of these skills. Assembly of tests with items that test identical subsets of skills provides unnecessary redundancy and may not provide appropriate diagnostic information. This issue is illustrated with a hypothetical example.

Let us suppose that our domain of interest (e.g., quantitative reasoning) has been deconstructed into five subskills (e.g., estimation, comparison). Our goal is to diagnose students' mastery of each skill based on item responses. Table 7.1 provides a sample design representing the skills measured by a pool of 10 test questions. This design matrix,

TABLE 7.1. *Q-matrix of 10-item pool measuring five subskills*

| | Subskill | | | | | |
Item	1	2	3	4	5	Inference from incorrect answer
1	1	1	0	0	0	Skills 1 and/or 2 not mastered
2	1	1	0	0	0	Skills 1 and/or 2 not mastered
3	1	1	0	0	0	Skills 1 and/or 2 not mastered
4	1	1	1	0	0	Skills 1, 2, and/or 3 not mastered
5	1	1	1	0	0	Skills 1, 2, and/or 3 not mastered
6	0	0	1	1	1	Skills 3, 4, and/or 5 not mastered
7	0	0	1	1	1	Skills 3, 4, and/or 5 not mastered
8	1	1	1	1	1	Any or all skills not mastered
9	1	1	1	1	1	Any or all skills not mastered
10	1	1	1	1	1	Any or all skills not mastered

often called a q-matrix, serves as a schematic representation of the cognitive skills model. Cells that contain a 1 indicate that the skill represented in that column is required to correctly solve the item designated in that row; a 0 indicates that the skill is not needed. As can be seen by the 1s and 0s in Table 7.1, every item measures two or more of the target skills, and every skill is measured by at least five items. For traditional testing purposes, this set of items would be appropriate to use given that all aspects of the construct are represented by items contributing to the overall ability estimate. However, for diagnostic purposes, the items are problematic. Closer examination of the rows in the q-matrix reveals that only four combinations of skills are represented by the items in the pool: 1,1,0,0,0; 1,1,1,0,0; 0,0,1,1,1; and, 1,1,1,1,1. At least two limitations of these patterns are clear. First, no items in the pool assess skill 1 in isolation from skill 2. Similarly, no items in the pool assess skill 4 without also measuring skill 5. These skills have been inextricably coupled in the item development process. The result of this skill coupling is that no item response pattern will allow an individual to make differential diagnoses about skills 1 and 2, or skills 4 and 5. Any skill diagnosis made from these items would be identical for skills 1 and 2 (i.e., skills 1 and 2 mastered or skills 1 and/or 2 not mastered), and identical for skills 4 and 5 (i.e., skills 4 and 5 mastered or skills 4 and/or 5 not mastered). Users who need to distinguish between individuals who have mastered skill 1, but not skill 2, would not gain the necessary information from these items. When selecting items, test developers should be aware of the skill combinations represented by the items in a pool and how unintentional skill coupling may limit the diagnostic utility of the test scores.

Computerized Adaptive Testing

With significant advances in computer technology, many educational testing programs now use computerized adaptive testing (CAT) systems. The advantage of CAT is its ability to reduce testing time without compromising accuracy. This is achieved by administering only test questions that provide information at an individual test taker's ability level. Of course, which items are most informative depends on the estimated ability of the test taker. Hence, each individual is likely to receive a different set of items. In a traditional testing situation for which scaling (ordering individuals on a single continuum) is the goal, the quality, or informativeness, of a test question is measured in terms of its ability to distinguish among possible estimates of a person's ability. In other words, a good item for a traditional CAT is one that helps accurately describe a person's overall ability. Statistically, this property is often described as the item's reliability, or discrimination.

The same benefits of CAT in a traditional testing environment could similarly be useful for diagnostic testing. Selecting items that are discriminating can improve the accuracy and efficiency of assessment. However, the meaning of "discriminating" changes somewhat depending on the purpose of the test. As previously mentioned, when the purpose of the test is to scale test takers, an item should discriminate between possible estimates of ability. In diagnostic assessment, the purpose of testing is to obtain a description of the individual's skills, processing, and knowledge. Therefore, a good diagnostic item should discriminate between various states of understanding, types of processing, and patterns of mastery (Henson & Douglas, 2005; Marshall, 1990). Few studies have examined CAT algorithms for selecting items based on a diagnostic interpretation of discrimination. Marshall (1981, 1990) proposes two Bayesian-based heuristics for diagnostic item selection. The first heuristic is a two-step process, the goal of which is to administer items whose responses reduce the posterior probability of several diagnostic states to zero. In other words, the heuristic selects items that maximally reduce the number of possible diagnoses. The second heuristic is similar to item information selection criteria. Information provided by each item is calculated based on the current probabilities of an individual's diagnosis. In general, items with correct response probabilities closest to .50 given prior item responses provide maximal information. Similar work by Henson and Douglas (2005) has also explored the use of a heuristic index (CDI•) for diagnostic CAT construction with some success. Unlike the information heuristic proposed by Marshall (1981), the CDI• is based on the Kullback-Liebler information for discriminating between two possible diagnostic states. Simulation studies of the CDI• suggest that under certain conditions, accurate classification for operational diagnostic CATs is feasible. However, further investigation of these and other item selection methods for computerized diagnostic assessment is still needed.

EVALUATING DIAGNOSTIC ITEMS USING COGNITIVE THEORY

Throughout the discussion of item and test development, emphasis has been placed on the importance of connections between behavioral observations and student inferences. The majority of the chapter thus far has described methods for developing and writing items based on a model of cognition. However, little guidance has been given as to how the cognitive model is developed and its relationship to items established. This is due in large part to the relative inattention to this topic in the psychometric literature. The majority of our statistical and psychometric methods assume that a cognitive model is in place at the outset of test development; test developers presumably fully understand what it is that they want to measure. The CDMs applied to assessment data, despite their mathematical sophistication, require a priori specification of a cognitive model. In other words, the cognitive model must be built *first* after which a statistical model can be applied. Although theory always provides a good basis for initial cognitive models of item processing, this assumes that theory exists. Unfortunately, many of the constructs of interest in achievement testing have been left unexamined by cognitive psychologists. Furthermore, as the use of new item types such as simulations, complex item formats, and ordered multiple-choice questions increases, new issues related to construct irrelevant variance are introduced (Sireci & Zenisky, 2006). In such situations, test developers must be resourceful and develop their own model. To more fully understand the constructs of interest to educators, researchers have drawn increasingly on qualitative research methodologies commonly employed in cognitive psychology to generate hypothetical models. Interviews with expert teachers, content experts, and even novice learners provide information to form a complete representation of a content domain. Several qualitative data collection methods are available for gathering the substantive information needed to develop a cognitive model. Two empirical methods borrowed from cognitive psychology are suggested to inform cognitive model development: verbal protocols and digital eye tracking.

Verbal Protocols

Verbal protocols are commonly employed in cognitive psychology to understand various aspects of human processing on complex tasks. Verbal protocols, or *think alouds*, consist of student verbalizations of response processes for an item either while solving a problem (*concurrent* or *online verbal protocols*) or once the item is completed (*retrospective verbal protocols*; Ericsson & Simon, 1993). They make explicit the processes that characterize human cognition. Several researchers have noted the potential for verbal protocols to inform theory and model building in assessment design (Embretson & Gorin, 2001; Gorin, 2006; Leighton, 2004). Leighton (2004) characterized traditional quantitative test analysis methods as "missed opportunities" that could be avoided with qualitative data collection methods such as verbal protocols. In the development of both NetPASS and the science OMC items, qualitative data collection was critical in the development of the underlying cognitive models (Briggs et al., 2006; Williamson et al., 2004). The development of the ECD student, evidence, and task models of NetPASS was informed by collecting verbal protocols from a small sample of examinees (Williamson et al., 2004). The construct map for the science OMC items required extensive interviews of teachers, content experts, and students, as well as the review of multiple educational texts relevant to the content (Briggs et al., 2006). Although qualitative investigations such as verbal protocols can be time consuming, they offer unique insight into human information processing that is indispensable for generating an accurate cognitive model.

Digital Eye Tracking

A technologically advanced method based on the same logic as verbal protocols, digital eye tracking has been useful in examining information processing during complex problem solving. Eye tracking methods record individuals' eye movement data during stimulus processing. The assumption of the technology is that the location of an individual's eye fixation corresponds to an allocation of visual attention and, in turn, cognitive processing resources (Rayner, 1998; Rayner, Warren, Juhasz, & Liversedge, 2004; Underwood, Jebbett, & Roberts, 2004). It has been recently argued that eye tracking data can be useful for gaining increased understanding of student interactions with test items. The general approach is to collect student eye movements during test taking and to examine these movements relative to a hypothesized processing model. Although fewer applications of eye tracking to educational

testing situations exist than in the psychological domain, several exam-
inations have helped identify specific problem-solving solution paths
that may be more or less effective (Diehl, 2004; Embretson, 1998; Gorin,
2006). For example, Gorin (2006) examined gaze trails for individuals solving multiple-choice reading comprehension items from the new
SAT-I. Three of these trails are shown in Figure 7.8. The lines and black
circles imposed on the test question represent the sequence and location
of visual gaze. It can be seen in the first diagram that the individual
solved this item by mapping information from the last paragraph of the
passage to the question and item responses. The second item was solved
by mapping information from the first paragraph of the passage. Finally,
when solving the third item, the individual solved the problem without even looking at the passage, even though that particular question
referred to vocabulary in the text with a given line number. Although
the pattern for each item was distinct, all three items were answered
correctly.

Of most interest is the fact that although the three items were intended
to measure the same construct, they appear to have been solved very
differently. This observation is consistent with much of the cognitive
research on expertise highlighting the use of multiple solution strategies in problem solving. Unfortunately, this finding can be quite problematic for diagnostic score interpretation. The assumption that observable behaviors can be linked to specific weaknesses in processing for
all individuals is dependent on the fact that all individuals are solving
problems in the same way; one cognitive model of processing for one
solution strategy. To the extent to which multiple strategies exist, multiple cognitive models are needed to provide accurate diagnosis for each
strategy group. The appropriate inferences to draw about an individual
student might depend significantly on which of the available models is
consistent with his or her solution strategy.

Further analysis of the eye patterns provided additional information
regarding student processing. As previously mentioned, across a small
set of individuals, different eye patterns were associated with correct
responses. Furthermore, the same eye pattern associated with a correct response for one student was observed for another who answered
the question incorrectly. This finding suggests that for these items, it is
not necessarily *where* an individual is looking when solving the problem, but rather *what* the individual does with the information. Based on
this finding, it seems unlikely that teaching students strategies about

(a) Item solved by mapping information from the end of the passage.

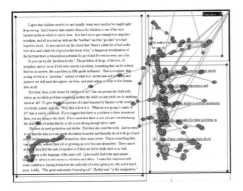

(b) Item solved by mapping information from the first paragraph of the passage.

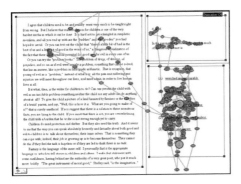

(c) Item solved with no direct mapping of information from passage checking.

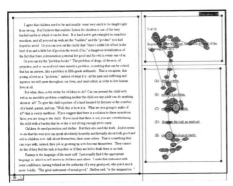

FIGURE 7.8. Illustrations of eye tracking patterns for three multiple-choice questions from a single reading comprehension passage.

where to look for information would be useful to improve student performance on the SAT. Rather, the most effective instruction might target skills related to processing and encoding information once it has been identified. Although this is a small example of early work with this methodology, eye tracking data such as that gathered on the SAT-I reading comprehension items may be useful for developing diagnostic test items. Information provided by eye patterns can assist test developers in generating and refining their cognitive models of item processing. Pilot testing of tasks with eye tracking could be useful to verify that students are engaging with the task as expected and to identify strategy differences that might not have been anticipated.

CONCLUSION

The process of test construction in education and psychology has been refined and re-refined to the point that there is considerable consistency in views on good test development practices. The effect of this process is evident in the extensive library of psychometrically sound tests available for almost any domain of interest. What is less available are tests designed appropriately for almost any use. When tests are properly designed, they are done so with a specific use in mind. Until recently, this use has rarely included diagnosis. This chapter examines how many of our existing test development procedures are, and are not, appropriately suited for test development for diagnosis.

In review, it appears that many procedures are the same. Construct definition is still central to item development. Statistical properties of the items such as reliability and validity remain critical for useful score interpretation. However, it has become clear that many of our existing testing construction methods must be adapted to meet the additional demands of diagnostic score use. Substantive exploration of item characteristics via exploratory and qualitative methods should be incorporated throughout the design process. As the technological constraints on test design are overcome, innovative item formats that provide opportunities for diagnosis should be explored. The use of tests in educational and psychological settings is ever increasing, as are the consequences of decisions made based on these tests. The potential for formative assessment to impact educational and psychological outcomes exists. Appropriate procedures for the development of diagnostic assessment tools must be further explored for us to achieve this promise.

References

American Educational Research Association (AERA), American Psychological Association, & National Council on Measurement in Education. (1999). *Standards for educational and psychological testing.* Washington, DC: AERA.

Behrens, J. T., Mislevy, R. J., Bauer, M., Williamson, D. M., & Levy, R. (2004). Introduction to evidence-centered design and lessons learned from its application in a global e-learning program. *International Journal of Testing, 4,* 295–302.

Bennett, R. E., Jenkins, F., Persky, H., & Weiss, A. (2003). Assessing complex problem solving performances. *Assessment in Education: Principles, Policy, & Practice, 10*(3), 347–359.

Briggs, D. C., Alonzo, A. C., Schwab, C., & Wilson, M. (2006). Diagnostic assessment with ordered multiple-choice items. *Educational Assessment, 11*(1), 33–63.

Champagne, A., Bergin, K., Bybee, R., Duschl, R., & Ghallager, J. (2004). *NAEP 2009 science framework development: Issues and recommendations.* Washington, DC: National Assessment Governing Board.

Cross, D. R., & Paris, S. G. (1987). Assessment of reading comprehension: Matching test purposes and test properties. *Educational Psychologist, 22*(3/4), 313–332.

DeVellis, R. F. (1991). *Scale development: Theory and applications.* Thousand Oaks, CA: Sage.

Diehl, K. A. (2004). Algorithmic item generation and problem solving strategies in matrix completion problems. *Dissertation Abstracts International: Section B: The Sciences and Engineering, 64*(8-B), 4075.

Embretson, S. E. (1994). Application of cognitive design systems to test development. In C. R. Reynolds (Ed.), *Cognitive assessment: A multidisciplinary perspective* (pp. 107–135). New York: Plenum Press.

Embretson, S. E. (1998). A cognitive design system approach to generating valid tests: Application to abstract reasoning. *Psychological Methods, 3,* 300–396.

Embretson, S. E. (1999). Generating items during testing: Psychometric issues and models. *Psychometrika, 64*(4), 407–433.

Embretson, S. E., & Gorin, J. S. (2001). Improving construct validity with cognitive psychology principles. *Journal of Educational Measurement, 38*(4), 343–368.

Ericsson, K. A., & Simon, H. A. (1993). *Protocol analysis: Verbal reports as data* (Rev. ed.). Cambridge, MA: MIT Press.

Frederiksen, N. (1990). Introduction. In N. Frederiksen, R. Glaser, A. Lesgold, & M. G. Shafto (Eds.), *Diagnostic monitoring of skill and knowledge acquisition* (pp. ix–xvii). Hillsdale, NJ: Erlbaum.

Gertner, A., & VanLehn, K. (2000). Andes: A coached problem solving environment for physics. In G. Gauthier, C. Frasson, & K. VanLehn (Eds.), *Intelligent tutoring systems: 5th International conference, ITS 2000* (pp. 131–142). Berlin: Springer.

Gorin, J. S. (2006). *Using alternative data sources to inform item difficulty modeling.* Paper presented at the 2006 annual meeting of the National Council on Educational Measurement. San Francisco, CA.

Hartz, S. M. (2002). A Bayesian framework for the unified model for assessing cognitive abilities: Blending theory with practicality. *Dissertation Abstracts International: Section B: The Sciences and Engineering, 63*(2-B), 864.

Henson, R., & Douglas, J. (2005). Test construction for cognitive diagnosis. *Applied Psychological Measurement, 29*(4), 262–277.

Leighton, J. P. (2004). Avoiding misconception, misuse, and missed opportunities: The collection of verbal reports in educational achievement testing. *Educational Measurement: Issues and Practice, 23*(4), 6–15.

Leighton, J. P., Gierl, M. J., & Hunka, S. M. (2004). The attribute hierarchy method for cognitive assessment: A variation on Tatsuoka's rule-space approach. *Journal of Educational Measurement, 41*, 205–237.

Marshall, S. P. (1981). Sequential item selection: Optimal and heuristic policies. *Journal of Mathematical Psychology, 23*, 134–152.

Marshall, S. P. (1990). Generating good items for diagnostic tests. In N. Frederiksen, R. Glaser, A. Lesgold, & M. Shafto (Eds.), *Diagnostic monitoring of skill and knowledge acquisition* (pp. 433–452). Hillsdale, NJ: Erlbaum.

Martin, J., & VanLehn, K. (1995). A Bayesian approach to cognitive assessment. In P. D. Nichols, S. F. Chipman, & R. L. Brennan (Eds.), *Cognitively diagnostic assessment* (pp. 141–167). Hillsdale, NJ: Erlbaum.

Messick, S. (1989). Validity. In R. L. Linn (Ed.), *Educational measurement* (3rd ed.; pp. 13–103). New York: American Council on Education/Macmillan.

Messick, S. (1995). Validity of psychological assessment: Validation of inferences from persons' responses and performances as scientific inquiry into score meaning. *American Psychologist, 50*, 741–749.

Mislevy, R. J. (1994). Evidence and inference in educational assessment. *Psychometrika, 59*, 439–483.

Mislevy, R. J., Steinberg, L. S., & Almond, R. G. (2002). Design and analysis in task-based language assessment. *Language Testing. Special Issue: Interpretations, intended uses, and designs in task-based language, 19*(4), 477–496.

Netemeyer, R. G., Bearden, W. O., & Sharma, S. (2003). *Scaling procedures: Issues and applications.* Thousand Oaks, CA: Sage.

No Child Left Behind Act of 2001, H.R. 1 Cong. (2001).

Pek, P. K., & Poh, K. L. (2004). A Bayesian tutoring system for Newtonian mechanics: Can it adapt to different learners? *Journal of Educational Computing Research, 31*(3), 281–307.

Rayner, K. (1998). Eye movements in reading and information processing: 20 Years of research. *Psychological Bulletin, 124*, 372–422.

Rayner, K., Warren, T., Juhasz, B. J., & Liversedge, S. P. (2004). The effect of plausibility on eye movements in reading. *Journal of Experimental Psychology: Learning, Memory, & Cognition, 30*, 1290–1301.

Sireci, S. G., & Zenisky, A. L. (2006). Innovative item formats in computer-based testing: In pursuit of improved construct representation. In S. M. Downing & T. M. Haladyna (Eds.), *Handbook of test development* (pp. 329–357). Mahwah, NJ: Erlbaum.

Tatsuoka, K. K. (1985). A probabilistic model for diagnosing misconceptions by the pattern classification approach. *Journal of Educational Statistics, 10*(1), 55–73.

Tatsuoka, K. K. (1995). Architecture of knowledge structures and cognitive diagnosis: A statistical pattern recognition and classification approach. In P. D. Nichols, S. F. Chipman, & R. L. Brennan (Eds.), *Cognitively diagnostic assessment* (pp. 327–361). Hillsdale, NJ: Erlbaum.

Tatsuoka, K. K., Corter, J. E., & Tatsuoka, C. (2004). Patterns of diagnosed mathematical content and process skills in TIMSS-R across a sample of 20 countries. *American Educational Research Journal, 41*(4), 901–926.

Underwood, G., Jebbett, L., & Roberts, K. (2004). Inspecting pictures for information to verify a sentence: Eye movements in general encoding and in focused search. *Quarterly Journal of Experimental Psychology A: Human Experimental Psychology, 57A*, 165–182.

U.S. Department of Education. (2003). *NAEP validity studies: Implications of electronic technology for the NAEP assessment* (Working Paper No. 2003–16). Washington, DC: Institute of Education Sciences.

VanLehn, K. (2001). *Olae: A bayesian performance assessment for complex problem solving.* Paper presented at the 2001 annual meeting of the National Council on Measurement in Education, Seattle.

Williamson, D. M., Bauer, M., Steinberg, L. S., Mislevy, R. J., Behrens, J. T., & DeMark, S. F. (2004). Design rationale for a complex performance assessment. *International Journal of Testing, 4*(4), 303–332.

Wilson, M. (2005). *Constructing measures: An item response modeling approach.* Mahwah, NJ: Erlbaum.

Wilson, M., & Sloane, K. (2000). From principles to practice: An embedded assessment system. *Applied Measurement in Education, 13*, 181–208.

PART III

PSYCHOMETRIC PROCEDURES AND APPLICATIONS

8

Cognitive Foundations of Structured Item Response Models

André A. Rupp and Robert J. Mislevy

> A construct-centered approach [to assessment design] would begin by asking what complex of knowledge, skills, or other attributes should be assessed, presumably because they are tied to explicit or implicit objectives of instruction or are otherwise valued by society. Next, what behaviours or performances should reveal those constructs, and what tasks or situations should elicit those behaviours?
>
> Messick (1994, p. 16)

INTRODUCTION

The quotation from Messick (1994) that opens this chapter eloquently lays out the essential narrative of educational assessment. Specifically, it captures how the design of tasks should be guided by the structure of the argument about learner competencies that one seeks to develop and eventually support with data from behaviors that activate these competencies. Moreover, the quote alludes to the fact that reasoning about learner competencies is a complex communicative act, which, like all communicative acts, requires the thoughtful integration of distinct pieces of information to construct a coherent, concise, and rhetorically effective argument.

Reasoning about learner competencies in educational assessment is both probabilistic and evidence based. It is probabilistic because it is concerned with developing an argument about one or more unobservable latent characteristics of learners. It is evidence based because the development of the argument must rely on data that are derived from aspects of examinees' observable behavior. However, such data provide only indirect information about latent characteristics, so the process of

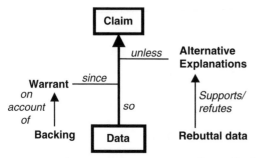

FIGURE 8.1. Argument structure according to Toulmin (1958). Reasoning about a *claim* is based on *data* by justification of a *warrant*, which, in turn, is supported by *backing*. The inference may be qualified by *alternative explanations*, which *rebuttal evidence* tends to support or refute.

reasoning about learner competencies requires an agreed-upon framework about which data patterns constitute relevant evidence in what manner (Schum, 1994).

Put differently, the construction of an evidentiary argument in educational assessment is achieved through a synthesis of logical and empirical information within a probabilistic framework of inference. Using terminology from Toulmin (1958), an evidentiary argument is constructed through a series of logically connected claims or propositions that are supported by data with warrants and can be subjected to alternative explanations (Figure 8.1). In educational assessment, *data* consist of learners' observed responses to particular tasks and the salient features of those tasks, *claims* concern examinees' proficiency as construed more generally, and *warrants* posit how responses in situations with the noted features depend on proficiency. Some conception of knowledge and its acquisition – that is, a psychological perspective – is the source of warrants, and shapes the nature of claims a particular assessment is meant to support as well as the tasks and data needed to evidence them.

The structure described thus far concerns the psychological and substantive rationale for inference but does not address the issues of *evaluating* and *synthesizing* the evidentiary value of a collection of typically overlapping, often conflicting, and sometimes interdependent observations. To aid in the complex process of synthesizing and evaluating potential pieces of evidence, the disciplines of statistics and psychometrics provide the required tools with which the probabilistic uncertainties in the evidentiary argument can be bounded. A psychometric model acquires meaning when a *correspondence* is established between its formal elements (i.e., its parameters and structural characteristics) and aspects of real world situations – a correspondence that depends on substantive theories, experience, and perspectives about the situations of interest. In educational assessment, a key discipline on which such correspondence is grounded is *psychology*. Traditionally, the dominant psychological perspectives had been trait and behavioral perspectives, but a *cognitive perspective* has become increasingly important. Consequently, psychometric models that operationalize elements of information processing theories from cognitive psychology through component variables and structural characteristics synergize the capacities of these two disciplines: a psychometric model guides probabilistic reasoning within the rhetorical framework of an evidentiary argument that concerns observable characteristics of learner behaviors as interpreted from a cognitive perspective.

Rather than being the focus of educational assessment itself, however, psychometric models play only a serving role in the construction of evidentiary arguments in the same way that linguistic competencies such as grammatical, lexical, or phonological knowledge play only a serving role in a communicative act. In other words, the appropriate development and utilization of psychometric models is a necessary, but not a sufficient, condition for developing a coherent, concise, and effective evidentiary argument about learner competencies. The structure of such an argument – and not the psychometric models – thus becomes the starting point for the design of an educational assessment that guides conceptual, analytical, and interpretative decisions (Mislevy, Steinberg, & Almond, 2003).

This chapter is about the theoretical underpinnings that guide the development and utilization of a specific group of psychometric models, namely, *structured item response theory* (SIRT) models, and the complex evidentiary arguments that can be constructed and supported with them. The structure of cognitive psychology as a discipline is briefly described in terms of its theoretical premises and methodological characteristics, with an emphasis on their implications for the construction of evidentiary arguments in educational assessment. Then, considerations of the grain size of feedback in educational assessment are presented that have an implication for the choice of the psychometric model and the interpretation of its parameters. The ways that theoretical perspectives in psychology guide the design, analysis, and interpretation of educational assessments are reviewed, and the implications of these perspectives for the development and utilization of psychometric models are discussed. A selection of representative SIRT models is presented briefly within this discussion to illustrate the key implications. Finally, two sample applications are provided, which were developed in the context of a national competency-based reform of the educational system in Germany. They underscore the natural fit and the benefits of integrating a cognitive psychology perspective into educational assessments to reason about learner competencies at a national level.

STRUCTURE OF COGNITIVE PSYCHOLOGY AS A DISCIPLINE

The formal and statistical machinery of educational measurement evolved in the first half of the 20th century under the aegis of *behavioral psychology* and *trait/differential psychology*. The forms of the models that were developed in those early days suited the nature of the claims one wanted to frame under in these perspectives. Briefly, educational assessment arguments under a behavioral perspective concern behaviors of learners in settings that are defined strictly in terms of observable behaviors. Under a trait/differential perspective, the focus of educational assessment arguments is on unobservable characteristics of learners, which are assumed to be relatively stable across time and revealed through systematic differences across individuals in various situations.

Cognitive psychology, which rose in importance as a response to those perspectives, asks questions about the nature, acquisition, and use of knowledge in ways that contrasted with those typically seen under behavioral or trait/differential perspectives on educational assessment: How do people represent the information in a situation? What operations and strategies do they use to solve problems? What aspects of problems make them difficult or call for various knowledge or processes? Specifically, the "cognitive revolution" during the 1960s and 1970s, exemplified by Newell and Simon's (1972) *Human Information Processing*, called attention to the nature of knowledge and how people acquire, store, and retrieve it – in other words, how people process different pieces of information (see van Lehn, 1989, for a readable overview of information processing theories). Strong parallels to computation and artificial intelligence characterize the theories of the time, and appeared in the use of rules, production systems, task decompositions, and means – ends analyses. The key characteristic that distinguishes an *information processing perspective* is that it models human problem solving in light of the capabilities and the limitations of human thought and memory that are revealed by psychological experiments. Contemporary cognitive psychology encompasses this information processing strand, as well as developmental, sociocultural, neuroscientific, and connectionist strands.[1] In particular, the view that the structures of information processing directly reflected the implementation of cognition has been largely supplanted by a connectionist view of learning (Clark, 1997). Yet, the information processing perspective can be seen as a complementary view, focusing on a higher-level analysis. It remains well suited to studying the nature, content, and utilization of much of the information people learn and use, particularly in the semantically rich domains of school and work (Greeno & Moore, 1993). As such, the information processing perspective forms the most important basis for the work on SIRT models, which is why it has a central place in this chapter.

To properly set the stage for more detailed discussions about SIRT models under an information processing perspective, we begin by discussing two complementary theoretical premises of cognitive psychology, along with their methodological implications.

Key Theoretical Premises in Cognitive Psychology

The first premise, which can be called the *universality of cognitive structures*, is that the cognitive structure and basic information processing mechanisms are essentially alike across all humans. Hence, all humans are equipped not only with remarkable capabilities, but also with equally remarkable limitations. For example, cognitively healthy humans learn multiple languages rapidly and effortlessly as toddlers but much more slowly and effortful as adults. They possess a virtually unlimited long-term memory capacity, but they have a working memory capacity of only about seven chunks of information. They are able to draw on numerous automatized skills for complex reasoning, but they fall prey to predictable cognitive biases.

One important consequence of the universality premise for educational assessment is that an explanation for an observable phenomenon that draws on principles from cognitive psychology cannot allow for

[1] See Bechtel, Abrahamsen, and Graham (1998) for a review that is both more historical and technical than the one here, and see the National Research Council's (2000) *How People Learn* for an overview aimed at education.

structurally idiosyncratic processing differences. In an assessment of reading comprehension ability, for example, any set of variables that is believed to capture essential characteristics of the cognitive processes learners engage in during the process of responding to a task must be consistently influential across learner groups to be reliable markers of this process from a cognitive psychology perspective. As discussed later in this chapter, the universality premise is consistent with different learners applying the same elemental processes with different information, strategies, or solution steps, some of which can be addressed with SIRT models. The premise does, however, constrain the space of possible explanations to those that are empirically or logically consistent with the power and limitations of a common set of processing capabilities.

It is, therefore, not surprising that researchers have generally been able to find consistent support for variables that can account for variation in operating characteristics of items such as item difficulty – as measured by a p-value, or percent correct, from classical test theory (e.g., Lord & Novick, 1968); a β-value, or item difficulty parameter, from item response theory (IRT) (e.g., van der Linden & Hambleton, 1997); or response time – only for those variables that are believed to directly index cognitive processes such as the depth of cognitive cycling and integration of information or the complexity of an information matching process (e.g., Gorin & Embretson, 2005; Mosenthal, 1996). In contrast, it is much more difficult to find consistent support for those variables whose influence on cognitive processes is more indirect and becomes more pronounced in interaction with other sets of variables such as the length of a text or the complexity of the wording of a prompt (e.g., Drum, Calfee, & Cook, 1981; Freedle & Kostin, 1993; Rupp, Garcia, & Jamieson, 2001). Therefore, researchers nowadays more frequently acknowledge the need to match the coding of selected characteristics of the stimulus material and the question material to theories of cognitive processing specific to different task types (e.g., Sheehan & Ginther, 2001; Sheehan & Mislevy, 2001) because it is believed that the cognitive processes for specific tasks types draw, in a similar vein, on the same processing capabilities.

The second premise of cognitive psychology, which can be called the *cultural specificity of information processing*, refers to the particularities of the contents of learning as they are expressed, learned, used, and transmitted within groups of people. That is, there are qualitative differences in the specifics of processing various pieces of culturally embedded information across learners despite their common mental architecture.[2] Models, concepts, symbol systems, representational forms, and associated processes for using them are developed, employed, and transmitted socially within a culture. The notion of "culture" in this context not only encompasses the common meaning of customs and artifacts of different societies, but also the distinct ways of thinking, talking, and interacting that are found in societal networks such as professions, workplaces, classrooms, interest groups, clubs, and families in which people share certain aspects of experience. Important implications of the cultural specificity premise for educational assessment include the need to account for the cultural symbolism of assessment tasks through variations in task design, to verify empirically that assessments are fair to learners from different cultural backgrounds, and to empirically connect information about the cognitive processes in task performance with explanatory information about the cultural background of the learners and the cultural context of learning.

The "principles and parameters" framework for cognitive grammars in psycholinguistics (e.g., Freidin, 1991) illustrates the interplay of the premises of universality and cultural specificity. It postulates that all languages in the world function according to a common set of "principles" that allow all humans to process "language" in a similar vein by drawing on similar mental resources, but that the linguistic context that a human is embedded in helps set the "parameters" for the particular language(s) he or she is exposed to and refines the specific information processing mechanisms in his or her particular context.

Methodological Characteristics

The complementary objectives of determining the universal components of mental operations in perception and attention as well as the culture-specific components of language and communication conceived of broadly have substantial implications for the types of research that are being conducted in cognitive psychology. Historically primary and continuing in importance are randomized designed experiments in laboratory settings. For example, Underwood and Bait (1996) synthesize a

---

[2] Note that this does not mean that the real world referents of information, such as the laws of physics, are culturally determined. Rather, the vast amount of information people work with is not innate but learned, expressed, and transmitted socially, in ways and forms that vary over time and across groups.

host of studies on tasks such as pattern recognition or priming effects for words, which serve to investigate the fundamental psycholinguistic processes in reading. These cognitive operations are mostly automatized and allow fluency in reading for healthy humans in the same way across languages, despite their differences in syntax and lexicon. However, the results from such studies are often at a level that is too atomic to be directly relevant to educational assessment, where stakeholders require information at a much coarser level of granularity with respect to the ability of learners to perform various culturally valued tasks across a wide range of contexts.

In the 1960s, influenced by the work of Newell and Simon, cognitive task analysis (CTA; Schraagen, Chipman, & Shalin, 2000) began to supplement experimental study. CTA addresses the differential organization of knowledge and structure of cognitive processes that come into play when subjects – often both experts and novices – carry out a given task. A cognitive task analysis in a domain seeks to shed light on (a) the essential features of the situations, (b) the internal representations of situations, (c) the relationship between problem-solving behavior and internal representation, (d) the ways in which problems are solved, and (e) the features that make problems difficult (Newell & Simon, 1972). Constructive in nature, CTA requires exhaustive observation and detailed analyses of minute aspects of behavior for a small number of subjects. Again, as with the results from designed experiments, the fine grain size of CTAs is poorly suited to the design of educational assessment without some translation of its results to a coarser grain size. Nevertheless, there are close connections between the goals of CTA and the construction of educational assessment tasks and the subsequent modeling of task performances with SIRT models.

As this brief discussion has highlighted, there is a general need of translating information from one informational grain size to another if the disciplines of cognitive psychology and educational assessment should benefit from one another. This need for articulation between cognitive psychology and educational assessment is a challenge in both directions. That is to say, task designers and measurement specialists have to find means to provide guidelines for task writing and for task coding that are, at once, consistent with theoretical predictions about information processing at a more fine-grained level and consistent with the practical resource constraints of the educational assessment process (see, e.g., Enright et al., 2000, pp. 2–7). However, as is shown in the next section, the level of grain size at which relevant information is articulated depends strongly on the grain size of the feedback that is desired from the educational assessment.

GRAIN SIZE AND PURPOSE OF FEEDBACK
IN EDUCATIONAL ASSESSMENT

Because evidentiary arguments are feedback mechanisms, it is useful to differentiate their rhetorical structure by jointly considering (a) the *granularity* of the feedback and (b) the *purpose* of the feedback. The notion of granularity itself is, of course, as imprecise as the notion of cognition because both concepts are latent characteristics of objects. This may appear theoretically disconcerting given the experimental precision of cognitive psychology as a discipline, but it is essentially unavoidable in practical application of its findings. More important, it can be largely overcome by careful mapping of the different granularity levels throughout the process of educational assessment design, analysis, and interpretation.

In terms of granularity, feedback can be given on a continuum that reaches from cognitively coarse, as in the case of summative statewide accountability reports (e.g., Baumert et al., 2001; Mullis, Martin, & Foy, 2005), to cognitively fine grained, as in the case of formative intelligent tutoring systems (e.g., Anderson & Gluck, 2001; van Lehn, 2004). The level of granularity in feedback that is developed through an evidentiary argument is driven primarily by the purpose for which the feedback is provided. One limitation that is shared by all SIRT models in this regard is the number of latent variables that can be reasonably modeled with real data. Although there is no conceptual limit to this number, this number most often ranges somewhere between four and eight attributes in practice. As the number of attributes increases additively, the number of possible competency classes increases exponentially, placing unreasonable demands on task design and task implementation. Therefore, applications of SIRT models typically operate at a coarse or very coarse grain size of cognitive granularity from the perspective of cognitive psychology. Subsequent interpretations retain their validity only if the linkage between subsumed cognitive processes and the coarser variables can be convincingly established.

In statewide accountability reports, for example, neither information about individual learners nor information about cognitive processes within individuals is typically relevant because the focus is on summarizing performance information at the class, school, province, or national level. In such cases, information about detailed cognitive processes that are required to successfully complete assessment tasks may be useful for constructing tasks and for investigating properties such as their difficulty and discriminatory ability, but information in these terms does not need to be looped back into the system to the learners, their teachers, or their parents. Hence, it is statistically more advantageous to analyze data with SIRT models that characterize students by more broadly defined proficiencies and that can accommodate the hierarchical structure of the data, the missingness patterns that arise from the matrix sampling design, and the multiple covariates at each level of the data hierarchy.

In contrast, the purposes of individualized performance reports such as those provided by intelligent tutoring systems or cognitively diagnostic tests administered in intact classrooms are to transcend the mere rank-ordering functionality of nondiagnostic assessments – even if these are contextualized via a myriad of background and contextual variables – and to provide a complex classification of learners into masters and non-masters on different attributes for criterion-referenced interpretations. Such classifications allow for the development of support systems for individual learners and for an adjustment of instructional strategies for entire classrooms. The grain size of SIRT models for such applications is coarser than a detailed process model of problem-solving activities from cognitive psychology, but it is intended to identify emergent capabilities and impasses consistent with such an analysis.

In many educational climates, there is a practical need to combine both levels of feedback, however. For example, in the current climate of implementing performance standards in countries such as the U.S., Germany, England, Austria, or Switzerland, it is politically acknowledged that one of the objectives of introducing national standards is the reform of educational practices to support students in optimal learning processes within a climate of systemwide accountability. As a consequence, feedback systems that can not only communicate current states of learner competencies, but also forecast potential remedial pathways toward mastery of previously unattained competencies, are needed for parents, students, teachers, and principals. One of the keys to facilitate this process is to react to the different communicative needs of this clientele through a translation of the diagnostic information that is provided by the assessments. Operationally, this requires the creation of tasks that can be banked on the basis of the demands they place on learner competencies so diagnostically optimal tests can be designed from them, data from these tasks can be analyzed with appropriate SIRT models, and different reporting mechanisms for stakeholders with different informational needs can be developed.

In sum, just as in other rhetorical structures, individual pieces of information are necessary, but not sufficient, for constructing a coherent, concise, and rhetorically effective assessment argument, whether it is for summative accountability reports or individualized diagnostic reports. It is only through the structure of psychometric models that are mapped onto the desired rhetorical structure of the evidentiary argument that such arguments attain those characteristics. It will be argued in the following sections that modern SIRT models with associated reporting mechanisms based on their parameter values provide promising tools to support this process. The next section shows how the structures of various SIRT models are aligned with psychological perspectives on learning and assessment.

PSYCHOLOGICAL PERSPECTIVES AND STRUCTURED ITEM RESPONSE THEORY MODELS FOR EDUCATIONAL ASSESSMENT

A variety of psychometric models from classical test theory and, predominantly, IRT are at the disposal of the measurement specialist at the beginning of the 21st century. Choosing among them can be a difficult task indeed. Although decisions about model choice are sometimes purely resource driven, psychometric models can be theoretically closely aligned with psychological perspectives on educational assessment that can support their choice through disciplinary, rather than logistical, considerations. Because the objective of this chapter is to showcase the advantages of SIRT models for developing complex evidentiary arguments from an information processing perspective, that psychological perspective will be discussed in most detail. However, to fully understand SIRT models, it is useful to examine their interpretative and developmental roots in the behavioral and trait/differential perspectives.

Precursor Developments for Structured Item Response Theory Under Behavioral and Trait/Differential Perspectives

Under a *behavioral perspective* on educational assessment, learning is viewed as occurring through contiguities of stimuli and responses. Educational assessments under a behavioral perspective need to provide opportunities for learners to display exactly those kinds of behaviors

Descriptive Title	Sample Item	General Form	Generation Rules
Basic fact; Minuend > 10	13 -6	A -B	1. $A = 1a$; $B = b$ 2. $(a < b) \, \varepsilon \, U$ 3. $\{H, V\}$
Borrow across zero	403 -138	A -B	1. # digits = $\{3, 4\}$ 2. $A = a_1a_2...; B = b_1b_2...$ 3. $(a_1 > b_1), (a_3 < b_3),$ $(a_4 \gtrless b_4), \, \varepsilon \, U_0$ 4. $b_2 \, \varepsilon \, U_0$ 5. $a_2 = 0$ 6. $P\{\{1,2,3\},\{4\}\}$

Capital letters represent numerals, lower case represent digits.
$x \, \varepsilon \, \{ -- \}$ means chose x with replacement from the set.
$U = \{1, 2,...,9\}$; $U_0 = \{0,1,...,9\}$.
$\{H,V\}$ means choose a horizontal or vertical format.
P means permutation of elements in the set. [Authors' note: The role of this rule in the present example is not clear to us.]

FIGURE 8.2. Two "item forms" from Hively, Patterson, and Page (1968).

about what decisions are to be made, which requires careful attention to the features of task situations strictly from the analyst's point of view. Figure 8.2 shows two item templates or "item forms" for generating mathematics subtraction items, which are taken from Hively, Patterson, and Page (1968).

The example shows how the rules for generating such – rather simple – terms are quite complex. Despite their complexity, they do not take into account how learners mentally process the items and solve them. Indeed, all that matters is that items such as these can be automatically generated so learners display the appropriate behavior, which, in this case, is performing correctly a subtraction of two numbers.

Psychometric models, commensurate with a behavioral perspective on educational assessment, address a learner's propensity to display the targeted behaviors in appropriate stimulus conditions. The variable of interest, typically a continuous latent variable denoted θ, is the unobservable probability of making the targeted response in a stimulus situation. Thus, even a relatively simple Rasch (1960/1980) model from traditional IRT can be used to model ratings of observations under a behavioral perspective. This model has the following form:

$$P(x_{ij} = 1 \mid \theta_i, \beta_j) = \frac{\exp(\theta_i - \beta_j)}{1 + \exp(\theta_i - \beta_j)}, \qquad (8.1)$$

where β_j is a continuous item location or "difficulty" parameter that marks the level of propensity to act that is required to be more likely than not to display the targeted behavior.

Of particular relevance to the discussions of SIRT models that follow, specifically the meaning of their constituent parameters, are three aspects of such psychometric models for behavioral assessment arguments. First, the meaning of the latent variable θ is not only determined by the form of the model or its parameters, but also by the specification of the stimulus settings and the identified aspects of the response. These are design decisions that lie *outside* the formal model structure per se and are driven by substantive considerations. Second, the meaning of θ is specifically related to the range of stimulus classes sampled. When several items generated from the same template comprise a test, θ refers to a specific class of behavior in a specific class of situations. If, however, a test is constructed by defining several item templates and items are generated for each of them, then θ refers to performance from a much broader and more heterogeneous domain. In that case, the model parameters support less precise inference about just what a learner can and cannot do, even though this does not diminish the fact that claims about behavior in the heterogeneous domain may prove useful and important for evaluating learning. Third, systematic relationships between item p-values and behaviorally relevant item features can be observed and modeled in both homogeneous and structured heterogeneous domains. For example, Guttman (1959, 1970), in his theory of "facet design," proposed that classes of items be built around systematic manipulation of key stimulus features similar to the item forms discussed previously. Domain theory motivated the designation of these features, and analysis of variance – based data analysis was used to analyze the impact of the stimulus feature variation on item characteristics. In a similar vein, Suppes and Morningstar (1972) modeled item p-values for computer-generated arithmetic items with a linear model based on stimulus features that defined and differentiated their item forms.

The aforementioned approaches to modeling the relationship between stimulus features and operating characteristics of items predate SIRT models, which formally integrate these relationships into a person-level model structure. A prominent model for this purpose is the *linear logistic test model* (LLTM; Fischer, 1973, Scheiblechner, 1972), a signal development in SIRT. The LLTM expresses the Rasch difficulty parameter of item j (see Equation 8.1) as the sum of basic parameters

$\mathbf{h} = (h_1, \ldots, h_K)$ that reflect additive contributions associated with specific item features that are present in the design of item j by known amounts $\mathbf{q}_j = (q_{j1}, \ldots, q_{jK})$ that can be collected in an item × feature Q-matrix. The formula for the decomposition of the difficulty parameter is as follows:

$$\beta_j = \sum_{k=1}^{K} q_{jk} h_k = \mathbf{q}'_j \mathbf{h}. \tag{8.2}$$

The LLTM is particularly attractive for statistical inferential work because it supports the same formal parameter estimation, model criticism, and hypothesis testing machinery that is brought to bear on basic IRT models (Fisher, 1997).

In contrast to a behavioral perspective on educational assessment, the focus of educational assessment under a *trait/differential perspective* is on unobservable latent characteristics of learners. They are assumed to be relatively stable across time and can be revealed through systematic differences across individuals in various different contexts, from the unique exigencies of everyday life to replicable observations in standardized settings. Under this perspective, psychometric models serve to numerically establish the link between the observed behavior and posited latent characteristics of the learners. Examples include models from classical test theory, which contain a latent true score, and the models of traditional IRT and confirmatory factor analysis.

Importantly, an IRT model used under a trait/differential perspective is formally identical to an IRT model used under a behavioral perspective, but the interpretation of model parameters now has a psychological layer. The latent trait variable θ is now viewed as reflecting more than simply the tendency to perform well in a specified domain of behavioral tasks. It reflects something about what a learner knows or can do that is brought to bear on the tasks at hand but that could also be brought to bear in a wider range of activities in everyday, academic, or occupational arenas. Item parameters are interpreted in terms of how much "resistance" the items offer against the proficiency so conceived. SIRT models come into play under a trait/differential perspective when stimulus features are formally related to response probabilities, as with the LLTM. The interpretation of model parameters now takes into account how the stimulus features cause learners to draw differentially on latent abilities or dispositions rather than on how the features induce them to act in a particular manner.

Structured Item Response Theory Models Under the Information Processing Perspective

Under an *information processing perspective* on educational assessment, unobservable mental *operations*, and not just mental characteristics, are brought to the foreground (Newell & Simon, 1972). These operations involve pattern recognition of external stimuli, the internal representation and retrieval of information, the comparison of different pieces of information, and the establishment of production rules. The focus of educational assessment under an information processing perspective is to design tasks whose successful accomplishment can be explicitly related to the requisite mental components and the differentiable cognitive processes that rely on these components, because, as expressed by Snow and Lohman (1989), "The evidence from cognitive psychology suggests that test performances are comprised of complex assemblies of component information-processing actions that are adapted to task requirements during performance" (p. 317). Thus, the information processing perspective widens the trait/differential perspective by sharpening the theoretical lens focused on decomposing how different latent characteristics of learners enable them to perform constituent cognitive processes for solving tasks.

Historically, researchers such as Carroll (1976) and Sternberg (1977) sought to model performance on psychological test items from an information processing perspective as early as in the latter half of the 1970s. Tasks were developed in light of features that were suggested by a theory of the domain to influence response processes and studies of peoples' problem solving in those situations. Researchers often focused on task features that had a direct impact on enabling cognitive processes such as the total memory load, the ease of retrieval of information, or the number of steps required to solve the task. This early research often focused on tests of psychological abilities and educational aptitudes such as analogies, spatial rotation, and analytic reasoning, rather than on pure knowledge tests. Although knowledge was unarguably required in solving many tasks, they were often constructed so differences among examinees depended more on the facility and accuracy with which examinees carried out elementary processes such as feature extraction and comparison of tokens rather than their ability to perform complex operations such as interpreting a particular statement. But the issue of what features of tasks to focus on is also a matter of the desired

TABLE 8.1. *Examples of production rules*

1) *If* the goal is to process a column in a subtraction problem,
   then write the difference between the numbers as the answer.

This production rule is based on the "smaller-from-larger" bug in whole number subtraction (van Lehn, 1990, p. 258). It gives the right answer for 785–324 but the wrong one for 724–385. A student solving subtraction problems with this rule does not distinguish the feature that the top number in the column is smaller than the bottom number, in which case an expert fires a sequence of production rules known collectively as "borrowing."

2) *If* the goal is to drive a standard transmission car
   and the car is in first gear
   and the car is going more than 10 miles per hour,
   then shift the car into second gear.

This production rule from Anderson (2000, p. 251) requires more detailed conditions to completely describe the action to be carried out. Different detailed production rules could be compiled to carry out the action, and, in fact, are necessary for gear shifters mounted on the floor and the steering column.

3) *If* an active path that includes the failure has not been created
   and the student creates an active path that does not include the failure
   and the edges removed from k are of one power class,
   then the student strategy is splitting the power path.

This production rule is used in an automated system to evaluate student strategy in the Hydrive intelligent tutoring system (Steinberg & Gitomer, 1996). A student is inferred to have used an expert strategy of space splitting if he or she has carried out a sequence of certain troubleshooting actions in a situation with certain conditions, including the results of actions he or she has taken previously.

grain size for representation, modeling, and reporting. As discussed in the previous section, finer grain sizes are more often seen in studies of the details of cognitive processes, whereas coarser grain sizes are more often associated with complex learning.

The choice of focus can be illustrated with the notion of a *production rule*, which triggers actions when specified conditions are satisfied. Table 8.1 shows three examples. These rules are particularly useful for studying differences between novices and experts from an information processing perspective because acquiring expertise in a domain means acquiring those production rules that are necessary to execute *effective* action in that domain. The development of expertise requires that learners distinguish more important from less important cues in the environment, organize information according to the principles and with the representational forms of the domain, reorganize smaller production rules into larger and more effective chunks, and automatize elementary cognitive processes to free resources for novel aspects of a problem (Anderson, 1995). Hence, detailed production rules about a process such as whole-number subtraction (e.g., van Lehn, 1990) are at a much finer level of cognitive granularity than notions such as strategies for sequencing production rules or schemas (e.g., Rumelhart, 1980) for organizing and recalling connected pieces of information.

However, the aims of formal education are not only to impart production rules or particular schemas for solving problems, but also to support the acquisition of broader domain knowledge, meta-cognitive awareness, and multiple learning strategies. Consequently, the features of tasks that are included in an SIRT model need to be relatable to the aspects of the higher-level declarative, procedural, and strategic knowledge structures that are the targets of instruction, as well as to aspects of the lower-level, more generally applicable, cognitive processes. An SIRT model within an information processing perspective on educational assessment thus mediates levels of cognitive grain size. For example, Tatsuoka's (1983) SIRT analysis of mid-level production rules in mixed number subtraction via the *rule-space methodology* is grounded on more detailed analysis of middle-school students' solutions in terms of flowcharts for alternative strategies and the procedures required in each (Klein, Birenbaum, Standiford, & Tatsuoka, 1981). Similarly, consider using the LLTM to model the relationship between stimulus features and item operating characteristics such as difficulty. Within an information processing perspective, the trait θ in such a model is interpreted as the capacity to bring to bear the posited cognitive processes. In terms of production rules, this may be the capability to recognize triggering conditions in a knowledge representation or a real world situation, to perform the appropriate action, or to organize a sequence of production rules in accordance with a strategy. Features of tasks that are modeled with a model such as the LLTM are similar to those that might appear in an application of the LLTM within a behavioral or trait/differential perspective, but they are specifically chosen to highlight knowledge or procedures in the unobservable cognitive activity that produces a response (see also Gierl, Leighton, & Hunka, this volume; Roussos et al., this volume).

Frequently, multivariate SIRT models for θ are needed to account for persons' performance in terms of profiles of knowledge and skill. Tasks may depend on one or more of these dimensions of proficiency, and different tasks may impose different profiles of demand on them. Substantive theory guides the construction of both the tasks and the probability model for analyzing the ensuing performances. For example, Adams, Wilson, and Wang's (1997) *multidimensional random coefficients multinomial logit model* (MRCMLM) is a multivariate generalization of the LLTM. Under the MRCMLM, the probability of a correct response for a dichotomous item is modeled as

$$P(x_{ij}|\,\theta_i, \mathbf{h}_j, \mathbf{a}_j, \mathbf{q}_j) = \Psi(\mathbf{a}'_j\theta_i + \mathbf{q}'_j\mathbf{h}_j). \tag{8.3}$$

Here $\mathbf{a}'_j\theta_i = a_{j1}\theta_1 + \cdots + a_{jD}\theta_D$, where θ is a D-dimensional vector and a_{jd} indicates the extent to which proficiency d is required to succeed on item j, the values depend on the knowledge and skill requirements that have been designed into each item.

In other models, abilities combine conjunctively with the cognitive response processes (e.g., de la Torre & Douglas, 2004; Formann, 1985; Haertel, 1989; Junker & Sijtsma, 2001; Maris, 1999). Collectively, these models are often called "cognitive diagnosis" models (see Nichols, Chipman, & Brennan, 1995), even though this labeling does not reflect the wider array of purposes to which they have been put (Rupp, 2006). In the *deterministic-input, noisy-and-gate* (DINA) model, for example, there is a one-to-one correspondence $a'_j\theta_i = a_{j1}q_{1} + \& + a_{jD}q_{D}$ between the features of items specified in a $\mathbf{Q}$-matrix and elements of learners' knowledge or skills, also termed cognitive "attributes." A person with all necessary attributes responds correctly with probability π_{j1}, and a person lacking one or more attributes responds correctly with probability π_{j0}, both of which are integrated into the following model structure:

$$P(x_{ij} = 1\,|\,\theta_i, \mathbf{q}_j, \pi_{j1}, \pi_{j0}) = \pi_{j0} + (\pi_{j1} - \pi_{j0})\prod_{k=1}^{K}\theta_{ik}^{q_{jk}}, \tag{8.4}$$

where θ_{ik} is a *discrete* latent variable that is 1 if person i possesses attribute k and 0 if not. Such models divide the learners into equivalence classes for each item and classify each learner into one of a fixed set of attribute classes, which assigns them a profile of which attributes they have most likely mastered and which ones they most likely have yet to master. Consequently, these models are also called *restricted latent class models* or *multiple classification models* (see, e.g., Haertel, 1989). Despite their complexity, they neither account for the strength with which information about individual latent variables is indexed by a task nor the completeness of the specification of the latent variable structure in the **Q**-matrix. This is more fully accomplished by models such as the *reparametrized unified model*, also called the *fusion model* (e.g., diBello, Stout, & Roussos, 1995; Hartz, 2002; Templin & Henson, 2005), and its extensions (e.g., Bolt & Fu, 2004; Templin, Roussos, & Stout, 2003).

Similar to these models, Embretson (1985) describes a *multicomponent latent trait model* (MLTM) and a *general component latent trait model* (GLTM) in which the successful completion of distinct subtasks is required to solve an overall task, and the probability of success for each subtask depends on a component of ability associated with that subtask. An "executive process" parameter *e* represents the probability that correct subtask solutions are combined appropriately to produce a successful response for the overall task, and a "guessing" parameter *c* represents the probability of a correct response even if not all subtasks have been completed successfully. For example, an MLTM with $e = 1$ and $g = 0$ was used in Embretson (1985) to model the probability that a learner solves an "analogy" task as the product of succeeding on the "rule construction" and "response evaluation" subtasks. Each subtask response was modeled by a dichotomous Rasch model as follows:

$$P(x_{ijT} = 1 \mid \theta_{i1}, \theta_{i2}, \beta_{j1}, \beta_{j2}) = \prod_{m=1}^{2} \Psi(\theta_{im} - \beta_{jm}), \qquad (8.5)$$

where x_{ijT} is the response to the overall task j by learner i and θ_{i1} and β_{j1} are the proficiency of the learner and the difficulty for subtask 1 (i.e., "rule construction"), whereas θ_{i2} and β_{j2} are the proficiency of the learner and the difficulty for subtask 2 (i.e., "response evaluation"). Under the GLTM, both subtask difficulty parameters β_{j1} and β_{j2} can be further modeled in terms of item features as in the LLTM (see Equation 8.2). Further theoretical extensions to such a SIRT model structure could include multivariate modeling in each step with MRCMLM or DINA building blocks.

SIRT *mixture models* incorporate multiple **Q**-matrices to specify the different approaches that may be used to solve tasks (Mislevy & Verhelst, 1990). Consider the case of *M* strategies; each person applies one strategy consistently to all items, and the item difficulty under strategy *m* depends on features of the task that are relevant under this strategy in accordance with an LLTM structure (see Equation 8.2). Denoting the proficiency of learner i under strategy m as θ_{im} and letting $\phi_{im} = 1$ if he or she uses strategy m and $\phi_{im} = 0$ if he or she does not, the response probability under such a model takes a form such as

$$P(x_{ij} = 1 \mid \theta_i, \phi_i, \mathbf{Q}_j, \mathbf{H}) = \prod_{m=1}^{M} \phi_{im} \left[\Psi \left(\theta_{im} - \sum_{k=1}^{K} q_{jmk} h_{mk} \right) \right]^{x_{ij}}$$

$$\times \left[1 - \Psi \left(\theta_{im} - \sum_{k=1}^{K} q_{jmk} h_{mk} \right) \right]^{1-x_{ij}}. \quad (8.6)$$

In addition to modeling differential strategies under an information processing perspective, it should be noted that this model has also been applied to the case of stage-like development (Wilson, 1989), again high-lighting that the structure of a SIRT model can accommodate different theoretical perspectives on educational assessment. In this case, stage membership is reflected by the ϕ_{im} parameters, and task features q_{jmk} are linked to proficiencies that appear at the various stages.

More generally, it is worth noting at this point that under such a *developmental perspective* on educational assessment it is posited that there exist different levels of integration of knowledge, different degrees of procedural skill, differences in the speed of memory access, and differences in the cognitive representations of the tasks one is to perform at various stages of learning (Glaser, Lesgold, & Lajoie, 1987, p. 77). The focus of educational assessment under a developmental perspective is on providing assessments that characterize growing knowledge structures with related cognitive processes and procedural skills that develop as a domain of proficiency is acquired. To discriminate developmental levels at a given point in time, psychometric models require observations that are differentially likely at various developmental levels so task performances can be assigned to distinct levels on a proficiency scale (e.g., the six scales of language proficiency of the *Common European Framework of Reference for Languages* [CEF; Council of Europe, 2001]). Models that additionally incorporate the hierarchical nature and explanatory variables of schooling as they relate to longitudinal analysis of development are discussed in Muthén (2002) and Skrondal and Rabe-Hesketh (2004).

SIRT models vary in the number of parameters that are estimated and the flexibility with which different variable types and relationships can be modeled. The previous examples concern dichotomous scores for discrete items, but we note that SIRT has also been adapted to ordered categorical item scores (e.g., Templin, He, Roussos, & Stout, 2003), observations evaluated by raters (e.g., Patz & Junker, 1999), and conditionally dependent clusters of item scores, so-called "item bundles" or "testlets" (e.g., Wainer & Wang, 2001; Wang, Bradlow, & Wainer, 2002; Wilson & Adams, 1995). Furthermore, as Templin and Henson (2004) show, any model that produces probability estimates for latent variable classification can be used, alongside the observed total score, to estimate what could be termed "pathways of optimal learning" (see also Tatsuoka, 1995). These pathways show how a continuous composite proficiency variable is related to the mastery of individual attributes and which attributes should be mastered next to trace the pathway most efficiently toward the mastery of all attributes. This kind of information is of high diagnostic value because it allows teachers to provide learners with tasks that are geared to their individual learning needs. Thus, SIRT is not so much a collection of particular set of models as a set of building blocks keyed to various aspects of students, tasks, and observational settings that can be assembled to address a wide range of inferential problems (Almond & Mislevy, 1999; de Boeck & Wilson, 2004; Rupp, 2002; von Davier, 2005).

Finally, it should be noted that the utilization of SIRT models is of two principal kinds in practice. On the one hand, these models can be applied a posteriori to assessments that were not designed to provide diagnostic information at a fine-grain level. Not surprisingly, problems in the convergence of the estimation routines or in the interpretations of predicted data patterns for these models often arise in practice because they are not able to extract precise information about distinct attributes due to the cognitive composition of these assessments (see, e.g., von Davier, 2005). On the other hand, these models can – and should – be applied to assessments whose design reflects a diagnostic purpose a priori (e.g., Templin & Henson, 2006). This means, for example, that the assessment reflects a balance of tasks that provide information about individual attributes and combinations of attributes in such a way that the attributes can be statistically discriminated.

Meaning of Component Latent Variables

As this chapter illustrates, it is essentially impossible to perform educational assessment without considering the *meaning* that can be given to the individual elements of the psychometric models because they are the foundations on which relevant interpretations will be built. No matter which SIRT model is chosen, there exists no "natural" or context-free meaning that is attached to its constituent latent variables. The latent variables in any model obtain their denotative and connotative meanings solely through the theory and psychological perspectives within which the variables themselves and the application of the model are embedded, and those are functions of the grain size of the feedback that is sought about learners and tasks. Consequently, it is fruitless to debate whether the label "attribute" for discrete latent variables is appropriate *generally*, but it *is* fruitful to debate whether it is appropriate *specifically* for the context at hand. In other words, any meanings attached to latent variables are *situated and not generic*.

This characteristic is, of course, shared with any latent variable model, especially those in traditional IRT, because the injection of one or several latent variables into a model, either discrete or continuous, is purely a statistical exercise (see, e.g., Junker, 1999, p. 10). In other words, just as there is no predetermined abstract meaning of continuous latent variables in traditional IRT models, there is no predetermined abstract meaning of continuous or discrete latent variables in diagnostic SIRT models. This implies that specialists for educational assessment need to consider factors such as the conditions of the observations, the accompanying theory that generated the assessment and its delivery, and the intended purposes of the assessment interpretations *en concerto*, all of which require logical and empirical evidence to establish the inferential validity that the quote at the beginning of the chapter asked for.

In the end, the construction of evidentiary arguments for educational assessments grounded in cognitive psychology is identical, in many respects, to other assessment contexts in the sense that an investigator is faced with a kaleidoscope of design and modeling choices that he or she has to decide among and justify. These choices have continued to increase in number due to the improved transfer of knowledge within and across disciplines and due to the technological advances for data collection, storage, and modeling. Not surprisingly, performing and justifying an educational assessment in a comprehensive manner has become even more challenging today, but at the same time it also affords a much richer explanatory rhetoric. To illustrate this potential along with some other key points made so far, the final section of the chapter presents two applications at slightly different levels of cognitive grain size.

ILLUSTRATIONS OF EDUCATIONAL ASSESSMENTS
GROUNDED IN COGNITIVE PSYCHOLOGY

The following examples should be prefaced by noting that cognitive psychology perspectives have, so far, found relatively little practical acceptance in the teaching community and in the international assessment community. We hope to be able to show that educational assessments informed by cognitive psychology can play an important role in educational reform by illustrating two applications in Germany where major changes to the educational system are currently underway.

German Context of Educational Reform

As a result of what was termed the "PISA-shock", namely, the unexpectedly poor performance of German secondary school students in all literacy domains on the PISA 2000 assessment, the national organization for school development, the *Standing Conference of the Ministers of Education and Culture* (KMK), released new educational standards for mathematics, the natural sciences, the German language, and the two foreign languages English and French, whose implementation has become mandatory across all 16 federal states. The national standards are a blend of *content and performance standards* (i.e., they are output oriented) and represent an important shift away from the traditional German curricular guidelines, which focused almost exclusively on didactics (i.e., they were input oriented). The new standards contain lists of "can do" statements that describe *competencies* that students should have acquired at a certain transitory point in their educational career (i.e., at the end of 4th, 9th, and 10th grades) and, in some cases, associated levels of performance. It is the mandate of the *Institute for Educational Progress* (IQB) in Berlin, Germany, to operationalize the national educational standards through tasks for classroom implementation and items for standardized national assessments. The descriptions of the competencies in the standards are grounded in theoretical models of domain expertise that incorporate information from different cognitive psychology frameworks, as discussed previously. The relationship between the theoretical models of competency and cognitive modeling endeavours are illustrated in the following for mathematics – with reference to summative evaluation – and French – with reference to formative evaluation.

Theoretical Models of Competencies for Mathematics and First Foreign Languages (English & French)

The national educational standards for mathematics extend the PISA 2003 framework for mathematical literacy (OECD, 2003) and define six *general mathematical competencies* at a moderate cognitive grain size: (a) to argue mathematically; (b) to solve problems mathematically; (c) to model mathematically; (d) to use mathematical representations; (e) to work with symbolic, formal, and technical aspects of mathematics; and (f) to communicate about mathematics. These competencies are activated during mathematical problem-solving tasks along with five *sets of domain-specific mathematical competencies* in the areas (a) numbers, (b) measurement, (c) objects and graphs, (d) functional relationships, and (e) probability and statistics. Depending on the cognitive processes involved in responding, each task can be classified as belonging to one of three complexity levels, which form, together with the competency areas, a three-dimensional space where tasks can be located (KMK, 2003, 2004). Task characteristics and task demands can now be used for developing a cognitively structured national item bank for standards-based assessment accordingly, which allows for the empirical evaluation of the postulated proficiency structures through SIRT models.[3]

The national educational standards for English and French as second languages are based on the CEF (Council of Europe, 2001), which was developed based on extensive syntheses of theories on second language acquisition, language use, and language assessment. Its rating scales for student performance were validated using qualitative analyses with committees of experts and a multifaceted Rasch scaling of the descriptors (North & Schneider, 1998). The CEF distinguishes four general competencies at a coarse cognitive grain size: (a) the ability to use knowledge about individual characteristics; (b) the ability to use declarative knowledge; (c) the ability to use procedural knowledge; and (d) the ability to learn in a self-regulated fashion, along with three communicative competencies at an equally coarse grain size: (a) linguistic, (b) sociolinguistic, and (c) pragmatic competencies. Similar to mathematics, these competencies get activated through problem-solving tasks, in this case involving communicative acts (i.e., reading, listening, writing, speaking, linguistic mediation). Each task that is being developed for the new national item bank for standards-based assessment of linguistic proficiency is coded according to these competencies.

[3] In fact, in accordance with the educational standards (KMK, 2003, 2004), each general mathematical competency was further broken down into finer levels of detail, resulting in 15 specific mathematical competencies. Each domain-specific mathematical competency was also further broken down into two levels, resulting in a total of 46 domain-specific mathematical competencies. However, this number is too large to be estimable with the models described in this chapter.

Traditional and Cognitive Diagnostic Approaches to Competency Scaling

For both mathematics and foreign language tasks, the standard proficiency scaling approach of national assessment data typically consists of a Rasch scaling or traditional IRT scaling of the tasks along one or multiple latent dimensions (e.g., OECD, 2003; Rost, 2004). With the aid of information about task features that impact processing characteristics, empirical information about item operating characteristics, and consensual standard-setting methods, proficiency scales are typically defined on the latent dimensions through supplementary analyses that lie outside the formal structure of the primary scaling models (e.g., Beaton & Allen, 1992; Cizek, 2001; Hartig & Frey, 2005). This leads to the definition of marker items that index proficiency levels along the latent continua of competency along which learners can be placed. In other words, this approach reflects both trait differential and developmental perspectives on educational assessments. This scaling approach is seen as a means of generating empirical yardsticks for comparison and as a means of empirically verifying the proposed model of competency. It also reflects an information processing perspective in terms of the substantive inferences about cognition that are desired.

Because the explicit objective of standards-based educational assessments is not only to merely provide a norm-referenced snapshot of learner performance, but also to provide maximally diagnostic information for students, parents, and teachers, alternative instructional and assessment frameworks for classrooms are sorely needed. Therefore, a modular system of instructional activities has been developed for implementation purposes in the domain of mathematics by the IQB, which illustrates how modifications of tasks in terms of supplementary materials, openness of questions, or level of abstractness result in varying cognitive demands. This allows teachers to construct their own tabular representations of which competencies are required and to what degree for each task they design and modify.

An example of such task variations is presented in Table 8.2, with associated representation of cognitive demands presented in Table 8.3. These specifications can now be used to carefully design classroom tests and, at a large-scale assessment level, to model the resulting data with a suitable diagnostic SIRT model such as the fusion model for polytomous attributes. In other words, an information processing perspective is applied to both the task design and, later, to the analysis and

TABLE 8.2. *Task variations for sample mathematics task*

Variation	Material	Question
I	---	The sides on a right-angled triangle are of length 3 cm and 5 cm. Compute the length of the hypotenuse.
II		In order to get from point A to B many drivers use the 'shortcut' through a side street rather than going around the corner on the main streets. In percent of the distance between A and B on the main streets, how much shorter is the shortcut?
III		In order to get from point A to B many drivers use the 'shortcut' through a side street rather than going around the corner on the main streets. If one can go, on average, 30 km per hour on the side street and 50 km per hour on the main streets, will the shortcut get one from A to B faster?
IV		In order to get from point A to B many drivers use the 'shortcut' through a side street rather than going around the corner on the main streets. Assume that you are allowed to go 30 km per hour on the side street. What is the maximum speed limit on the main streets that is allowable for the shortcut to save the driver time?

Variation	Material	Question
V		In order to get from point A to B many drivers use the 'shortcut' through a side street rather than going around the corner on the main streets. Assume that you are allowed to go 30 km per hour on the side street. What is the maximum speed limit on the main streets that is allowable for the shortcut to save the driver time? (a) Construct a table that shows the relationship between the unknown main street length (v) and the speed limit (u). (b) Explain - without formulas - that the relationship between u and v has a maximum at some point.
VI		In order to get from point A to B many drivers use the direct 'shortcut' through the Canalettostrasse and the Nicolaistrasse rather than going around the corner on the main streets Stuebelallee and Fetscherstrasse. Under which conditions is it advisable to use the shortcut? Explain your answer.

TABLE 8.3. *Cognitive task demands for sample mathematics task*

Variation	GM1	GM2	GM3	GM4	GM5	GM6	DM1	DM2	DM3	DM4	DM5
I	0	0	0	0	2	0	0	0	2	0	0
II	2	1	1	1	1	0	2	0	2	0	0
III	2	1	1	1	1	0	0	0	2	1	0
IV	2	1	1	1	1	0	0	0	2	2	0
V	2	2	2	2	2	2	0	0	2	1	0
VI	2	2	2	2	2	2	0	0	2	2	0

Notes: GM, general mathematical competency area; DM, domain-specific mathematical competency area; GM1, to argue mathematically; GM2, to solve problems mathematically; GM3, to model mathematically; GM4, to use mathematical representations; GM5, to work with symbolic, formal, and technical aspects of mathematics; GM6, to communicate about mathematics; DM1, numbers; DM2, objects and graphs; DM3, measurement; DM4, functional relationships; DM5, probability and statistics; 0, competency not required; 1, competency required but not essential; 2, competency required and essential.

interpretation of data collected from national student samples, with task information being directly integrated into the formal structure of the models used for proficiency scaling.

In the domains of English and French, the development of curricular activities is guided by the instructional framework of task-based learning (e.g., Nunan & Swan, 2004; Edwards & Willis, 2005), where each task spans multiple lessons and results in various observable behaviors concerning both the process and the product. Here, instructional design and resulting assessments also take into consideration a sociocultural perspective on learning. To validate the task demands empirically and to provide learners with direct formative feedback, research is conducted at the IQB to investigate how performance on the most effective tasks in the prepiloting phase can be modeled with SIRT models. This requires the interdisciplinary collaboration of the same consortium of didactic and measurement experts for French and English in Europe that was already involved in the process of task writing.

The cognitive variable structure for a sample interpretative reading task for a fictional text is presented in Figure 8.3, which uses the language of the ECD framework.[4]

To the left of the figure is the *student model*. Each node is a latent variable representing an aspect of competence, and the directed edges

---

[4] This is an integrative task in which the response would be typed. However, only the contribution of reading ability to the response is modeled for illustration purposes.

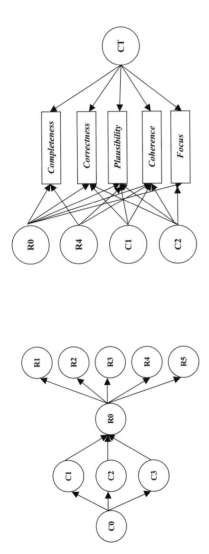

Student Model

C0 = Ability to develop, modify, and use enabling communicative competencies
C1 = Ability to obtain, retain, and use linguistic knowledge
C2 = Ability to obtain, retain, and use sociocultural knowledge
C3 = Ability to obtain, retain, and use pragmatic knowledge

Evidence Model

R0 = Ability to comprehend written texts
R1 = Ability to comprehend discrete information in texts
R2 = Ability to comprehend the basic information in texts
R3 = Ability to learn factual information from texts
R4 = Ability to interpret the meaning of texts
R5 = Ability to integrate information across texts

CT = Context variable to account for testlet effects

All variables except CT are coded on a six-point scale ranging from A1 = *Breakthrough* to C2 = *Mastery* (see CEFL, 2001, pp. 9-15 and pp. 22-25).

FIGURE 8.3. Graphical representation of cognitive variable structure for an interpretative French reading task.

233

represent dependencies among those variables. This graph reflects beliefs about learner competencies proposed by subject matter experts. The ability to develop, modify, and use enabling communicative competencies (C0) is viewed as influencing linguistic (C1), sociocultural (C2), and pragmatic (C3) communicative competencies. These competencies are the enabling linguistic foundations for global reading comprehension (R0), which can be broken down into five different aspects (R1–R5).

To the right of the figure is an *evidence model* for a particular task. The evidence model graph reflects subject matter experts' beliefs about several aspects of the assessment. The rectangles represent observable variables, that is, the features of performance that are evaluated. They are depicted as depending on a subset of the student model variables, the relationship conditioned by theoretically relevant features of the task (i.e., task model variables, not shown in this figure). Here, the overall reading ability (R0) is believed to influence all five observable variables whereas the specific interpretative reading ability (R4) is believed to influence the completeness, plausibility, and coherence of the response. Linguistic ability (C1) is believed to influence the correctness, plausibility, and coherence of the response, whereas sociocultural knowledge (C2) is believed to influence the correctness, coherence, and focus of the response. Finally, a context variable (CT) is added to the model to account for the response dependencies unique to this task, analogous to the Bradlow, Wainer, and Wang (1999) "testlet" model. This structure can now be modeled with, for example, the aid of a Bayesian inference network (e.g., Levy & Mislevy, 2004; Yan, Mislevy, & Almond, 2003) once sufficient amounts of data have been collected and can be tested against alternative representations of the student and evidence models.

In sum, the advantages of such cognitively motivated educational assessments are manifold. Probably most important is the fact that they make explicit the belief structure about competencies and task performance that is at the heart of the assessment design all along and that they allow for an empirical validation of this structure with a concurrent profiling of the learners. Educational assessments modeled in such ways strongly transcend the rank-ordering functionality of traditional assessments and can play a vital role in supporting the transformation of an instructional culture within a standards-based reform.

CONCLUSION

This chapter demonstrates how cognitive psychology can play an integral role in answering the questions that were laid out in the quote by

Messick (1984) at the beginning of the chapter. As advocated by numerous researchers (e.g., Embretson, 1994; Mislevy, 1996; Nichols, 1994), a cognitive psychology perspective should *not be overlaid a posteriori but integrated a priori* into the educational assessment design and be a prominent lens with which specialists think about their decision making. Although the level of grain size in the experimental tradition of cognitive psychology and the diagnostic tradition of educational assessment are certainly different, operationalizations of constructs and their relationships can be linked to one another with the help of SIRT models to create a coherent evidentiary rhetoric about learner competencies. Importantly, when educational assessments are carefully designed and viewed as interventions in the experimental sense, this distance can be shortened, which allows for a greater interchange and synergy between the two disciplines (see also Borsboom, Mellenbergh, & van Heerden, 2004, for a related discussion of the conceptualization of validity, and Borsboom & Mellenbergh, this volume).

Such endeavours were shown to be entirely compatible with competency-based performance standards in educational systems around the world that aim to (a) foster student learning, (b) provide insights into potential remedial pathways for learners, and (c) serve local and national accountability purposes. Although an integration of cognitive psychology into educational assessment design may be resource-intensive in terms of time, expertise, and infrastructure, its theoretical and practically realizable benefits typically warrant the investment. In general, it is also important to remember that even if challenges in modeling data from such assessments with sophisticated SIRT models arise in a given practical context, the assessment itself has certainly only benefited from a careful design and will retain its educational value despite any potential modeling limitations. In that sense, the integration of cognitive psychology into the process of designing, analyzing, and interpreting educational assessments represents an added value whose realization is certainly worth the necessary investments.

References

Adams, R., Wilson, M. R., & Wang, W.-C. (1997). The multidimensional random coefficients multinomial logit model. *Applied Psychological Measurement, 21,* 1–23.

Almond, R. G., & Mislevy, R. J. (1999). Graphical models and computerized adaptive testing. *Applied Psychological Measurement, 23,* 223–237.

Anderson, J. R. (1995). *Learning and memory: An integrated approach.* New York: Wiley.

Anderson, J. R. (2000). *Cognitive psychology and its implications* (5th ed.). New York: Worth.

Anderson, J. R., & Gluck, K. A. (2001). What role do cognitive architectures play in intelligent tutoring systems? In S. M. Carver & D. Klahr (Eds.), *Cognition and instruction: Twenty-five years of progress* (pp. 227–261). Mahwah, NJ: Erlbaum.

Baumert, J., Artelt, C., Klieme, E., Neubrand, M., Prenzel, M. Schiefele, U., Schneider, W., Stanat, P., Tillmann, K.-J., & Weiß, M. (Eds.). (2001). *[PISA 2000. Achievement of basic competencies for German students in an international comparison]*. Opladen: Leske & Budrich.

Beaton, A. E., & Allen, N. (1992). Interpreting scales through scale anchoring. *Journal of Educational Statistics, 17*, 191–204.

Bechtel, W., Abrahamsen, A., & Graham, G. (1998). Part I. The life of cognitive science. In W. Bechtel & G. Graham (Eds.), *A companion to cognitive science* (pp. 2–104). Boston, MA: Blackwell.

Bolt, D., & Fu, J. (2004, April). *A polytomous extension of the fusion model and its Bayesian parameter estimation*. Paper presented at the annual meeting of the National Council on Measurement in Education, San Diego.

Borsboom, D., Mellenbergh, G. J., & van Heerden, J. (2004). The concept of validity. *Psychological Review, 111*, 1061–1071.

Bradlow, E. T., Wainer, H., & Wang, X. (1999). A Bayesian random effects model for testlets. *Psychometrika, 64*, 153–168.

Carroll, J. B. (1976). Psychometric tests as cognitive tasks: A new structure of intellect. In L. B. Resnick (Ed.), *The nature of intelligence* (pp. 27–57). Hillsdale, NJ: Erlbaum.

Cizek, G. (2001). (Ed.). *Setting performance standards: Concepts, methods and perspectives*. Mahwah, NJ: Erlbaum.

Clark, A. (1997). *Being there: Putting brain, body and world together again*. Cambridge, MA: MIT Press.

Council of Europe (Europarat). (2001). *Common European reference framework for languages*. Accessed November 28, 2006, from www.coe.int/t/dg4/linguistic/CADRE˙EN.asp

de Boeck, P., & Wilson, M. (Eds.). (2004). *Explanatory item response models: A generalized linear and nonlinear approach*. New York: Springer.

de la Torre, J., & Douglas, J. (2004). Higher-order latent trait models for cognitive diagnosis. *Psychometrika, 69*, 333–353.

diBello, L.V., Stout, W. F., & Roussos, L. (1995). Unified cognitive psychometric assessment likelihood-based classification techniques. In P. D. Nichols, S. F. Chipman, & R. L. Brennan (Eds.), *Cognitively diagnostic assessment* (pp. 361–390). Hillsdale, NJ: Erlbaum.

Drum, P. A., Calfee, R. C., & Cook, L. K. (1981). The effects of surface structure variables on performance in reading comprehension tests. *Reading Research Quarterly, 16*, 486–514.

Edwards, C., & Willis, J. (Eds.). (2005). *Teachers exploring tasks in English language teaching*. Hampshire, England: Palgrave Macmillan.

Embretson, S. E. (1985). A general latent trait model for response processes. *Psychometrika, 49*, 175–186.

Embretson, S. E. (1994). Applications of cognitive design systems to test development. In C. R. Reynolds (Ed.), *Cognitive assessment: A multidisciplinary perspective* (pp. 107–135). New York: Plenum Press.

Enright, M. K., Grabe, W., Koda, K., Mosenthal, P., Mulcahy-Ernt, P., & Schedl, M. (2000). *TOEFL 2000 reading framework: A working paper* (TOEFL Monograph Series No. MS-17). Princeton, NJ: Educational Testing Service.

Fischer, G. H. (1973). The linear logistic test model as an instrument in educational research. *Acta Psychologica, 37*, 359–374.

Fischer, G. H. (1997). Unidimensional linear logistic Rasch models. In W. J. van der Linden & R. K. Hambleton (Eds.), *Handbook of modern item response theory* (pp. 221–224). New York: Springer Verlag.

Formann, A. K. (1985). Constrained latent class models: Theory and applications. *British Journal of Mathematical and Statistical Psychology, 38*, 87–111.

Freedle, R., & Kostin, I. (1993). The prediction of TOEFL reading item difficulty: Implications for construct validity. *Language Testing, 10*, 133–170.

Freidin, R. (1991). *Principles and parameters in comparative grammar.* Cambridge, MA: MIT Press.

Glaser, R., Lesgold, A., & Lajoie, S. (1987). Toward a cognitive theory for the measurement of achievement. In R. Ronning, J. Glover, J. C. Conoley, & J. Witt (Eds.), *The influence of cognitive psychology on testing and measurement: The Buros-Nebraska Symposium on Measurement and Testing* (Vol. 3; pp. 41–85). Hillsdale, NJ: Erlbaum.

Gorin, J. S., & Embretson, S. E. (2006). Predicting item properties without tryout: Cognitive modeling of paragraph comprehension items. *Applied Psychological Measurement, 30*(5), 394–411.

Greeno, J. G., & Moore, J. L. (1993). Situativity and symbols: Response to Vera and Simon. *Cognitive Science, 17*, 49–59.

Guttman, L. (1959). A structural theory for inter-group beliefs and action. *American Sociological Review, 24*, 318–328.

Guttman, L. (1970). Integration of test design and analysis. *Proceedings of the 1969 Invitational Conference on Testing Problems* (pp. 53–65). Princeton, NJ: Educational Testing Service.

Haertel, E. H. (1989). Using restricted latent class models to map the skill structure of achievement items. *Journal of Educational Measurement, 26*, 333–352.

Hartig, J., & Frey, A. (2005, July). *Application of different explanatory item response models for model based proficiency scaling.* Paper presented at the 14th international meeting of the Psychometric Society, Tilburg, The Netherlands.

Hartz, S. M. (2002). *A Bayesian framework for the unified model for assessing cognitive abilities: Blending theory with practicality.* Unpublished doctoral dissertation, University of Illinois at Urbana–Champaign, Department of Statistics.

Hively, W., Patterson, H. L., & Page, S. H. (1968). A "universe-defined" system of arithmetic achievement tests. *Journal of Educational Measurement, 5*, 275–290.

Junker, B. W. (1999). *Some statistical models and computational methods that may be useful for cognitively-relevant assessment.* Unpublished manuscript. Accessed November 28, 2006, from http://www.stat.cmu.edu/~brian/nrc/cfa

Junker, B. W., & Sijtsma, K. (2001). Cognitive assessment models with few assumptions, and connections with nonparametric item response theory. *Applied Psychological Measurement, 25,* 258–272.

Klein, M. F., Birenbaum, M., Standiford, S. N., & Tatsuoka, K. K. (1981). *Logical error analysis and construction of tests to diagnose student "bugs" in addition and subtraction of fractions* (Research Report 81–6). Urbana: Computer-Based Education Research Laboratory, University of Illinois.

KMK. (2003). [National educational standards for mathematics at the lower secondary level (Mittlerer Schulabschluss)]. Munich, Germany: Wolters Kluwe Deutschland.

KMK. (2004). [National educational standards for mathematics at the lower secondary level (Hauptschulabschluss)]. Munich, Germany: Wolters Kluwe Deutschland.

Levy, R., & Mislevy, R. J. (2004). Specifying and refining a measurement model for a computer-based interactive assessment. *International Journal of Testing, 4,* 333–369.

Lord, F. M., & Novick, M. R. (1968). *Statistical theories of mental test scores.* Reading, MA: Addison-Wesley.

Maris, E. (1999). Estimating multiple classification latent class models. *Psychometrika, 64,* 187–212.

Messick, S. (1994). The interplay of evidence and consequences in the validation of performance assessments. *Educational Researcher, 23*(2), 13–23.

Mislevy, R. J. (1996). Test theory reconceived. *Journal of Educational Measurement, 33,* 379–416.

Mislevy, R. J., & Verhelst, N. (1990). Modeling item responses when different subjects employ different solution strategies. *Psychometrika, 55,* 195–215.

Mislevy, R. J., Steinberg, L. S., & Almond, R. G. (2003). On the structure of educational assessments. *Measurement: Interdisciplinary Research and Perspectives, 1,* 3–67.

Mosenthal, P. B. (1996). Understanding the strategies of document literacy and their conditions of use. *Journal of Educational Psychology, 88,* 314–332.

Mullis, I. V. S., Martin, M. O., & Foy, P. (2005). *IEA's TIMSS 2003 international report on achievement in the mathematics domain: Findings from a developmental project.* Chestnut Hill, MA: TIMSS & PIRLS International Study Center, Boston College.

Muthén, B. O. (2002). Beyond SEM: General latent variable modeling. *Behaviourmetrika, 29,* 81–117.

National Research Council. (2000). *How people learn: Brain, mind, experience, and school.*Washington, DC:National Academy Press.

Newell, A., & Simon, H. A. (1972). *Human problem solving.* Englewood Cliffs, NJ: Prentice Hall.

Nichols, P. (1994). A framework for developing cognitively diagnostic assessments. *Review of Educational Research, 64,* 575–603.

Nichols, P. D., Chipman, S. F., & Brennan, R. L. (Eds.). (1995). *Cognitively diagnostic assessment.* Hillsdale, NJ: Erlbaum.

North, B., & Schneider, G. (1998). Scaling descriptors for language proficiency scales. *Language Testing, 15,* 217–262.

Nunan, D., & Swan, M. (2004). *Task-based language teaching.* Cambridge, UK: Cambridge University Press.

OECD. (2003). *PISA 2003 assessment framework: Mathematics, reading, science and problem solving knowledge and skills.* Retrieved November 28, 2006, from www.pisa.oecd.org/dataoecd/46/14/33694881.pdf

Patz, R. J., & Junker, B. W. (1999). Applications and extensions of MCMC in IRT: Multiple item types, missing data, and rated responses. *Journal of Educational and Behavioural Statistics, 24,* 342–366.

Rasch, G. (1960/1980). *Probabilistic models for some intelligence and attainment tests.* Copenhagen: Danish Institute for Educational Research. (reprint: Chicago: University of Chicago Press).

Rost, J. (2004). [Psychometric models to assess the attainment of national educational standards with models of competency]. *Zeitschrift für Pädagogik, 50*(5), 662–679.

Rumelhart, D. A. (1980). Schemata: The building blocks of cognition. In R. Spiro, B. Bruce, & W. Brewer (Eds.), *Theoretical issues in reading comprehension* (pp. 33–58). Hillsdale, NJ: Erlbaum.

Rupp, A. A. (2002). Feature selection for choosing and assembling measurement models: a building-block-based organization. *International Journal of Testing, 2,* 311–360.

Rupp, A. A. (in press). The answer is in the question: A guide for investigating and describing the theoretical foundations and statistical properties of cognitive psychometric models. *International Journal of Testing.*

Rupp, A. A., Garcia, P., & Jamieson, J. (2001). Combining multiple regression and CART to understand difficulty in second language reading and listening comprehension test items. *International Journal of Testing, 1,* 185–216.

Scheiblechner, H. (1972). [The learning and solution of complex cognitive tasks.]*Zeitschrift für experimentalle und Angewandte Psychologie, 19,* 476–506.

Schraagen, J. M., Chipman, S. F., & Shalin, V. J. (2000). *Cognitive task analysis.* Mahwah, NJ: Erlbaum.

Schum, D. A. (1994). *The evidential foundations of probabilistic reasoning.* New York: Wiley.

Sheehan, K. M., & Ginther, A. (2001). *What do passage-based MC verbal reasoning items really measure? An analysis of the cognitive skills underlying performance on the current TOEFL reading section.* Paper presented at the 2000 annual meeting of the National Council of Measurement in Education, New Orleans, LA.

Sheehan, K. M., & Mislevy, R. J. (2001). *An inquiry into the nature of the sentence-completion task: Implications for item generation* (GRE Board Report No. 95–17bP). Princeton, NJ: Educational Testing Service.

Skrondal, A., & Rabe-Hesketh, S. (2004). *Generalized latent variable modeling: Multilevel, longitudinal, and structural equation modeling.* Boca Raton, FL: Sage.

Snow, R. E., & Lohman, D. F. (1989). Implications of cognitive psychology for educational measurement. In R. L. Linn (Ed.), *Educational measurement* (3rd ed., pp. 263–331). New York: American Council on Education/Macmillan.

Steinberg, L. S., & Gitomer, D. G. (1996). Intelligent tutoring and assessment built on an understanding of a technical problem-solving task. *Instructional Science, 24,* 223–258.

Sternberg, R. J. (1977). *Intelligence, information processing and analogical reasoning: The componential analysis of human abilities.* New York: Wiley.

Suppes, P., & Morningstar, M. (1972). *Computer-assisted instruction at Stanford, 1966–68: Data, models, and evaluation of the arithmetic programs.* New York: Academic Press.

Tatsuoka, K. K. (1983). Rule-space: An approach for dealing with misconceptions based on item response theory. *Journal of Educational Measurement, 20,* 345–354.

Tatsuoka, K. K. (1995). Architecture of knowledge structures and cognitive diagnosis: A statistical pattern recognition and classification approach. In P. D. Nichols, S. F. Chipman, & R. L. Brennan (Eds.), *Cognitively diagnostic assessment* (pp. 327–360). Hillsdale, NJ: Erlbaum.

Templin, J. L., He, X., Roussos, L., & Stout, W. (2003). *The pseudo-item method: A simple technique for analysis of polytomous data with the fusion model.* Unpublished technical report draft for the ETS External Diagnostic Group. Department of Psychology, University of Illinois at Urbana-Champaign, IL.

Templin, J. L., & Henson, R. A. (2004). *Creating a proficiency scale with models for cognitive diagnosis.* Unpublished technical report for the ETS External Diagnostic Group. Department of Psychology, University of Illinois at Urbana-Champaign, IL.

Templin, J. L., & Henson, R. A. (2006). Measurement of psychological disorders using cognitive diagnosis models. *Psychological Methods, 11,* 287–305.

Templin, J. L., & Henson, R. A. (2005). *The random effects reparametrized unified model: A model for joint estimation of discrete skills and continuous ability.* Manuscript submitted for publication.

Templin, J. L., Roussos, L., & Stout, W. (2003). *An extension of the current fusion model to treat polytomous attributes.* Unpublished Technical Report for the ETS External Diagnostic Group. Department of Psychology, University of Illinois at Urbana-Champaign, IL.

Toulmin, S. E. (1958). *The uses of argument.* Cambridge, UK: Cambridge University Press.

Underwood, G., & Bait, V. (1996). *Reading and understanding.* Cambridge, MA: Blackwell.

van der Linden, W. J., & Hambleton, R. K. (1997). *Handbook of modern item response theory.* New York: Springer-Verlag.

van Lehn, K. (1989). Problem-solving and cognitive skill acquisition. In M. Posner (Ed.), *The foundations of cognitive science* (pp. 527–580). Cambridge, MA: MIT Press.

van Lehn, K. (1990). *Mind bugs: The origins of procedural misconceptions.* Cambridge, MA: MIT Press.

van Lehn, K. (2004, October). *The Andes intelligent physics tutoring system: Lessons learned about assessment.* Paper presented at the 4th ETS Spearman conference, Philadelphia.

von Davier, M. (2005). *A general diagnostic model applied to language testing data* (Research Report No. RR–05–16). Princeton, NJ: Educational Testing Service.

Wainer, H., & Wang, X. (2001). *Using a new statistical model for testlets to score TOEFL* (Technical Report No. TR-16). Princeton, NJ: Educational Testing Service.

Wang, X., Bradlow, E. T., & Wainer, H. (2002). *A general Bayesian model for testlets: Theory and applications* (Research Report No. 02–02). Princeton, NJ: Educational Testing Service.

Wilson, M. R. (1989). Saltus: A psychometric model of discontinuity in cognitive development. *Psychological Bulletin, 105,* 276–289.

Wilson, M. R., & Adams, R. J. (1995). Rasch models for item bundles. *Psychometrika, 60,* 181–198.

Yan, D., Mislevy, R. J., & Almond, R. G. (2003). *Design and analysis in a cognitive assessment* (Research Report No. RR-03–32). Princeton, NJ: Educational Testing Service.

9

Using the Attribute Hierarchy Method to Make Diagnostic Inferences About Examinees' Cognitive Skills

Mark J. Gierl, Jacqueline P. Leighton,
and Stephen M. Hunka

INTRODUCTION

Many educational assessments are based on cognitive problem-solving tasks. *Cognitive diagnostic assessments* are designed to model examinees' cognitive performances on these tasks and yield specific information about their problem-solving strengths and weaknesses. Although most psychometric models are based on latent trait theories, a cognitive diagnostic assessment requires a *cognitive information processing approach* to model the psychology of test performance because the score inference is specifically targeted to examinees' cognitive skills. Latent trait theories posit that a small number of stable underlying characteristics or traits can be used to explain test performance. Individual differences on these traits account for variation in performance over a range of testing situations (Messick, 1989). Trait performance is often used to classify or rank examinees because these traits are specified at a large grain size and are deemed to be stable over time. Cognitive information processing theories require a much deeper understanding of trait performance, where the psychological features of how a trait can produce a performance become the focus of inquiry (cf. Anderson et al., 2004). With a cognitive approach, problem solving is assumed to require the processing of information using relevant sequences of operations. Examinees are *expected* to differ in the knowledge they possess and the processes they apply, thereby producing response variability in each test-taking situation. Because these knowledge structures and processing skills are specified at a small grain size and are expected to vary among examinees within any testing situation, cognitive theories and models can be used to understand and evaluate specific cognitive skills that affect test performance.

This chapter introduces and describes the attribute hierarchy method (AHM) for cognitive assessment (Leighton, Gierl, & Hunka, 2004). The AHM is a psychometric method for classifying examinees' test item responses into a set of structured attribute patterns associated with different components from a *cognitive model of task performance*. This method helps link cognitive theory and psychometric practice to facilitate the development and analyses of educational and psychological tests. Results from AHM analyses yield information on examinees' cognitive strengths and weaknesses. Hence, the method has diagnostic value.

In Section I, we describe the diagnostic process and relate this process to cognitive diagnostic assessment. Then, we highlight some benefits of this testing approach. Finally, we define the phrase *cognitive model* in educational measurement, and explain why these models are important in the development and analysis of cognitive diagnostic assessments. In Second II, we present the AHM. We begin by focusing on the importance of specifying a cognitive model of task performance. A four-step approach for diagnostic testing is also described, where we define the cognitive model of task performance, use the cognitive model to direct test development, analyze and score the examinees' responses according to the cognitive model, and report examinees' scores using this model-based psychometric method. In Section III, we provide a summary and identify areas where additional research is required.

I. CHARACTERISTICS OF A DIAGNOSTIC INFERENCE

Diagnosis was described by the influential philosopher and evaluator Michael Scriven (1991) as:

The process of determining the nature of an affliction, of a putative symptom of disorder, or of poor performance, and/or the report resulting from the process. This may or may not happen to involve identification of the cause of the condition, but it always involves classifying the condition in terms of an accepted typology of afflictions or malfunctions, hence the terms it uses are evaluative. Diagnosis is not a primary type of evaluation; it presupposes that a true evaluation – such as the annual check-up – has already occurred, and has led to the conclusion that something is wrong. The task of diagnosis is classificatory. (p. 124)

This description is helpful for identifying some essential qualities in a cognitive diagnostic assessment. Three aspects of Scriven's description should be noted. First, diagnosis involves the process of determining the nature of poor performance and reporting the results from the process. Similarly, cognitive diagnostic assessment can be described as a process where test results yield information about examinees' cognitive skills and the results from this evaluation are reported. This approach to testing highlights the examinee-by-item interaction, in cognitive terms, where the knowledge, mental processes, and strategies used by an examinee to respond to test items are made explicit (Embretson, 1999; Nichols, 1994). One method of representing this interaction is with a cognitive model of task performance. Test score inferences anchored to a cognitive model should be more interpretable and meaningful for evaluating and understanding performance because the items are designed to measure the examinees' knowledge, processes, and strategies (National Research Council, 2001; Pellegrino, 1988; Pellegrino, Baxter, & Glaser, 1999). The diagnostic testing process used to link examinee performance to the cognitive model requires four steps: (a) specify the cognitive model, (b) develop items to measure the cognitive components described by the model, (c) analyze and score items according to the model, and (d) report the results.

Second, the diagnostic process should lead to the classification of cognitive skills using an accepted reporting system. Cognitive diagnostic assessment outcomes, therefore, should rely on a language for describing examinee thinking that is easily understood and that yields information about the examinees' cognitive problem-solving strengths and weaknesses that can be used by students, teachers, parents, and other stakeholders to understand the psychology of test performance. Cognitive diagnostic assessment information should also be reported to educational stakeholders in a manner that informs learning and instruction (Goodman & Hambleton, 2004).

Third, diagnosis is not a primary type of evaluation. Rather, diagnosis is one step in a much larger undertaking that occurs when a problem is suspected (Hunt, 1995). In other words, cognitive diagnostic assessment occurs as part of a much larger instructional process, where the goal is to identify learning problems and help remediate these problems. An effective cognitive diagnostic assessment must be well integrated into the learning environment, and it must be developed to help teachers understand how students think about and solve problems. These results also provide information that help teachers and students structure and classify cognitive skills. Thus, scores from cognitive diagnostic assessments should be viewed as one source of information that can be combined with other sources of information about the examinee (e.g., results from previous standardized tests, classroom tests, homework assignments, classroom observations) to make instructional decisions.

Potential Benefits of Cognitive Diagnostic Assessment

Cognitive diagnostic assessment may contribute to teaching and learning in two ways. First, it should increase our understanding of student test performance given many educational tests are based on cognitive problem-solving tasks. Test scores serve as merely an indicator of how students think about and solve educational tasks because cognitive performance cannot be observed directly. Instead, we assume that students who correctly solve a task use the appropriate knowledge, processes, and strategies. However, this assumption is rarely substantiated. In some cases, this assumption may be wrong. For example, researchers have demonstrated that examinees can generate correct answers using knowledge and skills that are unrelated to the target of inference specified in the items (e.g., Brown & Burton, 1978; Leighton & Gokiert, 2005; Norris, Leighton, & Phillips, 2004; Poggio et al., 2005). When this disjunction between the target of inference and actual student performance occurs, test score inferences may be inaccurate because the student did not use the knowledge and skills the developer intended to measure. Because cognitive test performance is both covert and often complex, a framework is required to link the examinees' problem-solving skills with interpretations of test performance. The development and use of a cognitive model of task performance provides one approach for identifying and measuring these skills so they can be connected with test performance and test score interpretations.

Second, cognitive diagnostic assessment provides one approach for linking theories of cognition and learning with instruction. Most large-scale educational tests yield little information for students, teachers, and parents about why some students perform poorly or how instructional conditions can be altered to improve learning (National Research Council, 2001). Increasingly, cognitive theory and research is improving our understanding of student performance on a wide range of academic tasks (Anderson, 2005; Anderson & Shunn, 2000; Bransford, Brown, & Cocking, 1999; Donovan, Bransford, & Pellegrino, 1999; Glaser, Lesgold, & Lajoie, 1987; Pellegrino, 1988, 2002; Pellegrino, Baxter, & Glaser, 1999).

This enhanced view of thinking has also lead to a better understanding of how assessment can be used to evaluate learning and improve instruction. Instructional decisions are made, in part, on how students think about and solve problems. Thus, teachers must draw on and, if possible, develop methods for making students' thinking overt so these cognitive skills can be evaluated. Instructional feedback can then focus on overcoming weaknesses. Cognitive models of task performance provide one method for representing thought. Because these models specify the knowledge structures and processing skills required to respond to test items, they can also be used to enhance test score interpretations and to guide instruction when the knowledge and skills specified in the model are identified as weak, given the examinees' test performance. In short, educators need tests that support inferences about examinees' cognitive skills on diverse academic tasks. Student performance on these tests, in turn, can help guide instruction (Pellegrino, 1988, 2002; Pellegrino et al., 1999). Because cognitive diagnostic assessments yield specific score inferences about the examinees' problem-solving strengths and weaknesses, these tests can help link what students' know (and do not know) in an academic domain with instructional methods designed to improve students' problem-solving skills in that domain.

Cognitive Models and Educational Measurement

To make specific inferences about problem solving, cognitive models are required. A cognitive model in educational measurement refers to a simplified description of human problem solving on standardized tasks at some convenient grain size or level of detail in order to facilitate explanation and prediction of students' performance, including their strengths and weaknesses (Leighton & Gierl, in press). These models provide an interpretative framework that can guide item development so test performance can be linked to specific cognitive inferences about examinees' knowledge, processes, and strategies. These models also provide the means for connecting cognitive principles with measurement practices, as Snow and Lohman (1989) explain:

As a substantive focus for cognitive psychology then, 'ability,' the latent trait θ in EPM (educational and psychometric measurement) models, is not considered univocal, except as a convenient summary of amount correct regardless of how obtained. Rather, a score reflects a complex combination of processing skills, strategies, and knowledge components, both procedural and declarative and both controlled and automatic, some of which are variant and some invariant across persons, or tasks, or stages of practice, in any given sample of persons or tasks. In other samples of persons or situations, different combinations and different variants and invariants might come into play. Cognitive psychology's contribution is to analyze these complexes. (pp. 267–268)

Cognitive processes represent a sequence of internal events where information in short- and long-term memory interacts. Short-term working memory is seen as a storage system associated with limited capacity, fast access, and conscious awareness. Long-term memory is seen as a storage system associated with unlimited capacity, slow access, and unconscious awareness. Verbal reports provide a description of the examinees' thought processes when the reported information enters short-term memory. Information in long-term memory can be made available to conscious awareness if it is transferred into short-term memory. However, until this information is accessed and attended to, it will not be consciously experienced. Given these assumptions, cognitive models of task performance can be generated by studying the cognitive processes used by examinees as they respond to items on tests. These models can be created by having examinees think aloud as they solve tasks in a specific domain or content area in order to identify the information requirements and processing skills elicited by the tasks (Ericsson & Simon, 1993; Leighton, 2004; Royer, Cisero, & Carlo, 1993; Taylor & Dionne, 2000; see also Leighton & Gierl, this volume). The model is then evaluated by comparing its fit to competing models using examinee response data from tests as a way of substantiating the components and structure. After extensive evaluation, scrutiny, and revision, the model may also generalize to other groups of examinees and different problem-solving tasks.

A cognitive model of task performance is specified at a small grain size because it magnifies the cognitive processes underlying test performance. Often, a cognitive model of task performance will also reflect a *hierarchy of cognitive processes* within a domain because cognitive processes share dependencies and function within a much larger network of interrelated processes, competencies, and skills (Anderson, Reder, & Simon, 2000; Dawson, 1998; Fodor, 1983; Kuhn, 2001; Mislevy, Steinberg, & Almond, 2003). Assessments based on cognitive models of task performance should be developed so test items directly measure specific cognitive processes of increasing complexity in the understanding of a domain. The items can be designed with this hierarchical order in mind so test item performance is directly linked to information about students' cognitive strengths and weaknesses. Strong inferences about examinees' cognitive skills can be made because the small grain size in these models helps illuminate the knowledge and skills required to perform competently on testing tasks. Specific diagnostic inferences can also be generated when items are developed to measure different components and processes in the model.

The strength of developing test items according to a cognitive model of task performance stems from the detailed information that can be obtained about the knowledge structures and processing skills that produce a test score (see Gorin, this volume). Each item is designed to yield specific information about the students' cognitive strengths and weaknesses. If the target of inference is information about students' cognitive skills, then the small grain size associated with these models is required for generating specific information. This specific information can be generated because the grain size of these models is narrow, thereby increasing the depth to which both knowledge and skills are measured with the test items. A cognitive model of task performance also requires empirical support with psychological evidence from the populations to which inferences will be targeted. Once this model is validated with the population of interest, items can be created that measure specific components of the model, thereby providing developers with a way of controlling the specific cognitive attributes measured by the test.

The weakness of developing items according to a cognitive model of task performance stems from the paucity of information currently available on the knowledge, processes, and strategies that characterize student performance in most testing situations. Moreover, some cognitive researchers believe this situation is unlikely to change in the near future because there is little interest in the outcomes from task analyses (Anderson & Schunn, 2000). Consequently, we have few detailed accounts of educational task performance. Because little is known about how students actually solve items on educational tests, relatively few models exist. And even when these models are available, they rarely guide psychometric analyses because they are usually restricted to a specific domain; they are expensive to develop initially and to refine over time because they require extensive studies of problem solving; and they require cognitive measurement expertise, which is relatively uncommon in educational testing.

II. INCORPORATING COGNITIVE MODELS INTO PSYCHOMETRIC PROCEDURES

Overview of the Attribute Hierarchy Method for Cognitive Assessment

The attribute hierarchy method for cognitive assessment (AHM; Leighton et al., 2004) is a psychometric method for classifying examinees' test item responses into a set of structured attribute patterns associated with different components specified in a cognitive model of task performance. This method illustrates how cognitive performance can be evaluated using an information processing approach because the AHM requires a cognitive model of structured attributes to evaluate examinee performance. These structured attributes, called the *attribute hierarchy*, define the psychological ordering among the attributes required to solve a test problem and, thus, serve as the cognitive model of task performance. The ordering of the attributes may be derived from cognitive considerations about the attribute structure. For example, attribute 1 is a prerequisite to attribute 2 and attribute 2 is a prerequisite to attribute 3, meaning that the attributes appear only once in the hierarchy. The test score inferences, therefore, focus on whether the attributes are present or absent. The ordering may also be derived from procedural considerations about the manner in which attributes are used during problem solving. For example, to solve an item, the examinee may need to use attribute 1 first, attribute 2 second, and then attribute 1 again, meaning the attributes may appear more than once in the hierarchy. The test score inference focuses on the presence of the attributes, as in the first case, but also on the application of these attributes in particular testing situation. By using the attribute hierarchy to create test items to measure the cognitive components described by the model, the test developer can orchestrate which attributes are measured by which items. By using the attribute hierarchy to interpret test performance, the test user achieves control over the scores and the inferences about processes and skills associated with performance. Hence, the hierarchy functions as a map indicating where examinees' have particular strengths and weaknesses. Consequently, the attribute hierarchy has a foundational role in the AHM because it represents both the construct and the knowledge and processing skills that underlie test performance. We describe the AHM according to the four-step diagnostic process presented earlier:

(a) specifying the cognitive model, (b) developing items to measure the model, (c) analyzing and scoring items according to the model, and (d) reporting the results.

Step 1: Specifying the Cognitive Model of Task Performance

The AHM is based on the assumption that test performance depends on a set of hierarchically ordered competencies called *attributes*. An attribute is a description of the procedural or declarative knowledge needed to perform a task in a specific domain. The examinee must possess these attributes to answer test items correctly. Attributes can be viewed as sources of cognitive complexity in test performance. But, more generally, attributes are those basic cognitive processes or skills required to solve test items correctly.

The quality of the test score inferences produced with the AHM depends on accurately identifying a cognitive model of task performance. This model specifies the psychological ordering of the attributes required to solve test items. This cognitive model, which in our case is an attribute hierarchy of test performance, serves a critical function: It provides a working representation of cognitive performance in the domain of interest. The attribute hierarchy is the most important input variable for the AHM because it is used to classify examinees' performance and to make inferences about their cognitive skills.

The cognitive model of task performance, as operationalized in the hierarchy of attributes, can be used to specify different structures of cognitive skills. Leighton et al. (2004) identified four forms of hierarchical structures, as shown in Figure 9.1, and described their possible implications for test development and construct representation. For each example, attribute 1 may be considered a hypothetical starting point because it represents the initial competencies that are prerequisite to the attributes that follow, or it may be considered a specific attribute. In Figure 9.1(A), the *linear hierarchy*, attribute 1 is considered prerequisite to attribute 2, attributes 1 and 2 are prerequisite to attribute 3, attributes 1 to 3 are considered prerequisite to attribute 4, attributes 1 to 4 are considered prerequisite to attribute 5, and attributes 1 to 5 are considered prerequisite to attribute 6. Specifying that attribute 1 is prerequisite to attribute 2 implies that an examinee is not expected to possess attribute 2 unless attribute 1 is present. In the linear hierarchy, the implication is also that if attribute 1 is not present, then all attributes that follow are not expected to be present. Figure 9.1(D), the *unstructured hierarchy*, represents the other extreme of possible hierarchical structures. In

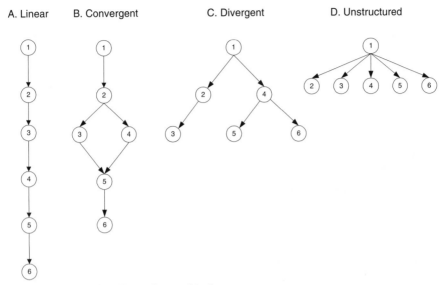

FIGURE 9.1. Four different hierarchical structures.

Figure 9.1(D), attribute 1 is considered prerequisite for attributes 2 to 6. However, unlike Figure 9.1(A), there is no ordering among attributes 2 to 6 in this hierarchy, and there is no unique relationship between the total score and the expected examinee response pattern. Many educational tests in use today could be characterized as an unstructured hierarchy of cognitive attributes because these tests clearly measure different knowledge components and processing skills, but the ordering of these attributes is not specified. Figure 9.1(B) represents the *convergent hierarchy*, where two different branches may be traced from 1 to 6. Attribute 2 is prerequisite to 3 and 4, but 3 or 4 are prerequisite to 5. This hierarchy, like Figure 9.1(A), ends at a single attribute. A convergent hierarchy describes the cognitive competencies leading to a single end state, where this state is represented as the most complex attribute measured by the test items. The final attribute in a convergent hierarchy is complex because its existence depends on all other attributes in the model. In contrast, Figure 9.1(C) represents a *divergent hierarchy* that describes the cognitive competencies leading to multiple end states consisting of two or more attributes that are hierarchically related.

The examples in Figure 9.1 can be expanded and combined easily to form increasingly complex networks of hierarchies, where the complexity varies with the cognitive problem-solving task. They can also be specified using cognitive (i.e., each attribute is used only once in the hierarchy) or procedural (i.e., each attribute may be used more than once in the hierarchy) assumptions. However, in each hierarchy, the same conditions are required to obtain a relationship between the examinees' expected and observed response pattern; namely, that the hierarchical relationships of attributes is a true model of the examinees' cognitive attributes, test items can be written to measure the attributes, and examinees respond without error or a "slip" given the relationship among the items that is specified in the attribute hierarchy (see Borsboom & Mellenbergh, this volume).

To illustrate an application of the AHM within the domain of mathematics, we developed a cognitive hierarchy to account for examinee performance in algebra. The algebra hierarchy is based on our review of the released items from the March 2005 administration of the SAT. Sample algebra items from the SAT Mathematics section can be accessed from the College Board Web site at www.collegeboard.com. The SAT is a standardized test designed to measure college readiness. Both critical thinking and reasoning skills are evaluated. The Mathematics section contains items in the content areas of Number and Operations; Algebra I, II, and Functions; Geometry; and Statistics, Probability, and Data Analysis. Only the items in Algebra I and II were evaluated and used to develop the algebra hierarchy.

In the "Cognitive Models and Educational Measurement" section of this chapter, we noted that cognitive models of task performance guide diagnostic inferences because they are specified at a small grain size, and they magnify the cognitive processes that underlie performance. But we also noted that few of these cognitive models currently exist. Ideally, an empirically tested (or supported) substantive theory of task performance would direct the development of a cognitive model of task performance. But, in the absence of such a theory, a cognitive model must still be specified to create the attribute hierarchy. Another starting point is to present examinees in the target population of interest with the task and, using verbal report methods, record the knowledge, processes, and strategies used by these examinees to solve the task. The model created from the task analysis can be assessed, initially, by evaluating its construct representation relative to the intended test score inferences and, as competing models are developed, by its fit and predictive utility relative to these competing models using examinee response data as a way of substantiating the model components and structure. In short, a task analysis can be used to create the first cognitive model of task performance by sampling items and examinees from the target

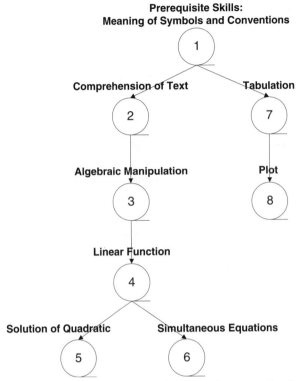

FIGURE 9.2. Cognitive model of task performance in algebra, specified as an attribute hierarchy.

population of interest when a theory or model of task performance is not available.

In conducting the task analysis of the SAT algebra items, we first solved each test item and attempted to identify the mathematical concepts, operations, procedures, and strategies used to solve each item. We then categorized these cognitive attributes so they could be ordered in a logical, hierarchical sequence to summarize problem-solving performance. Our cognitive model of algebra performance is presented in Figure 9.2. Because each attribute is only used once, our hierarchy is based on cognitive, not procedural, considerations about examinee performance. A summary of the component processes underlying each attribute, as identified in the task analysis, is presented in the Appendix. Our algebra hierarchy only serves as an example to illustrate an AHM analysis. Far more research is required to refine this model, including studies that focus on examinee performance using think-aloud methods (see Leighton & Gierl, this volume). The models generated from examinee-based studies could be used to evaluate the knowledge structures and processing skills specified for each attribute and the hierarchical structure of the attributes. Results from think-aloud studies would also help validate the attribute descriptions using both examinees and test items that are comparable to target populations of interest. Although the shortcomings of our task analysis limit the diagnostic inferences we can make about examinees using the algebra hierarchy, it does allow us to illustrate key concepts associated with the AHM. These concepts are presented next.

To calculate the expected examinee response patterns for a specific hierarchy in the AHM, a formal representation of the hierarchy is required. Our representation is guided by Kikumi Tatsuoka's rule-space approach where the adjacency, reachability, incidence, and reduced-incidence matrices are specified (Tatsuoka, 1983, 1995; see also Tatsuoka & Tatsuoka, 1989). To begin to illustrate the matrices associated with the algebra hierarchy, the direct relationships among attributes are specified by a binary adjacency matrix (A) of order (k, k), where k is the number of attributes. The A matrix for the algebra hierarchy in Figure 9.2 is specified as:

$$\begin{bmatrix} 0 & 1 & 0 & 0 & 0 & 0 & 1 & 0 \\ 0 & 0 & 1 & 0 & 0 & 0 & 0 & 0 \\ 0 & 0 & 0 & 1 & 0 & 0 & 0 & 0 \\ 0 & 0 & 0 & 0 & 1 & 1 & 0 & 0 \\ 0 & 0 & 0 & 0 & 0 & 0 & 0 & 0 \\ 0 & 0 & 0 & 0 & 0 & 0 & 0 & 0 \\ 0 & 0 & 0 & 0 & 0 & 0 & 0 & 1 \\ 0 & 0 & 0 & 0 & 0 & 0 & 0 & 0 \end{bmatrix}.$$

In the adjacency matrix, a 1 in the position (j, k) indicates that attribute j is directly connected in the form of a prerequisite to attribute k. The first row indicates, for example, that attribute 1 is a prerequisite to attributes 2 and 7.

To specify the direct and indirect relationships among attributes, a reachability matrix (R) of order (k, k), is used, where k is the number of attributes. The R matrix can be calculated using $R = (A + I)^n$, where n is the integer required for R to reach invariance and can represent the numbers 1 through k. A is the adjacency matrix, and I is an identity matrix. R can also be formed by a series of Boolean additions of rows of the adjacency matrix. The jth row of the R matrix specifies all the attributes, including the jth attribute, for which the jth attribute is a direct or indirect prerequisite. The R matrix for algebra hierarchy is given as:

$$\begin{bmatrix} 1 & 1 & 1 & 1 & 1 & 1 & 1 & 1 \\ 0 & 1 & 1 & 1 & 1 & 1 & 0 & 0 \\ 0 & 0 & 1 & 1 & 1 & 1 & 0 & 0 \\ 0 & 0 & 0 & 1 & 1 & 1 & 0 & 0 \\ 0 & 0 & 0 & 0 & 1 & 0 & 0 & 0 \\ 0 & 0 & 0 & 0 & 0 & 1 & 0 & 0 \\ 0 & 0 & 0 & 0 & 0 & 0 & 1 & 1 \\ 0 & 0 & 0 & 0 & 0 & 0 & 0 & 1 \end{bmatrix}.$$

For the R matrix, row 1 indicates that attribute 1 is a prerequisite to all attributes; row 2 indicates that attribute 2 is a prerequisite to attributes 2 through 6. The same interpretation applies to the other rows. The R matrix is used to create a subset of items based on the structure of the attribute hierarchy.

The set of potential items is considered to be a bank or pool of items that probes all combinations of attributes when the attributes are independent. The size of the pool is $2^k - 1$, where k is the number of attributes. It is described by the incidence matrix (Q) of order (k, i) where k is the number of attributes and i is the number of potential items. In the Q matrix, each item is described by the attributes that are required to respond correctly to the item or, conversely, the attributes required of an examinee for a correct answer. The columns of the Q matrix are created by converting the items ranging from 1 to $2^k - 1$ to their binary form. The Q matrix for the algebra hierarchy, which contains eight attributes, is of the order 8 by 255 (attributes by items). Because the matrix is large, it is not presented. Fortunately, the set of potential items can be reduced, often dramatically, when the attributes are related in a hierarchical structure because the hierarchy imposes dependencies among the attributes, resulting in a reduced Q matrix (Q_r). The Q_r matrix has great importance in the AHM because it specifies the cognitive blueprint for the test, as described in the next step.

Step 2: Developing Items to Measure the Cognitive Model
The hierarchy of attributes required to perform well in a domain must be identified prior to developing a test. This order of events is needed because the hierarchical organization of attributes must guide

the development of test items (Gierl, Leighton, & Hunka, 2000). By using the attribute hierarchy to develop test items, the developer achieves complete control over the specific attributes measured by each item. The Q_r matrix is produced by determining which columns of the R matrix are logically included in columns of the Q matrix, using Boolean inclusion.[1] The Q_r matrix for the algebra hierarchy is:

$$
\begin{bmatrix}
1 & 1 & 1 & 1 & 1 & 1 & 1 & 1 & 1 & 1 & 1 & 1 & 1 & 1 & 1 & 1 & 1 & 1 & 1 & 1 & 1 \\
0 & 1 & 1 & 1 & 1 & 1 & 1 & 0 & 1 & 1 & 1 & 1 & 1 & 1 & 0 & 1 & 1 & 1 & 1 & 1 & 1 \\
0 & 0 & 1 & 1 & 1 & 1 & 1 & 0 & 0 & 1 & 1 & 1 & 1 & 1 & 0 & 0 & 1 & 1 & 1 & 1 & 1 \\
0 & 0 & 0 & 1 & 1 & 1 & 1 & 0 & 0 & 0 & 1 & 1 & 1 & 1 & 0 & 0 & 0 & 1 & 1 & 1 & 1 \\
0 & 0 & 0 & 0 & 1 & 0 & 1 & 0 & 0 & 0 & 0 & 1 & 0 & 1 & 0 & 0 & 0 & 0 & 1 & 0 & 1 \\
0 & 0 & 0 & 0 & 0 & 1 & 1 & 0 & 0 & 0 & 0 & 0 & 1 & 1 & 0 & 0 & 0 & 0 & 0 & 1 & 1 \\
0 & 0 & 0 & 0 & 0 & 0 & 0 & 1 & 1 & 1 & 1 & 1 & 1 & 1 & 1 & 1 & 1 & 1 & 1 & 1 & 1 \\
0 & 0 & 0 & 0 & 0 & 0 & 0 & 0 & 0 & 0 & 0 & 0 & 0 & 0 & 1 & 1 & 1 & 1 & 1 & 1 & 1
\end{bmatrix}.
$$

The Q_r matrix has a particularly important interpretation: it represents the cognitive blueprint or specifications for the test. This blueprint is used to develop items that measure specific attributes outlined in the hierarchy. The 21 columns of the Q_r matrix indicate that at least 21 items must be created to reflect the relationships among the attributes in the hierarchy. For example, as shown in column 1 of the Q_r matrix, an item must be created to measure attribute 1. Similarly, for column 2, an item must be created to measure attributes 1 and 2. The remaining columns are interpreted in the same way. Some researchers claim that the impact of cognitive theory on test design is limited (Embretson, 1999; Gierl et al., 2000; National Research Council, 2001; Nichols & Sugrue, 1999; Pellegrino, 1988; Pellegrino et al., 1999). With the AHM, this limitation can be overcome when the cognitive requirements are described in the attribute hierarchy, and the items required to measure these attributes are specified in the Q_r matrix. That is, the Q_r matrix can serve as the test specification to guide item development, meaning that cognitive theory can have a clearly defined role in test design. This critical role also helps underscore the importance of correctly specifying the cognitive model in the form of an attribute hierarchy in step 1. Then, well-developed procedures for creating test content from the hierarchy-based

---

[1] Another method can also be used. Starting at the rightmost end of the Q matrix, select all columns requiring attribute 8 and do a Boolean addition of the eighth column of R. Any duplicate columns are redundant and therefore removed. This method makes it easy to identify the prerequisite conditions associated with attribute 8.

TABLE 9.1. *Expected response matrix and total scores for a hypothetical set of examinees based on the algebra hierarchy in Figure 9.2*

Examinee	Expected response matrix	Examinee attributes	Total score
1	100000000000000000000	10000000	1
2	110000000000000000000	11000000	2
3	111000000000000000000	11100000	3
4	111100000000000000000	11110000	4
5	111110000000000000000	11111000	5
6	111101000000000000000	11110100	5
7	111111100000000000000	11111100	7
8	100000010000000000000	10000010	2
9	110000011000000000000	11000010	4
10	111000011100000000000	11100010	6
11	111100011110000000000	11110010	8
12	111110011111000000000	11111010	10
13	111101011110100000000	11110110	10
14	111111111111110000000	11111110	14
15	100000010000001000000	10000011	3
16	110000011000001100000	11000011	6
17	111000011100001110000	11100011	9
18	111100011110001111000	11110011	12
19	111110011111001111100	11111011	15
20	111101011110101111010	11110111	15
21	111111111111111111111	11111111	21

test specifications can be used to produce items (Webb, 2006; see also Gorin, this volume).

Step 3: Analyzing and Scoring Items According to the Cognitive Model
Given a hierarchy of attributes, the expected examinee response patterns can be calculated. These patterns represent those responses that should be observed if the attribute hierarchy is true. Expected response patterns are produced by expected examinees. These hypothetical examinees possess cognitive attributes that are consistent with the hierarchy (when the hierarchy is based on cognitive considerations), and they apply these attributes systematically (when the hierarchy is based on procedural considerations). Expected examinees do not make errors or slips that produce inconsistencies between the observed and expected examinee response patterns. For the algebra hierarchy, the expected examinee response patterns and total scores associated with the expected examinees are shown in Table 9.1. The rows and columns of the expected

response matrix in Table 9.1 have distinct interpretations. Row 1 of the expected response matrix should be interpreted as follows: an examinee who only has attribute 1 – that is, (10000000) – is expected to answer only the first item correctly, producing the expected examinee response pattern (100000000000000000000). In contrast, column 1 of the expected response matrix should be interpreted as follows: an item that probes attribute 1 should be answered correctly by all examinees, producing the expected item response pattern (111111111111111111111). (The data from these column response patterns are used to estimate item parameters using an appropriate item response theory (IRT) model, as described later in this chapter.) The examinee's total score does not necessarily indicate which attributes are present. For example, a score of 10 may be obtained by having attribute patterns (11111010) or (11110110). If the algebra attribute hierarchy is true, then only 14 unique total scores across the 21 items will be produced for the expected examinees.

A total score can be used to rank or classify examinees, as is common with latent trait theories. However, this score does not indicate which attributes produce the examinees' observed response patterns. A cognitive diagnostic assessment attempts to link the test score with specific inferences about the examinees' problem-solving strengths and weaknesses. In the AHM, this means that the total score should be supplemented with information indicating which attributes are deficient so students and their teachers can take more specific instructional action when weaknesses are identified. When an attribute hierarchy has been identified, from which the Q_r matrix can be derived to guide the development of test items, the expected response patterns of examinees can also be defined. As a result, anomalous observed response patterns can be judged relative to the set of expected examinee response patterns. The AHM attempts to link an observed item response pattern to a hierarchy of cognitive attributes even when the observed response pattern is unusual in comparison to one of the expected examinee response patterns.

To classify an examinee's response pattern, the expected examinee response patterns that are logically contained within the observed response pattern must be evaluated.[2] When the expected pattern is included in the observed pattern, a "match" is noted; when the expected pattern is not logically included in the observed pattern, the likelihood

---

[2] This classification procedure is referred to as "Method B" in Leighton et al. (2004, pp. 219–220).

of slips are computed. Thus, slips are of the $1 \rightarrow 0$ form, meaning the examinees are expected to answer the item correctly, but for some reason they answer the item incorrectly. The product of the probabilities of each slip is calculated to give the likelihood that the observed response pattern was generated from an expected examinee response pattern for a given θ. Each expected θ is produced using data from an appropriate IRT model. To illustrate this approach, the two-parameter (2PL) logistic IRT model is used, as given by

$$P(u = 1 \mid \theta) = \frac{1}{1 + e^{-1.7a_i(\theta - b_i)}},$$

where a_i is the item discrimination parameter, b_i is the item difficulty parameter, and θ is the ability parameter. The a and b parameters are estimated for each item based on the expected item response patterns given by the columns of the expected response matrix in Table 9.1. Let V_j be the jth expected examinee response pattern for n items and X be an observed response pattern of the same length. Then, $d_j = V_j - X$ produces a pattern having elements ($-1, 0, 1$) corresponding to the type of error that may exist, where $d_j = -1$ [error of the form $0 \rightarrow 1$ with probability equal to $P_m(\theta)$], $d_j = 0$ (no error) and $d_j = 1$ [error of the form $1 \rightarrow 0$ with probability equal to $1 - P_m(\theta)$]. $P_m(\theta)$ probability of the mth observed correct answer when an incorrect answer was expected (i.e., $0 \rightarrow 1$ error) and $1 - P_m(\theta)$ is the probability of the mth observed incorrect answer when a correct answer was expected (i.e., $1 \rightarrow 0$ error). However, in the current classification example, interest is focused on the position of the 1s only as they indicate a $1 \rightarrow 0$ slip. Hence, the probability of m errors in the form $1 \rightarrow 0$ is given by

$$P_{jExpected}(\theta) = \prod_{m=1}^{M} [1 - P_m(\theta)],$$

where m ranges from 1 to M (i.e., the subset of items with the $1 \rightarrow 0$ error). In other words, the probabilities of negative slips ($1 \rightarrow 0$) at a given θ produce an estimate of the likelihood that an observed response pattern approximates an expected examinee response pattern at a given θ. The examinee is classified as having the jth set of attributes when the corresponding $P_{jExpected}(\theta)$ is high.

To demonstrate this classification method, two examples are presented. These examples are based on a sample of 2500 simulated examinees who possessed the total scores associated with each expected response pattern in Table 9.1, with the constraint that the scores be

TABLE 9.2. *Classification of observed response pattern (100000010000001000000)*

Theta		Slips	Expected response matrix	Examinee attributes
−2.0228	0.0000	3	000000000000000000000	00000000
−1.2927	*	0	100000000000000000000	10000000
−0.9432	0.0290	1	110000000000000000000	11000000
−0.5974	0.0000	2	111000000000000000000	11100000
−0.5967	0.0000	3	111100000000000000000	11110000
−0.5965	0.0000	4	111110000000000000000	11111000
−0.5965	0.0000	4	111101000000000000000	11110100
−0.5960	0.0000	6	111111100000000000000	11111100
−1.2865	*	0	100000010000000000000	10000010
−0.5960	0.0000	2	110000011000000000000	11000010
0.3770	0.0000	4	111000011100000000000	11100010
0.7861	0.0000	6	111100011110000000000	11110010
0.8074	0.0000	8	111110011111000000000	11111010
0.8074	0.0000	8	111101011110100000000	11110110
1.3761	0.0000	12	111111111111110000000	11111110
−1.2839	*	**0**	**100000010000001000000**	**10000011**
−0.5905	0.0000	3	110000011000001100000	11000011
0.7759	0.0000	6	111000011100001110000	11100011
1.4723	0.0000	9	111100011110001111000	11110011
1.4752	0.0000	12	111110011111001111100	11111011
1.4752	0.0000	12	111101011110101111010	11110111
2.2187	0.0000	18	111111111111111111111	11111111

normally distributed. The item parameters were estimated with the computer program BILOG-MG. Table 9.2 shows the results for the observed response pattern (100000010000001000000) with no slips. The attribute pattern associated with this observed response indicates that the examinee possesses attribute 1, 7 , and 8, meaning that the examinee posses the prerequisite skills to solve algebra items associated with understanding the meaning of symbols and conventions, as well as knowledge and skills required for tabulation and plotting (see Appendix for a more detailed description of the component processes required for each attribute). The asterisks in the $P_{jExpected}(\theta)$ column indicate that the expected examinee response pattern is logically included in the observed response pattern. Because the observed and expected response patterns match, the examinee is said to possess attributes 1, 7, and 8 at an ability level of −1.2839. No other attribute patterns are likely.

Table 9.3 contains the results for the observed response pattern (100000000000001000000) with one slip, meaning that the observed

TABLE 9.3. *Classification of observed response pattern (100000000000010000000)*

Theta		Slips	Expected response matrix	Examinee attributes
−2.0228	0.0000	2	000000000000000000000	00000000
−1.2927	*	0	100000000000000000000	10000000
−0.9432	0.02900	1	110000000000000000000	11000000
−0.5974	0.0000	2	111000000000000000000	11100000
−0.5967	0.0000	3	111100000000000000000	11110000
−0.5965	0.0000	4	111110000000000000000	11111000
−0.5965	0.0000	4	111101000000000000000	11110100
−0.5960	0.0000	6	111111100000000000000	11111100
−1.2865	**0.9634**	**1**	**100000010000000000000**	**10000010**
−0.5960	0.0000	3	110000011000000000000	11000010
0.3770	0.0000	5	111000011100000000000	11100010
0.7861	0.0000	7	111100011110000000000	11110010
0.8074	0.0000	9	111110011111000000000	11111010
0.8074	0.0000	9	111101011110100000000	11110110
1.3761	0.0000	12	111111111111110000000	11111110
−1.2839	**0.9500**	**2**	**100000010000001000000**	**10000011**
−0.5905	0.0000	5	110000011000001100000	11000011
0.7759	0.0000	8	110000111000011100000	11100011
1.4723	0.0000	11	111100011110001111000	11110011
1.4752	0.0000	14	111110011111001111100	11111011
1.4752	0.0000	14	111101011110101111010	11110111
2.2187	0.0000	19	111111111111111111111	11111111

response pattern differs from the expected examinee response patterns by one element on item 8 in the form $1 \rightarrow 0$. Many factors, including fatigue, diversion, or testwiseness, can affect an examinee's response to an item. As a result, any observed response pattern is subject to slips, producing a discrepancy with the expected examinee response patterns. Two reasons may account for the inconsistency between the observed and expected patterns in the Table 9.3 example. In line 9, there is a discrepancy in the eighth element of the form $1 \rightarrow 0$ between the expected and observed response patterns. The likelihood of this occurrence is .9634 for examinees with an ability estimate $\theta = -1.2865$ and an attribute pattern of (10000010). In line 16, there is also a discrepancy in the eighth element of the form $1 \rightarrow 0$ between the expected and observed response patterns. The likelihood of this occurrence is .9500 for examinees with an ability estimate $\theta = -1.2839$ and an attribute pattern of (100000011). Thus, we conclude that examinees with the observed response pattern (100000000000001000000) possess attribute 1 [as indicated by the * in the $P_{jExpected}(\theta)$ column]. But these examinees are also likely to possess attributes 7 and 8, given the high likelihood of the attribute patterns (10000010) and (100000011). Hence, an inference about the examinees' attribute mastery pattern can still be made, even when there is a discrepancy between the expected and observed response patterns, given the likelihood of alternative patterns.

Inevitably, slips will occur when the expected examinee response patterns are compared to the observed response patterns across a large sample of examinees. However, when many discrepant response patterns are identified, questions about model-data fit should also be considered. If the model, which produces the expected examinee response patterns, fails to match the observed data, then one must assess whether (a) the attributes were accurately identified, (b) the hierarchy was appropriately specified, (c) the items measure the attributes, and/or (d) the test was appropriate for the student sample. The hierarchy consistency index (HCI_i) can be used to evaluate model-data fit (Cui, Leighton, Gierl, & Hunka, 2006). The HCI_i evaluates the degree to which an observed examinee response pattern is consistent with the attribute hierarchy. Given K attributes and J items, the element q_{kj} of the reduced Q matrix indicates whether attribute k is required to solve the jth item. It can be expressed as:

$$q k_j = \begin{cases} 1 & \text{attribute } k \text{ required by item } j \\ 0 & \text{otherwise.} \end{cases}$$

Attribute mastery occurs when examinees correctly answer the items requiring the attribute. Thus, the HCI_i for examinee i is given as

$$HCI_i = 1 - \frac{2\sum_{j=1}^{J} \sum_{g \in S_j} X_j(1 - X_g)}{N},$$

where J is the total number of items, X_j is examinee i's score (1 or 0) to item j, S_j includes items that require the subset of attributes of item j, and N is the total number of comparisons for correct-answered items by examinee i. When examinee i correctly answers item j, $X_j = 1$. The examinee is also expected to answer item g that belongs to S_j correctly, $X_j = 1(g \in S_j)$. However, if $Xg = 0$, then $X_j(1 - X_g) = 1$, which is considered a misfit of the response vector i relative to attribute hierarchy. Thus, the numerator contains the number of misfits multiplied by 2. The HCI_i produces an index ranging from -1 to $+1$, which is easily interpreted. For example, when the examinee's observed response pattern matches the hierarchy, the numerator is 0 and the HCI_i will have a value of 1. Conversely, when the examinee's observed response pattern fails to match the hierarchy (i.e., a complete misfit where the examinee correctly answers one item but fails to answer any item that requires the subset of attributes measured by the correctly answered item), the numerator is $(2 \times N_{ci})$ and the HCI_i will have a value of -1. When low HCI_i values are produced for a sample of examinees, some aspect of the cognitive model may be inadequate. Further analyses are then required to evaluate whether the attributes are accurately identified, the hierarchy is appropriately specified, and/or the items properly measure the attributes.

To illustrate this approach, slips were added to the sample of 2500 simulated examinees who produced the total scores associated with each expected examinee response pattern in Table 9.1. The slips were based on the IRT probabilities. The IRT item response probabilities can be calculated for each expected response pattern at all values of θ. Because variation in the observed and expected examinee response patterns can be evaluated using the IRT probabilities (i.e., higher probabilities indicate a closer concordance between the two response patterns), two types of slips can be generated. First, slips can be created for the subset of items we expect examinees will answer incorrectly relative to the attribute hierarchy (i.e., slips of the form $0 \rightarrow 1$). These slips can be specified as the IRT item probability. Second, slips can be created for the subset of items we expect examinees will answer correctly relative to the attribute hierarchy (i.e., slips of the form $1 \rightarrow 0$). These slips can be specified as 1 minus the IRT item probability. Consider, for example, the frequency distribution used to generate the simulated data for this chapter: 87 of the 2500 examinees have the expected response pattern (100000010000001000000), which is associated with the attribute pattern (10000011). The item response probabilities for the 21 items can be computed at the θ value associated with this expected response pattern. If we only consider the probabilities for the first two items in the expected response pattern, the values are .9990 and .0332, respectively. Although every item will have an IRT probability, for illustration purposes, only the outcomes for the first two items are presented. Because $(1 - 0.9990) \times 87 = 0.0870$, no response vectors associated with attributes (10000011) will be randomly selected, and no changes of the form $1 \rightarrow 0$ will be introduced for item 1. The same 87 examinees are also expected to answer item 2 incorrectly. Thus, three slips of the form $0 \rightarrow 1$ will be randomly introduced into the simulated data, as $0.0332 \times 87 = 2.8884$. Using this data generation approach, 19.8% of all observed response patterns differ from the expected response patterns by a slip of either $0 \rightarrow 1$ or $1 \rightarrow 0$. The HCI_i for the slip-induced sample data is .8233, indicating there is moderate to strong model-data fit.

The classification and HCI_i results, taken together, can contribute to cognitive model development. We noted that cognitive models of task performance are often created by conducting empirical investigations of the cognitive processes used by examinees to solve test items. These models serve as a description of the thinking processes for a particular group of examinees on specific tasks. The model can be evaluated and possibly refined by comparing its fit using the slip likelihood from the classification results and the HCI_i outcome for different samples of examinees and different models of task performance.

Step 4: Reporting Cognitive Skills

Cognitive diagnostic assessment can be considered the process where test scores yield information about examinees' cognitive skills. The AHM can be used to classify examinees' cognitive proficiencies and report the classification results. The results from an AHM analysis should be combined with existing knowledge about examinees to identify problem-solving strengths and weaknesses. The attributes must be presented in a format that promotes the classification of cognitive proficiency, and the results from an AHM analysis must be reported in a manner that is easily understood by parents, students, teachers, and other stakeholders. Test score reporting is the primary method of providing information about the meaning and possible interpretations of test results to all stakeholders. As a result, reporting may serve as the *most critical step* in the diagnostic testing process for linking theories of cognition and learning with instructional practices. The general goals for test score reporting are clear:

Standard 5.10: When test score information is released to students, parents, legal representatives, teachers, clients, or the media, those responsible for testing programs should provide appropriate interpretations. The interpretations should describe in simple language what the test covers, what scores mean, the precision of the scores, common misinterpretations of test scores, and how scores will be used. (Standards for Educational and Psychological Testing, 1999, p. 65.)

The general characteristics of effective test score reports are also well documented (see Goodman & Hambleton, 2004, pp. 219). For example, score reports should be clear, concise, and visually appealing; reports should include readable text to support the interpretation of graphical information; the data should be presented in a succinct but complete manner so it is easily understood; key terms should be defined and statistical terms should be avoided; reports should be pilot-tested before they are used; reports should include detailed interpretative guides, where all sections of the report are explained; these guides also should include sample items and strategies for improving student performance.

Unfortunately, the specific goals and characteristics for cognitive diagnostic score reporting are neither clear nor well documented. As a result, little information exists on how to report scores from these types of tests. Clearly, detailed descriptions of the attributes, along with example items, are required to illustrate how the attributes are measured. Guidelines for interpreting the attributes are also needed because the test score inferences focus on specific cognitive skills at a small grain size. Implications for instruction should also be included by connecting the cognitive psychological literature to different performance outcomes using diagnostic student profiles, vignettes, and case studies (Pellegrino, 2002; van der Veen et al., in press). By identifying examinees' cognitive strengths and weaknesses, teachers may be in a better situation to understand how students think about and solve problems on tests, and to help students who encounter problems. However, this assessment information will only contribute to the teaching and learning process if it is first understood and then translated into effective interventions. Thus, the scores from cognitive diagnostic assessments must be reported carefully. Goodman and Hambleton (2004) note that little research exists on how student results from conventional large-scale tests are reported, despite the importance of the reporting process. No published research, to our knowledge, exists on the practices associated with score reporting for cognitive diagnostic assessments. Hence, additional research is needed on this important step in the cognitive diagnostic assessment process.

III. SUMMARY

In contemporary cognitive psychology, rooted in the information processing tradition, the focus is on the individual problem solver who brings an array of solution procedures to each problem and who selects an approach from these procedures as a result of the complex interaction between task and personal characteristics. This selection process is not easy to predict and need not be determined reliably by conventional item characteristics such as content or difficulty. Moreover, accuracy is not viewed as a good indicator of cognitive processing because a correct answer can be generated by testwise strategies or even in the presence of subtle misconceptions. Thus, cognitive theories are incompatible with many of the assumptions that underlie latent trait theories in educational and psychological measurement (Gierl, Bisanz, & Li, 2004; Glaser, Lesgold, & Lajoie, 1987; Mislevy, 1996; National Research Council, 2001; Pellegrino, 1988; Pellegrino et al., 1999). Because of this incompatibility, cognitive psychologists are now urging measurement specialists to develop assessment procedures for evaluating the patterns of an examinee's responses across a set of items or tasks. This pattern of observed responses can be interpreted relative to a cognitive model of task performance when the items are designed to measure the model. This approach to test design and analysis has tremendous potential for identifying examinees' cognitive strengths and weaknesses, particularly when the model provides a contemporary cognitive representation of the knowledge structures and processing skills that are believed to underlie conceptual understanding in a particular domain. Pellegrino et al. (1999), for example, claim that:

> it is the pattern of performance over a set of items or tasks explicitly constructed to discriminate between alternative profiles of knowledge that should be the focus of assessment. The latter can be used to determine the level of a given student's understanding and competence within a subject-matter domain. Such information is interpretative and diagnostic, highly informative, and potentially prescriptive. (p. 335)

The AHM for cognitive assessment is a psychometric method for classifying examinees' test item responses into a set of structured attribute patterns associated with different components specified in a cognitive model of task performance. Cognitive diagnostic assessment, conducted using the AHM, must be informed by theories of domain knowledge and skill acquisition so cognitive theory can be linked to measurement practice, thereby promoting cognitive inferences about examinees' performance. The AHM attempts to forge this link using a cognitive model to guide both the development of items and the interpretation of test scores. As cognitive diagnostic assessments continue to develop, they must also be informed by innovative new psychometric procedures that can measure performance and improve methods for reporting this performance in ways that are consistent with contemporary cognitive theory. Latent trait theories may be adequate for ranking examinees. However, if understanding and evaluating examinees' cognitive skills is primary to the test score inference, then new procedures that integrate cognitive theories with psychometric methods are required. That is, *a symbiotic relationship* between cognitive psychology and educational measurement is required if the challenges in cognitive diagnostic assessment are to be met.

We also note that a cognitive diagnostic assessment should not be conducted in isolation. Rather, it is expected to be an integral part of a much larger educational endeavour involving learning and instruction. Many large-scale educational tests provide students and teachers with little information on performance characteristics or skill attainment that can either directly improve learning or guide instruction. Cognitive diagnostic assessment, when it is integrated into a learning environment like the classroom, is an attempt to overcome this problem by providing specific information on examinees' cognitive strengths and weaknesses to help teachers understand how students think about and solve problems on tests. These diagnostic test results, in turn, may help teachers structure, classify, and understand students' problem-solving skills, which, when combined with other sources of information about the student, can inform and guide instruction.

Directions for Research

The AHM was described and illustrated within a four-step diagnostic process intended to increase the accuracy of our inferences about examinees. The results of this presentation, however, highlight some important challenges that must be met when the AHM is used for cognitive diagnostic assessment. One statistical problem concerns the accuracy of the classification method, given our assumption about the examinees' response state. A slip serves as an inconsistency between the observed and expected examinee response pattern, where we assume the examinee state is known with certainty. For example, a $1 \rightarrow 0$ slip indicates the examinee is expected to answer the item correctly but, for some reason, answers the item incorrectly. These slips can be attributed to factors such as fatigue, diverted attention, or testwiseness. Examinees' responses are then classified using the slip probabilities calculated from the IRT item and ability parameter estimates (see the "Step 3: Analyzing and Scoring Items According to the Cognitive Model" section). Item difficulty is another factor that may contribute to a slip. The notion of a slip, as it is currently used in the AHM, is based on the assumption that a slip is made from a known response state, meaning from $0 \rightarrow 1$ or from $1 \rightarrow 0$. However, this assumption about the examinees' response state may, in some cases, be inaccurate. For example, if a $1 \to 0$ slip occurs and $P(u = 1|\theta) = 0.90$, then the probability is high that the examinee's expected state is, indeed, a 1. However, if this slip occurs and $P(u = 1|\theta) = 0.10$, then the probability is low that the examinee's expected state is 1. Yet, using our classification approach, the expected state would still be considered a 1, even when $P(u = 1|\theta) = 0.10$ meaning the response probability is low. A more accurate representation would be probabilistic such as a slip of $1 \to 0$ occurring if the 1 state has a reasonable probability of existing, [e.g., a 1 state occurs only when $P(u = 1|\theta) \geq 0.50$)].

To address this challenge, we are studying how item difficulty may promote a better decision about the occurrence of a response slip. Item difficulty, the b_i parameter in the 2PL IRT model, is interpreted as the point on the ability scale where the probability of a correct response is 50%, meaning the greater the value of b_i, the higher the ability level required for an examinee to have a 50% chance of answering the item correctly. By considering item difficulty *in the context of a response slip*, the accuracy of our inference about the examinee's expected state may be increased. We are also investigating how non–IRT-based procedures for classifying and evaluating examinee response patterns can be used to complement existing IRT-based methods (see Gierl, Cui, & Hunka, 2007).

A second statistical challenge is posed by the calculation of attribute probabilities. Given an examinee's observed response vector, it would be useful to calculate the attribute probabilities directly because these results will yield specific information about an examinee's attribute mastery level. To estimate the probability that an examinee possesses specific attributes, we could assume the probability of a correct response to an item P_i is the product of the probabilities for the attributes p_k required to answer the item. Using logarithms, the expression can be rewritten in linear form as $Log[P_i(u = 1|\theta)] = \sum_{k=1}^{K} Log(p_i) + error$. For a simple attribute hierarchy of the form A1, A1 $\to$ A2, and A1 $\to$ A2 $\to$ A3, in which item 1 has the associated attribute vector (100), item 2 (110), and item 3 (111), the following three equations are produced

$$Log\, P_1 = Log(p_1),$$
$$Log\, P_2 = Log(p_1) + Log(p_2),$$
$$Log\, P_3 = Log(p_1) + Log(p_2) + Log(p_3).$$

The first equation states that the Log of the probability of item 1 being correct is equal to the Log of the probability that attribute A1 is present because item 1 involves attribute A1 only. The second equation states that the Log of the probability of item 2 being correct is equal to the sum of the logarithms of the probabilities that attribute A1 and A2 are present. The third equation states that the Log of the probability of item 3 being correct is equal to the sum of the logarithms of the probabilities that attributes A1, A2, and A3 are present. Using $X = AB$, where X is a column vector of length i containing $Log[P_i(u = 1 \mid \theta)]$, A is the transpose of the reduced Q matrix for items i, and B is the unknown attribute probabilities $Log(p_i)$, an exact solution can be had if A is square and nonsingular, and if the equations are consistent. The attribute probabilities produced using this approach could enhance the diagnostic value of the AHM because examinees would receive information about their attribute-level performance as part of the diagnostic reporting process. Hence, further research on the calculation and application of attribute probabilities seems warranted.

Of course, the diagnostic reporting process itself is also the source of many challenging problems. When the AHM is used, the attributes must be presented in a manner that promotes the classification of cognitive proficiency, and the results must be reported in a way that are easily understood by diverse stakeholders, including students, parents, and teachers. Reporting is also the primary method of providing information to these stakeholders about the interpretations of test scores and, thus, it may serve as the most important step in the diagnostic testing process for linking cognitive inferences with learning outcomes and instructional practices. Yet, Goodman and Hambleton (2004) found that a paucity of research exists on the practices associated with score reporting. Hence, much more research is needed to understand how cognitive diagnostic scores should be reported and, ultimately, used to enhance learning and instruction.

APPENDIX

Here, we provide a description of the attributes identified from a task analysis of the SAT Algebra items used to create the algebra hierarchy in Figure 9.2.

Attribute 1: Meaning of Symbols and Conventions
  a. Knows the arithmetic operations implied by +, −, x, =, |term|, square root, exponent, >, <, and signed numbers

    b. Implied operations in 2n, 2(term), (term)^2, n/2

    c. An inverse relationship exists between speed and distance traveled

Attribute 2: Comprehension of Text

    a. Knows meaning of the terms product, times, equals, result, squared, difference, sum, and total in a mathematical context

    b. From text, derive a mathematical expression when symbols representing one, two, or three unknown quantities are identified

    c. As in (b) but unknown symbols are not identified; examinee must assign symbols for identification of unknowns

    d. Can identify symbol for which solution is required

    e. Identifies relationships among unknowns (e.g., "b is 3 times greater than a" implies that $b = 3a$, $b/a = 3$, or $a = b/3$)

Attribute 3: Algebraic Manipulation

    a. Can manipulate terms on the rhs and lhs of an expression having signed values and signed unknowns

    b. Collection of common terms in an expression

    c. Can expand $(a + b)^2$

    d. Factoring

    e. Can rewrite square root terms using exponents

    f. Can move exponential terms from numerator to denominator and vice versa

Attribute 4: Linear Function

    a. Solve unknown in simple expression (e.g., $3a = 21$)

    b. Solve for more than one unknown in a simple expression when relationship among unknowns specified (e.g., $a + b = 21$ and $b = 2a$; may be considered simplest set of simultaneous equations)

    c. Recognizes the general form of linear function $y = a + bx$ and that it can be written as $f(x) = a + bx$

    d. Knows that "a" is the constant, and "bx" is b times x

    e. "x" is the independent variable and "y" the dependent variable

Attribute 5: Solution of Quadratic

    a. Knows the general form of a quadratic: $a x^2 + b x + c = 0$

    b. Can rearrange an expression into a quadratic form

   c. Solves for the unknown in a quadratic using factoring; recognizes that there may be more than one solution

   d. Solves quadratic form by using the equation $(-b \pm \text{Sqrt}(b^2 - 4ac))/2a$

   e. Can cross reference the terms a, b, and c to the expression at hand

Attribute 6: Simultaneous Equations

   a. As many equations as unknowns are required for the solution

   b. Multiplying an equation by nonzero constant does not change the solution

   c. Any linear combination of equations does not change the solution

   d. Recognizes no solution case: inconsistent equations, insufficient equations, linear dependency among equations; logical inconsistency (e.g., $2y + 3 = 4, 4y + 6 = 9$)

   e. Algebraic solution for 2 unknowns by solving one unknown in terms of the other and substituting

Attribute 7: Tabulation

   a. For an expression in one unknown, tabulate the result for a range of values

   b. Tabulate the result of a recursive expression (e.g., the $n + 1$ value is $1/2$ the nth value)

Attribute 8: Plotting

   a. Can construct a grid system with identified axes, origin, and tick marks

   b. Can read a coordinate point from the grid system

   c. Plot tabulated values of an expression

   d. For linear function $(y = a + bx)$, calculate "a" and "b"

References

American Educational Research Association (AERA), American Psychological Association, National Council on Measurement in Education. (1999) *Standards for educational and psychological testing*. Washington, DC: AERA.

Anderson, J. R. (2005). Human symbol manipulation within an integrated cognitive architecture. *Cognitive Science, 29*, 313–341.

Anderson, J. R., Bothell, D., Byrne, M. D., Douglass, S., Lebiere, C., & Qin, Y. (2004). An integrated theory of the mind. *Psychological Review, 111*, 1036–1060.

Anderson, J. R., Reder, L. M., & Simon, H. A. (2000). Applications and Misapplications of Cognitive Psychology to Mathematics Education. Retrieved June 7, 2006, from http://act-r.psy.cmu.edu/publications.

Anderson, J. R., & Shunn, C. D.,(2000). Implications of the ACT-R learning theory: No magic bullets. In R. Glaser (Ed.), *Advances in instructional psychology: Educational design and cognitive science* (Vol. 5, pp. 1–33). Mahwah, NJ: Erlbaum.

Bransford, J. D., Brown, A. L., & Cocking, R. R. (1999). *How people learn: Brain, mind, experience, and school.* Washington, DC: National Academy Press.

Brown, J. S., & Burton, R. R. (1978). Diagnostic models for procedural bugs in basic mathematics skills. *Cognitive Science, 2,* 155–192.

Cui, Y., Leighton, J. P., Gierl, M. J., & Hunka, S. (2006, April). *A person-fit statistic for the attribute hierarchy method: The hierarchy consistency index.* Paper presented at the annual meeting of the National Council on Measurement in Education, San Francisco.

Dawson, M. R. W. (1998). *Understanding cognitive science.* Malden, MA: Blackwell.

Donovan, M. S., Bransford, J. D., & Pellegrino, J. W. (1999). *How people learn: Bridging research and practice.* Washington, DC: National Academy Press.

Embretson, S. E. (1999). Cognitive psychology applied to testing. In F. T. Durso, R. S. Nickerson, R. W. Schvaneveldt, S. T. Dumais, D. S. Linday, & M. T. H. Chi (Eds.), *Handbook of applied cognition,* (pp. 629–66). New York: Wiley.

Ericsson, K. A., & Simon, H. A. (1993). *Protocol analysis: Verbal reports as data.* Cambridge, MA: The MIT Press.

Fodor, J. A. (1983). *The modularity of mind.* Cambridge, MA: MIT Press.

Gierl, M.J., Leighton, J. P., & Hunka, S. (2000). Exploring the logic of Tatsuoka's rule-space model for test development and analysis. *Educational Measurement: Issues and Practice, 19,* 34–44.

Gierl, M. J., Bisanz, J., & Li, Y. Y. (2004, April). *Using the multidimensionality-based DIF analysis framework to study cognitive skills that elicit gender differences.* Paper presented at the annual meeting of the National Council on Measurement in Education, San Diego.

Gierl, M. J., Cui, Y., & Hunka, S. (2007, April). *Using connectionist models to evaluate examinees' response patterns on tests using the Attribute Hierarchy Method.* Paper presented at the annual meeting of the National Council on Measurement in Education, Chicago.

Glaser, R., Lesgold, A., & Lajoie, S. (1987). Toward a cognitive theory for the measurement of achievement. In R. R. Ronning, J. A. Glover, J. C. Conoley, & J. C. Witt (Eds.), *The influence of cognitive psychology on testing* (pp. 41–85). Hillsdale, NJ: Erlbaum.

Goodman, D. P., & Hambleton, R. K. (2004). Student test score reports and interpretative guides: Review of current practices and suggestions for future research. *Applied Measurement in Education, 17,* 145–220.

Hunt, E. (1995). Where and when to represent students this way and that way: An evaluation of approaches to diagnostic assessment. In P. D. Nichols, S. F. Chipman, & R. L. Brennan (Eds.), *Cognitively diagnostic assessment* (pp. 411–429). Hillsdale, NJ: Erlbaum.

Kuhn, D. (2001). Why development does (and does not occur) occur: Evidence from the domain of inductive reasoning. In J. L. McClelland & R. Siegler

(Eds.), *Mechanisms of cognitive development: Behavioral and neural perspectives* (pp. 221–249). Hillsdale, NJ: Erlbaum.

Leighton, J. P. (2004). Avoiding misconceptions, misuse, and missed opportunities: The collection of verbal reports in educational achievement testing. *Educational Measurement: Issues and Practice, 23*, 6–15.

Leighton, J. P., & Gierl, M. J. (in press). Defining and evaluating models of cognition used in educational measurement to make inferences about examinees' thinking processes. *Educational Measurement: Issues and Practice.*

Leighton, J. P., Gierl, M. J., & Hunka, S. (2004). The attribute hierarchy model: An approach for integrating cognitive theory with assessment practice. *Journal of Educational Measurement, 41*, 205–236.

Leighton, J. P., & Gokiert, R. (2005, April). *The cognitive effects of test item features: Identifying construct irrelevant variance and informing item generation.* Paper presented at the annual meeting of the National Council on Measurement in Education, Montréal, Canada.

Messick, S. (1989). Validity. In R. L. Linn (Ed.), *Educational measurement* (3rd ed.; pp. 13–103). New York: American Council on Education/Macmillan.

Mislevy, R. J. (1996). Test theory reconceived. *Journal of Educational Measurement, 33*, 379–416.

Mislevy, R. J., Steinberg, L. S., & Almond, R. G. (2003). On the structure of educational assessments. *Measurement: Interdisciplinary Research and Perspectives, 1*, 3–62.

National Research Council. (2001). *Knowing what students know: The science and design of educational assessment.* Washington, DC: National Academy Press.

Nichols, P. (1994). A framework of developing cognitively diagnostic assessments. *Review of Educational Research, 64*, 575–603.

Nichols, P., & Sugrue, B. (1999). The lack of fidelity between cognitively complex constructs and conventional test development practice. *Educational Measurement: Issues and Practice, 18*, 18–29.

Norris, S. P., Leighton, J. P., & Phillips, L. M. (2004). What is at stake in knowing the content and capabilities of children's minds? A case for basing high stakes tests on cognitive models. *Theory and Research in Education, 2*, 283–308.

Pellegrino, J. W. (1988). Mental models and mental tests. In H. Wainer & H. I. Braun (Eds.), *Test validity* (pp. 49–60). Hillsdale, NJ: Erlbaum.

Pellegrino, J. W. (2002). Understanding how students learn and inferring what they know: Implications for the design of curriculum, instruction, and assessment. In M. J. Smith (Ed.), *NSF K-12 Mathematics and Science Curriculum and Implementation Centers Conference Proceedings* (pp. 76–92). Washington, DC: National Science Foundation and American Geological Institute.

Pellegrino, J. W., Baxter, G. P., & Glaser, R. (1999). Addressing the "two disciplines" problem: Linking theories of cognition and learning with assessment and instructional practices. In A. Iran-Nejad & P. D. Pearson (Eds.), *Review of Research in Education* (pp. 307–353). Washington, DC: American Educational Research Association.

Poggio, A., Clayton, D. B., Glasnapp, D., Poggio, J., Haack, P., & Thomas, J. (2005, April). *Revisiting the item format question: Can the multiple choice format meet the demand for monitoring higher-order skills?* Paper presented at the annual meeting of the National Council on Measurement in Education, Montreal, Canada.

Royer, J. M., Cisero, C. A., & Carlo, M. S. (1993). Techniques and procedures for assessing cognitive skills. *Review of Educational Research, 63,* 201–243.

Scriven, M. (1991). *Evaluation thesaurus* (4th ed.). Newbury Park, CA: Sage.

Snow, R. E., & Lohman, D. F. (1989). Implications of cognitive psychology for educational measurement. In R. L. Linn (Ed.), *Educational measurement* (3rd ed., pp. 263–331). New York: American Council on Education/Macmillan.

Taylor, K. L., & Dionne, J-P. (2000). Accessing problem-solving strategy knowledge: The complementary use of concurrent verbal protocols and retrospective debriefing. *Journal of Educational Psychology, 92,* 413–425.

Tatsuoka, K. K. (1983). Rule space: An approach for dealing with misconceptions based on item response theory. *Journal of Educational Measurement, 20,* 345–354.

Tatsuoka, K. K. (1995). Architecture of knowledge structures and cognitive diagnosis: A statistical pattern recognition and classification approach. In P. D. Nichols, S. F. Chipman, & R. L. Brennan (Eds.), *Cognitively diagnostic assessment* (pp. 327–359). Hillsdale, NJ: Erlbaum.

Tatsuoka, M. M., & Tatsuoka, K. K. (1989). Rule space. In S. Kotz & N. L. Johnson (Eds.), *Encyclopedia of statistical sciences* (pp. 217–220). New York: Wiley.

VanderVeen, A. A., Huff, K., Gierl, M., McNamara, D. S, Louwerse, M., & Graesser, A. (in press). Developing and validating instructionally relevant reading competency profiles measured by the critical reading section of the SAT. In D. S. McNamara (Ed.), *Reading comprehension strategies: Theories, interventions, and technologies.* Mahwah, NJ: Erlbaum.

Webb, N. L. (2006). Identifying content for student achievement tests. In S. M. Downing & T. M. Haladyna (Eds.), *Handbook of test development* (pp. 155–180). Mahwah, NJ: Erlbaum.

10

The Fusion Model Skills Diagnosis System

Louis A. Roussos, Louis V. DiBello, William Stout,
Sarah M. Hartz, Robert A. Henson, and
Jonathan L. Templin

1.0 INTRODUCTION

There is a long history of calls for combining cognitive science and
psychometrics (Cronbach, 1975; Snow & Lohman, 1989). The U.S. standards movement, begun more than 20 years ago (McKnight et al., 1987;
National Council of Teachers of Mathematics, 1989), sought to articulate
public standards for learning that would define and promote successful
performance by all students; establish a common base for curriculum
development and instructional practice; and provide a foundation for
measuring progress for students, teachers and programs. The standards
movement provided the first widespread call for assessment systems
that directly support learning. For success, such systems must satisfy a
number of conditions having to do with cognitive-science–based design,
psychometrics, and implementation. This chapter focuses on the psychometric aspects of one particular system that builds on a carefully
designed test and a user-selected set of relevant skills measured by that
test to assess student mastery of each of the chosen skills. This type of
test-based skills level assessment is called *skills diagnosis*. The system
that the chapter describes in detail is called the *Fusion Model system*.

This chapter focuses on the statistical and psychometric aspects of
the Fusion Model system, with skills diagnosis researchers and practitioners in mind who may be interested in working with this system.
We view the statistical and psychometric aspects as situated within a
comprehensive framework for diagnostic assessment test design and
implementation. We use the term "skills diagnostic tests" to refer to
tests that provide profiles of information on examinees: information

that is richer and more useful than a single score; information that is scientifically based and statistically sound; and information that can be effectively and readily acted on by students, parents, teachers, and others to improve teaching and learning. This work is based on the premise that periodic skills diagnostic testing, tuned to classroom needs, can greatly enhance teaching and learning, and can promote higher quality and greater accountability within educational and training programs. The Fusion Model system described here is an effective psychometric and statistical approach consisting of procedures and software for practical skills diagnostic testing.

In response to the assessment demands imposed by the standards movement, test manufacturers have redoubled their efforts to expand their test results beyond the reporting of standard global scores of student achievement in broad subject areas to more diagnostic scores indicating academic strengths and weaknesses on specific skills. Perhaps the best example in this regard is the recent development by Educational Testing Service (ETS) of a Score Report Plus™ for each student who takes the College Board's PSAT/NMSQT™ (Preliminary SAT/National Merit Scholarship Qualifying Test). In addition to the broad-based score report given in the past, the Score Report Plus includes a list of up to three important skills needed to perform well on the test and for which there is strong diagnostic information of lack of examinee mastery.

To provide the testing industry with practical tools for expanding standardized testing to include effective skills diagnosis, a research program initiated by the foundational modeling work of DiBello, Stout, and Roussos (1995); the subsequent developmental work of Hartz and Roussos (Hartz, 2002; Hartz & Roussos, in press); and recent ETS-supported research on refining these developments has resulted in a comprehensive skills diagnosis system, called the *Fusion Model skills diagnosis system* or, simply, the Fusion Model system.

The Fusion Model system includes the following four components:

1. An identifiable and interpretable item response function model, a reparameterization of the foundational Unified Model (DiBello et al., 1995)

2. A parameter estimation method referred to as *Arpeggio*,[1] which employs a Markov Chain Monte Carlo (MCMC) algorithm within

---

[1] The Arpeggio software system is owned by Educational Testing Service. Researchers can obtain this software by emailing Donna Lembeck at "dlembeck@ets.org." Information about use of the software and its performance characteristics is available through the authors.

a Bayesian modeling framework for model estimation, including item parameter estimation and ability distribution parameter estimation

3. A collection of model checking procedures, including statistical MCMC convergence checking, ability distribution and item parameter estimates with standard errors, model fit statistics, internal validity statistics, and reliability estimation methods

4. Skills-level score statistics, including mastery/nonmastery estimation, subscoring options for assessing mastery/nonmastery, and proficiency scaling statistics that relate test scores to skill mastery

This chapter provides a detailed description of each component, with particular focus on what a skills diagnostic practitioner needs to know.

Skills diagnosis, sometimes referred to as skills assessment, skills profiling, profile scoring, or cognitive diagnosis, is an application of psychometric theory and methods to the statistically rigorous process of (a) evaluating each examinee on the basis of level of competence on a user-developed array of skills, and (b) evaluating the skills estimation effectiveness of a test by assessing the strength of the relationship between the individual skills profiles and the observed performance on individual test items. Such examinee evaluation, ideally periodic throughout the teaching and learning process, can provide valuable information to enhance teaching and learning. It is primarily intended for use as *formative* assessment, in contrast to *summative* assessment, in that formative skills diagnosis is intended by its design and implementation to be used directly to improve learning and teaching. In contrast, summative assessment records examinee status at some point in time, usually at the end of an instructional unit, without any direct attempt to improve the examinees status on what was assessed.

Skills diagnosis can often be considered relatively low stakes from the perspective of the individual test taker. It affects decisions that have relatively short time horizons, such as deciding which problems to assign for tonight's homework or planning for tomorrow's lesson, as opposed to large life events, such as admission to college or selection for employment. The skills diagnostic score results, at least in principle, are well integrated within the classroom environment and constitute just one complementary element of an extensive store of teacher, peer, assessment, and instructional information. Of course, the distinction between formative and summative assessment is not sharp, and much effort is being devoted to aligning formative and summative assessments, and developing broad-based assessment systems that include both summative and formative components (The Commission on Instructionally Supportive Assessment, 2001). Because unidimensionally scaled assessment scores alone provide a relatively impoverished global overview of competence in any domain, such broad-based systems will likely rest on strategically conceived and well-designed skills diagnostic assessments.

There are two common types of applications of cognitive diagnostic methods. In some settings, it is important to revisit existing summative assessments and their data and apply diagnostic methods in a post-hoc attempt to extract some diagnostic information from these assessments (Birenbaum, Tatsuoka, & Yamada, 2004; Tatsuoka, Corter, & Guerrero, 2003; Tatsuoka, Corter, & Tatsuoka, 2004; Xin, 2004; Xin, Xu, & Tatsuoka, 2004). A related application is to employ diagnostic assessment models to existing assessment data in order to determine structural information about which skills underlie good performance on the assessment (DiBello et al., 2006). In contrast, the second type of application is on assessments that are specifically designed for the purpose of providing skills diagnosis. Most applications have been of the first kind, and a particularly well-done example is a study by Jang (2005) in which she applied the Fusion Model system to two forms of the ETS LanguEdge English Language Learning (ELL) assessment using data from a large-scale administration (about 1350 examinees per form) as well as data from a classroom setting (27 students). The LanguEdge was developed by ETS as a prototype for the latest version of its Test of English as a Foreign Language (TOEFL), but Jang defined a new classroom formative assessment purpose for the test and subsequently built a skills diagnosis framework for it to extract diagnostic information that was used by teachers and learners in a university-based summer ELL program. We refer to this particular example often throughout the chapter.

Instead of assigning a unidimensionally scaled ability estimate to each examinee as done in typical item response theory (IRT) model-based summative assessments, skills diagnosis model-based formative assessments partition the latent space into sufficiently fine-grained, often discrete or even dichotomous, skills and evaluate the examinee with respect to his or her level of competence on each skill. The term "skill" is used in a generic sense here and can refer to any relatively fine-grained entity associated with the examinee that influences item performance in the general subject area being tested. For example, suppose designers of an algebra test are interested in assessing student proficiencies with respect to a standard set of algebra skills (e.g., factoring, using the laws of exponents, solving quadratic equations, etc.). A skills diagnosis–based analysis attempts to evaluate each examinee with respect to each skill, whereas a standard unidimensional psychometric analysis typically evaluates each examinee only with respect to an overall scaled score on the algebra exam. We also note here that the decision about whether to use a set of user-defined skills or a unidimensional scale score in a given assessment depends largely on the intended purpose of the assessment. If the purpose of the algebra assessment described previously is only to separate the class into two groups – the group of students who are lagging behind, and all other students – then the assessment and reporting of individual skill competency levels is likely a distraction and an impediment. For such an assessment purpose, the best type of assessment would likely be a unidimensionally scaled assessment that reliably ranks examinees along a broad competency scale, representing in this case overall algebra ability.

Before we describe the details of the Fusion Model system, it is helpful to place the system within the context of a more general framework for skills diagnosis. Roussos, DiBello, Henson, Jang, & Templin (in press; see also Roussos, DiBello, & Stout, in press) described a framework for the entire implementation process for diagnostic assessment, elaborating on practical aspects of cognitively based assessment design and illuminating practical issues in regard to estimation and score reporting.

In particular, they described the diagnostic assessment implementation process as involving the following six steps:

1. Description of assessment purpose
2. Description of a model for the skills space
3. Development and analysis of the assessment tasks (e.g., test items)
4. Selection of an appropriate psychometric model for linking observable performance on tasks to the latent skill variables
5. Selection of statistical methods for model estimation and checking
6. Development of systems for reporting assessment results to examinees, teachers, and others

As discussed in Roussos, DiBello, Henson, et al. (in press), the steps of a successful implementation process are necessarily nonlinear, requiring considerable interaction and feedback between the steps and demanding close collaboration between users, test designers, cognitive psychologists, and psychometricians. This chapter focuses on the Fusion Model system, which provides components for implementation steps 4 to 6. Specifically, the Fusion Model item response function is a model that can

be selected in step 4 of the implementation process, the *Arpeggio* parameter estimation and model checking procedures could be employed in
step 5, and the Fusion Model system skills-level score statistics are
useful for developing score reports in step 6 of the implementation
process.

The first section of the chapter reviews the reparameterized unified
model (RUM), which is the item response function (IRF) that is used
in the Fusion Model system. The next section reviews the Monte Carlo
Markov Chain (MCMC) estimation procedure. The following section
describes the variety of model checking statistical techniques provided
by the Fusion Model system. The next section describes the last component of the Fusion Model system, the statistical techniques that have
been developed for use in score reporting. The last section of the chapter
summarizes the system, where to obtain more information, and future
areas of research and development. Throughout the chapter, our focus
is on describing the practical statistical aspects of the system so someone with test data would be able to apply the system intelligently and
know how to interpret the results, regardless of whether the application is a post-hoc analysis of existing summative test data or embedded within a full diagnostic framework beginning with the design of
the diagnostic instrument. We emphasize that the statistically focused
knowledge presented here is insufficient by itself for carrying out skills
diagnosis. In general, all steps of the implementation process described
previously are required for successful implementation, which includes
not only statistical analyses, but also substantive analyses and the interaction of the two. Readers are referred to Roussos, DiBello, Henson, et al.
(in press) and Roussos, DiBello, and Stout (in press) for more details on
the implementation process as a whole.

2.0 THE FUSION MODEL

Item response theory (IRT) provides a highly successful and widely
applied probabilistic modeling approach to assessment analysis and
scoring that is based on an item response function (IRF) model. IRT-
based cognitive diagnosis models, like all IRT models, define the probability of observing a particular response by examinee j to item i in
terms of examinee ability parameters and item parameters. Symboli-
cally, this probability is represented as $P(X_{ij} = x \mid \theta_j, \beta_i)$, where $X_{ij} = x$
is the response of examinee j to item i, θ_j is a vector of examinee j ability
parameters, and β_i is a vector of item i parameters. In this chapter, for
convenience, we restrict x to be dichotomous, indicating a correct ($x = 1$)

or incorrect ($x = 0$) response, but the Fusion Model can handle the poly-tomous case as well.

The fundamental assumption of IRT modeling is that, conditioned on the examinee ability parameters, an examinee response to any item i is independent of the examinee response to any other item i'. The distinguishing feature of cognitive diagnosis models from other IRT models is that the items $i = 1, \ldots, I$ relate to a prespecified, user-selected set of cognitive skills $k = 1, \ldots, K$ that are of particular interest to the skills diagnosis. This relationship is referred to as the Q matrix, where $q_{ik} = 1$ indicates that skill k is required by item i and $q_{ik} = 0$ indicates that skill k is not required by item i. The Q matrix notation was first introduced by Tatsuoka (1990), whose work highlighted the scientific development of the Q matrix as a critical component of skills diagnosis.

The Unified Model (DiBello et al., 1995) features both skills-based item parameters and skills-based examinee parameters. Furthermore, the Unified Model includes additional parameters to improve the fit of the model to the data. As discussed by Samejima (1994) in her Competency Space theory, let the examinee parameter $\theta = \{\alpha_Q, \alpha_b\}$ (examinee subscript j suppressed) denote the complete latent space of all relevant skills. Let α_Q be the vector of prespecified cognitive skills as denoted in the Q matrix. The remaining latent space, α_b, includes the relevant skills supplementary to those specified by the Q matrix. Samejima (1995) referred to α_b as skills associated with "higher-order processing" and suggested that these skills may be more substantively important than α_Q. From the Unified Model perspective, however, α_b does not need to be interpreted as higher-order processing; it is just a parametrically simple representation of the latent skills influencing examinee task performance that lie outside the user-specified Q matrix.

The Unified Model parameterizes ability for examinee j as (α_j, η_j), where α_j is a vector of skill mastery parameters corresponding one to one with α_Q, and η_j is conceptualized as a unidimensional composite of the elements of α_b (a projection of α_b onto a unidimensional scale). We call this η_j term the supplemental ability. The inclusion of this supplemental ability η_j in the Unified Model is connected to a type of item parameter that can be used to diagnose whether a test item is well modeled by the Q matrix skills that have been assigned to it. The explicit acknowledgment that the Q matrix is *not* necessarily a complete representation of all skill requirements for every item on the test differentiates the Unified Model from other skills diagnosis models.

For this chapter, we assume for convenience that the elements of α_j are dichotomous, that is, $\alpha_{kj} = 1$ if examinee j has mastered skill k, and

$\alpha_{kj} = 0$ if examinee j has not mastered skill k. In general, the Fusion Model can also handle more than two categories of skill mastery. On the other hand, η_j is modeled as a standard normal continuous variable. The ability distribution for the α_j parameters is assumed to be well modeled by its first- and second-order moments, namely, (a) the proportion of the population that has mastered each skill k – this proportion is denoted by $p_k, k = 1, \ldots, K$, and (b) the correlations between the K skill components of α_j. To facilitate better interpretability, tetrachoric correlations will be used instead of correlations to model the relationships between the dichotomous mastery variables.

Define $\pi_{ik} = P(Y_{ikj} = 1 \mid \alpha_{kj} = 1)$ and $r_{ik} = P(Y_{ikj} = 1 \mid \alpha_{kj} = 0)$, where $Y_{ikj} = 1$ refers to the unobserved event that examinee j correctly applies skill k to item i. (We restrict ourselves here to the case of dichotomous skill mastery, even though, as stated previously, the Fusion Model is also capable of handling more than two levels of skill mastery. Use of the latent variable Y_{ikj} is also used in the latent response models discussed by Maris, 1999.) The IRF for the Unified Model is given in Equation 10.1:

$$P(X_i = 1 \mid \underline{\alpha}_j, \eta_j) = d_i \prod_{k=1}^{K} \pi_{ik}^{\alpha_{jk} \cdot q_{ik}} r_{ik}^{(1-\alpha_{jk}) \cdot q_{ik}} P_{c_i}(\eta_j) + (1 - d_i) P_{b_i}(\eta_j),$$

$$(10.1)$$

where $P_h(\eta_j) = \{1 + \exp[-1.7(\eta_j + h)]\}^{1/2}$, a Rasch model (Rasch, 1961) with the difficulty parameter equal to the *negative* of h, where h stands for either c_i in the first term or b_i in the second term.

The product term in the model indicates two important aspects of the model. First is the statistical assumption of conditional independence of applying the skills, provided the Q-based strategy is used. The second is the cognitive assumption that the interaction of multiple skills within a given item is conjunctive. That is, a high probability of answering the item correctly requires successfully executing all the required skills. By further assuming local independence of the item responses, Equation 10.1 can be used to model the probability of any given response pattern, x. If k_i is the number of skills required for item i, then for each item i on the test there are $2k_i + 3$ item parameters: π_{ik} and r_{ik}, two IRT Rasch Model parameters c_i and b_i, and the final parameter d_i, the probability of selecting the Q-based strategy over all other strategies.

The Unified Model IRF not only models examinee responses as influenced by Q, but also allows non-Q skills to influence examinee response probability with the term $P_{c_i}(\eta_j)$, and allows for alternate non-Q

strategies with the term $P_{b_i}(\eta_j)$. As with the models of Maris (1999) and the general component latent trait model of Embretson (1984), the Unified Model has cognitively interpretable parameters, but unfortunately not all parameters are identifiable or, thus, statistically estimable.

The flexibility and interpretability of the Unified Model parameters led it to be chosen as the foundation for the Fusion Model skills diagnosis system described in this chapter. However, because nonidentifiable parameters existed in the original Unified Model (see Jiang, 1996), a reduction in the parameter space was required to make the model estimable. To accomplish this task, Hartz (2002) reparameterized the Unified Model to be identifiable in a way that retains interpretability of the parameters. To further reduce the complexity of the parameter space and to enhance the ability to estimate the parameters, the modeling of the possibility of alternate strategies was dropped by setting $d_i = 1$, $i = 1, \ldots, I$. The reduced model, referred to as the Reparameterized Unified Model (RUM), has $2 + k_i$ parameters per item compared to the $2k_i + 3$ parameters per item in the original Unified Model. The reduced model maintains the Unified Model's flexible capacity to fit diagnostic test data sets as compared to other skills diagnosis models, retaining the most substantively important components, such as the capacity for skill discrimination to vary from item to item and the residual ability parameter η, an additional and potentially important component of the original Unified Model that is missing from all other models. Equation 10.2 presents the RUM IRF, which is based on the same examinee parameters, α_j and η_j, that are used in the original Unified Model. The $P_{c_i}(\eta_j)$ term again refers to the Rasch model with difficulty parameter $-c_i$ [the lower the value of c_i, the lower the value of $P_{c_i}(\eta_j)$]

$$P(X_{ij} = 1 \mid \underline{\alpha}_j, \eta_j) = \pi_i^* \prod_{k=1}^{K} r_{ik}^{*(1-\alpha_{jk}) \times q_{ik}} P_{c_i}(\eta_j). \tag{10.2}$$

It is important for understanding and applying the Fusion Model that the interpretation of these parameters be clearly understood. Here,

$$\pi_i^* = P(\text{correctly applying } \textit{all} \text{ item } i \text{ required skills given}$$
$$\alpha_{jk} = 1 \text{ for all item } i \text{ required skills})$$

$$= \prod_{k=1}^{K} \pi_{ik}^{q_{ik}},$$

(under the assumption of conditional independence of individual skill application)

$$r_{ik}^* = \frac{P(Y_{ijk} = 1 \mid \alpha_{jk} = 0)}{P(Y_{ijk} = 1 \mid \alpha_{jk} = 1)}$$

$$= \frac{r_{ik}}{\pi_{ik}}, \text{ and}$$

$P_{c_i}(\eta_j) = P(\text{correctly applying skills associated with } \underline{\alpha}_b \text{ to item } i,$
conditional on η_j).

The $P_{c_i}(\eta_j)$ term refers to the Rasch model
(one-parameter logistic model, Rasch, 1961) with
difficulty parameter $-c_i$. Note that in our
parameterization, the lower the value of c_i,
the lower the value of $P_{c_i}(\eta_j)$.

where, $0 < \pi_i^* < 1$, $0 \leq r_{ik}^* \leq 1$, and $0 \leq c_i \leq 3$. (The bounds of 0 and 3 on the c_i parameter were chosen for convenience rather than because of any strict theoretical or logical constraint.)

The Fusion Model reparameterization replaces the $2k_i$ parameters π_{ik} and r_{ik} in the original Unified Model with $(1 + k_i)$ parameters π_i^* and r_{ik}^*. It is easy to show that the reparameterized model is mathematically equivalent to the original Unified Model, and the $(1 + k_i)$ parameters are now identifiable (DiBello, Stout, & Hartz, 2000). In addition to producing an identifiable parameter set, the new parameters are conceptually interpretable in a particularly appropriate way from the applications perspective. The parameter π_i^* is the probability that an examinee having mastered all the Q required skills for item i will correctly apply all the skills when solving item i. For an examinee who has *not mastered* a required skill k_0, her correct item response probability is proportional to $r_{ik_0}^*$. The more strongly the item depends on mastery of this skill, as indicated by a value of $r_{ik_0}^*$ closer to 0, the lower the item response probability for a nonmaster of the skill. Thus, r_{ik}^* is like an inverse indicator of the strength of evidence provided by item i about mastery of skill k. The closer r_{ik}^* is to zero, the more discriminating item i is for skill k. When most of the r_{ik}^* parameters for a skill are closer to zero (e.g., averaging less than 0.5), the test is said to display high cognitive structure for that skill, which is indicative of a test that is well designed for diagnosing mastery on the skill. Clearly, the r_{ik}^* parameters play an important role in evaluating the diagnostic capacity of an assessment instrument.

The distinctiveness of the π^* and r^* parameters in comparison to parameters in other models is important to note. Other models have indeed included components similar to π_{ik}^* and r_{ik}^*. The models in Maris (1999) have the π_{ik} and r_{ik} parameters of the Unified Model (DiBello et al., 1995), which are nonidentifiable. Conversely, the discrete MLTM of Junker (2000) has skill-based item parameters that are identifiable, but not item specific, so the influence of the skill on each individual item response probability is lost. This is especially important from the perspective of skills-based test design where one wishes to know for each skill which items are most effectively discriminating between examinee possession and non-possession of that skill.

The $P_{c_i}(\eta_j)$ component is an important unique component retained from the Unified Model because it acknowledges the fact that the Q matrix does not necessarily contain all relevant cognitive skills for all items. Interestingly, it is not present in any other skills diagnosis model. In this component, c_i indicates the reliance of the item response function on skills other than those assigned to that item by the Q matrix. As an approximation, these other skills are modeled, on average over all items, by a unidimensional ability parameter, η_j. When c_i is 3 or more, the item response function is practically uninfluenced by η_j because $P_{c_i}(\eta_j)$ will be very close to 1 for most values of η_j. When c_i is near 0, η_j variation will have increased influence on the item response probability, even with α_j fixed. Thus, the estimate of c_i can provide valuable diagnostic information about whether a skill is missing from the Q matrix or whether a skill already in the Q matrix needs to be added to a particular item's list of measured skills.

The Fusion Model assumes local independence (LI) given (α, η). If multiple skill-by-item assignments are missing from the Q matrix, then the influence of the missing multiple skills are unidimensionally captured by η. In this case, local independence with respect to (α, η) will only be approximate.

In summary, the Fusion Model enables the estimation of the most critical examinee parameters from the original Unified Model, while reparameterizing the Unified Model's item parameters so they are not only estimable, but also retain their skills-based interpretability, a feature that makes such models more attractive to users of educational tests in comparison to traditional unidimensional psychometric models.

3.0 METHOD OF ESTIMATION FOR THE MODEL PARAMETERS

After reparameterizing the Unified Model, a variety of possible methods for estimating the item parameters were explored. To increase the capacity of the RUM to fit the data and to simplify and improve the estimation procedures, a Bayesian modeling augmentation of the RUM was developed. Although using Bayesian Networks is one type of Bayesian approach that could have been adopted, we found that the probability structure of interest could be combined with relationships between the skills more directly by using a hierarchical Bayesian modeling approach instead. This Bayesian hierarchical structure, in effect, enhances the reparameterized Unified Model of Equation 10.2 by adding further parameters and their priors, where, as is common practice, the priors are either chosen to be uninformative, strongly informative, or estimated from the data (the empirical Bayes viewpoint). Thus, we describe the Bayesian modeling framework for the ability and item parameters, and then the MCMC procedure for estimating the parameters in the Bayesian framework.

3.1 Bayesian Framework for the Ability Parameters

The prior used for the η_j parameter was simply set to the standard normal distribution. However, the Bayesian model underlying the dichotomous skill mastery parameters required a more complicated approach.

The dichotomous α_{kj} ability parameters are modeled as Bernoulli random variables with probability of success p_k, the population proportion of masters for skill k. The prior for the dichotomous α_{kj} ability parameters consisted of the p_k parameter for each skill and the tetrachoric correlations between all skill mastery pairs. These parameters are modeled as hyperparameters in a hierarchical Bayes model.

In particular, raw correlations between the dichotomous skills are highly dependent on the differing proportions of masters for each skill. To deal with this problem, we used a well-known latent variable tool called *tetrachoric correlations*. Tetrachoric correlations model the relationship between two dichotomously measured variables, where it is assumed that a normally distributed latent variable generates each observed dichotomous variable (see, e.g., Hambleton & Swaminathan, 1985). The use of tetrachoric correlations was preferred over raw correlations between the dichotomous skills because raw correlations are highly dependent on the differing proportions of masters for each skill, thus making them more difficult to interpret as measures of the strength of relationship between two skills.

As stated, the tetrachoric correlations assume that continuous normal random variables underlie the dichotomous α_{kj} mastery variables. It is assumed that the continuous variables have been dichotomized by cut-point parameters. These continuous variables, which we denote symbolically as $\tilde{\alpha}_{kj}$, are viewed as continuous levels of skill competency that, when dichotomized by "cut points," determine mastery versus nonmastery of a skill. The cut-point parameters are denoted as κ_k and are related to the p_k parameters by the relation $P(\tilde{\alpha}_{kj} > \kappa_k) = p_k$, where $\tilde{\alpha}_{kj}$ is assumed to follow a standard normal distribution.

The correlations between η_j and the underlying $\tilde{\alpha}_j$ variables are, of course, modeled as nonnegative correlations. These correlations are estimated as hyperparameters (allowing the data to help estimate their joint distribution) and are given a Uniform prior, Unif(a, b), where a and b were set to 0.01 and 0.99, respectively, to prevent boundary problems. Numerical techniques for drawing the correlations in the MCMC algorithm were used to maintain positive definiteness, as is required of the correlation matrix (see Hartz & Roussos, in press, for details).

3.2 Bayesian Framework for the Item Parameters

Because the values of π_i^*, r_{ik}^*, and c_i can vary greatly for a given data set, the priors (distribution functions) for the three types of item parameters were each chosen to be a Beta distribution, allowing maximum flexibility of the shape the priors can take. Beta distributions are often used in Bayesian analyses because they naturally model parameters that are constrained to finite intervals, as is the case with π_i^* and r_{ik}^*. Even though, strictly speaking, c_i can be any real value, it makes practical sense to restrict its values for model parameter estimation to a finite interval. There are also mathematical reasons to prefer Beta distributions as priors. These reasons have to do with the Beta distributions being conjugates of the family of binomial distributions. To take advantage of the valuable flexibility of the Beta distribution, the parameters of the Beta priors are themselves estimated by assigning them priors and estimating the corresponding hyperparameters (the hierarchical Bayesian approach allowing the data to influence the estimated shape of the distributions, as is desirable). In the current version of *Arpeggio*, these hierarchical priors are fixed to be approximately uniform distributions.

3.3 Brief Description of MCMC

Largely due to the influence of the pair of Patz and Junker (1999a, 1999b) articles, MCMC has become popular in many skills diagnostic applications, in particular, for the fully Bayesian Fusion model (Roussos, DiBello, & Stout, in press) and the NIDA and DINA models (de la Torre

& Douglas, 2004). Although EM (expectation and maximization) algorithms are often much more efficient computationally than MCMC algorithms, EM algorithms are more difficult to extend to new models or model variants than are MCMC algorithms. As Patz and Junker (1999a) point out, EM algorithms are not as "straightforward" (p. 147; see also Junker, 1999, p. 70) to apply for parametrically complex models. Furthermore, one obtains a joint estimated posterior distribution of both the test's item parameters and the examinee skills parameters, which can be persuasively argued to provide better understanding of the true standard errors involved (as Patz & Junker, 1999a, 1999b, argued in their papers on MCMC uses in psychometrics).

Here, we provide a brief conceptual description of MCMC. First, a probabilistically based computational method is used to generate Markov chains of simulated values to estimate all parameters. Each time point (or step) in the chain corresponds to one set of simulated values. MCMC theory states that after a large enough number of steps (called the *burn-in phase* of the chain), the remaining simulated values will closely approximate the desired Bayesian posterior distribution of the parameters. It is important to note that obtaining this posterior distribution would almost always be impossible to compute analytically or approximate numerically, even using modern computational approximation methods because of the level of parametric complexity in our model. A solution to the analytical intractability is provide by implementing the Metropolis-Hastings procedure with Gibbs sampling that uses much simpler proposal distributions in place of the analytically complex full conditional distributions (see Gelman, Carlin, Stern, & Rubin, 1995). In the current version of *Arpeggio,* the *proposal distributions* (also called *jumping distributions*) take the form of moving windows (Henson, Templin, & Porch, 2004). The parameters defining these proposal distributions are already fixed by the program to appropriate values, and users should not change these values without first carefully consulting Henson, Templin, et al. (2004).

MCMC estimation is accomplished by running suitably long chains, simulating all parameters at each time point of the long chain, discarding the burn-in steps, and using the remaining steps in each chain as posterior distributions to estimate the parameter values and their standard errors. The practitioner must carefully choose the number of chains to be used, the total length of the chain, and the amount to be used for the burn-in. When a practitioner has little experience for a given analysis, we recommend the use of at least two chains of very long length and very long burn-ins (e.g., a chain length of 50,000 and a burn-in of 40,000). The next section in this chapter provides information on how to evaluate the MCMC results. The post–burn-in chains are estimates of the posterior distributions of the parameters. The *Arpeggio* software uses these distributions to provide EAP (expectation a posteriori) point estimates and posterior standard deviations as measures of variability.

It is interesting to note that MCMC could be used from either a partially Bayesian or a non-Bayesian perspective, and both are useful in different circumstances. A common application is fully Bayesian (as described here for the Fusion Model), often with hierarchical structure to give it an appropriate empirical Bayes flavor. The primary inferential outcome is the full posterior distribution of the joint item and examinee parameter distributions, as represented by a set of random draws from the joint distribution. Many argue that having these distributions and, in particular, the available estimated standard errors of each parameter, is of considerable value. Many MCMC references exist, and the Patz and Junker (1999a, 1999b) articles and the Gelman et al. (1995) book are especially recommended to interested readers considering parametrically complex models such as the models surveyed here.

4.0 MODEL CHECKING PROCEDURES

In this section, we discuss a variety of model checking methods that are available with the Fusion Model system, how to interpret the results of these methods, and what actions one might take in reaction to the results.

4.1 Convergence Checking

All statistical estimation methods that involve iterating until convergence to obtain a solution require checking for convergence – either convergence to within some specified tolerance, as in an EM iterative algorithm, or convergence to the desired posterior distribution, as in the case of MCMC. Because the statistical information one obtains from MCMC estimation (a full posterior distribution) is richer than that obtained from an EM algorithm (an estimate and its standard error), the evaluation of whether convergence has occurred is more difficult in the MCMC case.

In skills diagnosis applications, MCMC convergence may be difficult to obtain, depending on the complexity of the model and how well the design and assumptions of the model correspond to the reality of the data. In some cases, complex models may be statistically nonidentifiable. In other cases, identifiable models may be difficult to estimate well because of ill-conditioned likelihood functions. Of course, these modeling issues will cause problems for all estimation methods, not just for MCMC. In any case, the first thing that must be done after running the *Arpeggio* MCMC algorithm is to determine whether the chains converged to a stationary solution (presumed to be the posterior distribution of the parameters).

Although much has been written in the literature regarding the convergence of Markov Chains in MCMC estimation, there is no simple statistic that reliably evaluates whether the Markov Chain for each model parameter has converged. The Fusion Model system provides results for evaluating convergence in four ways: chain plots, estimated posterior distributions, autocorrelations of the chain estimates, and Gelman and Rubin $\hat{R}$ (Gelman et al., 1995), each of which is discussed in this section.

One important tool (perhaps the most important tool) for checking convergence is the chain plot for each parameter – a graph showing the value of the parameter for each step in the chain. In Figure 10.1, we give an example of an investigation by Jang (2005; Roussos, DiBello, Henson, Jang, & Templin, in press) of the effect of chain length on the estimation of an item parameter in the context of analyzing a 37-item test taken by about 1350 examinees using a Q matrix having nine skills, with an average of about two skills per item (which translates to an average of about eight items per skill). The plots show every 10th term in the chain to simplify the plots and reduce the sizes of the output. In this example, it seems evident from the chain plots that the first 1000 steps can adequately serve as the burn-in. The plots clearly indicate that the chains have settled into a stable distribution.

Also shown in Figure 10.1 are the posterior distributions. These graphs support the inference from the chain plots that convergence has occurred because there is little change in the posterior distribution after the first 1000 steps of the chain.

Figure 10.1 also shows the autocorrelation function, which can be used to determine the degree of independence between two groups of simulated data that are separated by a specified number of steps in the chain. The lower the autocorrelation is, the more information there is for a given chain length. Thus, if autocorrelation is relatively high, the chains must be run longer to estimate the posterior distribution with reasonable accuracy. Figure 10.1 indicates that there is little autocorrelation between

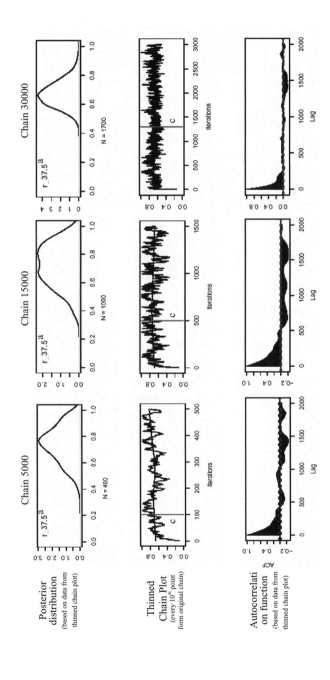

a. r_37.5 is an item parameters for items 37 and skill 5
b. N=number of post-burn-in points in thinned chain plot
C. vertical line denotes burn-in

FIGURE 10.1. Effect of chain length on item parameter estimation convergence. (From Jang, 2005; Roussos, DiBello, Henson, Jang & Templin, in press.)

291

chain estimates that are spaced 500 or more steps apart. This example illustrates good convergence results and is no doubt due to the careful model development by Jang.

Note that high autocorrelations do not necessarily imply MCMC non-convergence but, alternatively, may simply be indicating a relatively flat likelihood surface. This is a common problem with complicated models that are likely for almost any particular data set to have at least a few nonsignificant parameters, parameters whose values for the given data set are not significantly different from the values one would expect under an appropriate null hypothesis of no parameter influence (e.g., see Carlin, Xia, Devine, Tollbert, & Mulholland, 1999). This phenomenon is *not* the same as the nonidentifiability of overparameterized models. In such cases, the likelihood is relatively flat for *all* data sets.

In Figure 10.1, Jang (2005) looked at a single chain with varying chain lengths. Another important method supported by the Fusion Model system is to run *Arpeggio* for multiple chains and compare the results, including the chain plots, posterior distributions, and autocorrelations. If the chosen chain length has achieved convergence, then the results from different chains should be practically the same. Also, when you use multiple chains, the Gelman and Rubin $\hat{R}$ (the ratio of between-chain variance plus within-chain variance to within-chain variance; Gelman et al., 1995) will be reported in the results. Gelman et al. recommend that $\hat{R}$ values less than 1.2 are a necessary, but not sufficient, condition for convergence. In our experience, unfortunately, we have seldom seen $\hat{R}$ values greater than 1.2 in cases of nonconvergence. When we have, it has usually been an indication of a gross error we have made in one of our input or data files.

When convergence does not occur with the Fusion Model system, we have a few suggestions based on our own experiences. One frequent problem we have encountered is that when the c_i parameter (and its accompanying η_j ability parameter for the non-Q skills) is included in the model, estimation of the model parameters pertaining to the Q skills (i.e., the π_i^* and r_{ik}^* parameters) does not converge (or converges to a solution having most of the p_k parameters being very large). The reason this has occurred so frequently in our analyses is that most of our applications have been with tests having a single dominant dimension, and this allows the continuous η_j parameter to "soak up" most of the variance in the item responses. Conversely, we also sometimes have nonconvergence for the c_i parameters in cases in which many items have large numbers of skills required as specified in the Q matrix. In such cases, there is no variance left to be accounted for by the $P_{c_i}(\eta_j)$ part of the model. If either of these situations arises, a good solution is to drop the c_i parameter from all the items in the model – this is accomplished through a user set option that automatically sets all the c_i values equal to 10, which effectively makes the $P_{c_i}(\eta_j)$ term equal to 1 for all reasonable values of η_j. This reduced version of the Fusion Model is the version we often have used for analyzing real data.

If the c_i parameter is not in the model and nonconvergence occurs, the first thing to check is whether the burn-in phase of the MCMC chain was long enough to reach the posterior distribution phase. This can be checked by running an extremely long chain. If the longer chain still does not result in convergence, one can probably rule out chain length as the problem. In this case, one can revisit the model-building steps, and reconsider the Q matrix and the selected model to identify where changes may be warranted. For example, if the model assumes that a skill is difficult (small p_k), yet the skill is assigned to items having a large range of difficulty (including both hard and easy items), the MCMC algorithm may not be able to converge to a single level of difficulty for the skill.

There is much more to say, in general, about MCMC convergence. The reader is referred to Cowles and Carlin (1996) and a recent article by Sinharay (2004) for an excellent and thorough discussion.

4.2 Interpretation of Model Parameter Estimates

Given that the model estimation procedure has converged, the estimates for the ability distribution (for the skills) and item parameters should be evaluated.

4.2.1 Ability Distribution Parameters

A key issue for mastery/nonmastery diagnostic models is whether the proportion of examinees estimated as masters on each skill is relatively congruent with the user's expectations The Fusion Model system provides estimates of the p_k parameters and estimator standard errors for this purpose. If a skill turned out much harder or easier than expected, based on the p_k estimate and its standard error (e.g., harder or easier than desired from a formal standard-setting perspective, or relative to the difficulty of other skills), the Q matrix should be revisited and the item difficulty levels investigated for the items to which the skill has been assigned. In addition, the choice of tasks assessing that skill can be revisited to see if other more appropriate tasks can be found to either include or replace existing tasks. For example, if the proportion of masters for a skill is too low, one could try replacing the harder tasks for that skill with easier ones, adding easier ones, or both. Ultimately, the definition of the skill may need to be adjusted, for example, by suitable modification of Q or in a more basic way leading to a new set of tasks. For example, in Jang (2005, 2006; Roussos, DiBello, Henson, Jang, & Templin, in press), one of the skills was found by statistical analysis to be *much* easier than expected, whereas the other eight skill difficulties were ordered in a manner consistent with Jang's approximate expectations.

4.2.2 Item Parameters

The Fusion Model system also provides estimates and standard errors for the item parameters. The estimates for the π_i^*, r_{ik}^*, and, if present, the c_i parameters, should be inspected in detail because they play a key role in determining the success of the diagnosis. (The interpretive meaning of the item parameters is discussed previously and is thus only briefly repeated, as needed, here.)

First, we should repeat something we covered in Section 4.1. If the c_i parameters are included in the model and estimation convergence is obtained, the solution should be carefully investigated to determine whether the $P_{c_i}(\eta_j)$ part of the model dominates the fitted model. If that occurs, then most of the p_k parameters will be very large (artificially making nearly everyone a master on most of the skills) so most of the individual differences are explained by the η_j parameter. This has occurred frequently in our analyses because most of our applications have been with tests having a single dominant dimension, and this allowed the continuous η_j parameter to soak up most of the variance in the item responses. In this case, even if convergence has occurred, to obtain a diagnostically useful estimated model one needs to drop the c_i parameters from the model (see explanation in Section 4.1).

Assuming convergence has occurred and the estimates do not indicate any fundamental problem, as with the previous c_i parameters, the estimates for each type of item parameter will provide useful information on the performance of each item relative to its required skills.

The simplest item parameter to investigate is π_i^*, which indicates the probability that examinees have correctly executed all Q skills required by an item, conditional on having mastered all required skills. We want this value to be close to unity (1.0). In our applications, we have interpreted values of π_i^* less than 0.6 as indicating items that are overly difficult for the skills assigned to them. Either more skills or different (and likely more difficult) skills would need to be assigned to such items in order to have correct item response be indicative of mastery of the particular skills assigned to the item.

The remaining two types of item parameters, r_{ik}^* and c_i, give information on how well the items discriminate on the Q skills and the degree to which skills are missing in the Q assignments for an item, respectively. A low value of r_{ik}^* (0–0.5) is indicative of a highly discriminating item, and a low value of c_i (0–1.5) is an indication that either a Q skill is missing for the item or (if this occurs for many items) a skill is missing from the entire Q matrix. High values of r_{ik}^* and c_i are indicative of possible model simplifications. If r_{ik}^* is bigger than, say, 0.9, the item is not very discriminating for the corresponding skill and the Q matrix entry can be eliminated (1 changed to a 0), and if c_i is big, then the item is approximately "complete" and c_i can be dropped (i.e., set equal to 10).

It should be noted that a "1" entry in the Q matrix can be fully justified on substantive grounds – considering the definition of the skill and the coding procedures – and still show an estimated r_{ik}^* value that is very near 1.0. This is analogous to the situation in which a test item for a unidimensional test looks good on substantive grounds, but the discrimination parameter is very small, resulting in a relatively flat item characteristic curve. For diagnostic assessments, the high estimated r_{ik}^* value means that statistically the particular item is not contributing much information for distinguishing between masters and nonmasters of the given skill. So dropping the "1" entry from the Q matrix is not necessarily indicative of a "mistake" in the item coding. Instead, the decision is a statistically strategic one that bets on the gain in parameter estimation accuracy, with fewer parameters to be estimated and the resulting improvement in classification accuracy and interpretability (see later discussion) to be a worthwhile benefit to justify dropping the "1" entry in the Q matrix, even in light of the substantive rationale for the original "1" coding. Of course, if such cancellations occur for many of the items requiring a particular skill, the practitioner should interpret that as a signal that the skill or the skill coding procedure may need to be modified to bring the substantive coding and statistical behavior into better alignment.

The elimination of noninformative r_{ik}^* and c_i parameters is considered to be an important component of the Fusion Model system because it helps the model concentrate its statistical power where there is diagnostic information to be found. In other words, such reduction in the number of model parameters may be beneficial simply because fewer parameters can be better estimated (smaller standard errors) with the same observed data. However, more important, dropping nonsignificant Q matrix entries (which is what occurs when an r_{ik}^* is eliminated) reduces the possibility of examinee confusion that can arise from examinees labeled nonmasters performing nearly as well as those labeled masters on the items corresponding to the Q entries being eliminated. To this end, we have developed statistics to help identify statistically noninfluential r_{ik}^* and c_i item parameters.

To accomplish the goal of identifying noninfluential parameters, the Fusion Model system estimates the influence of r_{ik}^* and c_i on the item response function that uses that parameter. By employing a common probability scale for measuring this influence, the same statistical decision rule is used for both r_{ik}^* and c_i in determining whether the estimated influence is large enough to warrant keeping the parameter in the model. In our simulation studies, these decisions were based solely on a statistical hypothesis testing framework in which the null hypothesis is that the item parameter under investigation has negligible influence on the parameter's item response function. However, it is important to note that in practice, as discussed previously, such decision making would typically be based on an interaction of both statistical and substantive input. Because a Q matrix is often developed with strong theoretical arguments to back it up, the dropping of Q matrix entries needs not only strong statistical evidence, but also strong substantive arguments.

To estimate the influence of a particular item parameter, three different item response probabilities are calculated for each examinee from the Fusion Model IRF. With the other parameters fixed at their estimated means, three IRF probabilities are calculated: (a) with the parameter fixed at its null hypothesis (no influence) value (an r_{ik}^* would be fixed at 1.0, and a c_i would be fixed at 10.0), (b) with the parameter set to its estimated mean minus its estimated standard deviation, and (c) with the parameter set to its estimated mean plus its estimated standard deviation. For an r_{ik}^* parameter, the three IRF probability calculations are averaged over all examinees who are estimated as nonmasters of skill k (these are the only examinees for whom the r_{ik}^* would appear in their IRF). For a c_i parameter, the averaging is done using all examinees. When the average of item response probability (a) is close to that for either (b) or (c) (or both, depending on the preference of the practitioner), the parameter is said to be noninfluential and is dropped from the model.

The determination of whether two average probabilities are close is ultimately a subjective decision, but there still exists experience from other IRT domains of interest that can help guide decision making here.

The most common examples of such decision making with which we are familiar are in the context of differential item functioning (DIF) analyses. In DIF analyses, an average difference between IRFs of less than 0.01 is certainly considered to be a negligible amount, whereas a difference between 0.05 and 0.10 is often considered to be moderate and a difference greater than 0.10 is usually considered to be large (see, e.g., Dorans, 1989). In our simulation studies, we found that a relatively liberal approach (using cut-off values that are on the low side within the range of the typical DIF cut-offs) worked best for these particular studies. In particular, in our simulation studies, we declared that a c_i or r_{ik}^* is noninfluential for an item (and set the parameter to its null hypothesis value, thus dropping it from the model) when the average for (a) is within 0.03 of the average for (b) or within 0.01 of the average for (c).

Practitioners may, of course, choose other reasonable criteria and may choose to use only the difference between (a) and (b) or only the difference between (a) and (c). The former corresponds to a situation in which a practitioner is philosophically choosing a null hypothesis that the parameter belongs in the model and will only drop it out if the data provide strong evidence otherwise. The latter corresponds to a situation where the null hypothesis is that the parameter does not belong in the model and will only be included if the data provide strong evidence otherwise. Both philosophies are statistically valid, as is the combined use of both types of criteria. The choice is, as it should be, up to the practitioner.

Finally, because the item parameters across skills and items influence one another, we perform the calculations iteratively rather than all at once. On each run, we restrict ourselves to dropping a maximum of one parameter per item before rerunning the entire model and rechecking these statistics again (one can conduct this analysis in a repeated manner as in a stepwise regression). If more than one parameter appears noninfluential at the same time, then it is possible that the dropping of one parameter could cause another parameter to become influential. If both an r_{ik}^* and a c_i parameter are found to be noninfluential at the same step, the c_i parameter is preferentially dropped to favor the possibility of retaining skill mastery estimation in the item over the possibility of retaining estimation of η because skills diagnosis is the primary purpose of the analysis. Also, if two or more r_{ik}^* parameters for a particular item are found to be noninfluential, the parameter with the smallest average difference between the null hypothesis IRF probability (a) and the upper bound IRF probability (c) is dropped.

Even when a Q matrix is carefully developed for estimation of the Fusion Model with real data, or even when you generate simulated data and use the known Q matrix in your estimation model, there may be item parameters that, for the given data, are statistically insignificant.

For example, in a real data setting, a skill may be assigned by the Q matrix to an item, but it may be that examinees do not actually need or use the skill in correctly responding to the item (e.g., the item may require only a very elementary application of the skill and thus play an almost nonexistent role statistically, even though it is "required" for the item), or a skill may be needed to a much lower degree than other skills that also are delineated by the Q matrix. (This real data setting can be emulated in simulation studies by using a Q matrix in the estimation model that does not match the one used in simulating the data.)

An example of this situation is when data are simulated with low r_{ik}^* values and high π_i^* values (referred to as "high cognitive structure"), and moderate c_i values. In this case, the c_i parameters may not be well estimable because the item responses are largely determined by whether examinees have mastered the skills and are minimally affected by their proficiency on non-Q skills. Additionally, if an item measures both a hard skill and an easy skill, and the r_{ik}^* for the harder skill is very low, the r_{ik}^* for the easier skill will have little influence in the IRF.

An example of a real case in which parameter dropping was used is the analysis of Jang (2005, 2006; Roussos, DiBello, Henson, Jang, & Templin, in press). In this study, the estimated item parameters led Jang to eliminate about 9% of her Q matrix entries because certain items did not discriminate well on some of the skills that had been assigned to them. Specifically, the estimated parameters indicated that the ratio of skill performance by nonmasters to that by masters was 0.9 or more for about 9% of the item-skill combinations.

4.3 Model Fit Statistics

Once the Fusion Model has been calibrated from data, model fit is evaluated by using the fitted model to predict observable summary statistics that are compared to the corresponding observed statistics. The predicted statistics are obtained by simulating data from the fitted model and calculating the statistics on the simulated data. The item parameters used in the simulation model are the item parameter estimates (EAPs) from the real data analysis. The ability parameters used in the simulation model are probabilistically generated as follows. For each examinee in the calibration data set, the fusion model system provides a posterior probability of mastery (*ppm*) for each skill and an estimate of η. In the simulation, examinees are sampled with replacement from the calibration sample, and an $(\alpha_k, k = 1, \ldots, K)$ vector is simulated by generating an independent series of Bernoulli random variables, one for each skill, with the Bernoulli probability for each skill being equal to the sampled examinee's *ppm* for each skill. The resampled examinee's actual estimated η is used for the simulated value. The item parameters and ability parameters are then used in the standard way to generate simulated item responses. The resampling is done, say, 500,000 times, to obtain accurate predicted statistics. This type of approach is called posterior predictive model checking (see Gelman et al., 1995; Gelman & Meng, 1996; Sinharay, 2005; Sinharay & Johnson, 2003). The statistics that are typically calculated in the Fusion Model system are the proportion-correct scores on the items, the item-pair correlations, and the examinee raw score distribution (see Henson, Roussos, & Templin, 2004, 2005). The item pair correlations and the score distribution represent more demanding tests of data-model fit, and must be interpreted with care and in light of the diagnostic purpose of the assessment.

As a specific example, in the application of Jang (2005; Roussos, DiBello, Henson, Jang, & Templin, in press), the mean absolute difference (MAD) between predicted and observed item proportion-correct scores was 0.002, and the MAD for the correlations was 0.049, supporting the claim of good fit. One can also compare the fit between the observed and predicted score distributions. Figure 10.2 shows a comparison between the observed and the predicted score distributions from the

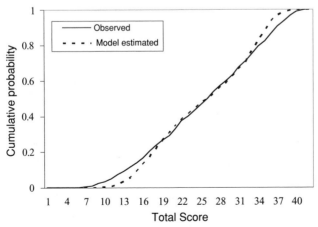

FIGURE 10.2. Comparison of observed and model estimated score distributions. (From Jang, 2005, 2006; Roussos, DiBello, Henson, Jang, & Templin, in press.)

real data analysis of Jang (2005, 2006; Roussos, DiBello, Henson, Jang, & Templin, in press). The misfit at the very lowest and highest parts of the distribution were expected as the mastery/nonmastery examinee model overestimated the scores of the lowest scoring examinees and underestimated the scores of the highest scoring examinees. Because the goal of the analysis was to estimate mastery/nonmastery rather than to scale examinees, this misfit actually had no effect on the mastery/nonmastery classification. Even though the lowest scoring examinees had overestimated scores, they were still all classified as nonmasters on all the skills. Similarly, although the highest scoring examinees had underestimated scores, they were still estimated as masters on all skills.

This is an example of a case in which one might discover that a simpler unidimensional model with a continuous ability parameter would fit the score distribution data better (i.e., produce predictions of total scores that look more like the observed data). But if such a model did not yield the desired mastery/nonmastery classification estimates without further work, it would not satisfy the diagnostic assessment purpose.

For a broader discussion of model diagnostic fit statistics relevant for cognitive diagnosis models, the reader is referred to Sinharay (2006). In his article, Sinharay demonstrates several model diagnostic approaches in the context of a real data analysis, and identifies several instances of poor model fit and severe nonidentifiability of model parameters. Although the Sinharay article involves a real data skills diagnosis that used a Bayes net approach, the model fit approaches he demonstrates are broadly applicable to any parametric skills diagnosis model, including the Fusion Model.

4.4 Internal Validity Checks

In general, broad conceptions of validity go beyond criterion validity in which model estimates and predictions are compared to observable data. For example, construct validity for an assessment instrument refers to the extent to which measurements of the instrument's construct(s) have expected relationships with other constructs in a wider nomothetic structure of related constructs; and consequential validity refers to the extent to which desired and positive consequences result from the use of assessment information.

Nevertheless, criterion validity based on observable data remains a critical component of the overall test validation process. We categorize criterion validity into two broad categories: internal validity (synonymous with internal consistency) and external validity. In the case of internal validity, the observable data come from the test data themselves. External validity statistics relate test-derived ability estimates to some other ability criterion external to the test – in particular, a criterion indicating whether the particular educational purpose of the skills diagnosis has been well served. The Fusion Model system includes internal validity checks, and users are also strongly encouraged to conduct external validity checks according to whatever criteria external to the test are most appropriate for the user's setting.

One kind of internal validity check is to measure the differences in observed behavior between examinees that are classified differently, and this idea provides the basis for the internal validity checks we have developed. Specifically, the Fusion Model produces two types of such statistics: *IMstats* for *item mastery statistics*, and *EMstats* for *examinee mastery statistics*.

IMstats describes how well, on an item-by-item basis and on average over all items, the *Arpeggio* MCMC estimates of examinee mastery of each skill correspond to the actual observed performance of the examinees on each item. Specifically, *for each item on the test*, the examinees are divided into three groups according to how many of the particular skills required by the item each examinee has been estimated as having mastered. Examinees who have mastered all skills required by item *i* are called the "item *i* masters." Examinees who are nonmasters on at least one, but not more than half, of the skills required for item *i* are called the "item *i* high nonmasters." Examinees who lack mastery on more than half the skills required for item *i* are called the "item *i* low nonmasters." This use of the terms "master" and "nonmaster" is different from our previous usage with respect to mastery of individual skills. Here mastery is discussed relative to *all* skills required for an item, not mastery relative to a single skill. Then, on an item-by-item basis, *IMstats* computes the observed proportion-right score on each item for the examinees falling into each of these three groups for that item. To determine whether the *Arpeggio* MCMC estimation procedure is working well in conjunction with the Q matrix, the results of *IMstats* are examined to see whether the item masters have performed decidedly better than item nonmasters and, similarly, whether the item high nonmasters have performed substantially better than the item low nonmasters. We consider this decision making to be fairly subjective in that it depends on what one considers to be a negligible difference in these proportions. We do not recommend a formal hypothesis testing approach here because these proportions are calculated over a large number of examinees, and their standard errors would be expected to be very small, making even nonconsequential small differences statistically significant.

EMstats stands for "examinee mastery statistics," and it is used to search for examinees who perform either unexpectedly poorly on the items for which they have mastered all the required skills or unexpectedly well on the items for which they have not mastered all the required skills. EMstats produces evaluation statistics on an examinee-by-examinee basis, as well as summary statistics over all examinees. After each examinee has been estimated as either mastering or not mastering each skill, the particular set of mastered skills for a given examinee provides the basis for dividing the examinee's items into three groups. Specifically, *for each examinee j,* the *items* on the test are divided into three groups (similar to the *IMstats examinee* groups), based on the proportion of each item's skills the selected examinee has been estimated as having mastered:

- **Examinee j's mastered items.** The set of items for which examinee j has been estimated as having mastered all Q matrix skills required for each item.
- **Examinee j's high nonmastered items.** The set of all items for which the examinee has been estimated as having nonmastered at least one, but not more than half, of the skills required by the item, according to the Q matrix.
- **Examinee j's low nonmastered items.** The set of all items for which the examinee has been estimated as having nonmastered more than half of the skills required by the item, according to the Q matrix.

The last two categories are also combined to form a fourth general category for all nonmastered items for this examinee. For each examinee, *EMstats* calculates the number of mastered, high nonmastered, and low nonmastered items for that examinee and the examinee's proportion-right score on each of these sets of items.

EMstats then compares the examinees observed proportion-right score for the examinee mastered items with a criterion value to determine whether this score is unusually low. Similarly, the scores on the examinees high nonmastered, low nonmastered items, and all nonmastered items together are also compared to criteria to determine whether these scores are unusually high. Because these observed proportion-right scores are frequently based on fairly small numbers of items, we decided that a hypothesis testing approach to the decision making was needed to avoid high type 1 error rates. Thus, for each examinee,

EMstats performs a one-tailed hypothesis test for each set of items. The hypothesis tests are one-tailed because for the mastered items we only care whether the examinee had an especially low proportion-right score, and for any of the sets of nonmastered items we only care whether the examinee had an especially high proportion-right score. The criterion values are either set by the user or are based on the observed item proportion-right scores for masters, high nonmasters, and low nonmasters from *IMstats*. The criterion values based on the latter case are used in this study.

The hypothesis tests are conducted in the following manner. First, the examinee's observed proportion-right score is subtracted from the appropriate criterion value. Then, under the assumption that the null hypothesis holds, the standard error is computed as $\sqrt{P_{c_i}(1 - P_{c_i}) \div n}$, where the summation is over the n items of interest and P_{c_i} is the criterion value for item i. Next, a simple z statistic is formed by dividing the difference by the standard error. Assuming that this z statistic is approximately normally distributed, the hypothesis test is performed by determining whether the calculated z statistic is less than -1.645 when the focus of the hypothesis test is on the mastered items or greater than 1.645 when the focus is on the nonmastered items.

To help ensure the validity of the assumption of approximate normality, we require that the number of items in a category be above some minimum level. Specifically, the minimum level is equal to the number of items needed for the hypothesis test to reject an observed difference of 0.2 or more at level 0.05.

As an example of the use of the *IMstats* internal validity check in a real data analysis, Figure 10.3 presents the *IMstats* results from Jang (2005, 2006; Roussos, DiBello, Henson, Jang, & Templin, in press) for one of the test forms she analyzed. These results clearly indicate a high degree of internal validity for the skills diagnosis because the mean score differences between item masters and item nonmasters are quite large for the vast majority of the items. The results also clearly point to certain problematic items, which Jang investigated. She discovered that these items tended to be either extremely easy or extremely hard. As noted by Jang, the test she used had been originally intended as a norm-referenced test, with the purpose of placing examinees on a continuous scale, thus requiring items of a wide range of difficulty. Jang quite rightly notes that such a test, developed for another purpose, is not necessarily a good one for doing skills diagnosis, and the identification of these problematic items through the internal validity analysis drove home this point.

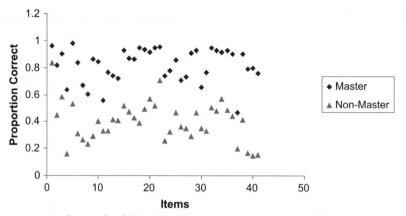

FIGURE 10.3. Internal validity check comparing performance difference between item masters and item nonmasters. (From Jang, 2005, 2006; Roussos, DiBello, Henson, Jang & Templin, in press.)

4.5 Reliability Estimation

Standard reliability coefficients, as estimated for assessments modeled with a continuous unidimensional latent trait, do not translate directly to discrete latent space modeled cognitive diagnostic tests. We note, however, that conceptions of reliability from first principles do still apply. Diagnostic attribute classification reliability can be conceptualized in terms of the twin notions of, on the one hand, the correspondence between inferred and true skills mastery state and, on the other hand, the consistency of classification if the same assessment were administered to the same examinee multiple times. It is this concept of consistency that is operationalized as the method for reliability estimation in the Fusion Model system.

Specifically, to estimate classification reliability, the calibrated model is used to generate parallel sets of simulated data and then to estimate mastery/nonmastery for each simulated examinee on each set. The simulation is carried out in the same way described previously for the model fit statistics in Section 4.3. For each skill, we calculate the proportion of times that each examinee is classified correctly on the test (estimation of correct classification rate) and the proportion of times each examinee is classified the same on the two parallel tests (estimated test–retest consistency rate). These rates are reported separately for true masters and true nonmasters of each skill, and also averaged over masters and nonmasters. The mastery/nonmastery estimation for a given skill is accomplished by calculating the *ppm* (posterior probability of mastery) for each examinee and declaring the examinee a master if $ppm > 0.5$. An option of using an indifference region is also provided, such that an examinee is declared a master if $ppm > 0.6$, nonmaster if $ppm < 0.4$, and unknown otherwise (the user can choose values other than 0.4 and 0.6 for the upper and lower boundaries of the indifference region). The use of an indifference region increases the reliability, at the cost of declaring a set of examinees to be of indeterminate mastery.

In any case, another set of statistics produced are a set of "pattern" statistics: the proportion of examinees whose estimated skill masteries are incorrect (estimated as a master when truth is nonmaster, or estimated as nonmaster when truth is master) for 0 skills, 1 skill, 2 skills, etc. This is a useful statistic because it can be used to judge how likely it is that an individual examinee has a certain number of errors in their estimated skill profile. For example, in an analysis by Henson, He, and Roussos (in press), 99% of the simulated examinees had one or no errors. Such statistics are easy for score users to interpret. When they get an estimated score profile, they can compare the results with their own records, keeping in mind that more than one incorrect skill mastery classification is extremely unlikely. Thus, if they find one skill classification that does not seem quite right, they should feel comfortable that they can disregard it without wasting precious time and effort trying to figure out the discrepancy. This seems like the kind of reliability estimation that teachers may be able to understand and use in their diagnostic score interpretations for a given skills profile – how many errors are there likely to be?

5.0 SCORE REPORTING STATISTICS

The last component in the Fusion Model system is the production of statistics that are useful for skills-level score reporting, which, for example, would be directed toward students, teachers, and parents in an educational diagnostic assessment setting.

Cognitive diagnostic analysis using the Fusion Model system can provide students and instructors with detailed skills-level student assessments that can be used to improve instruction and learning. Once a satisfactory calibration of a given test has been completed, then diagnostic scores can be provided in the classroom or across the Web by using either the *Arpeggio* MCMC procedure, with item and population parameters fixed to calibrated values, or the Bayesian posterior scoring program called the *Fast Classier*. The latter is the preferred method because it computes the mathematically correct maximum likelihood or maximum a posteriori estimates of the posterior probabilities of mastery and is computationally more efficient.

5.1 *ppm* and η

The basic set of statistics reported are the ability estimates: the estimate of α (α_k, $k = 1, \ldots, K$), and the estimate of η if the c_i parameters were included in the model.

As mentioned previously, the estimate of the α_ks are in the form of *ppm*s. These are obtained directly from the post–burn-in section of the MCMC chain for each skill. During the MCMC estimation at each step in the chain, α is proposed as a string of 1s and 0s for an examinee. After the chain has converged to the posterior distribution and has run for a large number of steps, the proportion of 1s in the chain for a particular skill is, by definition, the *ppm*, the posterior probability of mastery for the skill for that examinee. An examinee is then declared a master of a skill if *ppm* is above some user-provided upper threshold (0.5 or more), a nonmaster if *ppm* is below some user-provided lower threshold (0.5 or less), and is declared "indeterminate" if *ppm* is between the two thresholds. One interesting choice for the indifference region is (0.2, 0.8), which results in Cohen's kappa of at least 0.6 for all classifications, where 0.6 is regarded as a rule of thumb for a classification that is "substantial" relative to chance (on a scale of no agreement, slight, fair, moderate, substantial, and nearly perfect agreement; Landis & Koch, 1977).

From our experience, an examinee's *ppm* may fall into the indeterminate region typically for one or more of the following reasons: (a) the items were not very good for discriminating mastery from nonmastery for a particular skill, and/or (b) the examinee behaved inconsistently, neither like a master nor like a nonmaster but, rather, somewhere in between these two states (recall that the mastery/nonmastery dichotomy, although necessary for decision making, is a dichotomy of a more continuous or multicategory construct). If case (a) holds, the result may be a higher than desired proportion of examinees in the indifference region. The previous reliability calculation can help determine whether case (a) is occurring for a particular skill.

In regard to η_j, the Fusion Model system provides a Bayesian EAP estimate based on the MCMC estimated posterior distribution. In general, the estimate for η_j is not directly connected to the skills specified in the Q matrix and consequently is not used for diagnostic purposes.

5.2 Relating Scores to Skill Profiles: Proficiency Scaling

The *ppm*s mentioned in Section 5.1 are the primary (most direct) means for conveying skills-level diagnostic information to test takers and test users (e.g., students, parents, teachers, administrators). However, for test takers and users to have a high level of confidence in the *ppm*s, it is important that they have statistics that illuminate the relationship between skill mastery and the observed scores on the test – the scores being an entity with which they are much more familiar and can easily observe for themselves.

To this end, the Fusion Model system estimates the relationship between all possible test scores and all possible skill mastery patterns (all possible values of α, the vector of dichotomous mastery parameters for the K skills). The estimation method is based on simulating 100,000 examinee item responses from the fitted model, as described in Section 4.3 (for more details, see Henson, Roussos, & Templin, 2004, 2005). To make these results more interpretable, two sets of summary statistics are produced.

The first set of statistics summarizes the distribution of skill mastery patterns given a test score by reporting (a) the three most probable skill mastery patterns for each fixed score (and their associated probabilities in the simulated population at that score); (b) a count of the minimum number of skill mastery patterns whose probabilities sum to at least 50%, 75%, and 90% at each fixed score; and (c) the mean or expected *ppm* for each skill at each fixed score.

The second set of statistics summarizes the distribution of test scores for each possible skill mastery pattern. The Fusion Model system reports for each skill mastery pattern: (a) the expected score; (b) the standard deviation of the scores; and (c) the three most likely scores, the corresponding probability of each, and the sum of these three probabilities.

For well-designed tests and carefully implemented skills diagnosis, these statistics will help give users more confidence because they will see that an expected test score generally increases as the number of mastered skills increases. Furthermore, in knowing this conditional information, quick rudimentary estimates of skill mastery can be made from an examinee's test score.

Such information can largely be useful in low-stakes situations to give teachers additional information that can help in their approach to teaching and improving the learning environment. By knowing the relationship between test scores and skill mastery patterns, teachers can quickly evaluate each examinee's likely skill mastery pattern and determine what would be an appropriate focus for the examinee to improve his or her performance. However, such summaries of the joint distribution of test score and skill mastery pattern are not limited to those we have presented in this section. Others could be used for specific purposes that we have not yet addressed.

5.3 Use of Subscores for Estimation of Skill Masteries

In some test settings, practitioners may require an alternative to the *ppms* (see Section 5.1) that come from the *Arpeggio* MCMC scoring engine or from the Fast Classier. For example, a state testing program might mandate that mastery decision making be based on test cut-scores, the most easily interpretable information that can be transmitted to test users. This section discusses reasonable uses of subscores in cases in which we have performed a Fusion Model–based analysis of a test that has been well designed for cognitive skills diagnosis. We note that many commercially produced tests currently provide subscores as "diagnostic" score information, without any proper psychometric foundation. In contrast to these practices, we indicate here how we have constructed simplified subscoring systems that are based on a Fusion Model analysis and that can be shown to be close in accuracy to using the optimal Fusion Model–based *ppms*.

In some settings, we may have skills coded to items in such a way that each item has only one skill coded to it. We use the term "simple structure" for such Q matrices. One possible method for producing a subscore for each skill is to compute proportion correct or total scores over just the items coded to that skill. If the Q matrix for a given test includes items with multiple skills (as is often the case), we can still define a subscore for each skill in exactly the same way. Once we have a method for computing subscores, we need one more element to provide mastery/nonmastery classification scores. A cut-point in the proportion correct subscore is necessary to be able to translate the subscore into a mastery/nonmastery designation. The choice of a good cut-point is essential for good diagnostic performance of such a subscore method for producing diagnostic profiles (see Henson, Stout, & Templin, 2005) and is intimately related to standards setting.

In this section, we briefly discuss variations of a Fusion Model–based subscoring approach that uses the results of a Fusion Model parameter calibration to calculate appropriately weighted subscores and reasonable model-driven cut-points. We discuss how to achieve adequate performance, compared to optimal Fusion Model mastery/nonmastery scoring, by defining reasonable subscores (either based on a simple structure Q matrix as mentioned previously or a Q matrix that includes multiple skills per item) of some sort and user-selected cut-points as indicators of mastery. We note that a poor choice of cut-points or substantially suboptimal subscores (i.e., subscores that fail to incorporate a substantial portion of the information that would be provided about skills by a full Fusion Model system analysis) will likely produce substantially suboptimal skills classification accuracy (Henson, Stout, & Templin, 2005).

In the case of a nonsimple structure Q matrix, we have investigated methods for using the Fusion Model information to convert the nonsimple structure Q matrix into a suboptimal but reasonable simple structure Q matrix. Namely, each item with multiple skills is assigned to that skill k for which the estimated r_{ik}^* is smallest among all the skills assigned to the item by Q. Then that item will contribute only to the subscore for the *kth* skill. This is called simple structure subscoring. An alternative, and reasonable, approach is to leave the original Q matrix unchanged and allow items that are coded for multiple skills to contribute to multiple subscores.

We note that if the original Q matrix does include items with multiple skills, then both of these subscoring methods have been shown to be suboptimal compared to Fusion Model scoring (Henson, Stout, & Templin, 2005). Under the first subscore method, in which each item is assigned to only one skill, an item contributes "credit" (from a correct response) or "blame" (from an incorrect response) to only one of its originally coded skills, and the "credit" or "blame" for the other skills of that item are missing from their subscores. Under the second subscore method, in which the original nonsimple structure Q matrix is retained and each subscore adds up all items that are coded to it, an item that is answered incorrectly now contributes "blame" to the subscores for all theskills coded to that item. But in a conjunctive setting such as the Fusion Model, in which successful execution of all required skills is needed for correct item performance, the reason for the incorrect item response may be the lack of mastery on just one of the skills. The second subscore method has no mechanism for incorporating the fact that a given incorrect response on a multiple-skill item may be due to nonmastery on only one skill. Note that these missing credits or blames also hold for weighted subscoring, which we discuss in the next paragraphs. So the proper

question is how to make use of Fusion Fodel–based item information
to minimize the credit and blame problems, and when we do that, how
close do we come to the optimal Fusion Model mastery/nonmastery
scoring.

The first thing we do is use weighting that takes advantage of useful skill discrimination information contained in the estimated item
parameters. That is, some items are better indicators of mastery versus nonmastery when compared to others. For this reason, we suggest
sometimes using weighted subscores, where the item weights should
quantify how strongly each item measures the skill in question. We thus
have three ways of forming subscores: two producing ordinary (i.e.,
unweighted) subscores, and the third producing potentially more informative weighted subscores.

An intuitively reasonable choice of weights is $\delta_{ik} = \pi_i^*(1 - r_{ik}^*)$. For,
smaller r_{ik}^* values and larger π_i^* both indicate that the item is very informative about skill k mastery. The weight δ_{ik} ranges from 0 to 1 and can
be interpreted as an indicator of how strongly skill k influences the item
response function (0 means no impact, and 1 implies that it is impossible to get the item right when lacking skill k; Henson, Stout, & Templin,
2005). The reporting of these weights is useful even if *ppms* instead of
subscores are being used to decide mastery/nonmastery. When examinees receive a score report indicating mastery or nonmastery on a given
skill and are told which items measured the skill, they will naturally
examine their performance on those items and will typically notice both
correct and incorrect responses. The index can be used to better and
more easily interpret their item scores, for example, by listing the items
for them to inspect in order of highest to lowest δ_{ik} (see score reports
developed by Jang, 2006).

Using this weighting scheme, it is now possible to appropriately
define a weighted sum of items that is especially sensitive to the skill
k mastery/nonmastery dichotomy. Those items for which the kth skill
is most influential will have the largest weights. We define the *weighted
complex* skill k sum-score, W_{jk}, for the jth individual as a weighted sum
of those items required for skill $k(q_{ik} = 1)$ as follows:

$$W_{jk} = \sum_{i=1}^{I} \delta_{ik}(q_{ik}x_{ij}). \tag{10.3}$$

Unlike simple Q-based subscores, weighted Q-based subscores are
heavily influenced by those items with small r_{ik}^* values relative to those

with large r_{ik}^* values. For this reason, it is expected that the weighted (Q-based) subscores method of classification will have higher correct classification rates when compared to the ordinary (unweighted) Q-based subscore method, and simulation studies demonstrate this (Henson, Stout, & Templin, 2005). Based on these simulation results, it is also hoped that the performance of weighted subscores for many settings will be roughly as good as the correct classification rates produced by a full Fusion Model system analysis.

The next critical issue when using any weighted or unweighted subscoring approach is determining the cut-point at which a person is classified as a master. Henson, Stout, and Templin (2005) show that correct classification rates will be significantly lower than optimal if the cut-point for each subscore is selected in a way that ignores the Fusion Model parameters. In addition, Henson, Stout, and Templin (2005) show via simulation studies that by using a Monte Carlo estimation approach to determine the cut-point and using the aforementioned weighted subscores, the Fusion Model system's classification performance can be fairly well approximated.

The simulation method used in determining a cut-point for subscore-based mastery classification use is as follows. The Fusion Model system is used to obtain item parameter estimates and estimates of the joint distribution of the examinee skills space (see description in Section 4.3 or, for more details, see Henson, Stout, & Templin, 2005). Next, 100,000 simulated examinees and their simulated item responses are generated. Then, using a simple search, an appropriate cut-point for the weighted subscore is determined that maximizes correct classification rates for each skill, as determined in the simulated data set. This is possible because the true skill pattern for each of the simulated examinees is known.

In general, even if a full Fusion Model analysis is used to help design an effective skills-level test for diagnostics and then to calibrate the test, it may be unreasonable, or seen as undesirable or impractical in some settings, to do a full Fusion Model system–based classification. In such cases, the Fusion Model–based weighted subscoring approach can provide a relatively efficient, convenient, intuitively plausible, and inexpensive model-driven alternative. In these cases, although the Fusion Model is not directly used for skill pattern estimation, valuable information concerning the calibrated Fusion Model is used to determine the weights to use for the weighted subscores and the "optimal" cut-point. Henson, Stout, and Templin (2005) showed via simulation studies that although the Fusion Model system outperformed the subscoring approaches, in all cases the weighted subscoring Fusion Model–based method described previously provided a reasonable approximation. Henson, Stout, and Templin further showed that the unweighted subscoring approaches, perhaps mandated for the test setting, are clearly suboptimal relative to weighted subscoring but nonetheless can be reasonably effective. An upcoming paper by Henson and Templin (in press) will provide a detailed discussion of the subscoring approaches and the research results concerning them.

6.0 CONCLUDING REMARKS

This chapter has presented the Fusion Model skills diagnosis system, a comprehensive and ready-to-use data analysis system for conducting skills diagnosis. A detailed description of the Fusion Model system has been given in terms of four essential components required for a fully developed system: (a) the IRF model (RUM), (b) the MCMC estimation algorithm *Arpeggio* and its Bayesian modeling framework, (3) the collection of model checking procedures, and (4) the skills-level statistics that can be used for mastery/nonmastery scoring. Special emphasis was given to describing the probabilistic model and statistical methods constituting the Fusion Model system, outlining the user-focused results that the system reports, and explaining how to interpret and use these results. Although in this chapter the system was described as though it were restricted to dichotomously scored items and dichotomous skills (mastery vs. nonmastery), as noted at appropriate places in the chapter, the Fusion Model system is also applicable to polytomously scored items and/or polytomous skills (more than two levels of mastery). Indeed, the authors believe that these two polytomous directions will prove especially important in the future because of their potential to improve performance of diagnostic tests.

Educators have long implored the testing industry to more fully contribute to the formative assessment of learning, in particular by providing tests that can diagnose examinee mastery on skills of interest to teachers, parents, and other test users. Extensive research is underway to identify ways in which properly conceived and implemented assessment systems can improve teaching and learning, and lead to school improvement (see Pellegrino & Chudowsky, 2003; Popham, Keller, Moulding, Pellegrino, & Sandifer, 2005; Shavelson, Black, William, & Coffey, in press; Shepard, 2000). In the volatile accountability-focused standardized testing atmosphere that currently exists in the United States, it is especially important to understand how formative and summative assessment systems can be aligned, and how they can be mutually beneficial and supportive. The development of practical, effective psychometric and statistical models and approaches, such as the Fusion Model system, represents one essential component of this multifaceted problem. Many educational measurement specialists, including the authors of this chapter, see this formative assessment challenge providing psychometric solutions that will advance the effectiveness of formative assessment in classrooms as not only intellectually exciting from the research perspective, but also societally important from the educational perspective.

Motivated by this formative assessment challenge, this chapter presents in some detail one major attempt at providing the testing industry with a practical set of statistical tools sufficient for conducting educationally useful skills diagnosis, namely, the Fusion Model system. In particular, the Fusion Model system provides a comprehensive set of statistical and psychometric tools ready to provide effective formative assessment at a more fine-grained level than currently provided by the ubiquitous unidimensional test scoring currently used. The Fusion Model system also provides tools to help improve the design of diagnostic tests.

As noted herein, this systems performance has been heavily studied in simulation studies and has been applied in various real data settings. Particular applications include the briefly discussed Jang TOEFL work, as well as skills-level analyses of data from the PSAT/NMSQT and from the U.S. National Assessment of Educational Progress (NAEP). From the practitioner's perspective, the next necessary direction is the conducting of pilot studies and field studies of the Fusion Model system to investigate and develop procedures for the implementation of the system within the context of operational testing programs.

Indeed many such settings seem potentially ripe for such applied work. These include state and district K–12 standardized tests, development of periodically administered skills diagnostic tests intended for classroom use, and integration of diagnostic assessments into test preparation programs for high-stakes tests such as the undergraduate, graduate, medical, and other school or professional admissions testing. Applications in industrial and military training settings seem promising, too, especially because such training settings often have well-defined standards of what must be learned in order for students to be declared masters of the course material. Such standards would, of course, need to be converted into sets of skills by appropriately chosen experts. Future applications within 2- and 4-year colleges also seem promising. One example of a particularly intriguing and challenging application is the development of higher education courses in which diagnostic assessments serve the dual roles of formative assessment embedded in instruction and learning (based on student performance on periodically administered quizzes) and evaluation of overall summative assessment for traditional grading purposes.

Further psychometric and statistical challenges will arise in moving forward with the developments anticipated. However, the authors of this chapter believe that the status of the Fusion Model system is advanced enough to justify a concerted focus on the very real dual challenges of (a) learning to build effective diagnostic tests that are optimally tuned for strong diagnostic performance, and (b) addressing the substantial challenges in teacher professional development and development of curricular and instructional methods and systems that can benefit from such diagnostic assessment. Although our chapter focuses on the Fusion Model system, other systems at various stages of development are also available. Depending on their capabilities and performance properties, some of these systems will likely also be important in addressing this vital diagnostic educational challenge. Success in this diagnostic enterprise will depend vitally on high quality on at least three fronts simultaneously: the cognitive modeling of skills and skills acquisition; the preparation of teachers, curricula, and instructional programs and materials for a next generation classroom that is integrated with diagnostic assessment; and the psychometric quality of models and scoring procedures.

In summary, the Fusion Model system is well enough developed that it is ready for pilot-/field-testing in preparation for operational use, both (a) in existing settings where the summative test already exists and now needs enhanced scoring to carry out formative assessments, and (b) in contributing to the design of skills diagnostic formative assessments from scratch. Numerous interdisciplinary efforts are needed that draw on cognitive psychologists, teaching and learning experts, substantive curricular experts, practicing educators, and psychometricians to develop and make operational a new engineering science of informative skills level–based standardized testing. This chapter describes progress along the psychometric dimension specifically as represented by the Fusion Model system.

We conclude that the statistics and psychometrics concerning the Fusion Model system are advanced enough for developing a coordinated approach with the cognition, teaching, and learning components to significantly impact our vast and growing educational enterprise.

References

Birenbaum, M., Tatsuoka, C., & Yamada, Y. (2004). Diagnostic assessment in TIMMS-R: Between countries and within country comparisons of eighth graders' mathematics performance. *Studies in Educational Evaluation, 30*, 151–173.

Carlin, B., Xia, H., Devine, O., Tollbert, P., & Mulholland, J. (1999). Spatio-temporal hierarchical models for analyzing Atlanta pediatric asthma ER visit rates. In C. Gatsonis, R. Kass, B. Carlin, A. Carriquiry, A. Gelman, I. Verdinelli, & M. West (Eds.), *Case studies in Bayesian statistics* (Vol. IV, pp. 303–320). New York: Springer-Verlag.

The Commission on Instructionally Supportive Assessment. (2001, October). *Building tests to support instruction and accountability: A guide for policymakers.* Retrieved November 29, 2006, from http://www.testaccountability.org/

Cowles, M. K., & Carlin, B. P. (1996). Markov chain Monte Carlo convergence diagnostics: A comparative review. *Journal of the American Statistical Association, 91*, 883–904.

Cronbach, L. J. (1975). Beyond the two disciplines of scientific psychology. *American Psychologist, 30*, 116–127.

de la Torre, J., & Douglas, J.A. (2004). Higher-order latent trait models for cognitive diagnosis. *Psychometrika, 69*, 333–353.

DiBello, L. V., Stout, W. F., & Hartz, S. M. (2000, June). *Model parameterization and identifiability issues.* Paper presented at the international meeting of the Psychometric Society, University of British Columbia, Vancouver.

DiBello, L. V., Stout, W. F., & Roussos, L. A. (1995). Unified cognitive/psychometric diagnostic assessment likelihood-based classification techniques. In P. D. Nichols, S. F. Chipman, & R. L. Brennan (Eds.), *Cognitively diagnostic assessment* (pp. 361–389). Mahwah, NJ: Erlbaum.

DiBello, L. V., Stout, W. F., Roussos, L. A., Henson, R. A., Templin, J. L., & Fife, J. (2006). *Skill profiles for groups of students at a given NAEP scale level: Development and demonstration.* Unpublished project report, Educational Testing Service, Princeton, NJ.

Dorans, N. J. (1989). Two new approaches to assessing differential item functioning: Standardization and the Mantel-Haenszel method. *Applied Measurement in Education, 2*, 217–233.

Embretson, S. (1984). A general latent trait model for response processes. *Psychometrika, 49*, 175–186.

Gelman, A., Carlin, J. B., Stern, H. S., & Rubin, D. R. (1995). *Bayesian data analysis.* London: Chapman & Hall.

Gelman, A., & Meng, X.-L. (1996). Model checking and model improvement. In W. R. Gilks, S. Richardson, & D. J. Spiegelhalter (Eds.), *Markov chain Monte Carlo in practice.* Boca Raton, FL: Chapman & Hall/CRC.

Hambleton, R. K., & Swaminathan, H. (1985). *Item response theory*. New York: Kluwer-Nijhoff.

Hartz, S. M. (2002). *A Bayesian framework for the unified model for assessing cognitive abilities: Blending theory with practicality*. Unpublished doctoral dissertation, University of Illinois, Champaign.

Hartz, S. M., & Roussos, L. A. (in press). *The fusion model for skills diagnosis: Blending theory with practice* (ETS Research Report). Princeton, NJ: Educational Testing Service.

Henson, R. A., He, X., & Roussos, L. A. (in press). Cognitive diagnosis attribute level discrimination indices. *Applied Psychological Measurement*.

Henson, R. A., Roussos, L. A., & Templin, J. L. (2004). *Cognitive diagnostic "fit" indices*. Unpublished ETS Project Report, Princeton, NJ.

Henson, R. A., Roussos, L. A., & Templin, J. L. (2005). *Fusion model "fit" indices*. Unpublished ETS Project Report, Princeton, NJ.

Henson, R. A., Stout, W. F., & Templin, J. (2005). *Using cognitive model-based sumscores to do skills diagnosis*. Unpublished ETS External Team Project Report, Educational Testing Service, Princeton, NJ.

Henson, R. A., Templin, J. L., & Porch, F. (2004). *Description of the underlying algorithm of the improved Arpeggio*. Unpublished ETS External Team Project Report, Educational Testing Service, Princeton, NJ.

Henson, R. A., & Templin, J. L. (in press). Using model-based subscoring to do skills diagnosis. *Journal of Educational Measurement*.

Jang, E. E. (2005). *A validity narrative: Effects of reading skills diagnosis on teaching and learning in the context of NG TOEFL*. Unpublished doctoral dissertation, University of Illinois, Champaign.

Jang, E. E. (2006, April). *Pedagogical implications of cognitive skills diagnostic assessment for teaching and learning*. Paper presented at the annual meeting of the American Educational Research Association, San Francisco.

Jiang, H. (1996). *Applications of computational statistics in cognitive diagnosis and IRT modeling*. Unpublished doctoral dissertation, University of Illinois, Champaign.

Junker, B. W. (1999, November 30). *Some statistical models and computational methods that may be useful for cognitively-relevant assessment*. Prepared for the Committee on the Foundations of Assessment, National Research Council. Retrieved November 29, 2006, from http://www.stat.cmu.edu/~brian/nrc/cfa/.

Junker, B. (2000). *Some topics in nonparametric and parametric IRT, with some thoughts about the future*. Unpublished manuscript, Carnegie Mellon University, Pittsburgh.

Landis, J. R., & Koch, G. G. (1977). The measurement of observer agreement for categorical data. *Biometrics, 33*, 159–174.

Maris, E. (1999). Estimating multiple classification latent class models. *Psychometrika, 64*, 187–212.

McKnight, C., Crosswhite, F., Dossey, J., Kifer, E., Swafford, J., Travers, K., & Cooney, T. (1987). *The underachieving curriculum: Assessing U.S. school mathematics from an international perspective*. Champaign, IL: Stripes.

National Council of Teachers of Mathematics. (1989). *Assessment standards for school mathematics*. Reston, VA: Author.

Patz, R. J., & Junker, B. (1999a). A straightforward approach to Markov chain Monte Carlo methods for item response models. *Journal of Educational and Behavioral Statistics, 24*, 146–178.

Patz, R. J., & Junker, B. (1999b). Applications and extensions of MCMC in IRT: Multiple item types, missing data, and rated responses. *Journal of Educational and Behavioral Statistics, 24*, 342–366.

Pellegrino, J. W., & Chudowsky, N. (2003). The foundations of assessment. *Measurement: Interdisciplinary Research and Perspectives, 1*(2), 103–148.

Popham, W. J., Keller, T., Moulding, B., Pellegrino, J. W., & Sandifer, P. (2005). Instructionally supportive accountability tests in science: A viable assessment option? *Measurement: Interdisciplinary Research and Perspectives, 3*(3), 121–179.

Rasch, G. (1961). On general laws and the meaning of measurement in psychology. In J. Neyman (Ed.), *Proceedings of the fourth Berkeley symposium on mathematical statistics and probability* (Vol. 4). Berkeley: University of California Press.

DiBello, L. V., Roussos, L. A., & Stout, W. (2007). Review of cognitively diagnostic assessment and a summary of psychometric models. In C. R. Rao & S. Sinharay (Eds.), *Handbook of statistics: Volume 26, psychometrics* (pp. 979–1030). Amsterdam: Elsevier.

Roussos, L. A., DiBello, L. V., Henson, R. A., Jang, E. E., & Templin, J. L. (in press). Skills diagnosis for education and psychology with IRT-based parametric latent class models. In S. Embretson & J. Roberts (Eds.), *New directions in psychological measurement with model-based approaches*. Washington, DC: American Psychological Association.

Samejima, F. (1994, April). *Cognitive diagnosis using latent trait models*. Paper presented at the annual meeting of the National Council on Measurement in Education, New Orleans.

Samejima, F. (1995). A cognitive diagnosis method using latent trait models: Competency space approach and its relationship with DiBello and Stout's unified cognitive-psychometric diagnosis model. In P. D. Nichols, S. F. Chipman, & R. L. Brennan (Eds.), *Cognitively diagnostic assessment* (pp. 391–410). Mahwah, NJ: Erlbaum.

Shavelson, R. J., Black, P. J., William, D., & Coffey, J. (in press). On linking formative and summative functions in the design of large-scale assessment systems. *Educational Evaluation and Policy Analysis*.

Shepard, L. A. (2000). *The role of classroom assessment in teaching and learning* (CSE Technical Report 517). Los Angeles: National Center for Research on Evaluation, Standards, and Student Testing, University of California, Los Angeles.

Sinharay, S. (2004). Experiences with Markov chain Monte Carlo convergence assessment in two psycho-metric examples. *Journal of Educational and Behavioral Statistics, 29*, 461–488.

Sinharay, S. (2005). Assessing of unidimensional IRT models using a Bayesian approach. *Journal of Educational Measurement, 42*, 375–394.

Sinharay, S. (2006). Model diagnostics for Bayesian networks. *Journal of Educational and Behavioral Statistics, 31*, 1–33.

Sinharay, S., & Johnson, M. S. (2003). *Simulation studies applying posterior model checking for assessment of the common item response theory models.* (ETS Research Report No. RR-03-28). Princeton, NJ: Educational Testing Service.

Snow, R. E., & Lohman, D. F. (1989). Implications of cognitive psychology for educational measurement. In R. L. Linn (Ed.), *Educational measurement* (3rd ed., pp. 263–331). New York: Macmillan.

Tatsuoka, K. K. (1990). Toward an integration of item-response theory and cognitive error diagnoses. In N. Frederiksen, R. L. Glaser, A. M. Lesgold, & M. G. Shafto (Eds.), *Diagnostic monitoring of skill and knowledge acquisition.* (pp 453–488). Hillsdale, NJ: Erlbaum.

Tatsuoka, K. K., Corter, J., & Guerrero, A. (2003). *Manual of attribute-coding for general mathematics in TIMSS studies.* New York: Columbia University, Teachers College.

Tatsuoka, K. K., Corter, J., & Tatsuoka, C. (2004). Patterns of diagnosed mathematical content and process skills in TIMMS-R across a sample of 20 countries. *American Educational Research Journal, 41*, 901–926.

Xin, T. (2004). Latent trait and latent class models for multi-rater, multi-attribute agreement (UMI No. 3129052). *Dissertation Abstracts International, 65*(04), 1337A.

Xin, T., Xu, Z., & Tatsuoka, K. K. (2004). Linkage between teacher quality, student achievement, and cognitive skills: A rule-space model. *Studies in Educational Evaluation, 30*, 205–223.

11

Using Information from Multiple-Choice Distractors to Enhance Cognitive-Diagnostic Score Reporting

Richard M. Luecht

Unidimensional tests primarily measure only one proficiency trait or ability (Hambleton & Swaminathan, 1985). That is, we assume that a single proficiency trait can completely explain the response patterns observed for a population of test takers. However, most tests exhibit some multidimensionality (i.e., responses that depend on more than one proficiency trait or ability). Multidimensionality may be due to the cognitive complexity of the test items, motivational propensities of the test takers, or other more extraneous factors (Ackerman, 2005; Ackerman, Gierl, & Walker, 2003).

Diagnostically useful scores that profile examinees' strengths and weaknesses require well-behaved or principled multidimensional measurement information. This presents a challenge for established test development and psychometric scaling practices that are aimed at producing unidimensional tests and maintaining unidimensional score scales so accurate summative decisions can be made over time (e.g., college admissions, placement, or granting of a professional certificate or licensure). Any multidimensionality detected during the scaling process is treated as "nuisance factors" not accounted for when designing the test items and building test forms (e.g., passage effects due to choices of topics or method variance due to item types). In fact, most item response theory (IRT) scaling procedures regard multidimensionality and related forms of residual covariation in the response data as statistical misfit or aberrance (Hambleton & Swaminathan, 1985). Can this largely uncontrolled "misfit" or residual covariance be exploited for legitimate diagnostic purposes? Probably not.

It is one thing to detect subtle amounts of multidimensionality manifest in a data matrix for a large sample of test takers – most commonly using factor analytic techniques to detect patterns of residual covariance and then playing the "Name Those Factors" game.[1] And it is quite another to exploit it in a diagnostically useful way to produce reliable scales that will hold up across multiple test forms, subpopulations, and time.

Proficiency tests that are truly unidimensional are particularly problematic because virtually any subscores formed by combining content-related sets of the items using various attributes classification schemes determined by subject matter experts, tend to be highly correlated and substantially less reliable than the total test scores (Luecht, 2005a; Wainer et al., 2001). The reality is that any apparent fluctuations in the reported diagnostic subscore profiles probably reflect measurement errors and can lead to flawed diagnostic recommendations – essentially "chasing error" rather than suggesting useful remedial strategies. Conversely, if the subscores are highly reliable, or induced to be highly reliable by exploiting collateral information in other sets of items, the unidimensional nature of the response data will produce flat diagnostic profiles that are of little diagnostic utility beyond the total test scores.

The dilemma is that purely unidimensional tests apparently have little to share beyond the measurement information that goes into computing the total test scores, and tests that exhibit small amounts of extraneous multidimensionality may not be producing the proper type of measurement information to support diagnostically useful subscores. There are two potential solutions to this dilemma. The first solution entails the development of highly structured approaches to designing and writing/creating assessment tasks that will yield *stable* multidimensional information for two or more instructionally sensitive latent traits. This solution specifically involves the development of carefully engineered items, task designs, and templates, ideally based on

---

[1] Exploratory factor analysis reduces a set of statistical associations between different test items or components to a smaller collection of factors that are ultimately named by the researcher, who considers the logical categorization of groupings of items that load most strongly on each factor. Cliff (1987) has referred to this rather arbitrary process of estimating and then labeling statistically detectable factors as "the naming game". This approach is distinctly different than a confirmatory approach, which starts with a hypothesized factor structure (e.g., a subscore structure based on cognitively consistent tasks) and then attempts to validate that structure as fitting an observed correlation or covariance matrix.

empirical human factors and cognitive scientific research. This type of engineering-based design of test items and assessments has only recently gained impetus as a major research theme in measurement (e.g., Drasgow, Luecht, & Bennett, 2006; Ferrera et al., 2003; Huff, 2004; Irvine & Kyllonen, 2002; Leighton, 2004; Leighton, Gierl, & Hunka, 2004; Luecht, 2002; Mislevy & Riconscente, 2005). A more in-depth discussion of engineering solutions to test design problems is beyond the scope of this chapter.

The second solution involves taking advantage of multidimensional measurement information gleaned from additional data sources and is called *data augmentation*. Data augmentation can involve using any collateral information sources, including timing data, scores on other tests, or any other auxiliary data source that can be extracted and used in computing diagnostically useful score information. This chapter focuses on data augmentation mechanisms that make use of any measurement information hidden in meaningful distractor patterns for multiple-choice questions (MCQs). Results are presented from an empirical study that demonstrates that there are reasonable consistencies in MCQ distractor response patterns that might be detected and possibly exploited for diagnostic scoring purposes.

Dimensionality of Strengths and Weaknesses

It is important to question whether strengths and weaknesses are on the same metric or on *different* metrics before entering into a discussion of data augmentation. One argument is that most proficiency tests – by design and further reinforced as a consequence of commonly used psychometric scaling procedures such as IRT – only measure examinees' *strengths* along a single dimension of interest. That is, we sum the scored responses or model the probability of a correct response as a function of an underlying trait. If the examinee chooses the correct answers on the test, he or she demonstrates strength on the trait of interest. Under the strength-oriented perspective, weakness is merely considered to be the absence of, or negation of, strength. To further complicate matters, when the test is explicitly constructed to be unidimensional – which many tests are – the scored item response patterns tend to produce subscores that are strongly and positively correlated with the overall trait measured by the test. As a result, any skill profiles based on two or more diagnostic subscores that employ dichotomous correct/incorrect scoring will tend to be flat and uninformative (Luecht, 2005a, 2006; Luecht, Gierl, Tan, &

Huff, 2006; Wainer et al., 2001). That is, virtually any subscores computed from the data matrix will produce less reliable replications of the total test score, where any apparent scatter in the profile merely represents measurement errors.

Consider an alternative perspective where examinees' inherent weaknesses are believed to stem from faulty strategies, improper instantiations of rules, incomplete algorithms, incorrect procedural knowledge, or temporary slips in knowledge. That is, weaknesses are not only the absence of strengths, but also may involve the application of a *different*, albeit improper, constellation of knowledge and skill in the context of the particular task challenges posed by particular items. This weakness-oriented perspective suggests that we may be able to substantively explain the raw item response patterns by hypothesizing some underlying cognitive mechanisms and an associated different set of traits that cause the examinee to select particular, *incorrect* distractor options.

In the specific case of MCQs,[2] it should be possible to design the distractors to encourage specific response patterns based on differential states of understanding. This chapter discusses the feasibility of using MCQ distractor information – via data augmentation – for diagnostic scoring purposes. It is useful, however, to first address how the response data are transformed into the scored responses that are used in most psychometric scaling procedures.

Response Data, Scoring Evaluators, and Data Augmentation

Many psychometric scaling procedures deal with scored responses recoded into two or more integer values denoting "points." Dichotomous scoring typically converts the correct responses to ordered binary values: $u_i = 0$ if an item is incorrect, or $u_i = 1$ for a correct response. Polytomous scoring converts the responses to m ordered or partial credit categories ($u_i = 0$ for no credit, $u_i = 1$ for partial credit, $u_i = 2$ for full credit, etc.).

As discussed previously, a complication of dealing with a unidimensional test is that the dichotomously scored responses are only providing information about a single trait. Data augmentation implies the presence of additional data. This means obtaining an additional data source, besides the usual dichotomously scored response matrix,

---

[2] This chapter is limited to a discussion of MCQs. However, nothing presented is necessarily contradicted by considering more complex item types and scoring mechanisms.

$$U = \begin{array}{|l|}
\hline
110011101111111 \\
000111000010101 \\
010110001111111 \\
100011111111111 \\
110001001111101 \\
100101111111111 \\
100011010101100 \\
100000010100111 \\
000001110111100 \\
000001000101011 \\
\hline
\end{array}
\qquad
V = \begin{array}{|l|}
\hline
001100010000000 \\
111000110001010 \\
101000000000101 \\
011000000000000 \\
001010010000010 \\
010000000000000 \\
010100100000010 \\
011011000011000 \\
110110001000010 \\
110110011010100 \\
\hline
\end{array}$$

   Correct/Incorrect Matrix   *Augmented Data Matrix*

FIGURE 11.1. Two data matrices: **U**, correct/incorrect scores, and **V**, augmented data.

$\mathbf{U} = (u_1, u_2, \ldots, u_n)$. A simple example of data augmentation is displayed in Figure 11.1, which presents two dichotomously scored response matrices, **U** and **V**. Each matrix has 10 rows (persons) and 15 columns (items). The two matrices, however, refer to the same 10 test takers. That is, each row of **U** and each row of **V** represent two response vectors for the same test takers. **U** contains the usual correct/incorrect responses for a 15-item test. **V** is the augmented data matrix and might contain distractor-based scored responses.

  These two data matrices are separately computed using scoring mechanisms called *scoring evaluators* (Luecht, 2001, 2005a, 2005b). An MCQ item is typically scored by applying a simple pattern matching rule. The scoring evaluator is the software component that implements the scoring rule. The common correct answer key (CAK) scoring evaluator employs one or more pattern matching rules as a mathematical function that takes the form

$$u_{ij} = f(r_{ij}, a_i), \tag{11.1}$$

where r_{ij} is the response of examinee j to item i and a_i is the correct-keyed response for item i. For a simple CAK scoring evaluator, the function takes on one of two values (i.e., $u_{ij} = \in\{0,1\}$), where u_{ij} equals 1 if the test taker's response, r_{ij} equals the answer key, a_i, or u_{ij} equals 0, otherwise. However, as Luecht (2001, 2005b) discusses, more complex scoring evaluators can easily be devised for complex item types and pattern matches. Partial credit and polytomous scoring evaluators are also easy to conceptualize, extending this approach to almost any item types. For example, multiple-key scoring evaluators can be developed as a chain of single-key evaluators or operate on specified combinations from vector-valued arguments for the response variables and answer keys. The scoring evaluator's arguments, processing algorithm, and assigned point values can easily be represented as database structures to facilitate access for item analysis and scoring (Luecht, 2001, 2005b).

Some rather simple single-key modifications of the CAK scoring evaluator can be devised to demonstrate ways in which MCQ distractor response patterns can be exploited to generate a new answer key for each item. Other evaluators are possible, ideally based on cognitive scoring mechanisms devised to highlight weaknesses, misconceptions, and faulty instantiations. However, for purposes of illustration, two rather simple MCQ distractor-based scoring evaluators are (a) the popular incorrect key (PIK) method and (b) the strongest negative correlation (SNC) method.

The PIK scoring evaluator assumes that, for each item, at least one MCQ distractor is particularly *attractive* to lower-scoring examinees. That is, an incorrect response is assumed to be more than just a random choice or guess. Instead, the attractiveness of particular incorrect distractors is consistent enough across items to generate unique response patterns that will provide diagnostically useful information, especially for low-scoring examinees. Similar to the CAK evaluator, the PIK scoring evaluator can be expressed as

$$v_{ij} = f(r_{ij}, b_i), \tag{11.2}$$

where b_i is the most attractive distractor for low-scoring examinees. Note that a cutoff score must be selected on the criterion test – usually taken to be the total test score – in order to classify examinees as "low scoring" or not. For example, examinees below the 40th percentile might be classified as low scoring. The choice of a percentile cutoff is arbitrary and should be determined to ensure that sufficient numbers of examinees will be retained in the low-scoring group. The total test, number correct cut score[3] for each data set can be determined by a simple transformation, $x_{cut} = (z)\,s_x + \bar{x}$, using the total test score sample mean and standard deviation, where z corresponds to the percentile score for the cumulative-normal distribution of scores.

The SNC scoring evaluator assumes that the MCQ distractor having the largest negative correlation with the criterion score (total test score) is a good choice for extracting useful diagnostic information from the examinees' response patterns. We cannot definitively state why

---

[3] IRT score estimates can also be used.

examinees choose a particular distractor, only that endorsement of particular MCQ options that have the strongest negative relationship with total test performance may provide useful insights into weaknesses or faulty strategies that examinees might have employed. The SNC scoring evaluator is expressed as

$$v_{ij} = f(r_{ij}, c_i),$$ (11.3)

where c_i is the MCQ distractor that has the largest *negative* point-biserial correlation with the total test score.

Of course, any other rationale – ideally, one having a cognitive basis related to remediable weaknesses (e.g., Leighton, 2004; Leighton, Gierl, & Hunka, 2004) can be employed for purposes of identifying one or more auxiliary distractor patterns. The scoring evaluator concept makes it easy to implement even highly complex scoring rules involving incorrect responses across multiple items. In that case, $v_{sj} = f(\mathbf{r}_{sj}, \mathbf{c}_s)$, where $i \in s$ for a set of items, s, that share a particular vector of responses, $\mathbf{r}_{sj}$ and a vector or scorable attributes, $\mathbf{c}_s$. For example, choosing distractor option "B" on item 1 and "D" on item 3, would resolve to a simple, conjunctive pattern match:

$$v_{sj} = \begin{cases} 1, & \text{if } (r_{1j} = \text{"B"}) \cap (r_{3j} = \text{"D"}). \\ 0, & \text{otherwise} \end{cases}$$ (11.4)

These augmented data scoring evaluators will produce a new, dichotomously scored response vector for each examinee. The ensuing dichotomous response data matrix can subsequently be used to compute subscores or be otherwise analyzed like any dichotomous response matrix.

When applied to raw response data, these distractor-based scoring evaluators provide a new scored data matrix – the augmented data matrix, **V**. That data matrix can then be used alone or in conjunction with the CAK score data matrix to produce total test scores relative to the general trait being measured, and diagnostic measures of particular weakness-related traits.

Computing Diagnostic Subscores from Augmented Data

Recall that **U** denotes the traditional strength-related data matrix, scored using a CAK scoring evaluator. **V** is the augmented data matrix that is generated by another type of scoring evaluator. Simple sum scores can be computed for the appropriate elements within rows of the augmented data matrix, $\mathbf{V}$; that is, v_{ij}, for $i \in C_s$ items in scoring category C_s, and for $s = 1, \ldots, g$ categories. Unfortunately, as Luecht (2005a) and Luecht et al. (2006) have demonstrated, the resulting sum subscores based on PIK and SNC evaluators tend to be somewhat unreliable. Instead, it seems preferable to use the available data in $\mathbf{V}$, $\in$ and possibly incorporate additional information from $\mathbf{U}$, to compute more reliable subscores. That is, all data in $\mathbf{V}$ (and possibly in $\mathbf{U}$ as well) should be used in computing all subscores.

Wainer et al. (2001) presented an empirical Bayes estimation method called *augmented scoring* that is appropriate to use in these contexts. Other augmentation or collateral information–based methods might also be applicable (e.g., Folske, Gessaroli, & Swanson, 1999; Luecht, 1993; Nishisato, 1984). Wainer et al.'s (2001) method of augmented scoring incorporates a class of methods for computing subscores using the reliability as a means of weighting observed subscores to estimate true scores on a corresponding number of subscore scales. This class of methods extends from simple sum scores (e.g., number correct scores) to IRT scores, including Bayes mean and mode estimates (also see Vevea, Edwards, & Thissen, 2002).

Augmented scoring is a type of empirical Bayes scoring that, given p subscores, uses $p - 1$ of the subscores to predict the estimated true scores associated with the remaining variable. The estimation procedure is conceptually similar to *image analysis* in that the image matrix – here, the true score matrix – is estimated from the other $p - 1$ variables by minimizing the residuals (Gorsuch, 1983; Jöreskog, 1969). For Wainer et al.'s (2001) implementation, the augmentation process simultaneously regresses the (unknown) vector of p true scores on a vector of p observed subscores. The estimated coefficient matrix is then used as a set of regression weights for predicting the vector of true scores from the observed subscores. The regression equation used in augmented scoring can be written as

$$\hat{\tau} = \bar{\mathbf{x}}. + (\mathbf{x} - \bar{\mathbf{x}}.)\,\beta, \tag{11.5}$$

where $\hat{\tau}$, $\mathbf{x}$, and $\bar{\mathbf{x}}.$ are $N \times p$ matrices of true scores, observed scores, and means of the observed scores, respectively, and where β is $p \times p$ coefficient matrix. The coefficient matrix is computed as

$$\beta_{pp} = \Sigma_\tau \Sigma_x^{-1}, \tag{11.6}$$

where Σ_τ is the $p \times p$ population covariance matrix for the true scores, τ, and Σ_x is the $p \times p$ covariance matrix for the observed scores, x. In practice, β is estimated using the observed covariance matrix, $\mathbf{S}_x$, and given the true score covariance matrix, which is computed as follows

$$\mathbf{S}_\tau = \mathbf{S}_x - \mathbf{D}. \tag{11.7}$$

The matrix $\mathbf{D}$ is a diagonal matrix, $\mathbf{D} = diag(\mathbf{I} - \mathbf{R})\mathbf{S}^*_x$, where $\mathbf{R}$ is a p-length vector of reliability coefficients (e.g., Cronbach's α coefficients) and $\mathbf{S}^*_x$ is a $p \times p$ diagonal matrix containing the diagonal elements of $\mathbf{S}_x$.

The reliability coefficients for the augmented scores on component k ($k = 1, \ldots, p$) are estimated as

$$r^2_{\hat{\tau}_k, \tau_k} = \frac{\{a_{kk}\}}{\{c_{kk}\}}, k = 1, \ldots, p, \tag{11.8}$$

where $\{a_{kk}\}$ and $\{c_{kk}\}$ are, respectively, the diagonal elements of $\mathbf{A}_{pp} = \mathbf{S}_\tau \mathbf{S}_x^{-1} \mathbf{S}_\tau \mathbf{S}_x^{-1} \mathbf{S}_\tau$, the unconditional covariance matrix for the estimated true scores (i.e., the augmented scores) and $\mathbf{C}_{pp} = \mathbf{S}_\tau \mathbf{S}_x^{-1} \mathbf{S}_\tau$ (Wainer et al., 2001, p. 352). Finally, the conditional covariance of the augmented scores can be estimated as

$$\mathbf{S}_{\hat{\tau}|x} = \mathbf{S}_\tau - \mathbf{S}_\tau \mathbf{S}_x^{-1} \mathbf{S}_\tau, \tag{11.9}$$

and the square roots of the diagonal elements of $\mathbf{S}_{\hat{\tau}|x}$ are the conditional standard errors of the augmented score estimates, $\hat{\tau} \mid x$.

Although it is tempting, as alluded to previously, to augment the data and the scoring process – that is, to include both $\mathbf{U}$ and $\mathbf{V}$ in the empirical Bayes procedure –the proportionally higher reliability of the CAK-based observed test score scale, which is also negatively correlated with the PIK- and SNC-based scores, can potentially overwhelm any unique information produced by $\mathbf{V}$, producing an undesirable anomaly relative to the interpretation of the augmented weakness scores. This anomalous finding is demonstrated and discussed in the next section.

Empirical Study of Data Augmentation and Scoring

An empirical study was carried out using large-sample response data obtained from the 2003 field trial of the new SAT (nSAT; Liu, Feigenbaum, & Walker, 2004). Content for the nSAT was designed to align with curriculum and instructional practices in high school and college (O'Callaghan, Morley, & Schwartz, 2004; VanderVeen, 2004). The nSAT, like its predecessor, measures reasoning skills that have developed over time in the domains of mathematics and critical reading.

Three test forms with comparable data for the Mathematics and Critical Reading sections were used: Forms 2a, 2c, and 5. Each test form consisted of the same 54 mathematics items and the same 67 reading items, but with different orderings of the item blocks. Form 2a was administered to 2443 examinees. Form 2c was administered to 2336 examinees. Form 5 was administered to 2202 examinees. An essay was also administered during the field trial but was not investigated in this study.

The nSAT items are classified in several ways. The Mathematics items are classified by item type (comprehension, routine problem solving, or nonroutine analysis/computations) and by content (algebra, arithmetic, geometry, and miscellaneous). The Critical Reading items are classified by item type (passage based, sentence completion), passage type (long or short passage), and passage content. Although any of these classification schemas might have been used for creating diagnostic scores, it was decided to instead use experimental, cognitively based diagnostic categories for scoring purposes in this study.

Each item on the nSAT field trial forms was mapped into one of several cognitively based skill classifications. For Mathematics, the skill classifications included descriptions such as applying basic mathematics knowledge, applying advanced mathematics knowledge, managing complexity, and modeling/insight (O'Callaghan et al., 2004). For Critical Reading, the skill classifications had descriptions such as determining word meaning; understanding sentences; understanding larger sections of text; and analyzing purpose, audience, and strategies (VanderVeen, 2004).

These cognitively based item classifications are referred to as "skill categories" in this study. There were four skill categories for Mathematics and four skill categories for Critical Reading. Because of the experimental nature of the actual cognitive item classifications, these skills are not explicitly described and are simply labeled as skills "M1", "M2", "M3", and "M4" for Mathematics and as skills "CR1", "CR2", "CR3", and "CR4" for Critical Reading. Table 11.1 summarizes the item counts for each skill category. Forms 2a, 2c, and 5 had identical items and therefore had the same number of items in each category.

As noted previously, these classifications are experimental. Furthermore, like most item-level classification schemes, these are based on human subject matter experts' evaluations of the item content and task demands, and are therefore both fallible and less than optimal from a statistical perspective. The feasibility of using factor-derived diagnostic scores was also explored as a means of obtaining more statistically

TABLE 11.1. *Item counts by cognitive category for mathematics and critical reading*

Mathematics cognitive skill	Item count	Critical reading cognitive skill	Item count
M1	18	CR1	13
M2	8	CR2	24
M3	10	CR3	21
M4	18	CR4	9
Total	54	Total	67

optimal subscores. However, the factor analyses did not yield tangible psychometric benefits and greatly complicated the necessary comparisons among the three scoring evaluators. Despite their fallibility, the cognitive skill dimensions provided a convenient way of aggregating the results for purposes of comparison across the various scoring evaluators.

The 54 Mathematics items and 67 Critical Reading items were repeatedly scored using the CAK, PIK, and SNC scoring evaluators. This process provided three matrices of dichotomous item scores for each test form (Forms 2a, 2c, and 5). The dichotomous item-level scores were then summed for each examinee, using the appropriate item attributes corresponding to the four diagnostic skills for Mathematics and the four diagnostic skills for Critical Reading.

The data sets were initially kept separate by test form to evaluate the consistency (invariance) of the results with respect to sampling considerations. Table 11.2 displays the descriptive statistics (means and standard deviations) for the CAK-, PIK-, and SNC-based subscores for Mathematics (M1–M4) and Critical Reading (CR1–CR4) separated by test form. Similarly, Table 11.3 shows a descriptive summary of the four CAK-, PIK-, and SNC-based skill categories for Critical Reading.

The means and standard deviations indicate that, on average, reasonably parallel score profiles can be achieved across the three test forms for both Mathematics and Critical Reading. Note that higher values for the CAK-based subscores indicate *strengths* in the four skill domains. In contrast, the PIK and SNC scoring evaluators reward selection of a prescribed incorrect MCQ distractor (Equations 2 and 3). Therefore, higher PIK or SNC subscores imply greater degrees of weaknesses in each skill domain.

The reliability coefficients (Cronbach's α) for the CAK-, PIK-, and SNC-based subscores, broken down for the three test forms, are summarized in Table 11.4 (Mathematics on the left and Critical Reading

TABLE 11.2. *Means and standard deviations of CAK-, PIK-, and SNC-based diagnostic skill subscores in mathematics for Forms 2a, 2c, and 5*

Categories	M1			M2			M3			M4		
Form	2a	2c	5	2a	2c	5	2a	2c	5	2a	2c	5
CAK-Based Skill Category Subscores												
Mean	12.84	4.47	4.27	5.09	12.88	4.52	4.31	5.10	12.91	4.55	4.34	5.23
SD	3.90	2.26	2.47	3.75	3.89	2.23	2.38	3.75	3.96	2.23	2.45	3.85
PIK-Based Skill Category Subscores												
Mean	2.25	1.66	2.45	4.73	2.21	1.62	2.37	4.74	2.19	1.61	2.36	4.70
SD	2.09	1.38	1.64	2.83	2.04	1.38	1.61	2.84	2.06	1.37	1.65	2.81
SNC-Based Skill Category Subscores												
Mean	2.03	1.47	2.21	4.11	1.99	1.43	2.16	4.11	1.97	1.44	2.14	4.09
SD	2.13	1.34	1.58	2.67	2.06	1.31	1.55	2.66	2.09	1.34	1.61	2.68
N	2443	2336	2202	2443	2336	2202	2443	2336	2202	2443	2336	2202

on the right). The results are somewhat predictable. As shown in the second and sixth columns of Table 11.4, the reliability coefficients ranged from 0.68 to 0.84 for both the CAK-based Mathematics and Critical Reading subscores, indicating reasonable scoring accuracy, at least near the means of the respective subscore distributions. The reliability coefficients drop off noticeably for the PIK and SNC Mathematics subscores, with the largest decrease in reliability for the Critical Reading PIK subscores.

TABLE 11.3. *Means and standard deviations of CAK-, PIK-, and SNC-based diagnostic skill subscores in critical reading for Forms 2a, 2c, and 5*

Categories	CR1			CR2			CR3			CR4		
Form	2a	2c	5	2a	2c	5	2a	2c	5	2a	2c	5
CAK-Based Skill Category Subscores												
Mean	6.59	6.58	6.63	12.56	12.48	12.64	10.81	10.71	10.88	3.63	3.55	3.58
SD	2.81	2.77	2.76	5.18	5.11	5.08	4.54	4.43	4.33	2.30	2.27	2.26
PIK-Based Skill Category Subscores												
Mean	2.17	2.27	2.24	3.83	3.76	3.75	3.32	3.38	3.33	1.76	1.82	1.82
SD	1.54	1.58	1.54	2.50	2.47	2.48	2.10	2.04	2.06	1.29	1.32	1.32
SNC-Based Skill Category Subscores												
Mean	1.43	1.42	1.38	2.76	2.65	2.75	1.88	1.80	1.84	0.80	0.76	0.83
SD	1.55	1.52	1.54	2.41	2.40	2.54	1.91	1.81	1.89	1.05	1.03	1.05
N	2443	2336	2202	2443	2336	2202	2443	2336	2202	2443	2336	2202

TABLE 11.4. *Reliability coefficients for CAK-, PIK-, and SNC-based diagnostic subscores in mathematics and critical reading for Forms 2a, 2c, and 5*

	Mathematics				Critical reading		
Subscores	CAK	PIK	SNC	Subscores	CAK	PIK	SNC
M1	0.82	0.60	0.65	RC1	0.70	0.33	0.52
	0.83	0.59	0.64		0.70	0.31	0.50
	0.84	0.60	0.65		0.72	0.32	0.53
M2	0.70	0.40	0.43	RC2	0.84	0.52	0.61
	0.72	0.41	0.42		0.84	0.52	0.63
	0.72	0.39	0.45		0.84	0.52	0.66
M3	0.73	0.42	0.45	RC3	0.80	0.36	0.57
	0.68	0.42	0.44		0.79	0.38	0.54
	0.69	0.44	0.48		0.82	0.40	0.57
M4	0.68	0.63	0.63	RC4	0.68	0.21	0.39
	0.68	0.64	0.63		0.68	0.21	0.39
	0.68	0.63	0.64		0.68	0.19	0.375

If the disattenuated product-moment correlations between subscores are considered (i.e., the correlations between the M1, M2, M3, and M4 subscores for Mathematics and between the CR1, CR2, CR3, and CR4 subscores for Critical Reading), the aforementioned unidimensionality problem begins to emerge. Figure 11.2 plots the average disattenuated correlations and an associated error bar for the CAK-, PIK-, and

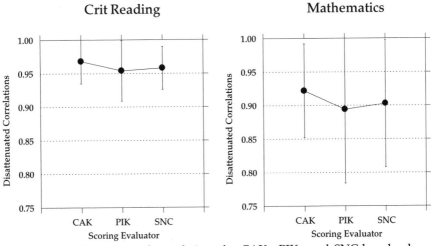

FIGURE 11.2. Disattenuated correlations for CAK-, PIK-, and SNC-based subscores for Mathematics and Critical Reading.

SNC-based subscores. The mean disattenuated correlations for CAK subscores are slightly higher than the PIK and SNC subscores. Also, the disattenuated correlations for Critical Reading are systematically higher than for Mathematics. However, on average, the correlations are nearer to 0.90 or higher, indicating that there is not a great deal of unique multidimensional information in U or V.

These results clearly support earlier comments implying that traditional use of the CAK scoring evaluator, when applied to an essentially unidimensional test like the nSAT, will produce subscores that are highly correlated with each other. Unfortunately, the data obtained from the PIK and SNC scoring evaluators exhibit a similar pattern of high disattenuated correlations. These high disattenuated correlations, combined with the lower reliability coefficients for the PIK- and SNC-based subscores (Table 11.4), suggest that using a single-key PIK or SNC scoring evaluators as the *sole* source of producing scored response information may actually sacrifice potentially useful measurement precision. Therefore, any additional "signal" present in V (and possibly U) must be considered.

Augmented Scoring

Augmented scoring was applied to the PIK and SNC data to improve the reliabilities of the subscores. Each of the three data sets for Forms 2a, 2c, and 5 were combined to produce a large data set for the two tests: Mathematics and Critical Reading ($N = 6981$ per combined data set).

The CAK-based total test observed score was initially included as a covariate in the empirical Bayes calculations[4] (i.e., the total observed CAK-based score for the 54 items in Mathematics and 67 items in Critical Reading). This set of computations resulted in *four* 5×5 observed score covariance matrices, along with four associated 5×1 reliability vectors for the following score combinations: (a) the Mathematics CAK-total test and the four PIK-based M subscores, (b) the Mathematics CAK-total test and the four SNC-based M subscores, (c) the Critical Reading CAK-total test and the four PIK-based CR subscores, and (d) the Critical Reading CAK-total test and the four SNC-based CR subscores.

---

[4] A small amount of autocovariance was obviously present among the scores because the CAK-based total test score shared partial information, via the response data for common items, with both PIK- and SNC-based subscores. However, this autocovariation was not sufficient to explain the anomalous results reported here.

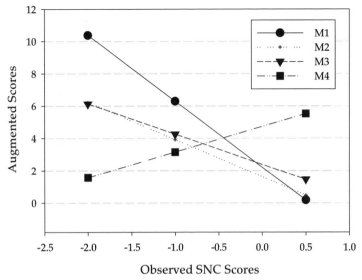

FIGURE 11.3. Anomalous results for augmented scores (SNC-based Mathematics) when the observed total test score is included.

Including the CAK-based observed total test score as a covariate produces an interesting but disturbing result that holds across the Mathematics and Critical Reading tests and for both the PIK- and SNC-based augmented subscores. The total test score scale reliability for Mathematics (CAK-based scores from **U**) was 0.928; the reliability for Critical Reading was 0.932. Because these reliability coefficients are so much higher than the reliabilities for the PIK and SNC subscore scales (Table 11.4), the empirical Bayes procedure results in a directional change of the latter weakness subscore scales, confounding interpretation. Figure 11.3 provides an example of this unexpected result for the augmented SNC-based subscores for Mathematics. The abscissa lists examinees having observed SNC-based subscores at three skill levels: two standard deviations below the mean, one standard deviation below the mean, and one-half of a standard deviation above the mean – all based on the means and standard deviations for the combined sample of 6981 examinees.

The anomaly is clearly demonstrated in Figure 11.3 by the apparent negative relationship between the observed SNC subscores and the augmented SNC subscores for M1, M2, and M3. Only M4 shows the proper positive relationship between the observed and augmented

TABLE 11.5. *Estimated β coefficient matrices for PIK- and SNC-based subscores for mathematics and critical reading*

β(PIK,M$_k$)	PIK-M1	PIK-M2	PIK-M3	PIK-M4
PIK-M1	0.409	0.234	0.206	0.069
PIK-M2	0.155	0.103	0.138	0.123
PIK-M3	0.182	0.185	0.151	0.129
PIK-M4	0.118	0.320	0.251	0.454
β(SNC,M$_k$)	SNC-M1	SNC-M2	SNC-M3	SNC-M4
SNC-M1	0.444	0.243	0.210	0.083
SNC-M2	0.159	0.103	0.147	0.121
SNC-M3	0.185	0.197	0.168	0.117
SNC-M4	0.143	0.317	0.228	0.437
β(PIK,CR$_k$)	PIK-CR1	PIK-CR2	PIK-CR3	PIK-CR4
PIK-CR1	0.129	0.186	0.095	0.095
PIK-CR2	0.333	0.313	0.247	0.184
PIK-CR3	0.153	0.221	0.191	0.196
PIK-CR4	0.079	0.086	0.102	0.090
β(SNC,CR$_k$)	SNC-CR1	SNC-CR2	SNC-CR3	SNC-CR4
SNC-CR1	0.243	0.177	0.145	0.115
SNC-CR2	0.340	0.325	0.293	0.305
SNC-CR3	0.195	0.206	0.258	0.265
SNC-CR4	0.067	0.093	0.115	0.155

SNC subscores. That is, because the SNC-based subscore scales are to be interpreted as skill *weaknesses,* the regression bias induced by incorporating the CAK-based observed total test scores actually alters the meaning of the subscore scales for M1, M2, and M3. Similar problems were apparent for the PIK-based data and replicated for Critical Reading.

The augmented scoring was carried out again, leaving the CAK-based total test scores out of the regression. The estimated coefficient matrices for these four sets of covariance matrices are presented in Table 11.5. The columns of each matrix demonstrate the relative weighting of the various scores when computing the linear composites (Equation 5).

Table 11.6 provides reliability coefficients for the PIK- and SNC-based subscores. The left-hand side of Table 11.6 shows the observed score reliability coefficients, whereas the right-hand side displays the reliability coefficients for the augmented scores. The observed score reliabilities are similar to the reliabilities reported in Table 11.4 for the form-specific PIK and SNC data but are now based on the larger combined sample.

TABLE 11.6. *Reliability coefficients (Cronbach's α) for observed and augmented scores*

Observed subscores				Augmented subscores			
Mathematics		Critical reading		Mathematics		Critical reading	
PIK	SNC	PIK	SNC	PIK	SNC	PIK	SNC
0.596	0.648	0.317	0.515	0.766	0.797	0.700	0.810
0.401	0.429	0.522	0.632	0.802	0.821	0.704	0.817
0.429	0.458	0.380	0.558	0.803	0.821	0.702	0.815
0.631	0.633	0.206	0.385	0.772	0.788	0.697	0.808

The reliability coefficients in Table 11.6 for the augmented scores demonstrate considerable accuracy improvements resulting from the empirical Bayes procedure. Even the lowest reliability coefficients are above 0.70. The augmented SNC-based subscores are slightly more reliable than the corresponding PIK-based subscores. However, it is important to keep in mind that the empirical Bayes scoring process induces higher correlations among the subscores. In fact, the product moment correlations between the estimated (augmented) true subscores ranged from 0.94 to 1.00 for Mathematics and from 0.98 to 1.00 for Critical Reading. The implication is that the improved reliability of the augmented scores comes at a cost – namely, diagnostic scores that converge toward a single composite score (Longford, 1997).

To provide a basis for comparison of the observed and augmented scores, observed subscores for the Mathematics skills were specified at three ability levels: −1.0 standard deviations, +0.5 standard deviations, and +1.5 standard deviations. The corresponding observed PIK- and SNC-based subscores were then computed using the large sample ($N = 6981$) means and standard deviations. Each observed subscore was subsequently transformed to an empirical Bayes estimate by using the appropriate β matrix (Table 11.5). Figure 11.4 displays the augmented scores as a function of the standardized observed scores. In this context, the standardization merely serves to align the plots relative to a common abscissa. Both the augmented PIK- and SNC-based subscores (M1−M4) exhibit the expected positive relationship – unlike the anomaly shown previously in Figure 11.3.

Figure 11.5 shows the corresponding augmented PIK- and SNC-based subscores for Critical Reading (CR1−CR4) as a function of the

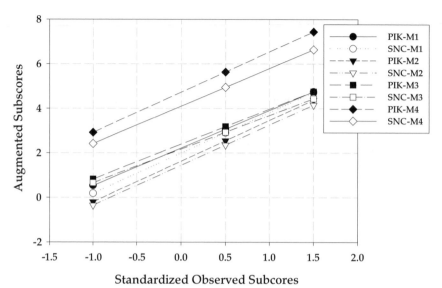

FIGURE 11.4. Plot of Mathematics augmented by standardized observed sub-scores (PIK and SNC).

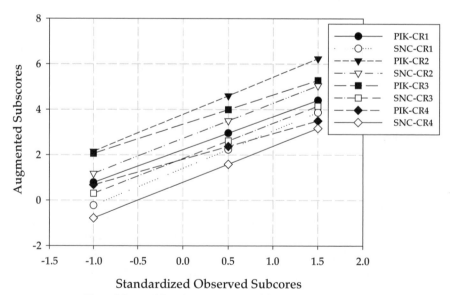

FIGURE 11.5. Plot of Critical Reading augmented by standardized observed sub-scores (PIK and SNC).

standardized observed scores ($z = -1.0$, $z = +0.5$, and $z = +1.5$). The patterns of relationships are positive and linear as expected and desired.

These examples certainly do not present overly compelling findings. The reason is simple. The nSAT data were largely unidimensional, and the choice of the PIK and SNC scoring evaluators merely capitalized on functions of the total test scores (i.e., the most popular distractor patterns for low-scoring examinees and the SNC with total test performance). Nonetheless, the process illustrated here seems to at least hint at the potential utility of a joint approach: augmenting the data, as well as using augmented or collateral information—based scoring to compute the diagnostic skill estimates. It is likely that this joint method will prove useful if multidimensional measurement information can be extracted via the distractor patterns.

DISCUSSION

Even the most sophisticated psychometric models cannot manufacture highly useful diagnostic information from a unidimensional test. The data itself must be multidimensional, and the extractable dimensional structure needs to hold up over time and contexts. Furthermore, the multidimensionality provided must support reliable metrics that are diagnostically useful and sensitive to remedial instruction and learning.

This chapter introduces some relatively simple, single-key scoring evaluators to isolate response information from MCQ distractor patterns, for purposes of scoring examinees with respect to diagnostically relevant skills. Both the PIK and the SNC evaluators produced item-level dichotomous scores that were shown to be consistent across the Mathematics and Critical Reading forms of the nSAT. That finding is the good news in that it suggests some additional information may generally be available in the patterns of incorrect answers. However, the results also suggested that the PIK- and SNC-based skill subscores only had poor to marginal reliability.

Augmented scoring was then introduced as a means of dealing with the inherent lower reliability associated with the diagnostic skill scores. The augmented scoring resolved the low-reliability issue but failed to adequately eliminate the inherent unidimensionality in the response data used here.

There are test development options to explore as part of future research. One option is to explore the use of other content-based or cognitive item coding schemes to classify items for purposes of determining skill category scores. However, a caution is warranted here. Almost any configuration of items mapped to skills domains, at least when the score response data are unidimensional, will probably remain unidimensional at least for single-key scoring evaluators such as the PIK and SNC evaluators. Other distractor pattern classification schemes could be used, in conjunction with multiresponse scoring evaluators, to generate augmented data matrices that actually exhibit useful multidimensionality. A second alternative is to explicitly design the distractors across clusters of items to be appealing to examinees who have systematic misconceptions, faulty strategies, and so on. That is, we want to directly tie incorrect response patterns to formatively relevant explanations. If classifying items into arbitrary taxonomies or "attribute matrices" is the sole process used to accomplish this mapping of tasks or test items to hypothetical cognitive domains, the results may never be completely adequate in terms of providing diagnostically relevant score information. However, if the item distractors (or item tasks in general) can be explicitly designed and experimentally verified to elicit specific information (i.e., linking task design to student models of understanding), it may be possible to actually design formative assessments that work.

ACKNOWLEDGMENTS

The author is indebted to the College Board for sponsoring key aspects of this research. All opinions and conclusions are solely those of the author.

References

Ackerman, T. A. (2005). Multidimensional item response theory modeling. In A. Maydue-Olivares & J. J. McArdle (Eds.), Contemporary psychometrics (pp. 3–25). Mahwah, NJ: Erlbaum.

Ackerman, T. A., Gierl, M. J., & Walker C. (2003). Using multidimensional item response theory to evaluate educational and psychological tests. *Educational Measurement: Issues and Practice, 22*, 37–53.

Cliff, N. (1987). *Analyzing multivariate data*. San Diego: Harcourt Brace Jovanovich.

Drasgow, F., Luecht, R. M., & Bennett, R. E. (in press). Technology in testing. In R. L. Brennan (Ed.), *Educational measurement* (4th ed., pp. 471–515). Washington, DC: American Council on Education and Praeger Publishers.

Ferrera, S., Duncan, T., Perie, M., Freed, R., Mcgivern, J, & Chilukuri, R. (2003, April). *Item construct validity: early results from a study of the relationship between intended and actual cognitive demands in a middle school science assessment.* Paper presented at the annual meeting of the American Educational Research Association, San Diego.

Folske, J. C., Gessaroli, M. E., & Swanson, D. B. (1999, April). *Assessing the utility of an IRT-based method for using collateral information to estimate subscores.* Paper presented at the annual meeting of the National Council on Measurement in Education, Montreal, Quebec, Canada.

Gorsuch, R. L. (1983). *Factor analysis* (2nd ed.). Mahwah, NJ: Erlbaum.

Hambleton, R. K., & Swaminathan, H. (1985). *Item response theory: Principles and applications.* Boston: Kluwer-Nijhoff.

Huff, K. (2004, April). *A practical application of evidence-centered design principles: coding items for skills.* Paper presented at the annual meeting of the National Council on Measurement in Education, San Diego.

Irvine, S. H., & Kyllonen, P. C. (2002). *Item generation for test development.* Mahwah, NJ: Erlbaum.

Jöreskog, K. G. (1969). Efficient estimation in image factor analysis. *Psychometrika, 34,* 183–202.

Leighton, J. P. (2004). Avoiding misconceptions, misuse, and missed opportunities: The collection of verbal reports in educational achievement testing. *Educational Measurement: Issues and Practice, 23,* 1–10.

Leighton, J. P., Gierl, M. J., & Hunka, S. (2004). The attribute hierarchy method for cognitive assessment: A variation on Tatsuoka's rule-space approach. *Journal of Educational Measurement, 41,* 205–237.

Liu, J., Feigenbaum, M., & Walker, M. E. (2004, April). *New SAT and new PSAT/NMSQT Spring 2003 field trial design.* Paper presented at the annual meeting of the National Council on Measurement in Education, San Diego.

Longford, N. T. (1997). Shrinkage estimation of linear combinations of true scores. *Psychometrika, 62,* 237–244.

Luecht, R. M. (1993, April). *A marginal maximum likelihood approach to deriving multidimensional composite abilities under the generalized partial credit model.* Paper presented at the annual meeting of the American Educational Research Association, Atlanta.

Luecht, R. M. (2001, April). *Capturing, codifying and scoring complex data for innovative, computer-based items.* Paper presented at the annual meeting of the National Council on Measurement in Education, Seattle.

Luecht, R. M. (2002, April). *From design to delivery: Engineering the mass production of complex performance assessments.* Paper presented at the annual meeting of the National Council on Measurement in Education, New Orleans.

Luecht, R. M. (2005a, April). *Extracting multidimensional information from multiple-choice question distractors for diagnostic scoring.* Paper presented at the annual meeting of the National Council on Measurement in Education, Montreal, Quebec, Canada.

Luecht, R. M. (2005b). Item analysis. In B. S. Everitt & D. C. Howell (Eds.), *Encyclopedia of Statistics in Behavioral Science,* London: Wiley.

Luecht, R. M. (2006, February). *Computer-based approaches to diagnostic assessment.* Invited presentation at the annual meeting of the Association of Test Publishers, Orlando, FL.

Luecht, R. M., Gierl, M. J., Tan, X., & Huff, K. (2006, April). *Scalability and the development of useful diagnostic scales.* Paper presented at the annual meeting of the National Council on Measurement in Education, San Francisco.

Mislevy, R. J., & Riconscente, M. M. (2005, July). *Evidence-centered assessment design: layers, structures, and terminology* (PADI Technical Report 9). Menlo Park, CA: SRI International.

Nishisato, S. (1984). A simple application of a quantification method. *Psychometrika, 49,* 25–36.

O'Callaghan, R. K., Morley, M. E., & Schwartz, A. (2004, April). *Developing skill categories for the SAT math section.* Paper presented at the annual meeting at the National Council on Measurement in Education, San Diego.

Wainer. H., Vevea, J. L., Camacho, F., Reeve, B. B., Rosa, K., Nelson, L., Swygert, K. A., & Thissen, D. (2001). Augmented scores – "Borrowing strength" to compute scores based upon small numbers of items. In H. Wainer & D. Thissen (Eds.), *Test scoring* (pp. 343–387). Mahwah, NJ: Erlbaum.

VanderVeen, A. (2004, April). *Toward a construct of critical reading for the new SAT.* Paper presented at the annual meeting at the National Council on Measurement in Education, San Diego.

Vevea, J. L., Edwards, M. C., & Thissen, D. (2002). *User's guide for AUGMENT v.2: Empirical Bayes subscore augmentation software.* Chapel Hill, NC: L. L. Thurstone Psychometric Laboratory.

12

Directions for Future Research in Cognitive Diagnostic Assessment

Mark J. Gierl and Jacqueline P. Leighton

In the Introduction to this volume, we began by describing key concepts that underlie cognitive diagnostic assessment (CDA) and by specifying some of the early ideas and precedents that guided the merger between cognitive psychology and educational measurement. Then, three distinct sections were presented where a host of esteemed contributors described research on topics related to CDA, theory, and practice. Chapters describing the foundations of CDA, principles of test design and analysis, and psychometric procedures and applications were presented. After surveying these chapters, we acknowledge that not all issues relevant to CDA were adequately covered. Some omissions occurred not because these topics are considered unimportant, but because, in some cases, the topics are not ready for discussion and, in other cases, the most appropriate authors were unavailable. Thus, in the final section, we highlight some of the important topics that were not covered in this book and, in the process, identify areas in which future research is required.

ISSUE 1: ROLE OF COGNITIVE MODELS
IN COGNITIVE DIAGNOSTIC ASSESSMENT

Every author in this volume claims that some type of cognitive model is required to make inferences about examinees' problem-solving skills. These models provide the framework necessary for guiding item development and directing psychometric analyses so test performance can be linked to specific inferences about examinees' cognitive skills. The foundation for generating diagnostic inferences, in fact, rest with cognitive theories and models. Hence, the veracity of the cognitive models and the validity of the diagnostic inferences must be evaluated. Borsboom and Mellenbergh (this volume) provided a concise review of test validity in cognitive assessment. They claim that a CDA is valid for measuring a theoretical attribute if variation in the attribute can be linked to variation in the measurement outcomes through the responses processes required by the test. Test validation, therefore, involves the process of evaluating whether the theoretical attribute has a causal effect on the test score. They also warn us that without substantive theory to link the attributes to the scores, we must be cautious when adopting the rhetoric of measurement and validity. Although their descriptions of validity and test validation are succinct and, seemingly, straightforward, they draw heavily on the strong program of validity, described as "the catch" in the Introduction; that is, we need explanatory information "with teeth" where the psychological attributes that link students' test performance to inferences about their cognitive skills are made explicit.

Norris, Macnab, and Phillips (this volume) add to the conceptual foundation laid by Borsboom and Mellenbergh by providing a philosophical analysis and justification for the use of cognitive models in CDA. Simply put, cognitive models help us operationalize the theoretical attributes, as well as response processes we are attempting to measure and make inferences about. Norris et al. also identify some of the limitations involved when using cognitive models in CDA, while maintaining that these models, when developed from data based on students' internal thoughts, can provide key insights into a student's understanding. Two methods that may be used to collect different types of psychological data on students' internal thoughts – protocol analysis and verbal analysis – were described in Leighton and Gierl (this volume).

Although these three chapters provide an excellent discussion of the conceptual issues and methods required to support cognitive diagnostic inferences, we still lack a collection of cognitive models, specifically, and psychological theories, more generally, on educational aptitudes and achievements that can serve CDA in a broad and useful manner. *What kinds of constructs can be measured with cognitive models and used to guide our diagnostic inferences? How can these constructs be identified and developed for CDA across grade levels and content areas? How do we develop instructional strategies to remediate deficiencies for CDA-based constructs?* Models and theories that can serve as theoretical attributes to guide diagnostic inferences, as well as the empirical studies to support these attributes and inferences, are slowly starting to emerge (see examples presented in Yang & Embretson, this volume, and Rupp & Mislevy, this volume). But despite these initial attempts, many more studies are still required on a range of educational constructs at different grade levels and in different domains before CDA will become relevant and applicable to more mainstream test users. Gierl et al. (this volume) provide this pointed summary:

> The weakness of developing items according to a cognitive model of task performance stems from the paucity of information currently available on the knowledge, processes, and strategies that characterize student performance in most testing situations. Moreover, some cognitive researchers believe this situation is unlikely to change in the near future because there is little interest in the outcomes from task analyses (Anderson & Schunn, 2000). Consequently, we have few detailed accounts of educational task performance. Because little is known about how students actually solve items on educational tests, relatively few models exist.

More general theories of cognition, as they pertain to the knowledge structures and cognitive processes, were not described in our volume either. Yet this is an area of great importance for the viability and longevity of CDA. But, as we claimed in our Introduction, the models and theories needed to support diagnostic inferences on educational tasks are unlikely to be developed by cognitive psychologists for use in educational measurement any time soon. Rather, it will be our responsibility to either adapt existing cognitive models or develop new cognitive models to guide the development and analysis of CDA. In fact, cognitive model development may be the single most important factor that contributes to the success or the failure of CDA – fortunately, it is a factor that we can influence. It is still too early to have fully functional and well-developed theories and models of cognition for educational measurement because these theories and models simply do not exist. In addition, presenting such theories without sufficient empirical evidence to show their appeal may, in fact, undermine the substantive component so important in CDA because these premature theories will have limited explanatory power. Hence, we must continue to conduct research into CDA by adapting more traditional educational and psychological models, while continuing to develop theories and models of cognition that can eventually be incorporated into our analytical models and methods.

ISSUE 2: USE OF PRINCIPLED TEST DESIGN FOR DEVELOPING COGNITIVE DIAGNOSTIC ASSESSMENTS

Calls for principled test design are increasing. A principled approach to test design and analysis requires some type of cognitive model to initially be identified and evaluated. Then, test items are developed using templates to measure the attributes or features in the model. Finally, model-based statistics are used to analyze the data, generate the scores, and guide the score interpretations. A more traditional approach to test design, by comparison, is guided by content specifications rather than a cognitive model of test performance. In this more traditional approach, item content and item formats are typically unstandardized and, thus, differ both within and between assessment tasks. Also, psychometric models are fit to the test data, post hoc, using exploratory statistical methods to identify appropriate scaling properties that can guide score reporting and interpretation. Despite the merits of principled test design over traditional test design, it is not a common approach for designing educational or psychological tests, and it has never been used, to our knowledge, in an operational testing situation.

Yet, when the goal is to develop a CDA, a principled test design approach is required because the purpose of the assessment is to identify and evaluate the examinees' cognitive skills as specified in a cognitive model of test performance. Most current applications of CDA rely on a *post-hoc* or *retrofitting* approach to test design where existing items are coded for cognitive attributes, and then analyzed. Although retrofitting items to cognitive models affords some conveniences, given that the items and the student response data are readily available, this approach is ultimately a poor one. If cognitive models are to gain an important role in CDA, then items must be developed to systematically measure the specific, microlevel components in the model – and items with these specifically cognitive characteristics are unlikely to exist on general purpose tests because item development is guided by content specifications and not an explicit cognitive model. Hence, the cognitive analysis of any existing test using retrofitting procedures will invariably produce a less than ideal fit between the cognitive model and the test data. This is most likely to occur because the tests were not designed from an explicit cognitive framework. At worst, the outcomes produced using a retrofitting approach are likely to yield weak diagnostic inferences, thereby undermining the value of a well-developed CDA. Luecht (this volume) believes that principled test design is critical to CDA, claiming that of the most promising approaches available, one is to

explicitly design the distractors across clusters of items to be appealing to examinees who have systematic misconceptions, faulty strategies, and so on. That is, we want to directly tie incorrect response patterns to formatively relevant explanations. If classifying items into arbitrary taxonomies or "attribute matrices" is the sole process used to accomplish this mapping of tasks or test items to hypothetical cognitive domains, the results may never be completely adequate in terms of providing diagnostically relevant score information. However, if the item distractors (or item tasks in general) can be explicitly designed and experimentally verified to elicit specific information (i.e., linking task design to student models of understanding), it may be possible to actually design formative assessments that work.

In other words, to overcome the inherent limitations associated with retrofitting, a more principled approach to test design and analysis is required. Gorin (this volume) provides an excellent description of test development practices for CDA. Other contributors provide descriptions and examples of different approaches to principled test design, such as evidence-centered design and the cognitive design system (Huff & Goodman; Yang & Embretson; Rupp & Mislevy; this volume).

But research into the theory and applications of principled test design is also developing rapidly. It is hoped that, eventually, these principled approaches to design and analysis will begin to affect the development of CDAs, as well as more traditional forms of educational assessment, thereby creating a more unified process where researchers and practitioners begin development with a clear sense of their analytical methods and reporting procedures. With this approach, test design is unified from the initial design stage to the final reporting stage. But the question still remains: *Will principled test design practices become more common in educational and psychological testing, particularly when cognitive models have such an important role in this approach?*

ISSUE 3: GRANULARITY AND SPECIFICITY OF COGNITIVE DIAGNOSTIC INFERENCES

CDA characterizes a testing approach where examinees' cognitive skills are evaluated, typically by specifying where in the underlying cognitive model the examinees' are believed to have particular strengths and weaknesses. But, as is evident from the chapters in this volume, the philosophical rationale required to create and validate these cognitive models, the principled test design procedures used to develop the assessment tasks, and, finally, the psychometric methods needed to analyze examinees' response data present us with a complex array of alternatives. As we try to maneuver through these alternatives, we must be guided by a clear sense of purpose. Unfortunately, the granularity or level of analysis issue that arises when using CDAs can easily throw us off track. Our contributors (e.g., Yang & Embretson; Gorin; Leighton & Gierl; Rupp & Mislevy; Roussos et al.) agree that, for diagnostic assessment, a fine grain size is required to make specific inferences about examinees' cognitive skills. Items must be developed that probe specific knowledge structures and psychological attributes. However, a cognitive analysis at a fine grain size may, by necessity, limit construct representation and content coverage. That is, depth of representation or coverage might be achieved at the expense of breadth of representation or coverage. Hence, it is fair to ask, *if developers are willing to create the detailed probes necessary for evaluating specific cognitive skills, are users willing to test more frequently and/or test more narrowly to acquire this detailed information?* Said differently, *will test users continue to demand CDAs when they realize that these assessments require more testing time or that these assessments yield less construct representation and content coverage in order to get the benefits associated with penetrating deeply into the student's understanding of the construct?*

Even when testing resources are available, CDAs must be specified at the appropriate grain size or level of analysis for a particular application or instructional use. Unfortunately, the factors required to identify the "appropriate" grain size are poorly defined – which, again, could contribute to some disillusion with CDA. With an attribute approach, like the attribute hierarchy method (Gierl et al., this volume) or fusion model (Roussos et al., this volume), the prerequisite skills specified in each attribute can easily be broken into much more specific attributes. Of course, more items would be required to measure these skills, thereby adding new and more specific attributes along with new cognitive structures. In other words, attributes can continually be specified at a smaller grain size, thus increasing the specificity of the cognitive inferences. However, this kind of specificity also requires that we increase the number of items to tap these attributes. Yang and Embretson note:

at what level should the construct be represented so that both adequacy of representation and generalizability of the diagnostic inferences are maintained? For example, the production rule system representation of the LISP encodes examinee's problem-solving process in such a detail that 80% of the errors in student performance can be captured (Anderson, 1990). So it is adequate in terms of the construct representation. In contrast, however, the fine-grained diagnoses that are afforded by the representation makes such inferences confined to the highly limited situation, which results in very limited generalizability (Shute & Psotka, 1996). Thus, depending on the purpose of the diagnostic assessment, setting the appropriate level of granularity in terms of the representation is crucial for the validity of the inferences that are made from testing results.

Grain size must be closely linked to the nature of the cognitive inference desired and type of reporting methods used (see Rupp & Mislevy, this volume). But the answer to the question, *what is the most appropriate grain size for evaluating examinees' cognitive skills?*, remains elusive without developing and applying more CDAs in different educational settings – and learning from our successes and failures. Little research and few concrete examples were presented in this collection that address this question directly. Hence, the granularity issue, which was also identified by DiBello, Stout, and Roussos (1995) as an important problem in CDA, still remains a key area of research.

ISSUE 4: REPORTING COGNITIVE
DIAGNOSTIC ASSESSMENT RESULTS

Score reporting is the interface between developer and user. Thus, reporting is another critical topic in CDA because score reports convey information about the meanings and possible interpretations of test results, often to a diverse audience of users. Standard 5.10 in the *Standards for Educational and Psychological Testing* (American Educational Research Association, American Psychological Association, National Council on Measurement in Education, 1999) describe the goals of score reporting:

When test score information is released to students, parents, legal representatives, teachers, clients, or the media, those responsible for testing programs should provide appropriate interpretations. The interpretations should describe in simple language what the test covers, what scores mean, the precision of the scores, common misinterpretations of test scores, and how scores will be used.

That is, CDA reports, which must appeal broadly, should contain a comprehensive, yet succinct, summary of the psychological outcomes from testing. However, satisfying these requirements pose a significant challenge, particularly when so little research exists on test score reporting. As we move away from reporting information that is content related and broad toward information that is cognitively rich and deep using cognitive models evaluated with sophisticated analytical methods (see Rupp & Mislevy, Gierl et al., Roussos et al., Luecht, this volume), the issues related to reporting become pressing indeed. Yet, little attention was devoted to CDA score reporting in this volume. This limitation must be overcome as more research is required on how to convey detailed, psychologically sophisticated information inherent to CDA for different types of users.

In addition to the nature of the psychological information we convey, the time required to deliver this information is also important. As Huff and Goodman (this volume) claimed, one important factor that detracts from the usefulness of diagnostic information is the significant delay students often experience between taking a test and receiving the results:

> The need to minimize lag time between administering the test and reporting results is something of which most assessment developers and policy makers are well aware. Still, it is the unfortunate reality that many large-scale assessment results are released months after the tests are administered, and often are not released until the subsequent school year (after students have moved on to another teacher and possibly to another school). If assessment developers want to provide educators with meaningful and useful diagnostic information, they must find ways to do this in a timelier manner, without sacrificing the quality and integrity of the assessments.

This issue is particularly relevant as we begin to develop more sophisticated psychometric procedures that yield specific cognitive inferences and, at the same time, require more elaborate input (e.g., attributes, hierarchies) and more complex estimation methods (e.g., Markov chain Monte Carlo estimation), thus affecting data processing and, ultimately, reporting times. These reporting issues inevitably lead us to the question, *how can we communicate sophisticated, psychologically based assessment information in a timely manner to a diverse audience of test users?*

ISSUE 5: INTEGRATING THEORIES OF COGNITION, LEARNING, INSTRUCTION, AND ASSESSMENT

The survey results presented by Huff and Goodman (this volume) indicate that stakeholders want more instructionally relevant assessment results. Our interest in CDA is fueled, in part, by the belief that this form of assessment can deliver relevant and helpful information about students' knowledge and processing. Many CDA researchers also believe that by providing more specific information on students' cognitive skills, assessments will help teachers understand how students think about and solve problems on tests that may help structure and direct instruction. But assessment must be situated in a much larger integrated educational context that also includes cognition, learning, and instruction. Our focus in this volume was on different aspects of the assessment component, specific to cognitive diagnostic testing. However, little attention was paid to the importance of aligning or integrating curriculum, instruction, and assessment to promote student learning using CDA. Because this topic is such a motivating factor for both the consumers and the producers of CDA, much more discussion is needed.

For instance, *can CDAs be developed for classroom testing?* We believe they can. Most current developments in CDAs, however, have focused on large-scale assessment. The development of CDAs mainly for large-scale testing suggest that enormous time, cost, and data requirements are needed to create and apply these types of assessments, along with the empirical scrutiny that is required to make diagnostic inferences defensible. As such, testing companies and government agencies are in a better position than classroom teachers to develop these complex measures of student performance. This is not to say, of course, that CDAs could not be developed to accompany smaller curriculum and instruction initiatives. In fact, classroom testing may be an ideal area to develop CDAs, as educators continue to espouse the need for high-quality formative classroom-based assessments. Some researchers, such as Roussos et al. (this volume), in fact, promote the view that CDA can contribute substantially to formative, classroom-level assessment:

Skills diagnosis, sometimes referred to as skills assessment, skills profiling, profile scoring, or cognitive diagnosis, is an application of psychometric theory and methods to the statistically rigorous process of (a) evaluating each examinee on the basis of level of competence on a user-developed array of skills, and (b) evaluating the skills estimation effectiveness of a test by assessing the strength of the relationship between the individual skills profiles and the observed performance on individual test items. Such examinee evaluation, ideally periodic throughout the teaching and learning process, can provide valuable information to enhance teaching and learning. It is primarily intended for use as *formative* assessment, in contrast to *summative* assessment, in that formative skills diagnosis is intended by its design and implementation to be used directly to improve learning and teaching. In contrast, summative assessment records examinee status at some point in time, usually at the end of an instructional unit, without any direct attempt to improve the examinees status on what was assessed . . . Skills diagnosis can often be considered relatively low stakes from the perspective of the individual test taker. It affects decisions that have relatively short time horizons, such as deciding which problems to assign for tonight's homework or planning for tomorrow's lesson, as opposed to large life events, such as admission to college or selection for employment. The skills diagnostic score results, at least in principle, are well integrated within the classroom environment and constitute just one complementary element of an extensive store of teacher, peer, assessment, and instructional information.

But can our current CDA models and methods truly satisfy those character-istics in formative, classroom assessment, as described by Roussos et al., that are deemed to be so important to teachers? Can our future CDA models and methods ever hope to meet the requirements of formative, classroom assessments? One innovative approach to testing that may provide some of the benefits of formative assessment is a computer-based CDA. With the rapid increase in computer technology, it is now feasible to provide an Internet-delivered, computer-based CDA at the classroom level. With computer-based approach, a CDA could yield diagnostic inferences on curriculum-specific content, delivered on-demand via the Internet, and provide immediate score reporting for the teacher and student. A computer-based CDA could also capitalize on other important testing advances such as the use innovative item formats (see Huff & Goodman and Gorin, this volume). The chapters in this book focused, mostly, on large-scale applications of CDAs using conventional modes of test administration. However, CDAs could be generalized to other levels of assessment. They could also incorporate advances in educational technology. With the enormous influence of technology on testing, research into inno-vative item formats, test designs, administration models, and scoring models with computer-based CDAs seem warranted.

As we consider the research presented in this volume and ponder the issues raised by our authors, one point is clear: significant changes are occurring in educational measurement. Developments in areas such as cognitive psychology, statistics, test design, educational technology, and computing science are just beginning to permeate the assessment field. Although some areas of education and psychology are becoming more specialized and, as a result, more narrow in scope, educational measurement is becoming more generalized and broader in scope due, in part, to these interdisciplinary forces. The diverse issues and areas of future research presented in the final chapter provide some support for this view. Hence, we believe that the success of CDA will not rely on any one factor, such as developing more sophisticated psychometric models and analytical machinery to process student response data. This view is much too narrow. Rather, CDA will be deemed a success when we can design items, analyze students' response patterns on these items, and provide detailed yet concise reports delivered in a timely fashion that allow us to make specific inferences about students. These outcomes will allow students, teachers, parents, and other educational stakehold-ers to gain new insights into how examinees' solve tasks on tests. That is, CDA must serve stakeholders by providing reliable, valid, and succinct information that can be used to understand, evaluate, and develop students' problem-solving skills.

More that 15 years ago, when Messick (1989) and Snow and Lohman (1989) hinted at the possibility of CDA, they highlighted the importance of both psychological theory and research for providing the necessary momentum in developing these assessments. Most educational and psychological tests are based on some form of cognitive problem-solving tasks. This fact is now widely acknowledged, as is the interest and the desire among a substantial number of measurement researchers and practitioners to study the cognitive basis of performance on these tasks using diverse theoretical frameworks and analytical methods from a range of disciplines. Added to these factors are the increasing calls among test users for instructionally relevant information that can be gleaned from what students think about and do when they solve items on tests. But to realize the goals that are being set for CDA, we must, first and foremost, be committed to making the psychological theory underlying these assessments explicit. This characteristic will help ensure that CDAs are *different* from more traditional forms of assessments. Such a commitment also requires that assessments, which are designed to diagnose cognitive skills, be put constantly under the cognitive microscope by pursuing a *strong program of validity.* We strongly believe that the time is right to pursue the strong program. And our proposal to follow this path could yield far more information about why students succeed and fail during learning, as well as what students do and do not understand during instruction, than has ever been possible.

References

American Educational Research Association (AERA), American Psychological Association, National Council on Measurement in Education. (1999). *Standards for Educational and Psychological Testing.* Washington, DC: AERA.

DiBello, L. W., Stout, W. F., & Roussos, L. A. (1995). Unified cognitive/psychometric diagnostic assessment likelihood-based classification techniques. In P. D. Nichols, S. F. Chipman, & R. L. Brennan (Eds.), *Cognitively diagnostic assessment* (pp. 361–389). Hillsdale, NJ: Erlbaum.

Messick, S. (1989) Validity. In R. L. Linn (Ed.), *Educational measurement* (3rd ed., pp. 1–103). New York: American Council on Education/Macmillan.

Snow, R. E., & Lohman, D. F. (1989). Implications of cognitive psychology for educational measurement. In R. L. Linn (Ed.), *Educational measurement* (3rd ed., pp. 263–331). New York: American Council on Education/Macmillan.

Author Index

Subject Index